VPK

English Grammar

(Simple, Practical yet Comprehensive)

with Multiple Examples, Exercises and Key

Revised Third Edition

Designed to move from the basic to the advanced and achieve mastery

Featuring

Parts of Speech, (Parts of) Sentence Structure
Phrases, Clauses and Sentences
Direct Speech and Indirect Speech
Inversion of Structural Elements
Phrasal Verbs, Idioms and Proverbs, Figures of Speech
Advanced Sentence Formation
&
much more.

An Interesting Innovative Scheme of Learning English

To follow us on facebook: https://www.facebook.com/spcEnglishGrammar

English Grammar (Simple, Practical yet Comprehensive)
To follow us on facebook: https://www.facebook.com/spcEnglishGrammar

First Edition: Dec. 2010,
Second Edition: April 2013
Third Edition: June 2014
Reprint: June 2015

Copyright: Author
　　　　　　　Registration No: L-37102/2011 dt. 12/01/2011
　　　　　　　(Copyright Office, Government of India)

Warning: No part of this book may be copied or reproduced commercially in any form without specific prior permission from the author.

Published by:　　　Notion Press Media Pvt Ltd,
　　　　　　　　　Old No. 38, New No. 6,
　　　　　　　　　McNichols Road, Chetpet,
　　　　　　　　　Chennai, Tamil Nadu
　　　　　　　　　India - 600031
　　　　　　　　　Phone: +91 44 42524252

Co-published by: **PALANI PUBLICATIONS**
　　　　　　　　　131/3, Emerald Flats
　　　　　　　　　Thirumangalam
　　　　　　　　　Chennai
　　　　　　　　　India - 600040
　　　　　　　　　Phone: +91 44 26157625, +91 9444177639

ISBN 978-93-84049-89-8

Price: ₹215

In fond memory of my grandma

(late) Mrs. Thiruvaai Seetharam

and

In dedication to my parents

(late) Mr. P. Palanichamy, M.A., M.Ed.
&
(late) Mrs. P. Muthulakshmi

In fond memory of my grandma

(late) Mrs. Thiruvasi Seetharam

and

In dedication to my parents

(late) Mr. P. Balasubramaniam, M.A., M.Ed

&

(late) Mrs. B. Arunachalaveni

FOREWORD

Dr. S. SHANMUGIAH, M.A., Ph.D. **Dt. 07-12-2009**
Registrar
Tamil Nadu Open University
Chennai

It is my proud privilege to record my appreciations for Mr. V.P. Kannan for his intense academic interest as it is very rare to see this kind of deep involvement in academic pursuit among non-academicians. The very fact that Mr. V. P. Kannan, a computer professional by himself, has chosen to write a book on grammar is quite suggestive of the realistic situation faced by students in the computer field. Most of our students, though endowed with great and appreciable computer and other technical skill, are not able to become successful in the job market as they lack communicative competence in English, both oral and written. It is in this context this book by Mr. V.P. Kannan assumes greater significance and relevance.

This is a book on grammar with a difference. Unlike the conventional books, the book is well-structured with units, wholesome by themselves and arranged in a logical sequence. Language experts have always insisted that any language should be learned in a natural way as that of the mother tongue. Mr. Kannan has made an earnest and effective attempt towards this end. The examples and exercises are presented in an informal way making the learning of grammar easy and natural.

With all these positive features, I am sure this book will be a boon not only to students but also to learners of the English language at all levels as the book is planned and designed in the most practical and natural way.

I wish the innovative attempt all success.

COMMENDATION

Prof. R. RAJA GOVINDASAMY, M.A., M.A.(USA) **Dt. 18-12-2009**
Principal
Thiagarajar College
Madurai

I congratulate Mr. V.P. Kannan on his success in bringing out a text book of English Grammar. I appreciate his initiative in working out a scheme of learning English that is interesting and easy to pursue. I am particularly happy about his resourcefulness in composing and compiling information in the form of mechanics and usage for practice. The book is comprehensive in that, in modular mode, it enables the learner to move from the basic to the advanced and achieve mastery by correct and consistent practice. All the grammar units have been dealt with in detail with appropriate examples and exercises.

Technology ensures that a process is carried out with an appropriate mechanism to yield a desired product. Under this circumstance, it is an interesting coincidence that a computer technologist engaged in software and hardware processes has mastered one significant aspect of soft skill, namely English communication skill, and reveals the secret of his success in the form of a text book on English grammar which is simple and complete in itself.

I commend the book to every teacher and learner.

FOREWORD

Mrs. FELICIA AUGSTINE M.A., M.Ed. **Dt. 23-01-2010**
Academic Supervisor
Dept. of English
SBOA School & Junior College
Annanagar West Extension, Chennai

    This book covers a variety of topics in grammar, and it is spread in an orderly way step by step like introduction to grammar, all the topics in grammar from Noun to Figures of speech, Grammar Exercises, key to Grammar Exercises and Appendices. Each topic is dealt with utmost care. There is an extensive treatment of each topic with a variety of exercises. This will be an excellent guide not only for the starter but also for a versatile person - a reference book. English plays a very important role as a tool for global communication. Effective communication holds the key to success in any career. Good & Correct English without any grammatical error is necessary to achieve progress in any sphere of life. Successful speakers and writers depend on their skill of grammatically correct language for noteworthy communication.

    This book can help school and college students improve their grammar. I am confident that this book will prove to be an asset to students and teachers. It will also be a source of support and guidance for parents who wish to prepare their wards for the examination and also help them to develop their proficiency in English Grammar.

    I wish Mr. V.P. KANNAN, the author of the book, a success and a bright future.

FOREWORD

Dr. Carl Perrin Ph.D.
Lakewood, NJ, USA

Dt. 29-01-2010

Email: drcarlperrin@yahoo.com

No matter how skillful people are in a profession, if they cannot explain what they are doing in correct language, others will doubt whether they are competent in their field. Employers judge job applicants not only for their vocational skills but by their language skills as well.

How we say something can be as important as what we say. A business communication might state that the writer is a proficient worker. However, if it contains of errors in grammar, readers get the idea that the author is careless and unprofessional. Readers do not have confidence in people who write ungrammatical messages.

Most business messages today are written on computers, which have the convenience of spell checks and grammar checks. These tools may help, but they are far from perfect. For example, spell checks don't recognize any difference between "see" and "sea." To write effectively, we need to know enough grammar to be able to verify what the grammar check tells us.

When we see grammatical errors in a web site, we move away from it because it lacks authority. It is unprofessional. The well-written message helps establish the writer's validity.

Ungrammatical communications lack clarity. When the language is wrong, the message becomes ambiguous. The reader has to check back to clarify the intent. Time is lost. Production suffers, and confidence diminishes. The worker who uses language effectively is always more competitive in looking for employment.

V P Kannan is a Technical Director for the Government of India. Since he is from a rural background, he is aware of the need for young job seekers from rural backgrounds to gain confidence in their English skills so that they can be successful in their careers and even in their lives. To help these young job seekers and other students, Kannan wrote English Grammar (Simple, Practical yet Comprehensive).

The book is indeed comprehensive and is designed in a way that will help students improve their knowledge of the way that the English language works. It progresses from the simple to the complex, from the alphabet to words to parts of speech to sentences. The book shows question words that help identify specific parts of speech. Who, whom, and what, for example, help recognize nouns. What and Which can point out adjectives.

The chapters on sentence structure look at the basic architecture of sentences: subject + verb + object or other complement. They also explain sentence types from a structural point of view: simple, compound, and complex, as well as the point of view of the mood: declarative, interrogative, imperative, and exclamatory.

After offering a thorough foundation of the basic structure of grammar, the book covers subjects like punctuation, figures of speech, and verbal phrases: gerunds, participles, and infinitives. It describes things like idioms, proverbs, and quotations. Each section contains multiple examples to illustrate the ideas. These examples help clarify the concepts in the text.

The second section of the book contains questions on each chapter of the first section. These allow students to test their own knowledge as they go along. A third section gives answers to the questions in Section Two. The book closes with a list of abbreviations arranged alphabetically and by topic. This arrangement will help readers find the abbreviation they seek.

Students will find *English Grammar (Simple, Practical yet Comprehensive)* very helpful as they work to improve their skill in English grammar. This skill and confidence in language will help them as they progress in their careers.

An Appreciable Effort

Thiru Dr. V. IRAI ANBU I.A.S. **Dt. 16-02-2010**
Secretary to Government
Tourism and Culture Department
Government of Tamil Nadu
Secretariat, Chennai - 600009

All the languages in the world have got prescriptions for usage. Grammar is not to be construed as a book codifying the mode of using a language. Even the spoken languages have rigorous discipline to be followed while conversing with others. Moreover, even a subtle difference can give a diametrically opposite meaning to the intended message. Intonation and facial expression are part of paralanguage signifying the connotations in which a person conveys the message.

Generally, we tend to accept the unwritten norm that the native speakers decide the grammar of a language. English has become the lingua-franca of India. Advancements recorded in other languages will hit the shelves of bookshops with English translation within a span of one month. The scope of English language is getting amplified by virtue of liberalization and globalization.

Thiru V.P. Kannan has brought out a nice manual covering all the aspects of grammar in a comprehensive manner with copious examples and adequate exercises. This book will be of immense help to the students who want to master the language. He has deliberately made it very simple to enhance the grasping of rural students who find English their 'Achilles heel'. He has adopted the question and answer approach to make it more interesting and absorbing.

I earnestly appreciate the efforts of the author who has churned out a book for students with commendable hard work and tremendous commitment.

About the Author

Mr. V. P. Kannan, M.Com., M.C.A., is presently working as a Scientist - E / Technical Director in National Informatics Centre (NIC), Tamil Nadu State Centre, Chennai under the Ministry of Communications and Information Technology, Government of India.

After finishing his primary schooling in his native village, Vettarampatty, a small hamlet at Tirunelveli District in Tamil Nadu, he had studied in St. Mary's Higher Secondary School, Vickramasingapuram, Tirunelveli District till plus two. Afterwards, he finished graduation and post-graduation in commerce from Yadava College, Madurai and Department of Commerce, Madurai Kamaraj University, Madurai respectively. Subsequently, immediately after post-graduation in commerce, he went on to complete post-graduation in computer applications from Thiyagaraja College of Engineering, Madurai.

After that, preceded by a brief interlude in a private concern in Bangalore, he joined NIC, Arunachal Pradesh State Unit, Itanagar as a Scientific Officer / Programmer and has been serving in different capacities in the different offices of NIC till his current position as Scientist - E / Technical Director in NIC, Chennai.

His interaction and experience with different types of people in different parts of our country from his school days to the present period has motivated him to write this book on English grammar in order to help the learners of English grammar from all walks of life, especially the students, young job seekers and those in the initial period of their career, to learn the grammar in a simple, practical and comprehensive way almost without anybody's help so that the learners of this grammar book develop a professional skill in English which is the gateway to the first step of success in the career of most of the people.

He can be contacted through the following e-mail addresses-

vpkannan6@yahoo.com

vppkannan@gmail.com

Preface

In addition to a good knowledge in our mother tongue / vernacular language, knowledge of English has become essential in all walks of life in everybody's life in our country. However, students of especially rural background, though otherwise well educated, could not gain confidence in English even after many years of attending the school and college because of many reasons, the author himself being an example of this anomaly during his school and college days and also the initial period of his career. Even most of the students of urban background, despite their ability to write and converse in English confidently, could not use English professionally because they study English just from the point of view of examination and do not have a real understanding of the grammar. When the students or even the other categories of people like parents and professionals realize their drawback in English and try to improve upon on their own, they could not do so easily because, among other reasons, a good self-tutoring grammar book that is simple, practical and comprehensive is not available. On the other hand, this book tries to bridge this gap between the interested learners of grammar and their goal of learning the grammar in a simple, practical and comprehensive way.

Generally, grammar books cannot be understood by students (or any learner of grammar) without guidance from a teacher or some experienced person. One striking feature of these books is the use / reference of topics from later chapters as if the reader know them or that the reader should jump to the later chapter from which the reader may again be redirected to another chapter and so on, thus creating a cyclic reading and finally confusing the reader beyond redemption. On the other hand, the approach of this book enables its readers to study grammar themselves almost without anybody's help and without frequently referring to other topics/ chapters. The approach of the book is a blend of the 'Question and Answer Approach' and the 'Linear Approach' because people, especially children, tend to learn the things by asking/forming questions, and also because it is easy to learn the topics one by one but one at a time as it instils confidence before moving on to the next. Therefore, the chapters in this book are organized in a logical and natural order and written with a minimum number of references to other chapters such that the reader reads its chapters sequentially, one by one, in accordance with the natural flow of thought of the learner. However, a reader can read / refer to any chapter directly also provided the reader has enough knowledge about the previous chapters. On the whole, the aim of the book is to help the reader learn English grammar more easily following the natural learning process.

At the same time, I take this opportunity to thank all, my parents, my teachers, my colleagues, my friends and relatives who supported me and made this book a reality by their invaluable contributions ranging from moral encouragement to suggestions and tips for improvement of the book to complete reading and pointing out the possible corrections. Specifically, I would like to register a few names in this regard.

First of all, I bow to God without whose Grace and Blessings I would not have been able to even attempt to write this book, let alone successful completion of the book. Secondly, I would like to thank my father Mr. P. Palanichamy, M.A., M.Ed., a retired Government Higher Secondary School Headmaster, who had taught me English grammar during my school days and aroused my interest in grammar. My special thanks are due to him for reading the manuscript several times completely, pointing out the corrections and suggesting the ways for improvement of the book. Master K. Padmanathan, my son and a student of middle schooling, deserves a special acknowledgement because it is my teaching experience with him at home which was the inspiration for writing this book. My wife, Dr. S. Pappathi, M.B.B.S., D.C.H., M.D., a Professor of Pathology in Madras Medical College, Chennai has been the motivation behind writing this book, and I would like to thank her for her support.

After my father, it is Mr. Carl Perrin, Ph. D. Lakewood, NJ, USA who taught me grammar and clarified my doubts on grammar. He has been helping me over INTERNET very promptly amid his busy schedule since 2008. I really admire him for his promptness and am highly indebted to him because, without his kind help, this book would not have been what it is today, and he has given a precious foreword pointing out the importance of the language skill of the people and the usefulness of the book.

Next, I would like to express my deep gratitude to Prof. Dr. S. Shanmugaiah, M.A., Ph.D., Registrar of Tamil Nadu Open University, who, regardless of his busy schedule, has kindly given a valuable foreword for this humble work to highlight the usefulness of this book to the learners of grammar in general and the student community in particular.

Then, I owe a debt of gratitude to Prof. R. Raja Govindasamy, M.A., M.A. (USA), Principal of Thiagarajar College, Madurai, for having kindly gone through the book amidst his tight line-up and having given a commendation suggestive of the unique features of the book and the usefulness of the book to students and even teachers.

Further, I am deeply indebted to Mrs. Felicia Augustine, M.A., M.Ed., Academic Supervisor, Department of English, SBOA School & Junior College, Chennai for her kind appraisal of the book and a noteworthy foreword which will certainly take the book forward to students, teachers and parents.

The Crescendo that it is, the appreciation from Thiru Dr. V. Irai Anbu I.A.S., Secretary to Government, Tourism and Culture Department, Government of Tamil Nadu has climaxed with a viewpoint that has very aptly described the book and set the ball (book) rolling. My heartfelt deep gratitude is due to Thiru Dr. V. Irai Anbu I.A.S. for his inspiring and eloquent appreciation for the book.

Finally, I request the readers, specifically the teachers, to comment on the book and to give a valuable feedback, pointing out the omissions and oversights, if any, and suggesting the ways to make the book more and more useful. I may be contacted through the following e-mail addresses of vpkannan6@yahoo.com and vppkannan@gmail.com .

Chennai
December, 2010

V P KANNAN

Table of Contents

Part I (Grammar)

1. Introduction to Grammar — 1-18
Parts of Speech - Sentence Structure - Parts of Sentence Structure - Phrases - Clauses - Phrasal Verbs, Idioms, Proverbs and Quotations - Functional Sentence Types - Direct Speech and Indirect Speech - Punctuation - Compound Words and Collocations - Figures of Speech

2. Nouns — 19-21
Types of Nouns - Aspects of Nouns

3. Pronouns — 22-25
Personal Pronouns - Reflexive Pronouns - Emphatic Pronouns - Reciprocal Pronouns - Demonstrative Pronouns - Indefinite Pronouns - Distributive Pronouns - Interrogative Pronouns - Relative Pronouns

4. Verbs - Basics — 26-45
Factors affecting the verb form - Action Verbs - Form of Finite Verbs for Tenses in Active Voice - Form of Finite Verbs for Tenses in Passive Voice - Uses of Tenses for Action Verbs - Modal Verbs - Be-Verbs - Action Verb cum Be-Verb - Action Verb cum Modal Verb - Action Verb cum Auxiliary Verb - Some Common Verbs

5. Negative Sentences — 46-46

6. Interrogative Sentences - Questions — 47-52
Yes/No Questions - Question-Word Questions - Questions for Passive Voice - Questions expressing Surprise - Tag Questions - Rhetorical Questions - Questions for Phrases and Clauses

7. Verbs - Advanced — 53-80
Conditional Sentences - Transitivity of Verbs - Stative Verbs - Dynamic Verbs - Causative Verbs - Perception Verbs - Thinking Verbs - Types of Other Complements - Mood - Extended Modal Verbs - Phrasal Verbs - Common Phrasal Verbs

8. Verbal Phrases - Gerunds, Participles and Infinitives — 81-89
Gerund Phrase - Compound Gerund - Participle Phrase - Absolute Phrase - Dangling Modifier/Phrase - Infinitive Phrase - Split Infinitive - Bare/Zero Infinitive

9. Conjugation of Verbs — 90-91

10.	**Contractions**	**92-97**

Contraction of Subject and Auxiliary Verbs - Questions with Contractions - Informal Contractions - Contractions with Tag Questions

11.	**Introductory Subjects - It and There**	**98-99**
12.	**Adjectives**	**100-114**

Position of Adjectives - Order of Adjectives - Degrees of Comparison - Pre-modifiers - Incomparable Adjectives - Adjective Phrase - Adjective Clause - Some Common Adjectives

13.	**Determiners and Articles**	**115-118**

Articles - Indefinite Articles - Definite Articles - Omission of Articles - Possessive Adjective Pronouns - Demonstrative Determiners - Quantifiers - Ordinal Determiners - Position and Order of Determiners

14.	**Adverbs**	**119-136**

Types of Adverbs - Adverb Phrase - Adverb Clause - Interrogative Adverbs - Relative Adverbs - Position of Adverbs - Special Uses of some Adverbs - Forms of Adjective-based Adverbs - Degrees of Comparison - Pre-modifiers

15.	**Prepositions**	**137-146**

Prepositional Object - Prepositional Phrase - Simple Preposition - Complex Preposition - Formation of Complex Preposition - Marginal Preposition - Usage of Common Prepositions - Omission of Prepositions - Ending a sentence with a Preposition

16.	**Phrases and Expressions**	**147-148**

Basic Phrases - Noun Phrase - Adjective Phrase - Adverb Phrase - Prepositional Phrase - Verbal Phrases - Post-modifier - Expressions

17.	**Clauses and Structural Sentence Types - Simple, Compound and Complex Sentences**	**149-177**

Independent/Main Clause - Dependent/Subordinate Clause - Relative Clause - Adverb Clause - Adjective Clause - Noun Clause - Simple Sentence - Compound Sentence - Complex Sentence - Compound-Complex Sentence - Transformation of Sentences - Mutually Dependent Clauses

18.	**Conjunctions**	**178-183**

Coordinating Conjunction - Subordinating Conjunction - Relative Conjunction - Correlative Conjunction - Parallel Construction - Conjunctive Adverb - Transitional Expressions

19.	**Direct Speech and Indirect (Reported) Speech**	**184-190**

Direct Speech - Indirect/Reported Speech - Divided Direct Speech

20.	**Inversion of Subject, Verb and Complement**	**191-193**

21.	Interrogative Sentences (Questions) - Advanced	194-196
22.	**Punctuation** Terminating a Sentence - Separating/Combining units of a Sentence - Omission of words/phrases - Capitalization	197-200
23.	**Advanced Sentence Formation** Using Participle Phrases - Loose Sentence - Periodic Sentence - Using Appositives - Parallel Structure - Fragments - Elliptical Sentences	201-206
24.	Same Words - Different Parts of Speech	207-212
25.	Compound Words, Compound Adjectives and Compound Adverbs	213-217
26.	Collocation and Patterns for words	218-221
27.	Idioms, Proverbs and Quotations	222-239
28.	**Other Word Groups/Types** Prefix - Suffix - Synonym - Antonym - Hyponym - Holonym - Homonym - Homograph - Homophone - Anagram - Alphagram - Palindrome	240-245
29.	**Figures of Speech** Simile - Metaphor - Hyperbole - Euphemism - Personification - Irony - Interrogation - Synecdoche - Metonymy - Antithesis - Oxymoron - Climax - Anticlimax	246-248

Part II (Grammar Exercises)

1.	Exercise for Chapter 2: Nouns	250-252
2.	Exercise for Chapter 3: Pronouns	253-255
3.	Exercise for Chapter 4: Verbs - Basics & Chapter 5: Negative Sentences	256-257
4.	Exercise for Chapter 6: Interrogative Sentences & Chapter 7: Verbs - Advanced	258-260
5.	Exercise for Chapter 8: Verbal Phrases - Gerund, Participle and Infinitive	261-262
6.	Exercise for Chapter 12: Adjectives & Chapter 13: Determiners and Articles	263-264
7.	Exercise for Chapter 14: Adverbs	265-266
8.	Exercise for Chapter 15: Prepositions	267-269

9.	Exercise for Chapter 16: Phrases and Expressions	270-270
10.	Exercise for Chapter 17: Clauses and Structural Sentence Types - Simple, Compound and Complex Sentences & Chapter 18: Conjunctions	271-274
11.	Exercise for Chapter 19: Direct Speech and Indirect (Reported) Speech	275-275
12.	Exercise for Chapter 20: Inversion of Subject, Verb and Complement	276-276
13.	Exercise for Chapter 29: Figures of Speech	277-277

Part III (Key to Grammar Exercises)

1.	Exercise for Chapter 2: Nouns	279-281
2.	Exercise for Chapter 3: Pronouns	282-283
3.	Exercise for Chapter 4: Verbs - Basics & Chapter 5: Negative Sentences	283-285
4.	Exercise for Chapter 6: Interrogative Sentences & Chapter 7: Verbs - Advanced	286-291
5.	Exercise for Chapter 8: Verbal Phrases - Gerund, Participle and Infinitive	291-292
6.	Exercise for Chapter 12: Adjectives & Chapter 13: Determiners and Articles	292-292
7.	Exercise for Chapter 14: Adverbs	293-293
8.	Exercise for Chapter 15: Prepositions	294-295
9.	Exercise for Chapter 16: Phrases and Expressions	296-297
10.	Exercise for Chapter 17: Clauses and Structural Sentence Types - Simple, Compound and Complex Sentences & Chapter 18: Conjunctions	297-301
11.	Exercise for Chapter 19: Direct Speech and Indirect (Reported) Speech	301-302
12.	Exercise for Chapter 20: Inversion of Subject, Verb and Complement	302-303
13.	Exercise for Chapter 29: Figures of Speech	303-303

Part IV (Appendices)

1.	Index	305-311
2.	Abbreviations - alphabetical order	312-312
3.	Abbreviations - topic-wise order	313-313

Part I

Grammar

Chapter 1
Introduction to Grammar

The aim of learning grammar is to speak and write correct language. In a language, sentences convey the complete meaning. Sentences are formed by combining a group of words to make a complete meaning. To form a grammatically correct sentence in English, we should know the types of words and their position and order in a sentence. The types of words are classified and grouped according to their function in sentences, called **Parts of Speech (POS)**. The position and order of the different (types of) words is defined by a set of rules called **Sentence Structures (SS)**.

Before going into the parts of speech and the sentence structures, let us briefly discuss the words, the alphabets and the sounds. A word is formed by combining alphabets. The alphabets represent the sounds of English, and they are divided into vowels, namely 'a, e, i, o and u' and consonants, the other alphabets. Besides, we should know that words can be divided into units/ subdivisions of closely related sounds containing a vowel and one or more consonants. Such a unit/subdivision is called a syllable. For example, 'do' is a single syllable word, and 'forever' has two syllables, namely 'for' and 'ever'. A good dictionary will be useful to identify the syllables.

In addition to Parts of Speech and Sentence Structure, other topics are also briefly discussed in this introductory chapter. The main topics dealt with in this chapter are:

I	Parts of Speech
II	Sentence Structure
III	Structural Elements
IV	Phrasal Verbs, Idioms, Proverbs and Quotations
V	Functional Sentence Types
VI	Direct Speech and Indirect Speech
VII	Punctuation
VIII	Compound Words and Collocations
IX	Other Word Groups/Types
X	Figures of Speech

Important: These topics are only briefly described in this introductory chapter and are described elaborately in later chapters. Not only in this chapter, but also in other chapters would it be mentioned that some topic is explained in detail in later chapters. However, you need not refer to the later chapter immediately and can continue to read the same chapter. The reference to a later chapter is given only to provide information and not to mean that you should know it before proceeding.

Tip: In the following discussion, <u>question words</u> are given against each element (parts of speech / structural elements) that is being discussed. The <u>answer to these question words</u> will point to the particular element, thus helping in understanding the element more clearly.

I Parts of Speech: Words are classified according to their functions in sentences. They are:

1) Noun, 2) Pronoun, 3) Adjective, 4) Determiner, 5) Verb, 6) Adverb, 7) Preposition, 8) Conjunction and 9) Interjection

A short description of these classifications and their functions is given below along with the abbreviations:

1) Noun (Naming Words): Abbreviation: **n**. The function of the noun is to tell the name of somebody or something.

Question Words for noun: Who, Whom and What - The answer to these question words in sentences is a noun / pronoun (explained next).

Examples	Question Words
<u>Ashoka</u> was a great King.	who? (person)
<u>Lion</u> is a wild animal.	what? (animal)
<u>Madurai</u> was the capital of Pandya Kings.	what? (place)
It is a <u>table</u>.	what? (thing)
<u>Rama</u> likes Lakshmana.	who? (person)
Rama likes <u>Lakshmana</u>.	whom? (person)
<u>Laughter</u> eases tension.	what? (idea)
Laughter eases <u>tension</u>.	what? (idea)
Children like <u>stories</u>.	what? (idea)

2) Pronoun (Substitute Words for nouns): Abbreviation: **pron**. Pronouns always refer to some noun, and it is convenient to use a pronoun instead of using a noun repeatedly. For example, in the sentence 'Balu is a tall boy, and **he** is a student', **he** is a pronoun referring to 'Balu'. Of course, the noun 'Balu' could have been used instead of **'he'**, but it would be odd.

Question Words for pronoun: Who, Whom and What - The answer to these question words in sentences can be a noun / pronoun.

Examples	Question Words
<u>I</u> am a boy. <u>We</u> are boys.	who?
<u>You</u> are a girl.	who?
<u>He</u> / <u>She</u> is a student. <u>They</u> are students.	who?
<u>It</u> is Chennai.	what?
<u>He</u> likes her.	who?
He likes <u>her</u>.	whom?

Chapter-1: Introduction to Grammar

3) Verb (Action Words / (State-of-) Being Words): Abbreviation: **v.** As action words, they tell what is happening, and as being words, they tell what is the condition / state of being of somebody/something in the sentence. <u>We cannot write any sentence without verb</u>.

Question Words for verb: What is happening and What is the condition / state of being - The answer to these questions in sentences is a verb. The verbs denoting 'Action' are called **Action Verbs**, and the verbs denoting the 'State' are called **Be-Verbs / Being Verbs**.

Examples	Question Words
I <u>am studying</u> grammar.	What is happening? - Action Verb
I <u>played</u> football yesterday.	What happened? - Action Verb
The earth <u>is</u> a planet, not a star.	What is the condition/state (of being) of 'the earth'? - Be-Verb
We <u>are</u> happy.	What is the condition/state (of being) of 'We'? - Be-Verb

4) Adjective (Describing Words for Nouns and Pronouns): Abbreviation: **adj.** They describe or give more information about noun/pronoun. In other words, they describe the quality of noun and pronoun.

Question Words for adjective: What type of, What kind of, Which and How + Be-Verb - The answer to these question words in sentences is an adjective.

Examples	Question Words
He is a <u>good</u> boy.	what type of (boy)?
She is <u>intelligent</u>.	what kind of (girl)?
I like the <u>blue</u> pen.	which (pen)?
Balu is <u>happy</u>.	How is (Balu)?

5) Determiner (similar to adjectives): Abbreviation: **d.** They refer to a particular noun. In other words, they determine the scope of noun such that they point to the particular noun, not any other noun. Determiners include the **articles** also, namely 'a, an and the.'

Question Words for determiner: Which and Whose - The answer to these question words in sentences can be a determiner.

Examples	Question Words
It is <u>her</u> pen.	which/whose (pen)?
<u>That</u> book is mine.	which (book)?
I like <u>all</u> the people.	which (people)?

A man came yesterday.   -   which (man)?: some man
I saw the man today also.   -   which (man)?: the same man

The main difference between Adjective and Determiner is that determiners can only be used attributively, not predicatively, but the adjectives can be used both ways as illustrated below:

A short girl came.   -   the adjective 'short' is used attributively,
i.e., before the noun 'girl'

She is short.   -   the adjective 'short' is used predicatively,
i.e., after the verb 'is' but not followed by a noun

Our book is good.   -   the determiner 'our' is used attributively,
i.e., before the noun 'book'

The book is our.   -   the predicative use of 'our' is wrong

6) Adverb (Describing Words for Verbs, Adjectives, other Adverbs and Sentences):
Abbreviation: **adv**. They describe or give more information about verbs, adjectives and other adverbs. Sometimes, the adverbs can modify the whole sentence also.

Question Words for adverbs in general: How, When, Where and Why. The specific form of question words are given below against what the adverb describes - The answer to these questions in sentences is an adverb.

Examples   **Question Words**

Adverbs describing verbs: How / When / Where / Why + Action Verb

He runs fast.   -   **How** does he *run*?
She moves quickly.   -   **How** does she *move*?
I meet him daily.   -   **How often** do I *meet* him?
He played yesterday.   -   **When** did he *play*?
We searched everywhere.   -   **Where** did we *search*?
He lied purposely.   -   **Why** did he *lie*?

Adverbs describing adjectives and adverbs: How + Adjective / Adverb

He is a very good boy.   -   **How** *good* is he?
He runs very fast.   -   **How** *fast* does he run?

Adverbs describing the sentence: How / When / Where / Why + Action Verb

Luckily, we won the game.   -   **How** did *we win the game*?

Chapter-1: Introduction to Grammar

7) Preposition (Position / Relationship Words): Abbreviation: **prep**. They describe the position/relationship of nouns/pronouns in relation to other nouns/pronouns, adjectives and verbs.

Question Words for preposition: preposition + What, How, When, Where, Why and Which - The answer to these questions in sentences can be prepositions.

Examples	Relationship	Question Words
There is a **book** <u>on</u> the **table**.	between noun and noun	on what? / where?
I like the **book** <u>on</u> the **table**.	between noun and noun	which (book)?
They are **good** <u>in</u> **dancing**.	between adjective and noun	in what?
The table **is made** <u>of</u> **wood**.	between verb and noun	of what? / how?
I **shall go** <u>in</u> the **morning**.	between verb and noun	when?
He can **play** <u>instead of</u> **me**.	between verb and pronoun	instead of whom?

Single-word prepositions are called <u>simple prepositions</u>, and multi-word prepositions are called <u>complex prepositions</u>. <u>Prepositions are always followed by noun/pronoun</u>.

8) Conjunction (Joining Words for words / groups of words / sentences): Abbreviation: **conj**. They are used to join two or more (group of) words or two or more sentences. Conjunction has **no question words**.

Examples

Paul <u>and</u> David will come tomorrow.	-	joining the words
We can take **tea** <u>or</u> **coffee**.	-	joining the words
It is **cold** <u>and</u> **wet**.	-	joining the words
We may reach **slowly** <u>but</u> **surely**.	-	joining the words
Abdul plays **before breakfast** <u>and</u> **after tea**.	-	joining the groups of words
I play tennis, <u>but</u> I don't play well.	-	joining the sentences
We can eat now, <u>or</u> we can wait till later.	-	joining the sentences

9) Interjection (Emotion Words): Abbreviation: **interj**. They are used to express sudden feelings and emotions and are not even words by themselves but some sounds. Interjection has **no question words**.

Examples

<u>Ah</u>! That is good.	-	Admiration	<u>Aha</u>! I am enjoying.	-	Pleasure
I got it. <u>Eh</u>!	-	Surprise	<u>Oh</u>! How beautiful!	-	Exclamation
<u>Ouch</u>! That hurts!	-	Pain	<u>Shit</u>! I have lost my keys.	-	Anger
<u>Yuck</u>! What a bad smell!	-	Disgust	<u>Hurray</u>! We won.	-	Happiness
<u>Hello/Hullo/Hi</u>! How are you?	-	Greeting	<u>Hey</u>! Be careful.	-	Attention
<u>Well</u>, I did not expect you.	-	Surprise	<u>Well</u>, What is he now?	-	Introductory remark

Note: It is to be noted that the same word can be used as different parts of speech as follows:

He has a fast car. (Adjective)   He can run fast. (Adverb)
Some people fast for festivals. (Verb)   They end the fast the next day. (Noun)

The question words to identify the different parts of speech are summarized below:

S.No	Parts of Speech	Question words
1.	Noun	Who, Whom and What
2.	Pronoun	Who, Whom and What
3.	Adjective	What type of, What kind of, Which and How + Be-Verb
4.	Determiner	Which and Whose
5.	Verb	What is happening and What is the condition / state
6.	Adverb	How, When, Where and Why
7.	Preposition	preposition + What, How, When, Where, Why and Which
8.	Conjunction	No question words
9.	Interjections	No question words

II Sentence Structure (SS): The sentence structure defines the position of the words (all parts of speech) in the sentences. The basic sentence structure is as follows:

Subject (S) + Verb (V) [+ Object (O)] [+ Other Complements (OC)].

The **square brackets** imply that the Object and the Other Complements are **optional**.

Subject (S) = Noun or Pronoun who performs the action or about whom something is stated.
Question Words: Who, What

Verb (V) = Same as Verb of Parts of Speech. The most important part of sentences.
Question Words: What is happening, What is the condition / state (of being)

Object (O) = Noun or Pronoun who receives the (effect of the) action of the subject.
Question Words: Whom, What

Chapter-1: Introduction to Grammar

Other Complement (OC) = It complements/adds more meaning to subject, object or verb, called **Subject Complement (SC), Object Complement (ObjC)** or **Verb Complement (VC)** respectively. It can be Noun, Pronoun, Adjective, Adverb and/or Preposition.

Question Words:

for Noun, Pronoun	-	Who, What
for Adjective	-	What type/kind of, How + Be-Verb
for Adverb	-	How, When, Where, Why
for Preposition	-	prep.+What, How, When, Where, Why, Which

For example,:

1)	n	v	n			--- POS (Parts of Speech) units
	Love	is	God.			
	S	V	OC(SC)			--- SS (Sentence Structure) units
2)	pron	v	adj			--- POS units
	She	is	good.			
	S	V	OC(SC)			--- SS units
3)	pron	v	pron			--- POS units
	She	likes	him.			
	S	V	O			--- SS units
4)	pron	v	n	prep	n	--- POS units
	He	plays	football	at	night.	
	S	V	O	OC(VC)		--- SS units
5)	pron	v	pron	adj		--- POS units
	It	makes	him	happy.		
	S	V	O	OC(ObjC)		--- SS units

Sentence Structure with Indirect Object:

Subject(**S**)+Verb(**V**)[+Object(**O**)+ 'to' +Indirect Object(**IO**)][+Other Complements(**OC**)].

or

Subject(**S**) + Verb(**V**) [+ Indirect Object(**IO**) + Object(**O**)] [+ Other Complements(**OC**)].

Indirect Object = Noun or Pronoun who receives the Object itself.
Question Words: to Whom, for Whom, to What, for What

The Object (O) receives the action or the effect of the action of the verb in a sentence as illustrated in the previous examples. The Indirect Object (IO) is the receiver of the Object (O) itself as illustrated below:

   Rama gave <u>a pen</u> to <u>Balu</u>.   Rama gave <u>Balu</u> <u>a pen</u>.
       O   IO   IO O

When there is an Indirect Object (IO), the Object (O) is sometimes referred to as Direct Object (DO). Moreover, it is to be noted that there must be an Object (O) to have an Indirect Object (IO) in a sentence. It is also to be noted that some verbs like **'give'** (illustrated above) can be used with both the structures while some verbs like **'explain'** (illustrated below) can be used with the former structure only. <u>A good dictionary can help you to identify the type of verb</u>.

   Rama explained Maths to her. (Right) Rama explained her Maths. (Wrong)

Besides, <u>when both the direct object and the indirect object are pronouns</u>, only the former structure is to be used as 'I gave it to them', not as 'I gave them it' or 'I gave it them.'

III <u>**Structural Elements / Parts of Sentence Structure**</u>: The basic sentence structure is discussed above. Various elements of sentence structures are explained below:

1) Sentence: A sentence is a group of words with (a minimum of) a subject and a verb and complete in meaning. For example,:

   I am a boy.   He is running.
   She wrote a letter quickly.   They are good.
   Balu has played football.   Education is important for children.

However, a longer sentence would have, in addition to the subject and the verb, one or more other structural elements including object, indirect object, other complements, phrase, clause and appositive which are all explained next.

2) Subject (S): Subject is a noun or pronoun who/that performs the action or about whom/what something is stated in a sentence. For example, the underlined words are subjects in the following sentences:

   <u>I</u> am a boy.   <u>He</u> is running.
   <u>She</u> wrote a letter quickly.   <u>They</u> are good.
   <u>Balu</u> has played football.   <u>Education</u> is important for children.

Chapter-1: Introduction to Grammar

3) Predicate: Predicate is all the other words than the subject. For example, the underlined words are predicates:

I <u>am a boy</u>.
She <u>wrote a letter quickly</u>.
Balu <u>has played football</u>.

He <u>is running</u>.
They <u>are good</u>.
Education <u>is important for children</u>.

Sometimes, only the verb of the sentence is referred to as predicate not including the object and the other complement.

4) Verb (V): Verb tells the action of the subject or the condition / state (of being) of the subject. For example, the underlined words are verbs in the following sentences:

She <u>wrote</u> a letter quickly.   -   tells the action of the subject
They <u>are</u> good.   -   tells the state (of being) of the subject

5) Object (O): Object is a noun or pronoun that receives the action or the effect of the action of a verb in a sentence. For example, the underlined words are objects in the following sentences:

Balu has played <u>football</u>.   She loves <u>him</u>.

6) Indirect Object (IO): Indirect Object is the receiver of the Object (O) itself. For example, the underlined words are indirect objects in the following sentences:

Rama gave <u>Balu</u> a pen.   He gave a gift to <u>her</u>.

7) Other Complements (OC): Other Complements refer to the part of the sentence that complements or adds more meaning to the basic structural elements of subject, verb or object. Basically, it can be a noun, pronoun, adjective, adverb or preposition. There can be many Other Complements in a sentence, and they are three types as explained below:

Subject Complement (SC): It complements or adds more meaning to the subject, and as such it can be a noun, pronoun or adjective. For example, the underlined word(s) is subject complement:

Love is <u>God</u>.   She is <u>good</u>.

Verb Complement (VC): It complements or adds more meaning to the verb, and as such it can be an adverb or a preposition followed by a noun/pronoun. It is also called **Adverbial.** For example, the underlined word(s) is verb complement:

She wrote a letter <u>quickly</u>.   She wrote a letter <u>*in* the morning</u>.

Object Complement (ObjC): Like subject complement, it is also a noun, pronoun or adjective; however, it complements or adds more meaning to the object and appears immediately after the object. For example, the underlined word(s) is object complement:

    Others made him <u>the leader</u>.   It made him <u>happy</u>.

Other complements are dealt with in detail in chapter 7 on Verbs - Advanced.

8) Phrase: A phrase is a group of words without verb but with some meaning. Any phrase will be functionally similar to a noun, adjective or adverb and called noun phrase, adjective phrase and adverb phrase respectively. For example, if a phrase functions like a noun, it is called a noun phrase and so on. The type of the phrase is determined by identifying the **key/head/main word** in the phrase. The head word will usually be the last word in the phrase. If it is a noun, it is a noun phrase, and if it is an adjective, it is an adjective phrase and so on. The types of phrases, namely **noun phrase, adjective phrase,** and **adverb phrase,** are collectively called **Basic Phrases.** *It is to be noted that a phrase can be used in the place of its equivalent part of speech*. For example, a noun phrase can be used instead of a noun. The basic phrases are described below where the phrase is underlined and the head word is in *italics*.

Noun Phrase (NP): It is a group of words in which the head word is a noun preceded by adjectives and determiners. For example,

    <u>An old *lady*</u> feeds the birds.

Adjective Phrase (AdjP): It is a group of words in which the head word is an adjective preceded by adverbs. For example,

    The car is <u>very *beautiful*</u>.

Adverb Phrase / Adverbial Phrase (AdvP): It is a group of words in which the head word is an adverb preceded by other adverbs. For example,

    He ran <u>very *quickly*</u>.

Prepositional Phrase (PP): In a prepositional phrase, the head word is a preposition followed by noun or pronoun. The noun or pronoun following the preposition is called **prepositional object (PO).** For example, in the following example, 'in the morning' is the prepositional phrase, and 'the morning' is the object of the preposition 'in'.

    They arrived <u>*in* the morning</u>.

Chapter-1: Introduction to Grammar

Functionally, prepositional phrases have <u>no independent function</u>, and they have to function like **noun phrase** or **adjective phrase** or **adverb phrase**. Use of prepositional phrase as noun phrase is explained in chapter 15 on Prepositions. If a prepositional phrase modifies/describes nouns, then it is an adjective phrase, and if it modifies/describes verbs, adjectives or adverbs, then it is an adverb phrase. They are illustrated below wherein the underlined phrases are prepositional phrases.

I saw the book *with* a cover. -   The prepositional phrase 'with a cover' modifies the noun 'book' with the possible question of '**Which** <u>book</u> did I see?' and the answer of 'the particular book with a cover', so it is an **adjective phrase**.

I play *in the evening*.   -   The prepositional phrase 'in the evening' modifies the verb 'play' with the possible question of '**When** do I play?' and the answer of 'in the evening', so it is an **adverb phrase**.

Moreover, a prepositional phrase functioning as noun phrase can be called **Prepositional Noun Phrase (PNP)**. Similarly, we have **Prepositional Adjective Phrase (PAdjP)** and **Prepositional Adverb Phrase (PAdvP)**.

<u>**Verbal Phrases:**</u> Verbal phrases are not (complete) verbs but some form of verb, functioning as either noun or adjective or adverb. Before proceeding, we should know the verb forms as illustrated below:

Base Form	**Present Form**	**Past Form**	**Past Participle Form**	**Present Participle Form**
love	love loves	loved	loved	loving

These forms are explained in detail in chapter 4 on Verbs - Basics. Now, we only need to know that some of these forms are used for verbal phrases. There are three types of verbal phrases, namely Gerund, Participle and Infinitive which are explained below:

Gerund / Gerund Phrase: The verb form of the gerund is Present Participle. They function as **noun** and can be used as such. Additionally, as it is a form of verb, it can take its own object and/or complement. For example,:

<u>Reading</u> is a good habit.   -   simple Gerund as subject
<u>Reading magazines regularly</u> improves our General Knowledge.
        -   Gerund Phrase as subject

Participle / Participle Phrase: The verb form of the participle is Present Participle or Past Participle. They function as **adjective** and can be used as such. Additionally, as it is a form of verb, it can take its own object and/or complement. For example,:

A <u>crying</u> baby gets attention immediately.	- simple Participle as Adjective modifying the noun 'baby'
<u>Crying all along</u>, the baby got tired.	- Participle Phrase as Adjective modifying the noun 'baby'
The building <u>destroyed by fire</u> needs repair.	- Participle Phrase as Adjective modifying the noun 'building'

Infinitive / Infinitive Phrase: The verb form of the infinitive is 'to' + Base Form. They function as **noun, adjective and adverb** and can be used as such. Additionally, as it is a form of verb, it can take its own object and/or complement. For example,:

Young boys always want <u>to play</u>.	- simple Infinitive as Object (noun)
We lack the determination <u>to win</u>.	- simple Infinitive as Adjective modifying the noun 'determination'
We must study <u>to get good marks</u>.	- Infinitive Phrase as Adverb modifying the verb 'study'

9) Expression (exp.): An expression is also a group of words, but unlike phrases, it need not function only like noun, adjective or adverb, but it can also function like other parts of speech like preposition, conjunction, etc. In a way, phrases can be considered as a kind of expression. Expressions functioning like other parts of speech are illustrated below:

I want a black pen <u>in addition to</u> the blue pen.	- expression as preposition
I will finish the work <u>as soon as</u> I can.	- expression as conjunction

10) Appositive: An appositive is a noun or a noun phrase placed immediately after another noun/pronoun to add additional information to the preceding noun or pronoun. For example, the underlined noun phrase in the following sentence is an appositive.

Bengaluru, <u>the capital of Karnataka</u>, is a garden city.

11) Clause: A clause is a group of words with subject and verb, and it is either complete or incomplete in meaning. If it is complete in meaning, it is called an **independent/main clause**, and if it is incomplete in meaning, a **dependent/subordinate clause**. For example,

<u>When he came back,</u> <u>the room was locked.</u>
subordinate clause   main clause

In the above example, the clause 'the room was locked' is a main clause because it can be written separately as a sentence because it would express a complete meaning. However,

Chapter-1: Introduction to Grammar

the clause 'When he came back' is a subordinate clause because it conveys only a partial meaning of the sentence, and something else (the main clause) has to be added to make it complete in meaning. Besides, the clause 'When he came back' cannot be written separately as a sentence because it would be incomplete in meaning.

The subordinate clauses start with a **conjunction**, and as such 'when' is used as a conjunction in the above subordinate clause 'When he came back'. As another example, in the sentence 'If you work hard, you can win', 'if' is a conjunction of the subordinate clause 'If you work hard'.

Like phrases, subordinate clauses can also be **noun clause (NCls)**, **adjective clause (AdjCls)** or **adverb clause / adverbial clause (AdvCls)**, depending on its function in the sentence.

Important: **Wherever a noun is used, its equivalent phrase or clause (i.e., noun phrase or noun clause) can also be used, and so are adjectives and adverbs as illustrated below:**

    Love is <u>God</u>.   Love is <u>the supreme God</u>.
      noun   noun phrase

    We know <u>the winner</u>.   We know **who** <u>will win the match</u>.
      noun phrase   noun clause

12) Pre-modifier vs. Post-modifier: The words that modify/describe other words are **modifiers**. For e.g., adjectives modify nouns and are modifiers for nouns. The modifiers placed before the other words they modify are called **pre-modifiers**, and the modifiers placed after the other words they modify are called **post-modifiers**. The difference is illustrated below:

    He is a <u>wealthy</u> man.   - pre-modifier: adjective used before noun

    He is a man <u>of wealth</u>.   - post-modifier: prepositional adjective phrase used after noun

    He is a man <u>who is wealthy</u>. - post-modifier: adjective clause used after noun

The terms pre-modifier and post-modifier can be applied to any modifier depending on the pre/post position of these modifiers.

13) Structural Sentence Types: Sentences can be classified according to the combination of independent clauses and dependent clauses. The following three are such sentence types:

Simple Sentence (SmpS): It is a sentence with only one independent clause. For example,

    <u>He got good marks</u>.
    independent clause

Compound Sentence (CpdS): A compound sentence consists of two or more independent clauses joined by conjunctions like 'and, but, or, etc.' For example,

<u>He had studied well</u>, **and** <u>he got good marks</u>.
  independent clause   independent clause

Complex Sentence (ClxS): A complex sentence contains one independent clause and at least one dependent clause.

<u>As he had studied well</u>, <u>he got good marks</u>.
  dependent clause   independent clause

IV <u>Phrasal Verbs, Idioms, Proverbs and Quotations:</u>

Phrasal Verb: A phrasal verb is a verb in its base form combined with an adverb and/or preposition and is treated as a single unit to give a different (new) meaning than the original meaning of the verb, adverb and preposition. For example,

He can easily <u>get across</u> his ideas to others.

The phrasal verb 'get across' is a combination of the verb 'get' and the adverb 'across' which means 'communicate something understandably to others'.

Idiom: An idiom is a group of words whose meaning as a group/single unit is different from the literal meanings of the individual words. For example, the group of words 'have a ball' is an idiom which means 'have a lot of fun/enjoyment' which is different from its literal meaning of 'having a ball in our hand physically' as illustrated below:

The party was great. We <u>had a ball</u>.

Proverb: A proverb is an expression or sentence, formed as a result of experience and observation, which conveys some general truth or advice that guides us to lead our life carefully, practically and satisfactorily. For example,

'<u>Face is the index of the mind</u>' is a proverb that tells us that the face reflects one's mind and that we can read it to know the state of his/her mind.

Quotation: A quotation is also similar to a proverb except that quotations are more direct in meaning and that quotations can be attributed to some particular person/author while a proverb cannot be attributed to somebody because the author is unknown. Moreover, the quotations can be on any topic/subject, not just on virtues and truths. For example,:

    Knowledge is Power.   -   Sir Francis Bacon
    Anyone who has never made a mistake
      has never tried anything new.   -   Albert Einstein

V Functional Sentence Types: Sentences can be classified according to their functions. Five types of sentences are given below:

Declarative Sentence / Assertive Sentence: It is used to form statements, both positive and negative. Most of our sentences belong to this type. For example,

    She invited him to her house.   She did not invite him to her house.

Interrogative Sentence: It is used to ask questions. For example,

    Did she invite him to her house?   When did she invite him to her house?

Imperative Sentence: It is used for requests and commands. For example,

    Please open the door.   Don't open the door.

It is to be noted that the subject in the imperative sentences is always 'you' and not explicitly mentioned.

Exclamatory Sentence: It is used to express emotions by emphasizing a declarative sentence or an imperative sentence and ends with an exclamation mark (!). For example,:

    How beautiful she is!   What a beautiful girl she is!
    How fast he runs!   What a beautiful girl!
    Get out!   I can't believe it!

Subjunctive Sentence: While the above types of sentences are used to express the facts, subjunctive sentences are used to express our wishes that may or may not become true. For example,:

    I wish that my favourite player play today.   It is essential that she write a letter.
    If I were rich, I would buy a car.   I wish I were rich.

Cleft Sentence / Emphatic Sentence: It is just a declarative sentence but written in such a way that it emphasizes/focuses a particular part like subject, object, verb, etc. of the original declarative sentence. Structurally speaking, cleft sentence is a simple sentence written as a complex sentence in order to emphasize/focus a particular part like subject, object, verb, etc. of the original simple sentence. For example,:

Declarative Sentence cum Simple Sentence	Cleft Sentence cum Complex Sentence
I wrote this book.	It was I who wrote this book.
He studied in Oxford University.	It was Oxford University where he studied.

He studied in Oxford University. The <u>university</u> where he studied was <u>Oxford</u>.
She worked throughout the day. All she did was <u>work</u> throughout the day.
She worked throughout the day. What she did was <u>work</u> throughout the day.

VI <u>**Direct Speech and Indirect (Reported) Speech:**</u> Direct Speech and Indirect Speech are two different ways of writing/telling to others at a later point of time what somebody has told earlier.

Direct Speech: In direct speech, what is told by somebody is simply reproduced without any change as illustrated below:

Balu said, "<u>I played football today</u>."

The words of Balu, i.e., "I played football today" are simply reproduced again without any change.

Indirect Speech / Reported Speech: In indirect speech, the speaker's words are expressed after converting them into as if it is told by the listener to a third person. For example,

<u>Balu told me that</u>   <u>he had played football that day</u>.
words of listener   converted words of speaker

Some words in direct speech are modified in indirect speech. For example, 'played' is changed to 'had played', and 'today' is changed to 'that day'. Moreover, though the above example shows the conversion of a declarative sentence from direct speech to indirect speech, the other types of functional sentences like interrogative sentences, imperative sentences, etc. can also be written using both direct speech and indirect speech as explained in chapter 19 on Direct Speech and Indirect Speech.

VII <u>**Punctuation**</u>**:** Punctuation is a set of symbols used to mark the different parts of sentences like the beginning of a sentence, end of a sentence, order of words, etc. and also to change the stress/rhythm of reading the sentences. Common punctuation marks/symbols include comma (,), period (full stop) (.), apostrophe (`), quotation mark (" "), question mark (?), exclamation mark (!), bracket (), dash (--), hyphen (-), ellipsis (…), colon (:) and semicolon (;). For example, the period (.) is used for terminating the declarative sentences, question mark (?) for interrogative sentences and exclamation mark (!) for exclamatory sentences as illustrated in the above examples of functional sentence types. The punctuation is explained in detail in chapter 22 on Punctuation.

VIII <u>**Compound Words and Collocations**</u>**:** When two or more words are combined together to form a single word, it is called a **compound word**. For example, 'newspaper' is a **compound noun** formed by combining the words 'news' and 'paper'. The compound words can be any parts of speech. If two or more words are combined with hyphens to form adjectives specifically, they are called **compound adjectives** as in '<u>a thickly-populated city</u>'. Similarly, **compound adverbs** are also formed by combining words with hyphen as in 'You can pay your loan <u>interest-free</u> now.'

Collocation: If two or more words tend to always occur or belong together, it is called a collocation. For example, we always say 'beautiful girl' and 'handsome boy' but not 'beautiful boy' or 'handsome girl' though they also would mean the same thing and are grammatically correct.

These topics are explained in detail in chapters 25 and 26 on 'Compound Words, Compound Adjectives and Compound Adverbs' and 'Collocation and Patterns for Words' respectively.

IX <u>**Other Word Groups/Types**</u>**:** We have learned that words are classified into different parts of speech, namely noun, pronoun, verb, etc. according to the similarity in their function in sentences. Words can be classified into other groups also based on some other similarities like their position, meaning, properties, etc. Such groups of words include prefixes, suffixes, synonyms, antonyms, hyponym, hypernym, holonym, meronym, homonym, homograph, homophone, anagram, alphagram and palindrome.

For example, 'inter' is a **prefix** because it is added to another word at the beginning to change the meaning of the original word as in 'interschool' which means 'between/among schools'. Similarly, 'ess' is a **suffix**, added at the end of another word, to form nouns of females as in 'poetess and lioness'. **Synonyms** are the words with same/similar meanings like 'box, case, chest, container, crate, pack, package, packet and trunk' while **antonyms** are words with opposite meanings like 'pass, success and triumph' to 'failure'.

They are all explained in chapter 28 on Other Word Groups/Types.

X <u>**Figures of Speech**</u>: Figures of speech refer to the style of using words in sentences in such a way that it means something different than what it would normally/literally mean and that the reader has to figure out the intended meaning. In short, when a sentence has a figurative meaning, it is said to be written with figures of speech. There are so many figures of speech. Some of the common figures of speech include simile, metaphor, hyperbole, euphemism, oxymoron, etc.

For example, **simile** is a way of comparing and <u>likening</u> something with something else because the first thing shows a property of the second thing as in '<u>She is like a rose</u>' wherein a girl is compared to a rose because she may be as beautiful or colourful as a rose.

Metaphor is also a way of comparing two things, but here one thing is <u>equated</u> to another thing because they are similar or exhibit almost the same property/behaviour as in '<u>Her heart is a stone</u>' wherein a girl's heart is compared/equated to a stone because her heart is also without any feeling just like a stone.

Figures of speech are explained in detail in chapter 29 on Figures of Speech.

What next?: Now, you have been introduced to almost all topics of grammar. The knowledge gained in this chapter would be helpful to read any of the following chapters straightaway. However, the chapters in this book are meant to be studied sequentially, one by one. On the other hand, if you have enough knowledge about the previous chapters, you can go to a particular chapter directly.

It is suggested that you spend more time on the chapters about verbs because, in author's opinion, verbs are the backbone of any language. Moreover, while the chapters on grammar topics, from chapter 1 to chapter 23, are to be studied very carefully, the other following chapters, mostly on words/vocabulary, can be skimmed through because it involves more of memorizing rather than understanding the concepts. In general, various vocabularies (list of words) given in various chapters like list of verbs, list of adjectives, etc. can simply be glanced through to avoid being held up in a particular chapter/topic. Besides, as you would already have found, the number of examples given in this book for each point is many more to help you understand the concepts better. However, if you want to complete the chapters quickly, you need not go through all the examples because even the first few examples of a concept/section could be sufficient to illustrate the point. Finally, my best wishes for your journey into the world of grammar in the following chapters.

Chapter 2
Nouns

Nouns are Naming Words. Abbreviation: **n**. They tell the name of somebody or something, namely persons, animals, places, things and ideas/feelings/conceptions.

Question Words for noun: Who, Whom and What - The answer to these question words in sentences is a noun/pronoun.

Examples	Question Words
<u>Ashoka</u> was a great King.	who? (person)
<u>Lion</u> is a wild animal.	what? (animal)
<u>Madurai</u> was the capital of Pandya Kings.	what? (place)
It is a <u>table</u>.	what? (thing)
<u>Laughter</u> eases tension.	what? (idea)
Laughter eases <u>tension</u>.	what? (idea)
<u>Raman</u> likes Lakshmanan.	who? (person)
Raman likes <u>Lakshmanan</u>.	whom? (person)
Children like <u>stories</u>.	what? (idea)

Some common nouns: time, year, month, week, day, person, man, woman, child, life, world, part, hand, eye, place, thing, school, class, teacher, student, work, case, point, government, company, number, group, problem and fact

I Types of Nouns: Nouns can be classified into the following types:

Proper Noun and Common Noun: A noun denoting a particular person, place or thing is called a proper noun, and a noun denoting a class/group of similar persons, places or things is called a common noun as illustrated below:

<u>Balu</u> is a good boy. -	proper noun
Balu is a good <u>boy</u>. -	common noun
<u>Chennai</u> is a city. -	proper noun
Chennai is a <u>city</u>. -	common noun

Concrete Noun and Abstract Noun: A noun denoting a physical (concrete) object that can be seen and touched is called a concrete noun. And, a noun denoting an idea/feeling/conception/quality which is formed in our mind but cannot be seen and touched is called an abstract noun. For example,:

<u>Children</u> play with <u>balls</u>. -	concrete nouns
There is a <u>fish</u> in the <u>fish-tank</u>. -	concrete nouns
<u>Laughter</u> eases <u>tension</u>. -	abstract nouns
<u>Honesty</u> is the best <u>policy</u>. -	abstract nouns
Treat children with <u>kindness</u>. -	abstract noun

Collective Noun: A noun denoting a collection of members/items is called collective noun. For example,:

The police controlled the traffic.	-	a collection of police men/women
They live in a good family.	-	a collection of family members
A big crowd gathered outside.	-	a collection of people

Countable Noun and Uncountable Noun: A noun denoting something which can be counted is called a countable noun, and a noun denoting something which cannot be counted is called an uncountable noun. For example,:

I have many books.	-	countable noun; plural allowed
You have a lot of knowledge.	-	uncountable noun; no plural
Apple is good for health.	-	countable noun; plural allowed
Milk is also good for health.	-	uncountable noun; no plural

II Aspects of Nouns: Nouns have mainly three aspects, namely number, gender and case which are explained below:

Number: When a noun denotes one person/thing, it is singular, and when it denotes more than one person/thing, it is plural. For example,:

Singular   **Plural**

I have an apple.   He has many apples.
A boy is walking along the road.   There are ten boys in the ground.

How to form plurals?: The guidelines for forming plurals are given below. However, it should be noted that they are only general guidelines, and the exact form can be confirmed using a good dictionary.

1) by adding 's' after nouns; e.g., car - cars, lamp - lamps
2) by adding 'es' after sibilant sounds of 'ch', 's', 'sh' and 'x'; e.g., beach - beaches, bus - buses, brush - brushes, box - boxes
3) by substituting 'y' preceded by consonant with 'ies'; e.g., city - cities
4) by adding 's' after 'y' preceded by vowel; e.g., boy - boys
5) by substituting 'f/fe' preceded by vowel with 'ves'; e.g., wife - wives, thief - thieves
6) by adding 's' after 'f' preceded by vowel; e.g., roof - roofs
7) by adding 's' or 'es' to nouns ending with 'o'; e.g., disco - discos, tomato - tomatoes
8) irregular plural forms; e.g., man - men, child - children, mouse - mice, tooth -teeth, goose - geese, foot - feet, ox - oxen
9) some nouns are always used as plurals; e.g., scissors, trousers, shorts
10) certain collective nouns are always used as plurals; e.g., people, cattle
11) some nouns have the same form in both singular and plural; e.g., sheep, dozen
12) by using the plural of the principal word in compound nouns; e.g., sons-in-law

Chapter-2: Nouns

Gender: A noun denoting a male person/animal is in <u>Masculine Gender</u>, and a noun denoting a female person/animal is in <u>Feminine Gender</u>. For example,:

Masculine Gender	**Feminine Gender**
I like my <u>father</u>.	I like my <u>mother</u>.
Some <u>boys</u> are naughty.	<u>Girls</u> work very hard.
The <u>cock</u> crowed.	<u>Hens</u> lay eggs.

A noun which can denote both male and female person/animal is in <u>Common Gender</u>. For example,:

The <u>child</u> is playing happily.   I have a good <u>friend</u>.
It is difficult to get a good <u>servant</u>.   Our <u>neighbours</u> do not cooperate.

A noun which denotes something which is neither male nor female, i.e., lifeless, is in <u>Neuter Gender</u>. For example,:

He does not have a <u>table</u> in his <u>house</u>.   <u>Books</u> are good friends.
I have a <u>computer</u> with <u>Internet</u>.   <u>Honesty</u> is the best <u>policy</u>.

A good dictionary can help you to know the different gender forms of a noun.

Case: When a noun is used as <u>subject</u>, it is in <u>subjective/nominative case</u>, and the question words for nouns in subjective/nominative case are 'Who and What'. Besides, when a noun is used as <u>object</u>, it is in <u>objective/accusative case</u>, and the question words for nouns in objective/accusative case are 'Whom and What'. For example,:

Subjective Case / Nominative Case	**Objective Case / Accusative Case**
<u>Balu</u> likes Ramu. (Who)	Balu likes <u>Ramu</u>. (Whom)
The <u>tiger</u> attacked the goat. (What)	The tiger attacked the <u>goat</u>. (What)

The form of the noun that shows ownership or possession is in <u>Possessive Case</u>, and the question word for nouns in possessive case is 'Whose'. For example,:

It is <u>Balu's</u> pen. (Whose)   That is a <u>hen's</u> egg. (Whose)

<u>How to form Possessive Case?</u>: The guidelines for forming possessive case are given below:

1) by adding "apostrophe + s" to singular nouns; e.g., Balu's pen, tiger's legs, boss's pen
2) by adding "apostrophe + s" to plural nouns not ending with 's'; e.g., men's wear
3) by adding only "apostrophe" to plural nouns ending with 's'; e.g., boys' bag

Chapter 3
Pronouns

Pronouns are Substitute Words for Nouns. Abbreviation: **pron**. Pronouns are used instead of (in place of) nouns. They always refer to some noun(s). For example, in the sentence 'Balu is a tall boy, and **he** is a student', '**he**' is a pronoun because it refers to the noun 'Balu'.

Question Words for pronoun: Who, Whom and What - The answer to these question words in sentences can be a noun / pronoun.

Examples		Question Words
I am a boy. We are boys.	-	who?
You are a girl.	-	who?
He / She is a student. They are students.	-	who?
It is Chennai.	-	what?
He likes her.	-	who?
He likes her.	-	whom?

I Personal Pronouns: The pronouns 'I, We, You, He, She, It, and They' are called personal pronouns because they refer to the particular person(s) being discussed in the sentence. Different forms (Cases) of the personal pronouns are used according to the position of its usage like Subject, Object, etc. as given below:

to read.

Subject Form (Nominative Case)	Object Form (Accusative Case)	Possessive Adjective Form * (Possessive Case)	Possessive Pronoun Form (similar to nouns) (Genitive Case)
First Person: The speaker refers to the 'self'			
I am a boy. We are boys.	Teachers like **me**. Teachers like **us**.	It is **my** bag. It is **our** bag.	**Mine** is red. **Ours** is red.
Second Person: The speaker refers to the person with whom the speaker is speaking to.			
You are a girl.	Teachers like **you**.	It is **your** bag.	**Yours** is blue.

Chapter-3: Pronouns

Third Person: The speaker refers to somebody else other than the 'self' and the listener.			
He is a boy. She is a girl. It is a cat. They are girls.	Teachers like him. Teachers like her. Children like it. Teachers like them.	It is his bag. It is her bag. This is its tail. It is their bag.	His is green. Hers is pink. Its is white. Theirs is pink.
Nouns are always Third Person:			
Balu is a boy.	Teachers like Balu.	It is Balu's bag.	Balu's is blue.
Question Words (Interrogative Pronouns):			
Who What	Whom What	Whose Which	Whose Which

* **Possessive adjective forms are classified under the heading 'Determiners'**

It is very important to note that the pronouns take different forms in different positions. Let's consider the sentence of 'He is a good student, and teachers like him.' Both 'He' and 'him' refer to the same person, but different forms/cases are used because 'He' is a subject, and 'him' is an object. **Finally, it is important to note that not only personal pronouns but also other types of pronouns (given below) have cases depending on the structural position of their usage in a sentence.**

II <u>**Reflexive Pronouns:**</u> They are the pronouns used as **objects** in sentences wherein the action of the subject reflects upon the subject itself as illustrated below:

I hurt **myself**.   We hurt **ourselves**.
You hurt **yourself**. You hurt **yourselves**.
He hurt **himself**. They hurt **themselves**.
She hurt **herself**.
It hurt **itself**.

III <u>**Emphatic Pronouns / Intensive Pronouns:**</u> They are the pronouns used to refer to the **subject** itself for emphasis as illustrated below:

I **myself** wrote the letter.   I wrote the letter **myself**.
We **ourselves** wrote the letter. We wrote the letter **ourselves**.
You **yourself** wrote the letter. You wrote the letter **yourself**.
You **yourselves** wrote the letter. You wrote the letter **yourselves**.

He **himself** wrote the letter.   He wrote the letter **himself**.
She **herself** wrote the letter.   She wrote the letter **herself**.
It **itself** ate the fruit.   It ate the fruit **itself**.
They **themselves** wrote the letter.   They wrote the letter **themselves**.

IV Reciprocal Pronouns: When two or more people (nouns) exchange something among themselves, reciprocal pronouns of 'each other' and 'one another' are used. 'Each other' is used for two people, and 'one another' is used for more than two people. For example,:

They love **each other**.   My friend and I shared **each other's** food.
Classmates support **one another**.   Students share **one another's** notes.

V Demonstrative Pronouns: Demonstrative pronouns point out at some nouns as illustrated below:

This is a pen given by my friend.   These are flowers for the temple.
That is wonderful.   Those are very beautiful.
Such was his strong faith.   He was new and treated as such.

Demonstrative pronouns can be used as determiners as explained in chapter 13 on Determiners.

VI Indefinite Pronouns: Indefinite pronouns can refer to everybody/everything of a group of nouns in a general way as illustrated below:

Everybody likes children.   You cannot give it to anybody.
    ('everybody' is used in positive sentences and 'anybody' in negative sentences)
Somebody will come tomorrow.   Nobody can win him.
Everything will be done.   He cannot do anything.
    ('everything' is used in positive sentences and 'anything' in negative sentences)
Something is going to happen.   Nothing can stop him.
One should be confident.   None can be so good.
All are singing national anthem.   Some are good.
You cannot meet any of them.   Each may donate ₹100.
Few will object to this.   Many will appreciate this.

Other indefinite pronouns include 'enough, fewer, less, little, much, several, more, most, both, either and neither'. Some of these pronouns like 'few and many' are used for countable nouns and some other like 'little and much' for uncountable nouns.

Chapter-3: Pronouns

VII Distributive Pronouns: Distributive pronouns refer to all persons/things in a group of nouns but one at a time as illustrated below:

    I will give you all <u>each</u> a chocolate.   <u>Each</u> of them will get a chocolate.
    We can buy bananas for ₹ 2 <u>each</u>.   We can buy <u>each</u> of these bananas for ₹ 2.
    <u>Either</u> of them can participate.   I like <u>neither</u> of them.

VIII Interrogative Pronouns: When the possible question words of pronouns, namely 'Who, Whom, Whose, What and Which' are used in questions, they are called interrogative pronouns. Questions are explained in chapter 6 on Interrogative Sentences - Questions.

IX Relative Pronouns: Relative pronouns are similar to interrogative pronouns but used in clauses as explained in chapter 17 on Clauses and Structural Sentence Types.

Chapter 4
Verbs - Basics

Verbs tell what is happening in the sentence or what is the condition / state (of being) of the subject in the sentence. Abbreviation: **v**. There are mainly two types of verbs, namely **'Action Verbs'** telling what is happening / what the subject is doing and **'Being Verbs / Be-Verbs'** telling what the condition / state (of being) of the subject is. For example,:

He <u>is playing</u> football.	-	Here, 'is playing' is an **'Action Verb'** because it shows the action of 'playing' and tells what is happening and what the subject 'he' is doing.
I <u>am</u> a boy.	-	Here, 'am' is a **'Being Verb / Be-Verb'** because it simply states that the subject 'I' is a boy and no action is involved.

As you would have noticed, verbs are called 'verbs' in both Parts of Speech and Sentence Structure.

I <u>Factors affecting the Verb Form:</u>

A verb is written in **different forms** according to many factors like **Person and Number of subject, Tense(time), Aspect(point of time and duration of time), Voice and Mood**. These factors are explained briefly below. Even if you don't understand these factors immediately, it is not a problem. You will understand them as you read on this chapter as well as the chapter 7 on Verbs - Advanced.

Person: It refers to the person of the subject, i.e., **First Person (fp), Second Person (sp) or Third Person (tp)**. These abbreviations are used against verb forms in our discussion to show that it determines the particular verb form.

Number: It refers to number of the subject, i.e., **Singular or Plural**.

Person and Number: Among other factors, the person and the number also determine a verb form together. In the following discussion, they are specified against each verb form to specify that a particular combination of person and number determines a specific form of verb. Abbreviations are used for this purpose. The abbreviations are as follows:

First Person Singular **(fps)**	First Person Plural **(fpp)**
Second Person Singular **(sps)**	Second Person Plural **(spp)**
Third Person Singular **(tps)**	Third Person Plural **(tpp)**

Chapter-4: Verbs - Basics

Tense: It refers to how a verb shows the time (**present, past** and **future**) of happening in the sentence.

Aspect: It refers to how a verb shows the duration of time in each tense. The duration of an action can be a point of time (**simple tense**), a certain continuous long duration (**continuous tense**), a certain long and completed duration (**perfect tense**) or a certain continuous very long duration (**perfect continuous tense**).

Voice: It refers to whether the subject acts (**active voice**), or the subject is acted upon and receives the effect of the action of the verb (**passive voice**).

Mood: Mood of the verb tells whether it expresses a fact/action using tenses (**indicative mood**), or it expresses a request/order (**imperative mood**), or it expresses just an intention/wish which may or may not happen (**subjunctive mood**).

Tense and Aspect: Among all the factors, the tenses and their aspects form the basis for writing verbs, also affected by other factors. Following are the tenses and their aspects:

Present Tense	Past Tense	Future Tense
Simple Present	Simple Past	Simple Future
Present Continuous	Past Continuous	Future Continuous
Present Perfect	Past Perfect	Future Perfect
Present Perfect Continuous	Past Perfect Continuous	Future Perfect Continuous

II <u>Action Verbs</u>: They are used to express what the subject is doing or what is happening in the sentence.

Finite Verb / Complete Verb: Action Verb should be written as a finite/complete verb in any sentence. The form of a finite/complete verb is as follows:

Finite/Complete Verb = Auxiliary Verb (if any) + Main Verb Form

As an example, **Main Verb Forms** are given below for the verb 'love':

Base Form	Present Form	Past Form	Past Participle Form	Present Participle Form
love	love loves (tps)	loved	loved	loving

The above verb 'love' and such verbs are called **regular verbs** because their Past Form and Past Participle Form are formed by adding 'ed' to the base form. Some other verbs are called **irregular verbs** because their Past Form and Past Participle Form are formed using different words not following any standard/pattern as illustrated below:

eat	eat eats (tps)	ate	eaten	eating

Auxiliary Verbs: Auxiliary verbs are used with the main verb forms to express the **person, number, tense and aspect** of the verb. They are listed below:

Tense / Aspect	Simple	Continuous	Perfect	Perfect Continuous
Present	do* does (tps)*	am (fps) is (tps) are (plural)	have has (tps)	have been has been (tps)
Past	did*	was (singular) were (plural)	had	had been
Future	shall (fp) will	shall be (fp) will be	shall have (fp) will have	shall have been (fp) will have been

* The auxiliary verbs of <u>do, does and did</u> are not used explicitly while writing positive sentences. They are used for writing negative and interrogative sentences which are explained in chapters 5 and 6 on these topics.

Examples of complete verb: The complete verb is illustrated below:

I <u>am reading</u> a book.

In the above sentence, 'am reading' is a complete verb in present continuous tense - i.e., am (auxiliary verb) + reading (Present Participle, the verb form for continuous aspect).

I <u>have read</u> that book.

In the above sentence, 'have read' is a complete verb in present perfect tense - i.e., have (auxiliary verb) + read (Past Participle, the verb form for perfect aspect).

I <u>have been reading</u> a book.

In the above sentence, 'have been reading' is a complete verb in present perfect continuous tense - i.e., have been (auxiliary verb) + reading (Present Participle, the verb form for perfect continuous aspect).

Chapter-4: Verbs - Basics

I <u>read</u> a book daily.

In the above sentence, 'read' is a complete verb in simple present tense - i.e., (no explicit auxiliary verb) + read (present form, the verb form for simple present aspect). As mentioned earlier, the auxiliary verb of 'do' for the simple present tense is not used explicitly. However, it will be used for negative and interrogative sentences as illustrated in 'I <u>do not read</u> a book daily' and '<u>Do</u> I <u>read</u> a book daily?'

Infinite Verb / Non-finite Verb / Incomplete Verb: Usage of other forms of verbs, i.e., the Participle forms without auxiliary verb and the infinitive ('to' + base form) are called infinite/non-finite/incomplete verbs which are also called verbal phrases. Verbal phrases are discussed in chapter 8.

III <u>Form of Finite Verbs for Tenses in Active Voice:</u> In Active Voice, 'subject' does some action, and the 'object' receives the effect as illustrated below:

<u>Shahjahan</u> <u>built</u> <u>the Taj Mahal</u>.
    S   V   O

The above example shows that the subject 'Shahjahan' performs the action of 'building', and the result/effect of the action is 'Taj Mahal'. The basic <u>sentence structure</u> for Active Voice is given below:

Subject(**S**)+[Aux.(**A**)]+Main Verb Form(**V**) [+ Object(**O**)] [+ Other Complements(**OC**)].

The form of complete/finite verb for various tenses in active voice is given below for the different subjects. <u>Examples for these tenses are given after explaining the passive voice also.</u>

Pronouns	**Simple Present**	**Simple Past**	**Simple Future**
I, We	present form	past form	shall + base form
You	present form	past form	will + base form
He, She, It, Singular noun	present form with 's' *(Third Person Singular needs 's' after verb)*	past form	will + base form
They, Plural noun	present form	past form	will + base form

Pronouns	Present Continuous	Past Continuous	Future Continuous
I, We	am/are + present participle	was/were + present participle	shall be + present participle
You	are + present participle	were + present participle	will be + present participle
He, She, It, Singular noun	is + present participle	was + present participle	will be + present participle
They, Plural noun	are + present participle	were + present participle	will be + present participle

Pronouns	Present Perfect	Past Perfect	Future Perfect
I, We	have + past participle	had + past participle	shall have + past participle
You	have + past participle	had + past participle	will have + past participle
He, She, It, Singular noun	has + past participle	had + past participle	will have + past participle
They, Plural noun	have + past participle	had + past participle	will have + past participle

Pronouns	Present Perfect Continuous	Past Perfect Continuous	Future Perfect Continuous
I, We	have been + present participle	had been + present participle	shall have been + present participle
You	have been + present participle	had been + present participle	will have been + present participle
He, She, It, Singular noun	has been + present participle	had been + present participle	will have been + present participle
They, Plural noun	have been + present participle	had been + present participle	will have been + present participle

Chapter-4: Verbs - Basics

IV <u>**Form of Finite Verbs for Tenses in Passive Voice:**</u> In Passive Voice, 'subject' receives the effect of or the result of some action performed by the 'subject' of the original sentence in active voice as illustrated below:

<u>Shahjahan</u> <u>built</u> <u>the Taj Mahal</u>. - Active Voice
    S   V   O

<u>The Taj Mahal</u>   <u>was built</u>   <u>by</u> <u>Shahjahan</u>. - Passive Voice
S (original object)   V   Prepositional Object (original subject)

The above example shows that the subject (original object) <u>'Taj Mahal'</u> receives the effect of or the result of the action 'building' performed by the prepositional object (original subject) 'Shahjahan'. The basic <u>sentence structure</u> for Passive Voice is given below:

Subject(**S**) + [Aux.(**A**)] + Past Participle(**V**) [+ 'by' + Prepositional Object(**PO**)] [+ **OC**].

When a sentence in active voice is written in passive voice, the original object becomes the subject, and the original subject becomes the prepositional object of 'by'.

Auxiliary Verbs for Passive Voice: They are listed below:

Tense / Aspect	Simple	Continuous	Perfect	Perfect Continuous
Present	am (fps) is (tps) are (plural)	am being (fps) is being (tps) are being (plural)	have been has been (tps)	*no passive voice*
Past	was (singular) were (plural)	was being (singular) were being (plural)	had been	*no passive voice*
Future	shall be (fp) will be	*no passive voice*	shall have been (fp) will have been	*no passive voice*

The form of complete/finite verb for various tenses in passive voice is given below for the different subjects. <u>Examples for these tenses in passive voice are given at the end of these forms of verbs</u>.

Pronouns	Simple Present	Simple Past	Simple Future
I, We	am/are + past participle	was/were + past participle	shall be + past participle
You	are + past participle	were + past participle	will be + past participle
He, She, It, Singular noun	is + past participle	was + past participle	will be + past participle
They, Plural noun	are + past participle	were + past participle	will be + past participle
Pronouns	**Present Continuous**	**Past Continuous**	**Future Continuous**
I, We	am being/are being + past participle	was being/were being + past participle	*no passive voice*
You	are being + past participle	were being + past participle	*no passive voice*
He, She, It, Singular noun	is being + past participle	was being + past participle	*no passive voice*
They, Plural noun	are being + past participle	were being + past participle	*no passive voice*
Pronouns	**Present Perfect**	**Past Perfect**	**Future Perfect**
I, We	have been + past participle	had been + past participle	shall have been + past participle
You	have been + past participle	had been + past participle	will have been + past participle
He, She, It, Singular noun	has been + past participle	had been + past participle	will have been + past participle
They, Plural noun	have been + past participle	had been + past participle	will have been + past participle
Pronouns	**Present Perfect Continuous**	**Past Perfect Continuous**	**Future Perfect Continuous**

No passive voice for the perfect continuous tenses

The following **example** shows the verb 'love' in different tenses and aspects under both Active Voice and Passive Voice.

Chapter-4: Verbs - Basics

<u>**Active Voice**</u>

Simple Present
I love her.
We love them.
You love me.
He/She/It loves you.
They love us.

Simple Past
I loved her.
We loved them.
You loved me.
He/She/It loved you.
They loved us.

Simple Future
I shall love her.
We shall love them.
You will love me.
He/She/It will love you.
They will love us.

Present Continuous
I am loving her.
We are loving them.
You are loving me.
He/She/It is loving you.
They are loving us.

Past Continuous
I was loving her.
We were loving them.
You were loving me.
He/She/It was loving you.
They were loving us.

Future Continuous
I shall be loving her.
We shall be loving them.
You will be loving me.
He/She/It will be loving you.
They will be loving us.

<u>**Passive Voice**</u>

Simple Present
She is loved by me.
They are loved by us.
I am loved by you.
You are loved by him/her/it.
We are loved by them.

Simple Past
She was loved by me.
They were loved by us.
I was loved by you.
You were loved by him/her/it.
We were loved by them.

Simple Future
She will be loved by me.
They will be loved by us.
I shall be loved by you.
You will be loved by him/her/it.
We shall be loved by them.

Present Continuous
She is being loved by me.
They are being loved by us.
I am being loved by you.
You are being loved by him/her/it.
We are being loved by them.

Past Continuous
She was being loved by me.
They were being loved by us.
I was being loved by you.
You were being loved by him/her/it.
We were being loved by them.

Future Continuous
no passive voice

Present Perfect
I have loved her.
We have loved them.
You have loved me.
He/She/It has loved her/him/it.
They have loved us.

Past Perfect
I had loved her.
We had loved them.
You had loved me.
He/She/It had loved her/him/it.
They had loved us.

Future Perfect
I shall have loved her.
We shall have loved them.
You will have loved me.
He/She/It will have loved her/him/it.
They will have loved us.

Present Perfect Continuous
I have been loving her.
We have been loving them.
You have been loving me.
He/She/It has been loving you.
They have been loving us.

Past Perfect Continuous
I had been loving her.
We had been loving them.
You had been loving me.
He/She/It had been loving you.
They had been loving us.

Future Perfect Continuous
I shall have been loving her.
We shall have been loving them.
You will have been loving me.
He/She/It will have been loving you.
They will have been loving us.

Present Perfect
She has been loved by me.
They have been loved by us.
I have been loved by you.
She/He/It has been loved by him/her/it.
We have been loved by them.

Past Perfect
She had been loved by me.
They had been loved by us.
I had been loved by you.
She/He/It had been loved by him/her/it.
We had been loved by them.

Future Perfect
She will have been loved by me.
They will have been loved by us.
I shall have been loved by you.
She/He/It will have been loved by him/her/it.
We shall have been loved by them.

Present Perfect Continuous
no passive voice

Past Perfect Continuous
no passive voice

Future Perfect Continuous
no passive voice

Chapter-4: Verbs - Basics

V <u>Uses of Tenses for Action Verbs</u>: Complementary words are given for each tense, and the presence of such words in sentences will normally indicate the use of a particular tense.

Simple Tenses:

Present: Regular habits and routines, truths, facts and feelings.
Complementary Words: usually, regularly, always, often, sometimes, rarely, never, seldom, daily, every, each, etc.

    e.g., She <u>brushes</u> her teeth twice **daily**.   -   habit
         I <u>go</u> to school **regularly**.   -   routine
         The sun <u>rises</u> in the east.   -   truth
         He **always** <u>likes</u> tea.   -   feeling

Past: Completed Actions
Complementary Words: yesterday, last week, last month, last year, etc.

    e.g., I <u>saw</u> him **yesterday**.

Future: Future Actions
Complementary Words: tomorrow, next week, soon, later, etc.

    e.g., They <u>will come</u> here **next week**.

Other ways of expressing the future:

    I am <u>going to</u> buy a car.   -   decided future action (present continuous tense is used here)
    Come quickly. The show is <u>about to</u> start. - immediate future (this usage is explained in the next chapter)

Continuous Tenses:

Present: Actions happening at the moment in the present; planned future.
Complementary Words: at the moment, now, today, this week, currently, etc.

    e.g., The boys <u>are playing</u> hockey **now**. - action at the moment
         We <u>are meeting</u> **this week**. - planned future/action

Past: Actions happening at that moment in the past.

    e.g., We <u>were playing</u> hockey at 5 pm yesterday.

Future: Actions happening at that moment in the future.

    e.g., We <u>shall be playing</u> hockey when you come tomorrow.

Perfect Tenses: In perfect tenses, the word 'Perfect' means 'Completed'.
Present: Past/Completed actions still having effect; actions just finished and the recent past.
Complementary Words: already, just, not yet, ever, never, so far, till now, etc.

>   e.g., I <u>have seen</u> the film 'Shivaji'.   - past action still having effect
>   He <u>has come</u> **just** now.   - action just finished
>   They <u>have arrived</u>.   - recent past action whose effect is still seen

Past: First past action of two past actions (Simple Past for second past action)

>   e.g., When we <u>reached</u> the station, the train <u>had left</u>.

Future: Actions that would be finished in the future
Complementary Words: by, in, etc.

>   e.g., We <u>shall have reached</u> Kolkata **by** 11 pm tomorrow.

Perfect Continuous Tenses:
Complementary Words: for, since, all

Present: Actions happening continuously till the present (moment) for some duration

>   e.g., They <u>have been living</u> here **since** 1970.
>   He <u>has been playing</u> **for** 5 hours.
>   I <u>have been experiencing</u> a problem of late.

Past: Actions happening continuously in the past for some duration and finished in the past itself

>   e.g., He <u>had been writing</u> a novel **for** 5 years.
>   I <u>had been waiting</u> for 10 minutes when the doctor came.

Future: Actions happening continuously since the past and till the future for some duration

>   e.g., By next year, we <u>shall have been living</u> here **for** 10 years.

VI <u>**Modal Auxiliary Verbs / Modal Verbs:**</u> Modal auxiliary verbs are very similar to the auxiliary verbs of 'shall' and 'will', or rather 'shall' and 'will' are also treated as part of modal verbs. The modal verbs 'shall' and 'will' are used to express the future (tenses) whereas other modal verbs are used to express the different conditions or feelings like obligation, possibility, ability, permission, necessity, hope, desire, etc. As you would have noticed, these modal conditions are also futuristic in time because they are neither finished (past) nor happening now (present) but should/may (not) happen after some time (future).

The following **examples** illustrate them:

I <u>shall</u> go. (future)	I <u>should</u> go. (obligation)
He <u>will</u> go. (future)	He <u>would</u> go. (possibility)
We <u>can</u> win. (ability)	We <u>could</u> win. (possibility)
They <u>may</u> win. (possibility)	They <u>might</u> win. (possibility)
She <u>must</u> come. (obligation)	You <u>ought to</u> learn. (obligation)

Chapter-4: Verbs - Basics

Other uses of modal verbs:

'Shall' used with second person and third person and 'will' used with first person mean certainty.

    I will help you. (certainty)   He shall help you. (certainty)

It is also to be noted that 'will' is used with all persons in modern English nowadays to express the future.

More uses:

It should solve the problem (certainty)   We should have studied. (past obligation)
Would you mind a minute? (request)   We would watch movies during our
                                            childhood. (past hobby)

Can you help me? (request)   Can I help you? (offer)
Can they attend the class? (permission)   They can attend the class. (permission)
Could you help me? (request)   Could I help you? (offer)
We could have studied. (past possibility)   We could win then. (past ability)
May I come in, please? (request)   We might have won. (past possibility)

Tip: As these modal verbs are similar to the auxiliary 'shall', they will also take the forms similar to 'shall be, shall have and shall have been'. For example, 'could be, could have and could have been' can also be used as auxiliary verbs.

VII Be-Verbs / Being Verbs: Be-Verbs, also called being verbs, are used to express the **condition or state (of being)** of something / somebody. They don't refer to any actions performed by something / somebody.

Various forms of be-verbs are given below:

Base Form	Present Form	Past Form	Past Participle Form	Present Participle Form
be	am, is, are	was, were	been	being

The sentence structure for be-verb is given below:

Subject(**S**) + Be-Verb(**V**) [+ Other Complements(**OC**)].

There is no Object(**O**) in the above sentence structure because the be-verbs cannot have object. For e.g.,

    She is a teacher.
    S   V   OC

The different forms of Be-Verbs under different tenses/aspects are as follows:

Tense / Aspect	Simple	Continuous	Perfect	Perfect Continuous
Present	am (fps) is (tps) are (plural)	am being (fps) is being (tps) are being (plural)	have been has been (tps)	---
Past	was (singular) were (plural)	was being (singular) were being (plural)	had been	---
Future	shall be (fp) will be	---	shall have been (fp) will have been	---
Modal	+ be	---	+ have been	---

<u>*Note:*</u> **Be-Verbs are also used as auxiliary verbs.**

Uses of Be-Verbs under different tenses: Be-Verbs are used to express the **condition/ state (of being)** of something / somebody at some time and its aspect.

Simple Tenses: express the state of being at a particular time.

      Present: e.g.,   I <u>am</u> a boy.
                                        She <u>is</u> a girl.
                                        We <u>are</u> students.

      Past: e.g.,   I <u>was</u> a boy.
                                        She <u>was</u> a girl.
                                        We <u>were</u> students.

      Future: e.g.,   I <u>shall</u> be a man.
                                        She <u>will</u> be a woman.
                                        We <u>shall</u> be masters.

Chapter-4: Verbs - Basics

Continuous Tenses: Be-Verbs are not used in continuous tenses. However, the various forms of be-verbs of continuous tenses are used as auxiliaries in passive voice.

Perfect Tenses: express the state of being over some time, but after it is finished.

Present:	e.g.,	I have been a student. / I have been to Mathura. She has been a student. / She has been to Mathura. We have been students. / We have been to Mathura.
Past:	e.g.,	I had been a student. / I had been to Mathura. She had been a student. / She had been to Mathura. We had been students. / We had been to Mathura.
Future:	e.g.,	I shall have been a student. / I shall have been to Mathura. She will have been a student. / She will have been to Mathura. We shall have been students. / We shall have been to Mathura.

VIII Action Verb cum Be-Verb (have): The verb 'have' can be used as both Action Verb and Be-Verb. Various forms of 'have' as action verb are given below:

Base Form	Present Form	Past Form	Past Participle Form	Present Participle Form
have	have has (tps)	had	had	having

The different forms of **'have' as Action Verb** under different tenses/aspects are as follows:

Tense / Aspect	Simple	Continuous	Perfect	Perfect Continuous
Present	have has (tps)	am having (fps) is having (tps) are having (plural)	have had has had (tps)	have been having has been having (tps)
Past	had	was having (singular) were having (plural)	had had*	had been having
Future	shall have (fp) will have	shall be having (fp) will be having	shall have had (fp) will have had	shall have been having (fp) will have been having
Modal	+ have	+ be having	+ have had	+ have been having

Note: **'Have' is also used as auxiliary verb.**

* The form 'had had' is very interesting because the first 'had' is an auxiliary verb and the second 'had' is the past participle form of the action verb 'have' as illustrated below:

I <u>had had</u> an old bike during my school days.
  A V

The different forms of **'have' as Be-Verb** are as follows:

Simple Present	Simple Past	Simple Future
have	had	shall have
has		will have
		(modal verb) + have

As you would have noticed, the form of **'have'** as both Action Verb and Be-Verb in simple tenses is the same. However, the meaning is slightly different as illustrated below:

Action Verb:	I <u>have</u> a ball.	=	I keep a ball with me.
	I <u>do not have</u> a ball.	=	I do not keep a ball with me.
Be-Verb:	I <u>have</u> a ball.	=	A ball is with me.
	I <u>have not</u> a ball.	=	A ball is not with me.

Apart from the meaning, the formation of negatives and interrogatives is different in each of these cases as illustrated in chapters 5 and 6 on these topics.

IX <u>**Action Verb cum Modal Verb (dare, need):**</u> The verbs 'dare and need' can be used as both Action Verb and Modal Verb. Various forms of these verbs are given below:

Base Form	Present Form	Past Form	Past Participle Form	Present Participle Form
dare	dare dares (tps)	dared	dared	daring
need	need needs (tps)	needed	needed	needing

The uses of **'dare and need'** as Action Verb are like any other action verb, and as **Modal verb,** they are generally used in negative and interrogative sentences; as,

Chapter-4: Verbs - Basics

Base Form	Past Form
I <u>dare</u> not play.	I <u>dared</u> not play.
How <u>dare</u> you oppose me?	---
He <u>need</u> not go.	He <u>needed</u> not go.
	He <u>need not have</u> gone.
Need I go?	---

X <u>**Action Verb cum Auxiliary Verb (do):**</u> The verb '**do**' is used as both Action Verb and Auxiliary verb. Various forms of 'do' are given below:

Base Form	Present Form	Past Form	Past Participle Form	Present Participle Form
do	do does (tps)	did	done	doing

The forms of **'do' as Auxiliary-Verb** are as follows:

Simple Present	Simple Past	Simple Future
do does	did	---

The auxiliary verbs of <u>do, does and did</u> are not used explicitly while writing positive sentences. They are used for writing negative and interrogative sentences as illustrated in chapters 5 and 6 on these topics. However, when they are used explicitly while writing positive sentences, they are used to emphasize the action expressed by the main verb as illustrated below:

I study every day.	-	simply states that I study every day
I <u>do study</u> every day.	-	strongly states that I (certainly) study every day
I sent a letter.	-	simply states that I sent a letter
I <u>did send</u> a letter.	-	emphatically states that I (surely) sent a letter

XI <u>**All Auxiliary Verbs:**</u> From the above discussions, it can be concluded that the auxiliary verbs include be-verbs, modal verbs and the (action) verbs 'have' and 'do'.

XII **Some Common Verbs:** In the following list of verbs, regular verbs are in normal font; *irregular verbs are in italics*, and **antonyms are in bold**.

Base/Present Form	Past Form	Past Participle Form	Present Participle Form = Base Form + ing
accept	accepted	accepted	accepting
agree	agreed	agreed	agreeing
refuse	**refused**	**refused**	**refusing**
reject	**rejected**	**rejected**	**rejecting**
allow	allowed	allowed	allowing
forbid	*forbade*	*forbidden*	*forbidding*
arrange	arranged	arranged	arranging
cancel	**cancelled**	**cancelled**	**cancelling**
ask	asked	asked	asking
reply	**replied**	**replied**	**replying**
begin	*began*	*begun*	*beginning*
start	started	started	starting
stop	**stopped**	**stopped**	**stopping**
become	*became*	*become*	*becoming*
believe	believed	believed	believing
disbelieve	**disbelieved**	**disbelieved**	**disbelieving**
borrow	borrowed	borrowed	borrowing
lend	*lent*	*lent*	*lending*
break	*broke*	*broken*	*breaking*
make	*made*	*made*	*making*
bring	brought	brought	bringing
take	*took*	*taken*	*taking*
burn	burnt	burnt	burning
buy	bought	bought	buying
sell	*sold*	*sold*	*selling*
call	called	called	calling
carry	carried	carried	carrying
change	changed	changed	changing
clean	cleaned	cleaned	cleaning
soil	**soiled**	**soiled**	**soiling**
close	closed	closed	closing
shut	*shut*	*shut*	*shutting*
open	**opened**	**opened**	**opening**
comb	combed	combed	combing
come	*came*	*come*	*coming*

Chapter-4: Verbs - Basics

go	*went*	*gone*	*going*
complain	complained	complained	complaining
cough	coughed	coughed	coughing
count	counted	counted	counting
cut	*cut*	*cut*	*cutting*
dance	danced	danced	dancing
decide	decided	decided	deciding
do	*did*	*done*	*doing*
draw	*drew*	*drawn*	*drawing*
drink	*drank*	*drunk*	*drinking*
drive	*drove*	*driven*	*driving*
eat	*ate*	*eaten*	*eating*
explain	explained	explained	explaining
fall	*fell*	*fallen*	*falling*
feel	*felt*	*felt*	*feeling*
fill	filled	filled	filling
empty	**emptied**	**emptied**	**emptying**
find	*found*	*found*	*finding*
finish	finished	finished	finishing
fit	*fit*	*fit*	*fitting*
fix	fixed	fixed	fixing
fly	*flew*	*flown*	*flying*
fly	flied	flied	flying
follow	followed	followed	following
forget	*forgot*	*forgotten*	*forgetting*
remember	**remembered**	**remembered**	**remembering**
remind	reminded	reminded	reminding
get	*got*	*got, gotten*	*getting*
give	*gave*	*given*	*giving*
take	**took**	**taken**	**taking**
happen	happened	happened	happening
hear	*heard*	*heard*	*hearing*
help	helped	helped	helping
trouble	**troubled**	**troubled**	**troubling**
disturb	**disturbed**	**disturbed**	**disturbing**
hold	*held*	*held*	*holding*
hurt	*hurt*	*hurt*	*hurting*
join	joined	joined	joining
separate	**separated**	**separated**	**separating**
keep	*kept*	*kept*	*keeping*
know	*knew*	*known*	*knowing*
leave	*left*	*left*	*leaving*

arrive	**arrived**	**arrived**	**arriving**
lift	lifted	lifted	lifting
drop	**dropped**	**dropped**	**dropping**
like	liked	liked	liking
dislike	**disliked**	**disliked**	**disliking**
hate	**hated**	**hated**	**hating**
listen	listened	listened	listening
live	lived	lived	living
lose	*lost*	*lost*	*losing*
gain	**gained**	**gained**	**gaining**
win	*won*	*won*	*winning*
mean	*meant*	*meant*	*meaning*
meet	*met*	*met*	*meeting*
move	moved	moved	moving
need	needed	needed	needing
organize	organized	organized	organizing
pay	*paid*	*paid*	*paying*
receive	**received**	**received**	**receiving**
play	played	played	playing
promise	promised	promised	promising
put	*put*	*put*	*putting*
question	questioned	questioned	questioning
answer	**answered**	**answered**	**answering**
rain	rained	rained	raining
read	*read*	*read*	*reading*
run	*ran*	*run*	*running*
say	*said*	*said*	*saying*
tell	*told*	*told*	*telling*
see	*saw*	*seen*	*seeing*
seem	seemed	seemed	seeming
look	looked	looked	looking
send	*sent*	*sent*	*sending*
set	*set*	*set*	*setting*
show	showed	showed	showing
hide	**hid**	**hidden**	**hiding**
sign	signed	signed	signing
sing	*sang*	*sung*	*singing*
sit	*sat*	*sat*	*sitting*
stand	**stood**	**stood**	**standing**
sleep	*slept*	*slept*	*sleeping*
wake	**woke**	**woken**	**waking**
smoke	smoked	smoked	smoking

Chapter-4: Verbs - Basics

speak	*spoke*	*spoken*	*speaking*
spell	spelled	spelled	spelling
spell	*spelt*	*spelt*	*spelling*
spend	*spent*	*spent*	*spending*
save	**saved**	**saved**	**saving**
study	studied	studied	studying
succeed	succeeded	succeeded	succeeding
fail	**failed**	**failed**	**failing**
suggest	suggested	suggested	suggesting
swim	*swam*	*swum*	*swimming*
talk	talked	talked	talking
teach	*taught*	*taught*	*teaching*
learn	**learned**	**learned**	**learning**
think	*thought*	*thought*	*thinking*
translate	translated	translated	translating
travel	travelled	travelled	travelling
try	tried	tried	trying
turn	turned	turned	turning
type	typed	typed	typing
understand	*understood*	*understood*	*understanding*
use	used	used	using
wait	waited	waited	waiting
walk	walked	walked	walking
want	wanted	wanted	wanting
watch	watched	watched	watching
work	worked	worked	working
worry	worried	worried	worrying
write	*wrote*	*written*	*writing*

Chapter 5
Negative Sentences

Negative sentences are formed by adding 'not' between the auxiliary verb and the main verb form. The <u>sentence structure</u> for the negative sentences is given below with examples.

Subject(**S**) + Aux.(**A**) + **'<u>not</u>'** + Main Verb Form(**V**) [+ Object(**O**)]
[+ Other complements(**OC**)].

He is coming.	-	Positive Sentence
He is <u>not</u> coming.	-	Negative Sentence
He will come.	-	Positive Sentence
He will <u>not</u> come.	-	Negative Sentence
Football is played here.	-	Positive Sentence
Football is <u>not</u> played here.	-	Negative Sentence

If there is more than one word in the auxiliary, 'not' should be added after the first word of the auxiliary as illustrated below:

He has been playing.   -   He has <u>not</u> been playing.

The **negative auxiliaries** are normally formed by adding 'not' after the auxiliary verb as in 'is not', 'will not', 'may not', 'do not', etc.; however, <u>the negative of 'can' is 'cannot', not 'can not'</u>.

If there is no explicit auxiliary, the implicit auxiliary should be used as illustrated below where the implicit auxiliary is given in bold:

I play football.	-	I **do** <u>not</u> play football.
He plays football.	-	He **does** <u>not</u> play football.
We played football.	-	We **did** <u>not</u> play football.

As given above, though auxiliaries are not written explicitly for simple present tense and simple past tense, they exist implicitly and should be used for forming negative sentences. It is very important to know them because they will be used in forming questions also. They are given below:

Present Form	=	do + Base Form	(e.g., do + play)
Present Form with 's'	=	does + Base Form	(e.g., does + play)
Past Form	=	did + Base Form	(e.g., did + play)

For **be-verbs**, 'not' is added just after the single-word be-verb and after the first word of the multi-word be-verb. For e.g.,

He is a teacher.	He is <u>not</u> a teacher.
They will be strong.	They will <u>not</u> be strong.

46

Chapter 6
Interrogative Sentences - Questions

I Yes/No Questions: Yes/No Questions are called so because the answer for these questions always start with 'Yes or No'. They are formed by inverting the auxiliary and the subject. The sentence structure for the 'Yes/No' interrogative sentences is given below with examples:

Aux.(A) + Subject(S) + ['not'] + Main Verb Form(V) [+ Object(O)] [+ Other Complements(OC)]?

He is coming.	-	Positive Sentence
Is he coming?	-	Yes/No Interrogative Sentence
Yes, He is coming.	-	Positive answer
No, He is not coming.	-	Negative answer
He will come.	-	Positive Sentence
Will he come?	-	Yes/No Interrogative Sentence
Yes, he will come.	-	Positive answer
No, he will not come.	-	Negative answer

If there is no explicit auxiliary, the implicit auxiliary should be used as illustrated below where the implicit auxiliary is given in bold:

I play football.	-	Positive Sentence
Do I play football?	-	Yes/No Interrogative Sentence
Yes, I play football.	-	Positive answer
No, I do not play football.	-	Negative answer
He plays football.	-	Positive Sentence
Does he play football?	-	Yes/No Interrogative Sentence
Yes, he plays football.	-	Positive answer
No, he does not play football.	-	Negative answer
We played football.	-	Positive Sentence
Did we play football?	-	Yes/No Interrogative Sentence
Yes, we played football.	-	Positive answer
No, we did not play football.	-	Negative answer

If there is more than one word in the auxiliary, the first auxiliary and the subject should be inverted as illustrated below:

He has been playing.	-	Positive Sentence
Has he been playing?	-	Yes/No Interrogative Sentence
Yes, he has been playing football.	-	Positive answer
No, he has not been playing football.	-	Negative answer

The same rule, inverting the first auxiliary and the subject, is followed for negative sentences also as illustrated below:

He is not coming.	-	<u>Is</u> he <u>not</u> coming?
He will not come.	-	<u>Will</u> he <u>not</u> come?
I do not play football.	-	<u>Do</u> I <u>not</u> play football?
He does not play football.	-	<u>Does</u> he <u>not</u> play football?
We did not play football.	-	<u>Did</u> we <u>not</u> play football?
He has not been playing.	-	<u>Has</u> he <u>not</u> been playing?

II Question-Word Questions: Question words are used to question the subject (S), object (O) or other complement (OC), and in the question, the part of the sentence being questioned is dropped. The general sentence structure for questions is given below:

Question-Word (**QW**) + Yes/No Question? i.e.,

Question-Word (**QW**) + Aux. (**A**) + Subject (**S**) + [**'not'**] + Main Verb Form (**V**)
[+ Object (**O**)] [+ Other Complements (**OC**)]?

Question words include <u>What, Which, Who, Whom, Whose, How, When, Where and Why</u>. The particular question word to be used depends on the part of the sentence that is being questioned. Different types of question-word questions are described below:

1. Questions referring to Subject: The questions for subject have a different sentence structure than the above one as explained just next. The question word *'Who / What / Which'* is to be used in the place of the subject *without inverting the auxiliary and the subject.*

<u>She</u> played football yesterday.	-	<u>Who</u> played football yesterday?

2. Questions referring to Object: The question word *'Whom / What / Which'* is to be used with the corresponding Yes/No question, omitting the object.

She played <u>football</u> yesterday.	-	<u>What</u> did she play yesterday?

3. Questions referring to Possessive Determiner: The question word *'Whose / Which'* is to be used with the noun described by the possessive determiner, omitting the possessive determiner.

Chapter-6: Interrogative Sentences - Questions

Possessive determiner of subject:

His team won the match.	-	Whose team won the match?
This book is better.	-	Which book is better?

Possessive determiner of object:

He kicked my bag. - Whose bag did he kick?

4. Questions referring to Attributive Adjective: It is similar to the questions referring to possessive determiner. The question word 'Which / What type of / How + adjective' is to be used with the noun described by the attributive adjective, omitting the attributive adjective.

Attributive adjective of subject:

A tall boy is running fast.	-	Which boy is running fast?
Five people are required now.	-	How many people are required now?

Attributive adjective of object:

I like the green pen.	-	Which pen do I like?
You have spent ₹100.	-	How much money have you spent?

5. Questions for Other Complement: In the following discussion, the terms noun, adjective and adverb mean their phrases and clauses also.

a. Subject Complement: It complements or adds more meaning to the subject, and as such it can be a noun, pronoun or adjective. The question word for noun or pronoun is 'Who / What' and for adjective, 'What type (of) / How + adjective / How'. These question words are to be used with the corresponding Yes/No question, omitting the subject complement.

She is a teacher.	-	What is she?, Who is she?
She is good.	-	What type is she?
	-	How is she?
She is a good girl.	-	What type of girl is she?
I am 10 years old.	-	How old am I?
He has five apples.	-	How many apples does he have?
It is 5 pm.	-	What time is it?

b. Verb Complement: It complements or adds more meaning to the verb, and as such it will be adverb. The question word 'How / When / Where / Why / How + adverb / preposition + What' is to be used with the corresponding Yes/No question, omitting the verb complement.

She wrote a letter <u>quickly</u>.	<u>How</u> did she write a letter?
She played football <u>yesterday</u>.	<u>When</u> did she play football?
She has written a letter <u>in the morning</u>.	<u>When</u> has she written a letter?
He played <u>yesterday</u> in the school.	<u>When</u> did he play in the school?
He played yesterday <u>in the school</u>.	<u>Where</u> did he play yesterday?
He studied hard <u>to get good marks</u>.	<u>Why</u> did he study hard?
It takes <u>just 10 minutes</u> to the beach.	<u>How long</u> does it take to the beach?
It is just <u>3 km</u> to the beach.	<u>How far</u> is it to the beach?
He meets me <u>daily</u>.	<u>How often</u> does he meet me?
I like him <u>because he is my favourite hero</u>.	<u>Why</u> do you like him?
The ball is <u>on the table</u>.	<u>Where</u> is the ball?
She wrote a letter <u>with a pencil</u>.	With what / <u>How</u> did she write a letter?

c. Object Complement: It complements or adds more meaning to the object, and as such it can be a <u>noun, pronoun or adjective</u>. It is similar to questions for object.

Others made him <u>the leader</u>.	<u>What</u> did others make him?
It made him <u>happy</u>.	<u>How</u> did it make him?

III Questions for Passive Voice: It is also similar to the questions of active voice as it also requires the similar inversion of the auxiliary and the subject and also the use of appropriate question words depending on the structural element being questioned.

The plane was hijacked.	<u>Was the plane</u> hijacked?
The plane was not hijacked.	<u>Was the plane</u> not hijacked?
The plane was hijacked <u>yesterday</u>.	<u>When</u> was the plane hijacked?
<u>The plane</u> was hijacked by terrorists.	<u>What</u> was hijacked by terrorists?
The plane was hijacked <u>by terrorists</u>.	<u>By whom</u> was the plane hijacked?
The plane was hijacked <u>for ransom</u>.	<u>Why</u> was the plane hijacked?

IV Questions with Question-Words expressing surprise: Question words expressing surprise include 'Whatever, Whichever, Whoever, Whomever, Whosever, However, Whenever, Wherever and Whyever' and 'Whatsoever, Whosoever, Whomsoever, Whosesoever, Howsoever, Whensoever, Wheresoever and Whysoever'. These question words express a bit of surprise when used to ask questions and are illustrated below:

Whatever do you say?	Whichever has he chosen?
Whoever has done this?	Whomever do you love?
Whosever book was stolen?	However has he done this?
Whenever have you come?	Wherever has he gone now?
Whyever did you do this?	

The 'whatsoever, whosoever, whomsoever, whosesoever, howsoever, whensoever, wheresoever and whysoever' are stronger form of their corresponding 'ever' question words.

Chapter-6: Interrogative Sentences - Questions

V Tag Questions: A contracted question asked/placed at the end a statement is called a tag question, and it is used to confirm whether what is stated in the statement is true or not as illustrated below:

Milk is white, isn't it?   -   "isn't" is the contraction of 'is not' and the contraction is explained in chapter 10 on Contractions.

He has not come, has he?

Sentence Structure for Tag questions: Structures are given below with examples.

1) Positive Statement, Negative Tag? (Negative Tag = negative auxiliary + subject?)
2) Negative Statement, Positive Tag? (Positive Tag = positive auxiliary + subject?)

I am a teacher, aren't I? (It is 'aren't I', not 'amn't I')	I am not a teacher, am I?
You are a student, aren't (are not) you?	You are not a teacher, are you?
Children go to school, don't (do not) they?	Parents do not go to school, do they?
He is coming, isn't (is not) he?	He is not coming, is he?
She has done it, hasn't (has not) she?	She has not done it, has she?
Farmers have been living here, haven't (have not) they? - (please note that the full auxiliary 'have been' is not used for tag question and that only the first auxiliary word 'have' is used.)	
They played football, didn't (did not) they?	They did not play football, did they?
We had helped you, hadn't (had not) we?	We had not helped you, had we?
You will help us, won't (will not) you?	You will not help us, will you?

3) Positive Statement, Positive Tag?
4) Negative Statement, Negative Tag?

Sometimes, the same type of tags is more meaningful as illustrated below:

Let's go, shall we?

Answering Tag questions: A simple 'Yes' or 'No' would answer the tag questions. However, the entire question tag can be repeated, reversing it, along with Yes or No. Besides, it is very important that the answer should be 'Yes (positive answer)' or 'No (negative answer)' according to the intention of the answer, not according to the type of question, i.e., positive or negative question. For example,:

You are not helping him, are you?
- if you do not want to help, the answer is 'No' or 'No, I am not', and you should not say 'Yes' or 'Yes, I am' thinking that you agree with the questioner/question.
- if you want to help, the answer is 'Yes' or 'Yes, I am.'

You are helping him, aren't (are not) you?
- if you want to help, the answer is 'Yes' or 'Yes, I am'
- if you do not want to help, the answer is 'No' or 'No, I am not.'

VI Rhetorical Questions: It is a question asked not to get a reply but to effectively state something, and if the question is answered, then the answer would be just the confirmation of the intention of the speaker. For example,:

Have you not done that?   Why bother?
How worse is the situation?   Who cares?

Sometimes, tag questions are also used in this way as illustrated below:

You have not done that, did you?

VII Questions for Sentences with phrases and clauses: Such questions are explained in chapter 21 on 'Interrogative Sentences (Questions) - Advanced'. An example is given below, showing how to question the subject of the subordinate clause:

I believe that **he** is the best student.   -   **Who** do you believe is the best student?

Chapter 7
Verbs - Advanced

In this chapter, we are going to discuss some advanced uses and aspects of verbs.

I Usage of verbs in Conditional Sentences: Conditional sentences are used to express a situation in which something will happen only when something else happens or something else is true. They are formed using the sentence structure of complex sentences with an 'if-clause' (a subordinate clause starting with 'if') and a main clause. The 'if-clause' specifies the condition, and the main clause tells what will/would happen if the condition succeeds. There are four types of conditional sentences as explained below:

First Conditional Sentence: It is used for conditions that are very likely to happen. For example,

If he studies well, he will get good marks.
    present tense   future tense

Second Conditional Sentence: It is used for conditions that are least likely to happen or are not likely to happen. For example,:

If I won a lottery, I would buy a car.   -   least likely but still possible
    past tense   would + base form

If he were a girl, he would wear a frock.   -   impossible
    past tense   would + base form

Third Conditional Sentence: It is used for conditions that were likely to happen but did not happen. For example,

If he had studied well, he would have got good marks.
    past perfect tense   would have + past participle

Zero Conditional Sentence: It is used for talking about general truths.

If you heat the ice, it melts.
    present tense   present tense

II Usage of 'some Action Verb + Present Participle (-ing form of verb)': We use the following sentence structures for this purpose:

1) **go + present participle**: It is a short form for 'go + for + present participle' and used for doing outdoor activities.

    I go shopping today.   She went searching for her dog.
    He goes swimming.   Let's go surfing.
    We can go diving.   They may go fishing.

2) **keep + present participle**: It is a short form for 'keep + on + present participle' and used for doing activities continuously.

<table>
<tr><td>Keep writing to me.</td><td>We keep worrying unnecessarily.</td></tr>
<tr><td>He keeps watching movies.</td><td>Do not keep asking the same question.</td></tr>
</table>

2) **stop / finish + present participle**: It is used for continuous activities.

<table>
<tr><td>Finish writing.</td><td>Stop worrying unnecessarily.</td></tr>
</table>

III <u>**Classification of Verbs based on the Transitivity:**</u> As we have studied earlier, verbs are generally of two types viz. action verbs and be-verbs. Verbs can be divided into **transitive verbs, intransitive verbs** and **linking verbs** also based on whether they transfer the result/effect of the verb to the object or not as explained below:

Transitive Verb: An action verb is a transitive verb if it has an object because the action passes from the subject to the object as illustrated below:

He ate an apple.   -   'ate' is transitive because it has the object 'an apple'

Intransitive Verb: An action verb is an intransitive verb if it has no object, and also, the other complement, if any, is verb complement, i.e., an adverb or prepositional adverb phrase. For example,:

<table>
<tr><td>He is sleeping.</td><td>-</td><td>'is sleeping' is intransitive because it has neither an object nor an other complement.</td></tr>
<tr><td>Paddy grows in fields.</td><td>-</td><td>'grows' is intransitive because it has no object and the other complement is the prepositional adverb phrase 'in fields'.</td></tr>
<tr><td>He ate quickly.</td><td>-</td><td>'ate' is intransitive because it has no object and the other complement is the adverb 'quickly'. It should be noted that the verb 'ate' was used as transitive verb in the example given for transitive verb while the same verb is used as intransitive verb in this example. Therefore, <u>it may be noted that some verbs like 'eat' can be used as both a transitive verb and an intransitive verb</u>.</td></tr>
</table>

Linking Verb / Copula Verb: Linking Verbs tell the state of being, not action. As such, be-verbs are linking verbs. However, some action verbs are action verbs in form only but have no action and just tell the state of being. Such verbs are functionally linking verbs, and their other complement will be subject complement, i.e., noun, pronoun or adjective placed immediately after the verb. It is to be noted that some action verbs can function as both linking verbs and transitive and/or intransitive verbs. <u>The main difference between a linking-action verb and a pure be-verb is that a pure be-verb can have both a subject complement and a verb complement whereas a linking-action verb can have only a subject complement</u>. For example,:

Chapter-7: Verbs - Advanced

She <u>is beautiful</u>.	-	'is' is a linking verb because it is a be-verb.
The cat <u>smells</u> the food.	-	'smells' is used as a <u>transitive verb</u> because it has the object 'food'.
The dog <u>smells</u> quickly.	-	'smells' is used as an <u>intransitive verb</u> because there is no object and the other complement is an adverb 'quickly'.
The food <u>smells good</u>.	-	'smells' is used as a <u>linking verb</u> because the subject does not do any action but simply tells the state (of being) of the food that the smell of the food is good, and also, the other complement 'good' is an adjective.
He <u>appears unwilling</u> to help me.	-	'appears' is used as a <u>linking verb</u> because the other complement is an adjective 'unwilling'.
He <u>appeared from behind the screen</u>.	-	'appeared' is used as an <u>intransitive verb</u> because there is no object and the other complement is a prepositional adverb phrase.

<u>Following are the common linking verbs</u>:

be-verbs, become, seem	-	always linking verbs
look, sound, smell, taste, feel	-	represent senses of our body and can be both linking verb and action verbs.
appear, grow, turn, prove, remain	-	both linking verb and action verb

Transitive Verb and Verb Complement/Object Complement: A transitive verb with its object can be followed by both verb complement and object complement which should be identified correctly. For example,:

The people made him <u>popular</u>.	-	the other complement 'popular', being an adjective and appearing after the object, complements the object, so it is an object complement.
She wrote the letter <u>in the morning</u>.	-	'in the morning', being a prepositional adverb phrase, complements the verb, so it is a verb complement.

IV <u>Classification of Action Verbs based on the Continuance</u>: The action of some verbs can continuously happen for some time at length, whereas the action of some other verbs cannot. Based on whether an action verb can or cannot continuously happen for some time at length, action verbs are divided into stative verbs and dynamic verbs.

Stative Verbs: Such verbs that cannot continuously happen for some time at length but simply state something or feel the state of something are called stative verbs. They cannot be used in continuous tenses. For example,:

    I like banana.   I agree with you.
    He owns two cars.   I can't satisfy you.

They include verbs of Perception (see, hear, smell, taste, feel, look, seem, etc.), Opinion (assume, believe, consider, doubt, think, suppose, etc.), Mental States (forget, imagine, know, mean, notice, recognize, remember, understand, etc.), Emotions/Desires (envy, fear, dislike, hate, hope, like, love, mind, prefer, regret, want, wish, etc.) and Measurement (contain, cost, hold, measure, weigh, etc.)

Dynamic Verbs: Verbs that are used to denote continuous action for some time at length are called dynamic verbs. They can be used in continuous tenses also. For example,:

    He is running.   I am playing chess now.

Some verbs can be both stative and dynamic. They are illustrated below:

    The cake tastes great. (stative)   The boy is tasting the cake. (dynamic)

V Classification of Action Verbs based on their purpose / intention: Action verbs can be classified according to the purpose of their uses as follows:

a. Verbs of our own actions: They are used to specify our own actions performed by us physically with our own body like eating, walking, writing, etc., but not the ideas felt or thought about in our mind. For e.g.,

    We are playing.   I fixed the door myself.

b. Causative Verbs: Normally, we do our work, and sometimes we want or make somebody else do our work. When we do the work, we use the 'verbs of our own actions' to specify the action, but when we cause others to do our work, we use causative verbs. The sentence structures for using causative verbs and examples are as follows:

Causative Verbs with Active Voice:

1) Subject + Causative Verb + Object/Agent (somebody else) + Base Form of Action Verb + Object of Action Verb.

He had the carpenter fix the door. - It is in the active voice because the agent does the work of fixing the door. At the same time, please note that the agent is the object of the causative verb.

Chapter-7: Verbs - Advanced

Causative Verbs with Passive Voice:

2) Subject + Causative Verb + Object + Past Participle of Action Verb + by + Agent.
                                                                    (somebody else)

He <u>had</u> the door <u>fixed</u> by the carpenter.   -   It is in the passive voice because the object is acted upon by the agent.

3) Subject + Causative Verb + Object + Past Participle of Action Verb.

He <u>had</u> the door <u>fixed</u>.   -   It is in the passive voice because the object is acted upon, rather than acting.

The 'Agent' in the above structures is also called 'Actor' sometimes.

List of Causative Verbs: Causative verbs include have, make, let and get. Their meanings and structures are given below:

have	means simply causing the agent to do the work; e.g., You can <u>have</u> the mechanic <u>repair</u> the bike.
make	means compulsorily causing the agent to do the work; e.g., The teacher <u>made</u> the student <u>write</u> the test.
let	means allowing the agent to do the work; e.g., She will <u>let</u> him <u>go</u>.
get	means simply causing the agent to do the work and the following action verb will have the 'to' form, i.e., infinitive verb form; e.g., I will <u>get</u> him <u>to pick</u> me up.

Other causative verbs include 'advise, allow, appoint, ask, assist, cause, convince, employ, encourage, force, help, hire, implore, instruct, invite, incite, motivate, order, permit, require, remind, teach and tell' which all require the agent/actor to be followed by the 'to' form, i.e., infinitive verb form. At the same time, these causative verbs can be used as normal action verbs also as in 'He made a mistake.'

Causative Verbs with Be-Verbs: Can we use the causative verbs with be-verbs when we want others (agents/actors) to be in a particular state? Let's see some examples:

I will make him (<u>to be</u>) a good dancer.   -   Be-Verb not required
I will motivate him <u>to be</u> a good dancer.   -   Be-Verb required

It is to be noted that the first example does not require a Be-Verb after the agent because the whole action is the responsibility of the subject, whereas in the second example, the responsibility lies with both the subject and the agent.

Causative Verbs and Object Complement: It is important to note that the object complements can be used after the object of the causative verbs only.

    Others made him <u>the leader</u>.   It made him <u>happy</u>.

Intrinsic Causative Verbs: Some verbs are intrinsically causative and are transitive verbs as illustrated below:

    He <u>sat</u> me in the front row.   He <u>walks</u> his pet dog.

c. <u>Perception Verbs</u>: Perception verbs are those verbs which are used to express the senses of our sense organs or our feelings. Such verbs include 'see, look, look at, watch and seem; hear and sound; smell and sniff; taste; and feel and touch'. For e.g.,

He <u>is looking</u> at the paper.	She <u>saw</u> the sunrise.
It <u>seems</u> strange.	They <u>are watching</u> TV.
Can you <u>hear</u> the noise?	That song <u>sounds</u> strange.
The boy <u>smells</u> the cake.	The dog <u>sniffed</u> at the plate.
The cake <u>tastes</u> great.	Their sufferings <u>touch</u> our heart.
I <u>feel</u> great today.	

Some perception verbs are used to express the fact that one observes/watches some agent (somebody else / something else) doing something. The <u>sentence structures</u> for this purpose are similar to that of causative verbs and are given below with examples:

1) Subject + Perception Verb + Object/Agent + Base Form of Verb.

    I <u>saw</u> him <u>play</u>.   -   'saw' is emphasized, and 'play', the verb showing the action of the agent, is in active voice

2) Subject + Perception Verb + Object/Agent + Participle Form of Verb.

    I <u>saw</u> him <u>playing</u>.   -   'playing' is emphasized and it is in active voice
    I <u>saw</u> him <u>being beaten</u>.   -   'being beaten' is emphasized and it is in passive voice

3) Agent as Subject + Perception Verb in Passive Voice + Participle Form of Verb.

    He <u>was seen</u> <u>playing</u>.   -   'playing' is emphasized and in active voice

Chapter-7: Verbs - Advanced

4) Agent as Subject + Perception Verb in Passive Voice + 'To' Form of Verb.

He <u>was heard</u> <u>to leave</u>.	-	'was heard' is emphasized, and 'to leave' is in active voice
He <u>was heard</u> <u>to be leaving</u>.	-	'to be leaving' is emphasized and it is in active voice
He <u>was heard</u> <u>to have been beaten</u>.	-	'to have been beaten' is emphasized and it is in passive voice

Perception verbs that can be used in this fashion are 'see, look at, listen to, hear, watch, feel and sense'.

<u>Note</u>: **The main difference between "Causative Verbs" and "Perception Verbs of others' Actions" is that the former causes the agent to do something while the latter simply observes the agent doing something.**

d. <u>Thinking Verbs and Verbs of Opinion / Knowledge:</u> Some perception verbs are used to express our thinking, ideas, opinion or the perception of our mind about others. Our ideas / perceptions in our mind about others can involve 'the state (of being) of somebody/something' or 'some action'. The <u>sentence structures</u> for this purpose are given below with examples:

1) Subject + Perception Verb + Agent +'to' Form of Be-Verb.

I <u>consider</u> him <u>to be a genius</u>.	-	state (of being) of somebody i.e., a genius
I <u>consider</u> him <u>a genius</u>.	-	'to be' can be dropped

2) Agent as Subject + Perception Verb in Passive Voice + 'To' Form of Be-Verb.

He <u>was considered</u> <u>to be a genius</u>.	-	state (of being) of somebody i.e., a genius
He <u>was believed</u> <u>to be a saviour</u>.	-	state (of being) of somebody i.e., a saviour

3) Agent as Subject + Perception Verb in Passive Voice + 'To' Form of Action Verb.

He <u>was believed</u> <u>to have taken the key</u>.	-	'action' (to have taken) in active voice
He <u>was believed</u> <u>to have been kidnapped</u>.	-	'action' (to have been kidnapped) in passive voice

The verbs that can be used to express our thinking / perception include 'agree, believe, consider, know, learn, like, mean, think, understand, want, wish, etc.' Such verbs also use the sentence structure of a complex sentence wherein such verbs are used in the main clause and the knowledge/opinion is expressed in the subordinate clause starting with 'that' as illustrated below:

I think/believe that he is the best student.
   main Clause   subordinate clause

I believe him.   - used without subordinate clause

He thinks/believes that he will get the first rank.
   main Clause   subordinate clause

You know   that she has made a mistake.
  main Clause   subordinate clause

You know her very well.   - used without subordinate clause

We learned   that grammar is an interesting subject.
  main Clause   subordinate clause

We learned some important subjects last year.   - used without subordinate clause

We should understand that our mother tongue is very important.
   main Clause   subordinate clause

She understands English very well.   - used without subordinate clause

The leaders knew that people would oppose the price rise.
   main Clause   subordinate clause

VI **Type of Other Complements: Easy Identification:** As we have already learned, the basic sentence structure is as follows:

Subject (**S**) + Complete Verb (**V**) [+ Object (**O**)] [+ Other Complements (**OC**)].

As it shows, a simple sentence structure will be-   S + V.
If object is also included, it will be-   S + V + O.
If other complements are also included, it will be-   S + V + O + OC.
If other complements are added without object, it will be- S + V + OC.

Chapter-7: Verbs - Advanced

When the other complement is included, it should complement (add more meaning to) either subject (S), verb (V) or object (O). If it complements the subject, it is called Subject Complement (SC); if it complements the verb, it is Verb Complement (VC); and if it complements the object, it is called Object Complement (ObjC). <u>In short, a sentence can have a subject, a verb, an object and their complements.</u>

<u>Now, the question is how to easily identify the type of complement?</u> One way is to equate/relate the other complement to the subject, the object and the verb semantically (i.e., by meaning) in the given order, and if it equates with the subject, it is subject complement and so on.

The other way is to syntactically (i.e., by grammar rules) identify the parts of speech of the other complement and their position and, then, identify the type of complement accordingly. The set of rules defining what can follow a verb, as explained in the sections from S.No. II to S.No. V of this chapter, is called **Verb Pattern**. (A good dictionary would give the verb pattern of each verb.) For example, if a noun, pronoun or adjective is placed after the linking/be-verb, it is subject complement. It is illustrated below:

<u>She</u> <u>is</u> <u>a teacher</u>.　　　　　She = a teacher, so subject complement
　S　V　　OC　　　　　　　　- besides, the noun phrase 'a teacher' appears
　　　　　　　　　　　　　　　　after the be-verb 'is'.

On the other hand, if a noun, pronoun or adjective is placed after the object, it is object complement. Please remember that only causative/perception verbs can have object complement. For e.g.,

<u>She</u> <u>makes</u> <u>him</u> <u>happy</u>.　　　him = happy, so object complement
　S　V　　O　OC　　　　　　　- besides, the adjective 'happy' appears after
　　　　　　　　　　　　　　　　the object 'him', and the verb 'make' is used
　　　　　　　　　　　　　　　　as a causative verb.

Similarly, an adverb or prepositional (adverb) phrase placed after the verb is verb complement. Please remember that any verb, transitive, intransitive or be/linking, can have verb complement. For e.g.,

<u>She</u> <u>was</u> <u>in her room</u>.　　　- the prepositional phrase 'in her room' appears
　S　V　　OC　　　　　　　　　after the be-verb 'was', and therefore a verb
　　　　　　　　　　　　　　　　complement.

<u>She</u> <u>ran</u> <u>very fast</u>.　　　　ran => very fast, so verb complement
　S　V　　OC　　　　　　　　　- besides, the adverb phrase 'very fast' appears
　　　　　　　　　　　　　　　　after the intransitive verb 'ran'.

<u>She</u> <u>wrote</u> <u>a letter</u> <u>quickly</u>.　　wrote => quickly, so verb complement
　S　V　　O　　OC　　　　　　- besides, the adverb 'quickly' appears after
　　　　　　　　　　　　　　　　the transitive verb 'wrote', though not
　　　　　　　　　　　　　　　　immediately after the verb.

Some more examples are given below:

<u>She</u> <u>is</u> <u>kind</u>.
 S V OC

She = kind, so subject complement
- besides, the adjective 'kind' appears after the be-verb 'is'.

<u>She</u> <u>looks</u> <u>so happy</u>.
 S   V   OC

She = so happy, so subject complement
- besides, the adjective phrase 'so happy' appears after the linking verb 'looks'.

<u>She</u> <u>made</u> <u>him</u> <u>a leader</u>.
 S   V   O   OC

him = a leader, so object complement
- besides, the noun phrase 'a leader' appears after the object 'him', and the verb 'made' is used as a causative verb.

<u>She</u> <u>wrote</u> <u>a letter</u> <u>quickly</u> <u>in the office</u>.
 S   V   O   OC   OC

wrote => quickly, so verb complement
- besides, the adverb 'quickly' appears after the transitive verb 'wrote', though not immediately after the verb.

wrote => in the office, so verb complement
- besides, the prepositional phrase 'in the office' appears after the transitive verb 'wrote', though not immediately after the verb.

Like words and phrases, even clauses can also be identified as to the type of complement as illustrated below:

<u>She</u> <u>was writing</u> <u>when he came</u>.
 S   V   OC

was writing => when he came, so verb complement
- besides, 'when he came' is an adverb clause appearing after the verb 'was writing'.

VII Mood: Mood refers to the attitude or the intention of the verb and the sentence. It can also be said to refer to the type of the function of the verb and the sentence. There are three moods as explained below:

Indicative Mood: It is used to make statements and questions and as such Declarative Sentences and Interrogative Sentences are in indicative mood. *Sentences in indicative mood only have tenses, not any sentences in any other moods.* For example,:

She invited him to her house.   She did not invite him to her house.
Did she invite him to her house?   When did she invite him to her house?

Chapter-7: Verbs - Advanced

It is to be noticed that an exclamatory sentence is also a kind of declarative sentence written differently for emphasis or for expressing strong feelings as illustrated below:

What a beautiful girl she is!	=	She is a stunningly beautiful girl.
How fast he runs!	=	He runs very quickly.

Imperative Mood: It is used to make requests and orders, and as such Imperative Sentences are in imperative mood. The verbs in imperative mood have no tense. For example,:

    Please open the door.   Don't open the door.

It is to be noticed that the subject in the imperative sentences is always 'you' and not explicitly mentioned.

Subjunctive Mood: It is used to express wishes that may happen or may not happen, fifty-fifty, but somebody wishes that it should happen. It is also used to express wishes that cannot happen or are least likely to happen, but somebody wishes that it should happen. As such, Subjunctive Sentences are in subjunctive mood. Though the subjunctive sentences are declarative sentences in form, sometimes they are written in the form of imperative sentences and exclamatory sentences as explained below. The verbs in this mood have no tense. The verb forms and the sentence structures used to write sentences in subjunctive mood are explained below:

1) Wishes or Conditions that may happen or may not happen, fifty-fifty:

<u>Verb Form:</u> The required verb form is base form like come, go, be, etc., for all types of nouns and pronouns including third person singulars that normally require 's' after verbs in present tense.

<u>Sentence Structure:</u> The required sentence structure is a Complex Sentence, i.e., Main Clause in indicative mood with usual verb forms + Subordinate Clause in Subjunctive Mood with base verb form. For example,

    <u>He *suggests*</u>   <u>that she **attend** the meeting</u>.
    Main clause   Subordinate clause

Like the verb 'suggest' (used in the above example), the following verbs are also typically used in the main clause of the subjunctive sentences, namely 'ask, command, demand, insist, propose, recommend and request' followed by 'that'. For example, 'demand that', 'request that' and so on. Let's take another example,

    <u>It is *essential*</u>   <u>that she **be** present in the meeting</u>.
    Main clause   Subordinate clause

Like the adjective 'essential' in the above example, the following adjectives are also typically used in the main clause of the subjunctive sentences, namely 'desirable, important, necessary and vital' followed by 'that', for example, 'desirable that', 'vital that' and so on.

2) Wishes or Conditions that cannot happen or are least likely to happen, 10:90 :

Verb Form: The required verb form is Past Form like 'came' for 'come', 'went' for 'go', 'were' (not was) for be-verbs, etc. for all types of nouns and pronouns.

Sentence Structure: The required sentence structure is a Complex Sentence, i.e., either of the Main Clause or the Subordinate Clause in Subjunctive Mood with past verb form + the other clause in Indicative Mood with usual verb forms. For example,

  If I **were** rich,   I *would buy* a car.
  Subordinate clause Main clause

As you would have noticed, it is exactly the same as Second Conditional Sentence and as such all Second Conditional Sentences are in subjunctive mood.

  I *wish*   (that) I **won** the match. - 'that' is usually omitted.
  Main clause Subordinate clause

Some other examples are:

  If I **were** you, I *would* go.   She *behaves* <u>as if</u> she **were** a queen.

3) Imperative Sentences or Exclamatory-Imperative Sentences expressed as wishes;

  Long live our King! = Let/May our King live long.
  God bless you! = (Let/May) God bless you.

In such sentences, the expression 'Let/May' is usually omitted. An interesting point (difference) to be noted here is illustrated below:

  God bless you! - It is in subjunctive mood because it is a wish.
  God blesses you. - It is in indicative mood because it is expressed as a fact.

Chapter-7: Verbs - Advanced

VIII Extended Modal Verbs: In chapter 4, we have already discussed the modal verbs. Now, we are going to see some additional expressions/phrases which are not exactly modal verbs in form but modal in meaning and function.

Some Fixed Expressions as Modal Verbs: They can be used in simple present tense only and are listed below:

1. had better: You <u>had better</u> stay at home.   -   <u>suggestion</u>
You <u>had better not</u> stay at home.
(Note that 'not' is used after the entire expression 'had better', not just after the first word 'had' as it would have been with the normal auxiliary verbs.)

2. would rather: I <u>would rather</u> study (than play). -   <u>preference</u>
I <u>would rather not</u> study (than play).
(Note that 'not' is used after the entire expression 'would rather', not just after the first word 'would' as it would have been with the normal auxiliary verbs.)
<u>Would</u> you <u>rather</u> study?

Action Verbs as Modal Verbs:

1. have to, has to, had to: It means 'should' and is used in simple tenses only as follows:

Simple Present :	I <u>have to</u> study.		Do I <u>have to</u> study?
	I <u>do not have to</u> study.		Do I <u>not have to</u> study?
	He <u>has to</u> study.		Does he <u>have to</u> study?
	He <u>does not have to</u> study.		Does he <u>not have to</u> study?
Simple Past :	They <u>had to</u> study.		Did they <u>have to</u> study?
	They <u>did not have to</u> study.		Did they <u>not have to</u> study?
Simple Future :	You <u>will have to</u> study.		Will you <u>have to</u> study?
	You <u>will not have to</u> study.		Will you <u>not have to</u> study?

2. have got to, has got to, had got to: It also means 'should', and it is in perfect tense format and is used as such as follows:

Present Perfect :	I <u>have got to</u> study.		Have I <u>got to</u> study?
	I <u>have not got to</u> study.		Have I <u>not got to</u> study?
	He <u>has got to</u> study.		Has he <u>got to</u> study?
	He <u>has not got to</u> study.		Has he <u>not got to</u> study?

Past		They had got to study.	Had they got to study?
Perfect	:	They had not got to study.	Had they not got to study?
Future		You will have got to study.	Will you have got to study?
Perfect	:	You will not have got to study.	Will you not have got to study?

3. used to: It is used to express the past habits as illustrated below:

Past		I used to smoke.	Did I use to smoke?
Habit	:	I did not use to smoke.	Did I not use to smoke?

4. get used to: It is used to express making (new) habits and is mostly used as follows:

Present	:	She is getting used to exercise.	Is she getting used to exercise?
		She is not getting used to exercise.	Is she not getting used to exercise?
Past	:	She has got used to exercise.	Has she got used to exercise?
		She has not got used to exercise.	Has she not got used to exercise?
Future	:	She will get used to exercise.	Will she get used to exercise?
		She will not get used to exercise.	Will she not get used to exercise?

5. going to: It is used to express the things that we shall do in the (implied) future and is used in continuous tenses as follows:

Present Continuous:	Balu is going to play.	Is Balu going to play?
	Balu is not going to play.	Is Balu not going to play?
Past Continuous:	Balu was going to play.	Was Balu going to play?
	Balu was not going to play.	Was Balu not going to play?

'Be-Verb + to' as Modal Verbs: Some Be-Verbs are used as modal verbs below to illustrate the usage.

1. **am to:**	I am to meet him.	Am I to meet him?
= (required to) :	I am not to meet him.	Am I not to meet him?
2. **is to:**	She is to meet him.	Is she to meet him?
= (required to) :	She is not to meet him.	Is she not to meet him?
3. **were to:**	They were to have met him.	Were they to have met him?
= (required to) :	They were not to have met him.	Were they not to have met him?

Chapter-7: Verbs - Advanced

'Adjective expressions' as Modal Verbs: Adjective expressions in the form of 'be-verb + adjective + to' can be used with modal sense. For example,

is able to	=	can	He is able to swim.	Is he able to swim?
			He is not able to swim.	Is he not able to swim?

be used to: It is used to express the familiarity with something and is mostly used in simple tenses as follows:

Present Habit	:	I am used to exercise.	Am I used to exercise?
		I am not used to exercise.	Am I not used to exercise?
Past Habit	:	I was used to exercise.	Was I used to exercise?
		I was not used to exercise.	Was I not used to exercise?
Future Habit	:	I shall be used to exercise.	Shall I be used to exercise?
		I shall not be used to exercise.	Shall I not be used to exercise?

Other adjective expressions with modal sense are as follows:

be about to	=	going to happen		**be bound to**	=	should
be certain to	=	sure to		**be due to**	=	have to
be likely to	=	may		**be sure to**	=	should
be meant to	=	have to		**be obliged to**	=	should
be supposed to	=	have to		**be required to**	=	have to

IX Phrasal Verbs: Generally, a verb is a single word in its base form. A phrasal verb is a multi-word verb which acts like a single verb. Phrasal verbs are formed by adding an adverb and/or preposition to the base form of a verb to give a different meaning than the meaning of the original base form as illustrated below:

1) verb (base form): For example, **'go'** means 'move from one place to another place'.

2) verb (base form) + adverb: For example, **'go on'** means 'continue'. Please note that the word 'on' can be used as both preposition *(with meaning of 'on the top of')* and adverb *(with the meaning of 'continuously')* and that it is used as an adverb here as illustrated below:

   Farmers go on working despite the rain.

3) verb (base form) + preposition: For example, **'go towards'** means 'use something (money) as payment for (buying) something' as illustrated below:

   This money can go towards our new TV.

4) verb (base form) + adverb + preposition: For example, **'go out of'** means 'no longer present' as illustrated below:

   Buses will go out of the road tomorrow for the drivers' strike.

Particles: When the adverbs or the prepositions are used as part of phrasal verbs, they are called particles.

Verb Forms of Phrasal Verbs: Though phrasal verbs are multiword verbs, only the base form of the phrasal verb inflects (changes) as illustrated below:

Base Form	Present Form	Past Form	Past Participle	Present Participle
go	go goes (tps)	went	gone	going
go on	go on goes on (tps)	went on	gone on	going on
go towards	go towards goes towards (tps)	went towards	gone towards	going towards
go out of	go out of goes out of (tps)	went out of	gone out of	going out of

Separable Phrasal Verbs vs. Inseparable Phrasal Verbs: As phrasal verbs are multiword verbs, a question arises as to whether the words in a transitive phrasal verb can be separated so that the object of the phrasal verb can be written in between. It is explained as follows:

1) Phrasal verbs ending with preposition: They cannot be separated, and like prepositional phrases, objects always follow the preposition as illustrated below:

    She is looking after the child.   -   Correct
    She is looking the child after.   -   Incorrect

2) Phrasal verbs ending with adverb: When they are used as transitive verbs with a noun as an object, they may or may not be separated. It is just a matter of one's style. However, if the object is a pronoun, they must be separated. These points are illustrated below:

    Turn on the radio.   -   Correct
    Turn the radio on.   -   Correct
    Turn it on.   -   Correct
    Turn on it   -   Incorrect

<u>**Warning:**</u> As many prepositions can be used as adverbs also, the type of the particle as a preposition or as an adverb should be ascertained before applying the above rules.

Chapter-7: Verbs - Advanced

Some Common Phrasal Verbs:

As we have learned, phrasal verbs are formed by combining particles with verbs. Though a particle can be used with many verbs, it would have the same meaning in general. The general meaning of some common particles is given below. However, these meanings should not be taken literally on being used as part of phrasal verbs.

Particle		Meaning
about / around	-	do something aimlessly (e.g., fiddle about/around)
across	-	do something which involves the other/opposite side (e.g., get across)
along	-	do something together or beside with somebody/something (e.g., get along)
away	-	do something such that it results in keeping something away (e.g., clear away)
back	-	do something as a reaction (e.g., give back)
by	-	do something somehow, not exactly (e.g., drop by)
down	-	do something involving downward movement (e.g., cool down)
up	-	do something completely; increase in size/effect (e.g., eat up / add up)
for	-	do something with an aim/target (e.g., look for)
in	-	do something such that it results in keeping something in (e.g., drop in)
into	-	do something with inward movement (e.g., break into); do something with involvement or after getting into it (e.g., draw into)
on	-	do something continuously; stick to something (e.g., drag on)
over	-	avoid something without getting into it; again (e.g., get over / do over)
through	-	get into and succeed (e.g., get through)
with	-	do something with (the help of) somebody/something (e.g., get on with)
out	-	do something to finish (e.g., blow out)
off	-	happen successfully; out of something (e.g., come off)
under	-	receive the result of doing something; submit oneself (e.g., come under)

Phrasal Verb	Meaning	Example
account for	explain	How can you account for your performance?
act on/upon	take action	The police acted on the tips from the public.
act for	represent on behalf of	He acts for his wife.
act up	behave badly	The rogues acted up rudely in the market.
add to	increase	The rising prices add to our woes.
add up	calculate	Add up all the amounts.
	make sense	His explanation does not add up now.
add up to	make a total of	The figures add up to 100.
allow for	consider	We must always allow for contingencies.
ask after	enquire about	He always asks after her.
ask around	ask many people	I will ask around for the information.
back out	withdraw	They may back out from the competition.
back up	support	He may back you up in your demands.

Phrasal Verb	Meaning	Example
bail out	rescue	The ministry had to bail out a minister.
bang about	move around noisily	A rogue student banged about in the school.
bang into	crash into/hit	I banged into the gate.
bang on	hit/slam/bump	She banged on the door angrily.
bang on about	talk a lot about something	He always bangs on about his car.
bank on	rely	You can bank on his support.
bear on	affect	His attitude bears on his health.
bear with	be patient	Kindly bear with her mistakes.
beat up	hit hard	He was badly beaten up.
beat down	shine with heat	The sun beats down today.
bend (somebody) to	force	You cannot bend me to your ideas.
blow out	put out a flame	Blow out the candle.
blow up	explode	The bomb blew up in a shop.
bog down	get entangled	They were bogged down on trivial issues.
boil over	get angry	She is boiling over at his attitude.
boil down to	finally point to	Everything finally boils down to money.
book in/into	arrange to stay	I booked into the hotel at 7 AM.
border on	come very close to	Your anger borders on madness.
break up	separate into pieces	The glass broke up as it fell down.
break off	end suddenly	Their agreement broke off suddenly.
break into	enter with force	The police broke into the locked house.
break through	succeed	Scientists break through in their research.
break down	fail	Their car broke down on the way.
break away	leave a group	The dissidents may break away tomorrow.
breeze through	do something easily	She breezed through the exam.
bring up	raise	You can bring up the issue now.
bring around	persuade to agree	The leader can bring around the dissidents.
bump into	meet by chance	I bumped into my old friend in the market.
bundle out	defeat completely	India bundled out England in the first innings.
burst into	start suddenly with force	She burst into tears suddenly.
burst out	speak/do suddenly and loudly	He burst out laughing.
buy into	believe something	I will not buy into your tricks.
buy up	buy all or much	Buy up everything in the market.
butter up	flatter	He is buttering up his boss.
call off	cancel	The meeting was called off.
call upon	formally invite	He called upon the chairman to speak.
call for	need	The situation calls for help from others.
call up	telephone somebody	The operator called up the customer.
call on	meet (officially)	The ministers called on the PM.
carry on	continue	Carry on with your work.
carry out	execute/complete	We should carry out our duty carefully.
cash in on	make use of	The party tried to cash in on the price rise issue.

Chapter-7: Verbs - Advanced

catch on	pick up easily	She finds it easy to catch on new things.
catch up	join / reach something though started late	I could catch up with my seniors.
check in/into	report and occupy a room	I checked in at the hotel at 7 AM.
check out	leave the hotel	I shall check out at 9 PM.
chew out	scold severely	His father chewed him out yesterday.
chill out	relax	You have to chill out now.
chip in	contribute	All students chipped in for the victims.
churn out	produce in large quantity	We churn out only ideas.
clam up	become quiet suddenly	She clammed up suddenly in the class.
close in	get closer to / intensify	The animal closed in on its prey.
close down	closes permanently	That shop is likely to be closed down.
come across	find / meet by chance	I may come across my old friends.
come down with	become ill	She came down with flu last week.
come down to	finally points to	His point comes down to money finally.
come of	result	Nothing came of their discussion.
come off	get out of / fall	The handle came off the bike.
cool down	become calm	She cooled down after some time.
count on	rely	You cannot count on him.
count out	exclude	We should count him out of this.
cozy up	be friendly	He will cozy up to you now.
crack down	take action against	The police cracked down on some shops.
crash out	lose a game and exit	Team A crashed out against Team B.
crop up	appear / come up	Your name cropped up in their discussion.
cross out	strike out	You can cross out the items you don't want.
cut across	be common to many	Recent opinions cut across the party lines.
cut back	reduce	You should cut back on coffee.
cut down	reduce	He is advised to cut down on drinking.
dash off	rush	Dash off a letter to your father.
dawn on	begin to realize	It dawned on him that the mistake was his.
die down	become less gradually	The anger died down among us.
dig up	unearth (discover)	People like to dig up others' private life.
do away with	abolish	We should do away with very old items.
do over	do again	I think we have to do it over again.
drag on	continue for too long	They want to drag on the issue.
draw into	get involved slowly	You are drawn into the novel.
draw up	arrive and stop	Our car drew up outside our house.
drill down	go into the deeper aspect	We should drill down into the matter.
drop in	visit informally	Why don't you drop in on us sometimes?
drop by	visit informally	Please drop by our house.
drop out	stop attending	He dropped out of school at a young age.
dwell on / upon	think / talk a lot	Don't dwell on the past forever.

Phrase	Meaning	Example
ease off / up	become less	The traffic eased off by late evening.
eat away	erode	The coast is eaten away gradually by the sea.
eat into	take away	The last bill has eaten into our savings.
eat out	eat outside the home	Let's eat out tonight.
edge out	move out gradually	She may be edged out soon.
embark on / upon	get into / start newly	We may embark on our new project now.
end up	finally arrive / do	He ended up doing everything all over.
face up to	accept the reality	We should face up to the real situation.
fall apart	separate and stop functioning	Their team fell apart.
fall back on	have as support	He has some savings to fall back on.
fall down	fail	His theory fell down finally.
fall for	fall in love	They fell for each other.
fall through	fail / not happening	Their plan fell through for want of money.
feed on	eat and live	Herbivores feed on plants.
feed up	give more food to make fatter	Feed up your skinny husband.
feel up to	strong enough to do	Do you feel up to going out?
fend for	take care of	We have to fend for ourselves.
fiddle about/around	keep doing unimportant things	Don't fiddle around and waste time.
fight out	not giving in but fight	They had to fight it out in the court.
figure out	understand and find	I can't figure out the truth.
find out	know / discover	It is difficult to find out the answer.
finish off	complete	Why can't you finish off immediately?
fit in	be part of some environment	It is difficult to fit in the new office.
fix up	arrange	Can you fix up a meeting with him?
fizzle out	fail finally	His plan has fizzled out finally.
flare up	become worse	Suddenly, his illness flared up.
flip through	turn the pages quickly	She flipped through the magazine.
fold up	fold to reduce the size	He always folds up the papers inside her bag.
follow up	check again to ensure	You must follow up his behaviour.
fool around	not be serious	Be alert! He may just fool around.
freak out	react very strongly	She will freak out if she sees you now.
frown on/upon	disapprove	Boss can frown upon your decision.
gear up	get ready	My son gears up for the tight schedule.
get across	communicate	I can get it across to you.
get ahead of	move past others	She may get ahead of others soon.
get along	be friendly	He can get along with anybody.
get around	overcome/avoid	It is not easy to get around this problem.
get away with	escape after doing wrong	He could get away with the offence.
get back to	contact again	I shall get back to you afterwards.
get by with	somehow manage/live	She had to get by with little money.
get by	be unnoticed	He could get by after criticizing the boss.
get down	leave a vehicle	He has just got down from the bike.

Chapter-7: Verbs - Advanced

get in	come/go inside	Get in, Sir.
get into	get involved	Don't get into others' matter.
get on	enter a vehicle	She got on the plane.
get on with	continue with	I am able to get on with the work.
get off	leave a vehicle	She got off the plane.
	escape punishment	He could get off though he was guilty.
get out	leave a place/escape	He has got out just now.
get out of	leave a vehicle	She got out of the car.
	stop some activity	He is trying to get out of smoking.
get over	overcome a problem	Can we get over the problem?
	finish	When does the class get over?
get through	finish / succeed	She got through the test.
get together	meet socially	We can get together next Sunday.
get up	wake up from sleep	I will get up around 5 AM.
get up to	do something naughty or wrong	He would get up to this.
give away	distribute for free	You can't just give away your savings.
give back	return	He will give back your money.
give in	surrender	Don't give in so easily.
	submit homework	Have you given in the homework?
give into	yield to	Don't give into pressure.
give up	stop / surrender	He gave up smoking.
gloss over	treat a mistake as nothing	He glossed over his friend's mistake.
go after	chase	He always goes after her.
go against	be against	The verdict went against them.
go ahead with	proceed further	You can go ahead with the plan.
go back on	break a promise	She can go back on her own words.
go off with	run away with someone	She has planned to go off with him.
go on with	continue doing	He wants to go on with the usual work.
go out with	have a relationship	She goes out with the neighbourhood boy.
go past	cross a place without stopping	The bus went past the stopping.
go through	read / examine	He is going through the report.
go with	accept / date	It goes with your idea.
		She goes out with him.
goof around	doing nothing	He is only goofing around.
goof off	be lazy	I am only going to goof off at the weekend.
grow apart	no longer be closer	They have grown apart now.
grow out of	grow too large for clothes	You have grown out of this dress.
grow up	become matured	You should grow up in your behaviour.
gun for	look for an opportunity to blame, attack, entrap, etc.	She is gunning for a slip on your part.
	trying seriously for	He is gunning for the top post.
hack into	break the software security of a computer and corrupt the data	Criminals may hack into the computers in any office.

Phrasal Verb	Meaning	Example
hand down	pass onto next generation	The skill was handed down by his father.
hand in	submit	You should hand in the assignment today.
hand out	distribute	The teacher handed out the papers.
hand over	give	The boss will hand over the keys to you.
hang on	wait / continue	Despite the trouble, he hangs on.
hang up	end a phone call	He suddenly hung up the phone.
harp on	talk about something repeatedly in a boring way	Don't harp on your success story.
head for	move towards	She is heading for Hyderabad.
heat up	make something warm	Heat up the rice.
hinge on/upon	depend completely	His fate hinges on the result.
hit back	retaliate	Hit back if required.
hit out at	respond angrily	The manager hit out at the allegations.
hold back	prevent / control	She could not hold back her feelings.
hold on	wait / stop for a while	Hold on a minute please.
hold up	delay while travelling	We were held up in the traffic.
home in on	target and achieve	The police could home in on the suspect.
hook up	arrange to meet	Why don't you hook him up with me?
hunt down	search to punish	He was hunted down by the rogue.
hush up	hide / keep as a secret	She tried to hush up her mistake.
iron out	mutually resolve the differences	We can iron out the issues.
jack up	raise	We had to jack up the car to change the tyre.
jot down	write quickly	She jotted down the points of the discussion.
jump at	accept eagerly	He jumped at the offer.
jump all over	scold severely	The boss jumped all over him.
keep away/off	be away	You must keep away from smoking.
keep on	continue	He keeps on writing to magazines.
	follow	Keep on him until he does it.
keep up	maintain	She must keep up the performance.
key in	type in a keyboard	She can key in data faster.
kick out	send (throw) out forcibly	The boss kicked him out.
knock out	hit and make unconscious	The thieves knocked him out.
lash out	criticize angrily	Suddenly, he lashed out at his critics.
lay off	stop employing the workers	The factory may lay off the workers.
lead to	result	Your attitude will lead to confusion.
leak out	become known	The questions leaked out yesterday.
leave on	not turned off	Leave the radio on.
leave out	not included	You may be left out of the team.
let down	not supported	She felt let down by her husband.
let out	release	The suspect was let out finally.
lie down	take rest	I want to lie down now.
light up	illuminate/burn	She is going to light up the lamp.

Chapter-7: Verbs - Advanced

live up to	meet the expectation	He lived up to his father's wish.
lock up	put in prison	The culprit will be locked up soon.
	close all doors and windows	We have to lock up our house at night.
log into/on	start working on a computer identifying yourself	Have you logged into the computer?
log out/off	stop working on a computer	You must log out before closing the computer.
look after	take care	He looked after his parents.
look back	think about the past	Sometimes, we should look back.
look down on	think low about	Don't look down on others.
look for	search	I am looking for my pen.
look forward to	anticipate enthusiastically	I look forward to my appointment.
look into	examine and act on it	Please look into the problem.
look out	be careful	Look out for rain before going out.
look up	refer to	She looked up the dictionary.
look up to	respect	Everyone looks up to him.
lord it over	behave like a boss	People like to lord it over others.
lose out	lose the game/work	He lost out to a compatriot.
luck out	be very lucky	She really lucked out on the job.
make up	create / invent	Don't make up reasons.
make up for	compensate	He could not make up for the damages.
make up with	be friendly again	She made up with her husband again.
mark up	increase the price	They are going to mark up the prices soon.
mark down	reduce the price	They may mark down the prices.
mess up	spoil / ruin	Don't mess up the room.
miss out on	lose a chance	She missed out on her promotion.
mix up	become confused	We got mixed up and lost our way.
mull over	think about / consider	I have to mull it over before deciding.
nag at	criticize repeatedly	She always nags at me.
nail down	force somebody to give a definite reply	He was nailed down finally.
name after	give a name of somebody	The bridge was named after the captain.
nod off	fall asleep unintentionally	The lecture made many nod off.
note down	write the points	We have to note down the points.
occur to	form an idea in the mind	It occurred to me very late.
opt out	choose not to be part of	He opted out of the competition.
own up	accept	Nobody owned up to the bomb blast.
pack off	send somebody away	He was packed off to another place.
pack up	stop working / finish	We can pack up early today.
pair up	form a pair	They paired up for the function.
pass away	die	His mother passed away last month.
pass for	be accepted	His debut passed for brilliance.
pass through	cross a place without stopping	The train passes through the station.

pass to	change the ownership	His property passed to his relatives.
patch up	do some repair work and try to restore	We cannot even patch our old dress up.
pay off	pay back a loan completely	The loan can be paid off easily.
phase in	introduce gradually	Reforms can be phased in two years.
phase out	remove gradually	The foreign aid may be phased out slowly.
pick out	select / choose	You can pick out your new dress.
pick up	learn quickly	She can pick up languages easily.
	take	You had better pick up your items.
	take somebody on the vehicle	I shall pick you up later.
pile up	accumulate	Newspapers are piling up.
pin down	find out exactly	It is difficult to pin down the cause.
pin up	fix to a wall	The notice is pinned up on the board.
pit against	confront	Business has pit them against each other.
play back	play music, film etc.	Please play back the song.
play down	make something less important	The industry tries to play down the crisis.
play upon	exploit a weakness	The rich plays upon the poverty of the poor.
plough back	reinvest the money	The chairman may plough back the profit.
plug in	connect to electricity	Plug in the gadget first.
point out	make it aware to others	He has correctly pointed out the problem.
pop up	appear suddenly	The problem can pop up again.
pour down	rain heavily	It poured down heavily yesterday.
print out	print from computer	You can print out the document.
pull apart	destroy	His theory was pulled apart by her.
pull down	demolish	The old building was pulled down.
pull off	mange to do something difficult	She pulled off the game.
pull out	withdraw	The military has begun to pull out.
pull over	stop/park a vehicle to the side of a road	The police asked me to pull over.
pull oneself together	regain control of emotions	You must pull yourself together now.
put across	convey a message	He could finally put across his points.
put off	postpone	The meeting is put off.
put on	get fat	She has recently put on weight.
put on	wear	Put on your coat now.
put up	allow to stay	I can put you up. Where are you put up?
put up with	tolerate	She had to put up with the problem.
rack up	acquire a lot	He has racked up a lot of wealth.
rake up	bring back old problems	The press have raked up old scandals.
reach out	stretch the arm	He reached out and held the pipe.
read out	read aloud	Read out the question.
rein in	control	They had to rein in the crowd.

Chapter-7: Verbs - Advanced

ride out	survive a difficult time	The industry tries to ride out the crisis.
ring up	telephone somebody	I shall ring up when it is over.
ring back	return a telephone call	She will ring back afterwards.
rip off	charge too much / cheat	Don't go there. They will rip you off.
roll out	launch / introduce	The new model car was rolled out.
roll back	retreat	They rolled back later.
romp in	win easily	The No. 1 player romped in easily.
root out	remove the root cause	The society tries to root out the problem.
rope in	get help from	She could not rope in her sister.
rough up	assault	He was roughed up by some stranger.
round off	approximate to a whole number	10.53 is rounded off to 10.50.
rule out	exclude a possibility	Help from her brother is ruled out.
run after	chase	The police ran after the thief.
run against	oppose / make it difficult	His own points are running against him.
run down	hit a pedestrian with vehicle	The car ran down an old man.
run into	cost	The project can run into crores.
run on	be powered by	This car runs on diesel.
run out of	nothing left	We ran out of sugar.
sail through	succeed, pass easily	I sailed through the exam.
save on	reduce expenses on an item	We cannot save on food.
screen out	exclude	Some applications are screened out.
screw up	do badly	They screwed up the plan.
see off	bid good-bye at airport, etc.	He has gone to see her off.
see through	not getting deceived	The police could see through the plan.
sell out	completely sold	All tickets were sold out within an hour.
send for	send somebody to bring somebody else / search for somebody else	They had to send for the doctor.
send off	say bye at airport, etc.	He has gone to send her off.
set aside	save something	She set aside some money every month.
	cancel a verdict/decision	The appeal court set aside the verdict.
set forth	start a journey	We set forth in the morning.
set off	explode a bomb	The bomb was set off with a remote.
set out	display / show	New products are set out in the market.
set up	arrange/establish	Set up a meeting to discuss setting up a factory.
settle down	start living in a place	It is difficult to settle down in this area.
settle for	accept what is available	He settled for a small flat.
shoot up	increase quickly / grow	The prices shot up suddenly.
show off	do something to attract others.	Don't show off.
shrug off	disregard something	He shrugged off the problems.
shut down	close a shop / computer	The shop is shut down at 9 PM.
shut out	exclude	He was shut out from the party.

shut up	stop talking	Shut up your mouth.
shy away from	avoid due to lack of confidence	She always shies away from the boss.
side with	support somebody	Nobody can side with him.
sign for	sign on behalf of	You cannot sign for your wife.
sign in	register in a hotel/office	Please sign in here.
sign off	stop doing and leave	The project is to be signed off soon.
sign up	enlist to study a course of study	Why don't you sign up for M.A.?
sit back	relax in a chair	Don't worry, sit back and think again.
sit for	pose for an artist	She sat for a famous artist.
sit on	be a member	She regularly sits on the committee.
sit out	be out	He had to sit out the committee.
slip up	make an error	I slipped up in calculation.
smack of	appear to have negative quality	It smacks of hypocrisy.
sniff at	disapprove / be scornful	Don't sniff at the opportunity.
sniff out	find something by smell	Police dog can sniff out the thief.
sort out	resolve a problem	We can sort out the problems.
spark off	cause to happen	His remarks sparked off the controversy.
spell out	explain in detail	He does not want to spell out the plan.
spit out	say something angrily	Don't spit out words unnecessarily.
split up	divide into groups	The class was split up into many teams.
squeeze up	have too many people in a room	We have to squeeze up in the car.
stack up	accumulate	Files are stacked up in the manager's room.
stand by	support	I shall stand by you in difficulty.
stand out	be extraordinary	She stands out in the crowd.
stand up to	stick to the principles	You must stand up to what you believe.
start out	begin a journey	They started out yesterday evening.
start over	start and do again	You have to start over if required.
stem from	originate	The problem stemmed from you.
step down	reduce / resign	He may step down today.
step up	increase	You have to step up the pressure.
step in	get involved	Somebody else has to step in now.
stick to	not changing	He decided to stick to his plan.
stir up	make trouble	Don't stir up the issue now.
stop by	visit briefly	I must stop by the market.
storm out	leave a place angrily	He stormed out of the room.
strike upon	form an idea	It didn't strike upon immediately.
stumble across/upon	find accidentally	I stumbled upon the lost ring.
sum up	summarize	The points were summed up in the end.
swear by	have great confidence	I can swear by his words.
swing around	change the opinion quickly	They will have to swing around soon.
take after	look like / resemble	My sister takes after our father.
take back	return	I must take back the book tomorrow.

Chapter-7: Verbs - Advanced

take down	write notes	Students take down notes in the class.
take off	remove (a wear)	Take off your cap inside the room.
	be absent from work	He may take tomorrow off.
	plane departing	The flight will take off now.
take on	assume responsibility	You may have to take on more work.
take over	assume control	The new chairman will take over soon.
take up	occupy time or space	Meetings take up all the time.
	start newly	He has lately taken up swimming.
talk down	make something less important	She is trying to talk down the matter.
talk into	persuade to do	He always talks me into the new work.
talk over	discuss	We can talk over the problems.
tap into	exploit a resource	The company can tap into the new market.
tear down/up	demolish/destroy	The old town will be torn up soon.
tell apart	see the difference	I can tell apart between them.
tell off	speak angrily at	She told him off yesterday.
tick off	mark it completed	You have to tick off as you finish them.
throw out	make somebody leave	He was thrown out for his behaviour.
tip off	secretly inform the police	The neighbours tipped off the police.
tire of	get bored	I am tired of these activities.
top up	refill something	We have to top up the coolant oil.
touch upon	mention	The main points are not touched upon.
track down	find after search	It was difficult to track them down.
trickle down	pass the benefit	The benefit of reforms began to trickle down to the poor people also.
trade off	bargain	We should trade off now itself.
try out	test	You should try out before buying.
tuck in	keep clothes' ending inside	You have to tuck in your shirt.
tune into	watch/listen to a TV/Radio program	Why don't you tune into FM?
turn against	become against	The public turned against the mob.
turn around	change position/direction to face the other way	The doctor asked me to turn around.
turn down	reject an offer	She turned down the job offer.
turn on	start a machine	Turn on the TV.
turn off	stop a machine	Turn off the TV.
turn out	result / produce	Everything turned out well at the end.
turn up	come / appear	She has not turned up so far.
use up	finish / consume	We used up all the jam.
venture into	take risks	He always ventures into new areas.
wade through	get to the end with difficulty	I managed to wade through the book.
wait on	serve people	He waits on customers in the restaurant.
wait upon	wait for a result	We have to wait upon the result of the test.
wake up	stop sleeping	I usually wake up at 6 AM.

Phrasal verb	Meaning	Example
walk away with	win easily	He walked away with the first prize.
warm up	do exercises before a game	He warms up 15 minutes before the match.
wash away	flood removing something	The recent flood washed the shed away.
wash out	cancel an event due to rains	The match was washed out.
watch out for	be careful	Watch out for dogs here.
watch over	keep an eye on somebody	The teacher watches over the students.
wear out	stop working/be tired	The machine wore out completely.
whip up	rouse	He can whip up the crowd with his speech.
whisk away	take somebody somewhere suddenly and quickly	The suspect was whisked away by the police suddenly.
wind up	close a business/company	The company was wound up last year.
wipe out	destroy completely	Some disaster has wiped out the dinosaurs.
work on	develop further	They are working on the project.
work out	solve a problem	You should work out all problems.
wrap up	dress warmly	He wraps up while sleeping.
	finish	We can wrap up the work today.
write down	make notes	Students write down the class notes.
write off	no longer useful/valid	You can write off that debt.
write up	report in writing	He must write up his business dealings.
yield to	surrender	Don't yield to temptation.
zero in on	focus	Finally, the police has zeroed in on him.
zonk out	fall asleep quickly	I zonked out as soon as I got home.
zoom in (on)	focus more closely	The camera zoomed in on him.
zoom out	focus on more area	The camera zoomed out to show more area.

Chapter 8
Verbal Phrases - Gerunds, Participles and Infinitives

A verbal phrase is not a complete/finite verb but some form of verb functioning as a phrase. Like any other phrase, a verbal phrase should also function as a noun (phrase) or an adjective (phrase) or an adverb (phrase). The different forms of verbs with 'love' as an example are given below:

Base Form	Present Form	Past Form	Past Participle Form	Present Participle Form
love	love loves	loved	loved	loving

The Base Form, Past Participle Form and Present Participle Form cannot be used as complete verb without auxiliary verbs, and therefore, are used as verbal phrases. There are three types of verbal phrases, namely Gerund, Participle and Infinitive, which are explained below:

I Gerund / Gerund Phrase: Gerunds take the form of Present Participle and refer to the act of doing something. They function as **noun (phrase)** and can be used wherever a noun can be used including subject, object, subject complement, object of preposition, etc., and being a form of verb, it can take its own object and/or complement. For example,:

<u>Reading</u> is a good habit.	-	simple Gerund as subject
<u>Reading magazines regularly</u> improves our General Knowledge.	-	Gerund Phrase as subject
She doesn't like my <u>singing</u>.	-	simple Gerund as object
My main habit is <u>walking in the beach daily</u>.	-	as subject complement.
The police can arrest you for <u>violating the traffic rules</u>.	-	Gerund phrase as object of preposition.

Compound Gerund: Compound Gerunds are formed by combining the Present Participle of the verb 'be', i.e., being or 'have', i.e., having, with Past Participles as illustrated below. The context of tenses in which a particular form of gerund can be used is given within brackets.

	Action Verbs		Be-Verbs
	Active Voice	Passive Voice	No voice
Simple Aspect *(Simple Present Tense)*	loving	being loved	being
Continuous Aspect (*Present Continuous, Present Perfect Continuous, Past Continuous and Past Perfect Continuous tenses*)	loving	being loved	---
Perfect Aspect (*Present Perfect, Simple Past and Past Perfect tenses*)	having loved	having been loved	having been

Note: **Future Tenses are handled with Infinitive.**

Being loved is a great feeling.   - Passive Compound Gerund as subject.
He was tired of having worked continuously.   - Active Compound Gerund Phrase
                                                                              as object of preposition.

Examples for Gerund of Be-Verb: The gerund of be-verb is generally used with complement only as illustrated below:

Being a teacher is interesting.
Having been to Mecca at least once is important for Muslims.

II **Participle / Participle Phrase:** Abbreviation: **prt**. Participles take the form of Present Participle and Past Participle. They function as **adjective (phrase)** and can be used wherever an adjective can be. Being a form of verb, it can take its own object and/or complement. Different forms of the participles are illustrated below. The context of tenses in which a particular form of participle can be used is given within brackets.

	Action Verbs		Be-Verbs
	Active Voice	Passive Voice	No voice
Simple Aspect *(Simple Present Tense)*	loving	loved	being
Continuous Aspect	loving	being loved	---
(Present Continuous, Present Perfect Continuous, Past Continuous and Past Perfect Continuous tenses)			
Perfect Aspect	having loved	having been loved	having been
(Present Perfect, Simple Past and Past Perfect tenses)			

Note: **Future Tenses are handled with Infinitive.**

The **different uses** of the participles are illustrated below with examples:

1) Like adjectives, they can be used both attributively and predicatively.

A crying baby gets attention immediately.   -   simple Participle with the Present Participle form used attributively as an Adjective modifying the noun 'baby'

We should not use the folded paper to write.-   simple Participle with the Past Participle form used attributively as an Adjective modifying the noun 'paper'

In the above examples, it is to be noted that the participles are used attributively and that the present participle is active in meaning and the past participle is passive in meaning.

He looks worried.   -   simple Participle with the Past Participle form used predicatively as an Adjective modifying the pronoun 'He'

She is excited about her marks.   -   Participle Phrase with the Past Participle form used predicatively as an Adjective modifying the pronoun 'She'

It is interesting.   -   simple Participle with Present Participle form used predicatively as an Adjective modifying the pronoun 'It'

Chapter-8: Verbal Phrases - Gerunds, Participles and Infinitives

2) They can be used entirely at the beginning of a sentence, at the end of a sentence, or in apposition.

<u>Walking along the beach</u>, I saw her. - Participle Phrase used in the beginning of the sentence modifying the pronoun 'I'

I saw her <u>walking along the beach</u>. - Participle Phrase used in the end of the sentence modifying the pronoun 'her'

I saw her, <u>walking along the beach</u>. - Participle Phrase used in the end of the sentence (preceded by comma) modifying the pronoun 'I'

In the above three examples, please note the difference in the meaning of the same participle phrase depending upon its position and the use of comma just before it in the third example.

Note: **The participle phrase used in the beginning of the sentence can also be considered to modify, like an adverb, the whole sentence or the main clause.**

<u>Loudly shouting slogans</u>, the crowd passed by. - Participle Phrase used in the beginning of the sentence modifying the noun 'the crowd'

Everybody pitied the innocent victims <u>killed in the blast</u>. - Participle Phrase used in the end of the sentence modifying the noun 'victims'

<u>Driven by determination</u>, they could win the game. - Participle Phrase used in the beginning of the sentence modifying the pronoun 'they'

They, <u>watching a boring movie on TV</u>, fell asleep. - Participle Phrase used in apposition modifying the pronoun 'They'

The building, <u>destroyed by fire</u>, needs repair. - Participle Phrase used in apposition modifying the noun 'the building'

The project <u>benefiting the citizens the most</u> will get an award. - Participle Phrase used in apposition modifying the noun 'the project'

In the last two examples, please note that the first sentence has the participle phrase set off with commas because it is **non-essential** while it is not set off with commas in the second sentence because it is considered to be an **essential** part of the sentence.

Absolute Phrase: A participle phrase used in the beginning of a sentence normally modifies the subject of the sentence as illustrated in the previous examples. Sometimes, the participle phrase will have its own subject and modifies the entire sentence. Such participle phrases are called absolute phrases. They are illustrated below:

God <u>willing</u>, we can get over the problem.   -   Participle 'willing' having its own subject 'God' and modifying the sentence

The train <u>having arrived</u>, all became happy.   -   Participle 'having arrived' having its own subject 'The train' and modifying the sentence

Dangling Modifier/Phrase: A participle phrase used in the beginning of a sentence normally modifies the subject of the sentence as illustrated in the previous examples. But, if the participle phrase is written in such a way that it neither has its own subject nor modifies the main subject/object of the sentence, it is called the error of dangling modifier which is illustrated below:

<u>Having worked hard</u>, the work was completed.   -   The participle phrase in the above sentence neither has its own subject nor modifies the subject 'the work'. Therefore, it is a dangling modifier. The sentence can be rewritten as follows:

<u>Having worked hard</u>, they completed the work.   -   Now, the participle phrase modifies the subject 'they'.

<u>Running across the road</u>, the bus hit him.   -   It can be written as:
<u>Running across the road</u>, he was hit by the bus.

Participles used as Adverbs: Participles are generally used as adjectives. However, they can be treated as adverbs also if they modify the verb rather than a noun as illustrated below:

He came <u>running</u>.   -   'running' modifies the verb 'came' and therefore an adverb.

Similarly, absolute phrases are also adverbs because they modify the entire sentence.

Examples for Participle of Be-Verb: The participle of be-verb should be used with complement only as illustrated below:

<u>Being a teacher</u>, she is happy.
<u>Mala having been nice to students</u>, everybody liked her.

Tip: **Like participles, the adjectives may also be used as phrases modifying the subject or the whole main clause as illustrated below:**

<u>Tall and very beautiful</u>, she is liked by all.

Of course, it can also be written with the participle of the be-verb as follows:

<u>Being tall and very beautiful</u>, she is liked by all.

Chapter-8: Verbal Phrases - Gerunds, Participles and Infinitives

III <u>**Infinitive / Infinitive Phrase:**</u> Abbreviation: **inf**. An infinitive takes the base form of a verb preceded by the word 'to', i.e., 'to + base form' as in 'to love'. Infinitives can function as **noun (phrase), adjective (phrase) or adverb (phrase)**. Being a form of verb, it can take its own object and/or complement. Different forms of the infinitives are illustrated below. The context of tenses in which a particular form of infinitive can be used is given within brackets.

	Action Verbs		Be-Verbs
	Active Voice	Passive Voice	No voice
Simple Aspect *(Simple Future Tense)*	to love	to be loved	to be
Continuous Aspect *(Future Continuous Tense)*	to be loving	---	---
Perfect Aspect *(Present Perfect, Past Perfect and Future Perfect tenses)*	to have loved	to have been loved	to have been
Perfect Continuous Aspect *(Future Perfect Continuous Tense)*	to have been loving	---	---

<u>*Note*</u>: Generally used with futuristic meaning, infinitives in perfect aspect refer to completed actions of intent in all tenses.

The **different uses** of the infinitives are illustrated below with examples wherein the <u>infinitives are underlined</u> and the word complemented by the infinitive is in **bold**:

Example	Explanation	Question Word
1. Young boys always **want** <u>to play</u>.	- simple Infinitive as object **(noun)**	What?
2. <u>To play daily</u> is a good habit.	- Infinitive Phrase as subject **(noun)**	What?
3. **Her ambition** is <u>to win the cup</u>.	- Infinitive Phrase as subject complement **(noun)**	What?
4. We lack the **determination** <u>to win</u>.	- simple Infinitive as **Adjective** modifying the noun 'determination'	What kind of?
5. The teacher **allowed** us <u>to play</u>.	- simple Infinitive as **Noun/Adjective** being the object complement	What?
6. We must **study** <u>to get good marks</u>.	- Infinitive Phrase as **Adverb** modifying the verb 'study'	Why?
7. It is **nice** <u>to meet you</u>.	- Infinitive Phrase as **Adverb** modifying the adjective 'nice'	How nice?
8. I was **about** <u>to go out</u>.	- simple Infinitive as object **(noun)** of the preposition 'about'	What?
9. The doctor **asked** me <u>to take the medicine</u>.	- Infinitive Phrase as **Noun/Adjective** being the object complement	What?

Now let us study these sentences in detail to understand how to characterize an infinitive as noun, adjective or adverb.

First, compare the first(1) and the sixth(6) sentences. It is to be noted that though the infinitives follow the verb in both of them, the infinitive in the first(1) sentence is a **noun**, and the infinitive in the sixth(6) example is an **adverb**. Why is it so? It is due to the question word required to be used for the Infinitive. If the question word is 'What', it is a **noun**, and if the question word is 'Why', then it is an **adverb**. In other words, if the infinitive is object or subject complement, it is **noun**, and if it is verb complement (conveying some purpose in this example), then it is an **adverb**.

Secondly, the infinitive in the second(2) example is a **noun** because it is the subject of the sentence, and in the third(3) example also, it is a **noun** because it is the subject complement following the *linking verb* 'is'.

Thirdly, compare the fourth(4) and the fifth(5) sentences. It is to be noted that though the infinitives follow the noun/pronoun in both of them, the infinitive in the fourth(4) sentence is an **adjective**, and the infinitive in the fifth(5) example is a **noun/adjective**. Why is it so? In the fourth(4) example, it is an **adjective** because it modifies the preceding noun 'determination' and the question word is 'what kind of'; and in the fifth(5) example, it is a **noun/adjective** because it immediately follows object 'us' describing the object itself and the question can be 'What did the teacher allow us?'

Moreover, if the infinitive follows an adjective as in the seventh(7) example, then also it is an **adverb** because it modifies the adjective. Like a noun, the infinitive can be the **object of prepositions** as illustrated in the eighth(8) example.

Finally coming to the ninth(9) example, you would have noticed that it is similar to the fifth(5) example and that the infinitive is a **noun/adjective**. Besides, like the fifth(5) example, it is to be noted that the sentence is in the form of a **causative sentence** with the causative verb 'ask' and the actor 'me' with its action verb as the infinitive 'to take'. Besides, similar to participles in absolute phrases, the actor 'me' can be characterized as the subject of the infinitive phrase 'to take medicine'. However, treating the actor as the **subject of the infinitive phrase** is somewhat misleading because the actor itself, i.e., 'me', would be the object of the causative verb, 'asked'. Whatever may be our analysis or treatment of the elements of these kind of sentences, the fact is that it is basically a causative sentence.

When an infinitive phrase is used as a noun phrase, it can be called an **Infinitive Noun Phrase (INP)**; as an adjective phrase, an **Infinitive Adjective Phrase (IAdjP)** and as an adverb phrase, an **Infinitive Adverb Phrase (IAdvP)**.

Some more examples for infinitives:

His aim is to become a champion.
A good coach to teach him the tricks of the game is his immediate need.
He is happy to be undergoing training under an experienced coach.
He is happier to have been congratulated by his coach.
He is the happiest to have become the champion.

Chapter-8: Verbal Phrases - Gerunds, Participles and Infinitives

Actor or No Actor? :

When should we or should not we use 'actor' before the infinitive? The answer is simple. If the verb is a causative verb, we should use the actor, and if the verb is a non-causative verb (or self-causative?), we should not.

<u>Causative verbs</u> including **'advise, allow, appoint, ask, assist, cause, convince, employ, encourage, force, get, help, hire, implore, instruct, invite, incite, motivate, order, permit, require, remind, teach and tell'** require the agent/actor to be followed by the 'to' form, i.e., infinitive verb form as illustrated below:

> He has **advised** me <u>to study well</u>.
> The teacher may **instruct** you <u>to write the assignment again</u>.
> The court **ordered** him <u>to be present in the court next time</u>.

Please note that a causative verb causes its object to do the action/work that is implied by the infinitive.

<u>Non-Causative verbs</u> cause/require the subject itself to do the work implied by the infinitive. Therefore, these verbs require the infinitives to immediately follow the verb (non-causative) as illustrated below:

> The players **agreed** <u>to play again</u>.   -   both actions, agree and to play, are performed by the subject
>
> He **pretends** <u>to suffer from headache</u>   -   both actions, pretend and to suffer, are performed by the subject

Now, compare the above two non-causative sentences with the following causative sentences:

> The umpire **advised** the players <u>to play again</u>. - the action 'advise' is done by the subject 'the umpire' and the action 'to play' by the object 'players'
>
> The teacher **instructed** him <u>to write again.</u>   - the action 'instruct' is done by the subject 'the teacher' and the action 'to write' by the object 'him'

The non-causative verbs include **'agree, begin, continue, decide, fail, hesitate, hope, intend, learn, neglect, offer, plan, prefer, pretend, promise, refuse, remember, start, and try'**.

Some verbs can be <u>both causative and non-causative</u>. They include **'ask, expect, like and want'** and can be used in both ways as illustrated below:

> I **expected** him <u>to win</u>.   -   causative usage
> I **expected** (myself) <u>to win</u>.   -   non-causative usage

Infinitive (Phrase) as Adverb modifying the whole sentence/main clause: Like adverbs, infinitive phrases can be used to modify the whole sentence/the main clause. When it is used in this way, it should be set off with a comma as illustrated below:

> <u>To get his degree</u>, he had to study very hard.

Split Infinitives: Normally, the infinitive should not be split to include other words between 'to' and 'base form'. However, a single-word adverb may be accepted between 'to' and 'base form' as illustrated below:

Non-causative verbs require the infinitives **to immediately follow** the verb.

Expressions with Infinitives after Question Words: Expressions combining question word + infinitives can be used with some verbs (called **Learning Verbs**) like 'understand, learn, know, ask, decide, explain, show, tell and forget' which are used to learn and probe. The question words include 'who, whom, what, how, when, where and why'. Such expressions can be formed with the conjunction 'whether' also. They function as nouns in sentences. They are illustrated below:

We should understand what to do and what not to.   I know who/whom to meet.
You should learn how to play the keyboard.   She asked me when to switch on the TV.
The boss will tell you where to go today.   You decide yourself whether to play or not.
The boss explained why to follow a particular method.

Bare Infinitive / Zero Infinitive: Normally, the form of infinitive is 'to + base form of verb'. However, bare infinitive is just the base form without 'to'. Bare infinitives are used in the following patterns:

1. <u>After the verb 'help'</u>: The verb 'help' can take both infinitive and bare infinitive after it as illustrated below:

Do you help your wife to cook?   Do you help your wife cook?
He helps me to prepare for the exam.   He helps me prepare for the exam.

2. <u>In cleft sentences with 'do' as the verb</u>:

What I did was listen in the class.   -   It is equivalent to saying 'What I did was listening in the class'; however, the former one is more natural/idiomatic.

All we can do is just wait.

3. <u>Before the second infinitive when two infinitives are connected by conjunctions like and, but, etc.</u>:

I want to sing and (to) dance.
You can try to solve the problem now or (to) wait until later.
I would like to study now rather than (to) watch TV.

4. <u>Strictly after certain verbs (let, make, hear, see)</u>:

I can **hear** them talk to each other.
Can you **see** them play there?

Chapter-8: Verbal Phrases - Gerunds, Participles and Infinitives

Let us **pray** for the welfare of the world.
You cannot **make** anybody work by force.

Please note that **'hear** and **see'** are **Perception Verbs** and **'let** and **make'** are **Causative Verbs**.

5. <u>Making suggestions with the question word 'Why'</u>: as;

Why <u>waste</u> time on minor issues?   Why <u>not try</u> it?   Why <u>bother</u>?

Examples for Infinitive of Be-Verb: The infinitive of be-verb should be used with complement only as illustrated below:

She wanted <u>to be a good teacher</u>.
She was happy <u>to have been nice to students</u>.

IV <u>Using Gerund and Participle with Infinitive to express the future</u>:
Expressing future actions with gerund or participle can be done by combining the gerund or the participle with infinitive as illustrated below:

Going to become a teacher makes her very happy.   - gerund + infinitive
Going to become a teacher, she is very happy.   - participle + infinitive

V <u>Verb Pattern for using Gerund vs. Infinitive as Nouns</u>:
Both gerunds and infinitives can be used as nouns. However, how do we decide when to use gerund and when to use infinitive? When the proposed verbal phrase purely refers to the act of doing something, i.e., a continuous action or a pure action without any reference to the tense (time), then gerund must be used. On the other hand, if the proposed verbal phrase is futuristic in nature or is used to express an intention, the infinitive must be used. For example,:

You should avoid <u>drinking</u>.	-	Correct
You should avoid <u>to drink</u>.	-	Incorrect
You plan <u>to save some money</u>.	-	Correct
You plan <u>saving money</u>.	-	Incorrect

Verbs going with infinitives: Some verbs, mostly stative verbs and futuristic in meaning, take only infinitives as objects (noun). They include 'agree, continue, decide, expect, hesitate, learn, need, promise, neglect, hope, want, plan, attempt, propose, intend and pretend'.

Verbs going with gerunds: Some verbs take only gerunds as objects (noun) because they don't express the future or the intention. On the other hand, they deal with pure nouns/ pronouns, and as such can take only gerunds. They include 'admit, avoid, appreciate, consider, deny, delay, detest, enjoy, finish, give up, insist on, keep, keep on, mind, miss, postpone, practice, put off, quit, recommend, recall, regret, suggest, stop, think of and tolerate'.

Verbs going with both infinitives and gerunds: Some verbs go with both and they include 'begin, continue, hate, like, love, prefer, remember, start and try'.

Chapter 9
Conjugation of Verbs

Having learned all the important aspects of verbs, it is time to learn the conjugation of verbs. Conjugation of a verb shows the various forms that a verb could take to mark a Person, Number, Tense, Voice, Mood and the derivatives of verbs, namely, Infinitives, Gerund and Participle. Let's see the conjugation of the verb 'love' to illustrate:

Tenses	Active Voice	Passive Voice
Simple Present	I/We/You love	I am loved
		We/You are loved
	He/She/It loves	He/She/It is loved
	They love	They are loved
Present Continuous	I am loving	I am being loved
	We/You are loving	We/You are being loved
	He/She/It is loving	He/She/It is being loved
	They are loving	They are being loved
Present Perfect	I/We/You have loved	I/We/You have been loved
	He/She/It has loved	He/She/It has been loved
	They have loved	They have been loved
Present Perfect Continuous	I/We/You have been loving	*no passive voice*
	He/She/It has been loving	
	They have been loving	
Simple Past	I/We/You loved	I was loved
		We/You were loved
	He/She/It loved	He/She/It was loved
	They loved	They were loved
Past Continuous	I was loving	I was being loved
	We/You were loving	We/You were being loved
	He/She/It was loving	He/She/It was being loved
	They were loving	They were being loved
Past Perfect	I/We/You had loved	I/We/You had been loved
	He/She/It had loved	He/She/It had been loved
	They had loved	They had been loved

Chapter-9: Conjugation of Verbs

Past Perfect Continuous	I/We/You had been loving He/She/It had been loving They had been loving	*no passive voice*
Simple Future	I/We shall love You will love He/She/It will love They will love	I/We shall be loved You will be loved He/She/It will be loved They will be loved
Future Continuous	I/We shall be loving You will be loving He/She/It will be loving They will be loving	*no passive voice*
Future Perfect	I/We shall have loved You will have loved He/She/It will have loved They will have loved	I/We shall have been loved You will have been loved He/She/It will have been loved They will have been loved
Future Perfect Continuous	I/We shall have been loving You will have been loving He/She/It will have been loving They will have been loving	*no passive voice*

Imperatives: love   be loved

Gerund Phrase:

			Be-verb
Simple/Continuous Aspect	loving	being loved	being
Perfect Aspect	having loved	having been loved	having been

Participle Phrase:

Simple Aspect	loving	loved	being
Continuous Aspect	loving	being loved	---
Perfect Aspect	having loved	having been loved	having been

Infinitive Phrase:

Simple Aspect	to love	to be loved	to be
Continuous Aspect	to be loving	---	---
Perfect Aspect	to have loved	to have been loved	to have been
Perfect Continuous Aspect	to have been loving	---	---

Chapter 10
Contractions

Contractions are the abbreviated/short form of word(s) formed by leaving out one or more letters from the word(s) and replacing the missing letter(s) with an apostrophe. They are not used in formal speeches and formal written English. Contractions are illustrated below, and their pronunciations are given as their equivalent words within the brackets. Though standard pronunciation symbols are normally used to specify the pronunciation of the words, the equivalent words are used here to make it simpler for the readers. A good dictionary can be referred to for the exact pronunciation.

I **Contraction of Subject (Pronoun) and Auxiliary Verbs:**

Positive Form		Negative Form	
Long Form	Short Form	Long Form	Short Form

Present Tense Form

Long Form	Short Form	Long Form	Short Form
I am	I'm (aaim)	I am not	I'm not (aaim not)
We are	We're (wee-er)	We are not	We're not (wee-er not)
			We aren't (we arent)
You are	You're (youre)	You are not	You're not (youre not)
			You aren't (you arent)
He is	He's (heez)	He is not	He's not (heez not)
			He isn't (he izant)
She is	She's (sheez)	She is not	She's not (sheez not)
			She isn't (she izant)
It is	It's (its)	It is not	It's not (its not)
			It isn't (it izant)
They are	They're (there)	They are not	They're not (there not)
			They aren't (they arent)
I do	---	I do not	I don't (i doent)
We do	---	We do not	We don't (we doent)

Chapter-10: Contractions

You do	---	You do not	You don't (you doent)
He does	---	He does not	He doesn't (he daznt)
She does	---	She does not	She doesn't (she daznt)
It does	---	It does not	It doesn't (it daznt)
They do	---	They do not	They don't (they doent)
I have	I've (aaiv)	I have not	I've not (aaiv not)
			I haven't (i havent)
We have	We've (weeve)	We have not	We've not (weeve not)
			We haven't (we havent)
You have	You've (youve)	You have not	You've not (youve not)
			You haven't (you havent)
He has	He's (heez)	He has not	He's not (heez not)
			He hasn't (he hazant)
She has	She's (sheez)	She has not	She's not (sheez not)
			She hasn't (she hazant)
It has	It's (its)	It has not	It's not (its not)
			It hasn't (it hazant)
They have	They've (theyve)	They have not	They've not (theyve not)
			They haven't (they havent)

Past Tense Form

I was	---	I was not	I wasn't (i wazant)
We were	---	We were not	We weren't (we werent)
You were	---	You were not	You weren't (you werent)
He was	---	He was not	He wasn't (he wazant)
She was	---	She was not	She wasn't (she wazant)
It was	---	It was not	It wasn't (it wazant)
They were	---	They were not	They weren't (they werent)

I/We/You/He/She/It/ They did		I/We/You/He/She/It/ They did not	I/We/You/He/She/It/ They didn't (didnt)
I had	I'd (aaid)	I had not	I'd not (aaid not) I hadn't (i hadnt)
We had	We'd (weed)	We had not	We'd not (weed not) We hadn't (we hadnt)
You had	You'd (youd)	You had not	You'd not (youd not) You hadn't (you hadnt)
He had	He'd (heed)	He had not	He'd not (heed not) He hadn't (he hadnt)
She had	She'd (sheed)	She had not	She'd not (sheed not) She hadn't (she hadnt)
It had	It'd (itd) *	It had not	It'd not (itd not) * It hadn't (it hadnt)
They had	They'd (theyd)	They had not	They'd not (theyd not) They hadn't (they hadnt)

Future Tense/Modal Verb Form

I shall	I'll (aail)	I shall not	I'll not (aail not) I shan't (i shant)
We shall	We'll (weel)	We shall not	We'll not (weel not) We shan't (we shant)
You shall	You'll (youl)	You shall not	You'll not (youl not) You shan't (you shant)
He shall	He'll (heel)	He shall not	He'll not (heel not) He shan't (he shant)
She shall	She'll (sheel)	She shall not	She'll not (sheel not) She shan't (she shant)

Chapter-10: Contractions

It shall	It'll (itl)	It shall not	It'll not (itl not) It shan't (it shant)
They shall	They'll (theyl)	They shall not	They'll not (theyl not) They shan't (they shant)
I/We/You/ He/She/It/ They should	---	I/We/You/ He/She/It/ They should not	I/We/You/He/She/It/ They shouldn't (shouldnt)
I will	I'll (aail)	I will not	I'll not (aail not) I won't (i wont)
We will	We'll (weel)	We will not	We'll not (weel not) We won't (we wont)
You will	You'll (youl)	You will not	You'll not (youl not) You won't (you wont)
He will	He'll (heel)	He will not	He'll not (heel not) He won't (he wont)
She will	She'll (sheel)	She will not	She'll not (sheel not) She won't (she wont)
It will	It'll (itl)	It will not	It'll not (itl not) It won't (it wont)
They will	They'll (theyl)	They will not	They'll not (theyl not) They won't (they wont)
I would	I'd (aaid)	I would not	I'd not (aaid not) I wouldn't (i wouldnt)
We would	We'd (weed)	We would not	We'd not (weed not) We wouldn't (we wouldnt)
You would	You'd (youd)	You would not	You'd not (youd not) You wouldn't (you wouldnt)
He would	He'd (heed)	He would not	He'd not (heed not) He wouldn't (he wouldnt)
She would	She'd (sheed)	She would not	She'd not (sheed not) She wouldn't (she wouldnt)

It would	It'd (itd) *	It would not	It'd not (itd not) *
			It wouldn't (it wouldnt)
They would	They'd (theyd)	They would not	They'd not (theyd not)
			They wouldn't (they wouldnt)
I/We/You/He/She/It/They can	---	I/We/You/He/She/It/They cannot	I/We/You/He/She/It/They can't (caant)
I/We/You/He/She/It/They could	---	I/We/You/He/She/It/They could not	I/We/You/He/She/It/They couldn't (couldnt)
I/We/You/He/She/It/They may	---	I/We/You/He/She/It/They may not	I/We/You/He/She/It/They mayn't (maynt) *
I/We/You/He/She/It/They might	---	I/We/You/He/She/It/They might not	I/We/You/He/She/It/They mightn't (mightnt) *
I/We/You/He/She/It/They must	---	I/We/You/He/She/It/They must not	I/We/You/He/She/It/They mustn't (muzant)

* These contractions are rarely used.

II Questions with contractions: The contractions cannot be used for making questions when the contracted word has the subject also as part of it. However, when the contracted word is a separate word from the subject, it can be used for making questions. These points are illustrated below:

We're boys.	-	're we boys? (Wrong)
	-	Are we boys? (Correct)
We aren't boys.	-	Aren't we boys? (Correct)
	-	Are we not boys? (Correct)

Chapter-10: Contractions

III Informal contractions: They are shorter/merged form of some words used together and are used almost only in informal spoken English. They are seldom used in writing. Some are given below:

ain't	=	am not / is not / are not / have not / has not
gimme	=	give me
gonna	=	going to
gotta	=	(have) got a / (have) got to
kinda	=	kind of
lemme	=	let me
wanna	=	want a / want to
whatcha	=	what are you / what have you
ya	=	yes / you

IV Contractions with Tag Questions: Tag question, a mini question asked/placed at the end of a statement, generally uses contractions wherever possible as illustrated below:

Milk is white, isn't it? -   (Tag questions are described elaborately in chapter 6.)

Chapter 11
Introductory Subjects - It and There

The words 'It' and 'There' are used as introductory subject/word before the 'Be-Verbs' when the real subject follows as complement.

I 'It' as the introductory word/subject:

1) <u>As substitute for long subjects:</u> 'It' is used as introductory subject/word when the actual/real subject is (very) long because long subjects are difficult to express as well as to understand. For example,:

<u>It</u> <u>is</u> <u>interesting</u> <u>to read stories written by authors of children's books.</u>
S V   OC   OC: actual subject
     =   <u>To read stories written by authors of children's books</u> <u>is</u> <u>interesting</u>.
              actual subject   V   OC
     =   <u>Reading stories written by authors of children's books</u> <u>is</u> <u>interesting</u>.
              actual subject   V   OC

<u>It</u> <u>is</u> <u>unpredictable</u> <u>whether the train would come on time at this station.</u>
S V   OC   OC: actual subject
     =   <u>Whether the train would come on time at this station</u> <u>is</u> <u>unpredictable</u>.
              actual subject   V   OC

<u>It</u> <u>was</u> <u>an achievement</u> <u>that our school won the cup in the tournament.</u>
S V   OC   OC: actual subject
     =   <u>That our school won the cup in the tournament</u> <u>was</u> <u>an achievement</u>.
              actual subject   V   OC

<u>It</u> <u>was</u> <u>actually he</u> <u>who won the cup for our school.</u>
S V   OC   OC: actual subject
     =   <u>One who won the cup for our school</u> <u>was</u> <u>actually he</u>.
              actual subject   V   OC

2) <u>As impersonal pronoun:</u> Impersonal pronoun of 'it' is generally used when both the subject and the verb have the same/similar words. For example,:

It is raining. It rains.	-	'It' refers to 'the rain'
It stinks.	-	'It' refers to 'the stink of something'
It thunders.	-	'It' refers to 'the thunder'
It pains me to hear the news.	-	'It' refers to 'the pain in me'
It is very kind of you to help.	-	'It' refers to 'the kindness in you'

Chapter-11: Introductory Subjects - It and There

3) <u>For expressing weather and time:</u> The nouns of weather and time are not used as subjects, and instead, 'it' is used to refer to them. For example,:

It is winter now.	-	'It' refers to 'the season'
It is 5 pm.	-	'It' refers to 'the time'
It should be too hot there.	-	'It' refers to 'the climate'
It is Sunday.	-	'It' refers to 'the day'

II '<u>There' as the introductory word/subject:</u> The word **'there'**, usually an adverb, can also be used as introductory subject/word in sentences with Be-Verb / Linking Verb, and the actual subject will follow the verb. 'There' is used when a general statement is made without referring to the specific details of the information as well as the source of the information in the sentence. It is illustrated below:

<u>There is a marriage</u> in the hall tomorrow. - some marriage
  S   V   actual subject

<u>There seems</u> to be <u>a commotion</u> in the playground. - some commotion
  S   V   actual subject

<u>There is a book</u> on the table.   <u>There are some books</u> on the table.
  S   V actual subject   S   V   actual subject

    - please note the use of the verbs. Singular verb 'is' is used for singular subject 'a book', and plural verb 'are' is used for plural subject 'some books'.

Chapter 12
Adjectives

Adjectives are Describing Words (Modifiers) for Nouns and Pronouns. Abbreviation: **adj**. They describe or tell more information about noun/pronoun. In other words, they describe the quality/characteristic/feature/attribute of noun and pronoun.

Question Words for adjective: What type of, What kind of, Which and How + Be-Verb - The answer to these question words in sentences is adjective.

Examples	Question Words
He is a good boy. (used **attributively**, i.e., before noun)	what type of (boy)?
She is intelligent. (used **predicatively**, i.e., after verb)	what kind of (girl)?
The blue pen writes well. (used **attributively**, i.e., before noun)	which (pen)?
Balu is happy. (used **predicatively**, i.e., after verb)	How is (Balu)?

Adjectives of quantities, namely 'Many, Much, Few, Little, etc.': Most of the adjectives are used to express the qualities of the noun/pronoun. However, 'Many, Much, Few and Little' are used to the express the quantities, 'Many and Few' with countable quantities and 'Much and Little' with uncountable quantities as illustrated below:

There are many apples. (countable)	He has few apples only. (countable)
There is much sugar. (uncountable)	She has little sugar only. (uncountable)

<u>Synonyms of Many and Much:</u> The expressions 'a great deal of', 'a lot of' and 'lots of' are used as synonyms for 'much', and some of them are informal as follows:

She has much courage. (formal)	She has a great deal of courage. (formal)
She has a lot of courage. (informal)	She has lots of courage. (informal)

Similarly, the expressions 'a lot of' and 'lots of' are used as synonyms for 'many', and they are informal as follows:

She has many dresses. (formal)	She has a lot of dresses. (informal)
She has lots of dresses. (informal)	

Adjectives as Nouns: Adjectives can be used as nouns by placing 'the' before the adjective, denoting a group of nouns as illustrated below:

The rich are enjoying, but the poor are suffering. - denoting the group of people who are rich or poor

Chapter-12: Adjectives

Adjectives are used as nouns in certain expressions as follows:

<u>In **short**</u>, they are wrong.   They are discussing <u>in **secret**</u>.
We will meet <u>before **long**</u>.   At **present**, I am in business.
He left the school <u>for **good**</u> (permanently).   It will be over tomorrow <u>at **best**</u>.
The situation is going <u>from **bad** to **worse**</u>.   Give your statement <u>in **black** and **white**</u>.

Nouns as Adjectives: Nouns can be used as adjectives as illustrated below. When nouns are used as adjectives, they are called **Noun Adjuncts**.

She is a <u>college</u> **girl**.   The <u>village</u> **girl** is innocent.

Participles as Adjectives: The participle form of verb, both the present participle and the past participle, can be used as adjectives as illustrated below:

A <u>crying</u> baby gets immediate attention.   -   present participle
We should not write on <u>folded</u> papers.   -   past participle

The use of participles as adjectives is explained in chapter 8 on Verbal Phrases.

I <u>Position of Adjectives</u>: Adjectives can be used <u>attributively</u>, i.e., before nouns, as well as <u>predicatively</u>, i.e., after verb as illustrated below:

He is a <u>good</u> boy. (attributively)   The boy is <u>good</u>. (predicatively)

When used <u>attributively</u>, adjectives are generally placed before nouns; however, they are <u>placed after indefinite pronouns</u> like 'somebody, anybody, nobody, something, anything and nothing' as illustrated below:

Anybody <u>rich</u> can buy **anything** <u>expensive</u>, but **nobody** <u>sensible</u> would call it as **something** <u>useful</u> for **somebody** <u>poor and needy</u>.

In certain expressions, the adjective comes after the noun as follows:

president <u>elect</u>, time <u>immemorial</u> and heir <u>apparent</u>.

Similarly, **the adjective 'else'** is also used after the noun it modifies with the meaning of 'other than' as illustrated below:

Somebody <u>else</u> has done it.   What <u>else</u> do you want?

When two or more adjectives are used, they can be placed after the noun/pronoun (i.e., in apposition) <u>for emphasis</u> as illustrated below:

The minister, <u>rich and powerful</u>, can do anything.

Some adjectives, all starting with the letter 'a' like **'ablaze, afloat, afraid, aghast, aglow, alike, alive, alone, aloof, asleep, awake, averse and aware'** are used <u>only predicatively</u> as illustrated below:

The forest has been <u>ablaze</u> since yesterday.   She always remains <u>aloof</u>.
His face looks <u>aglow</u>.   The child is <u>asleep</u>.

II <u>Order of Adjectives</u>: The adjectives can be classified into the following types/classes, namely <u>Determiner (determiners are a kind of adjective), Opinion, Size/Shape, Age, Colour, Origin, Material and Purpose</u>, and when many adjectives are used consecutively, they can be placed/ordered in the order as given above, i.e., DOSA-COMP/DosaComp, the acronym with the first letter of the name of the above types. For example,

He has a <u>beautiful</u> <u>big</u> <u>new</u> <u>grey</u> <u>Indian</u> <u>plastic</u> <u>race</u> car.
      d   opinion   size   age   colour   origin   material   purpose

When we use adjectives belonging to the same type/class, we can put 'comma' between the adjectives and 'and/but' before the last adjective but nothing between the last adjective and the noun as illustrated below:

It is a   <u>small, long and oval-shaped</u> table.
      d   size   size   size

III <u>Degrees of Comparison</u>: Adjectives can be compared with reference to its intensity in one use/situation to another use/situation. This is the degrees of comparison of adjectives. In other words, it is the comparison of the intensity of the adjectives under different situations. There are three ways of comparison as follows:

Example	-	Type of comparison and Degrees of Comparison
Raghu is <u>tall</u>.	-	no comparison
Raghu is **as** <u>tall</u> **as** Ram.	-	comparison of <u>equality</u> between two; **positive degree**
Raghu is <u>taller</u> **than** Ravi.	-	comparison of <u>inequality</u> between two; **comparative degree**
Balu is **the** <u>tallest</u> of all.	-	comparison of <u>superiority</u> among all; **superlative degree**

Forms of adjectives for comparison: Three forms of comparison, namely Positive Degree, Comparative Degree and Superlative Degree, are used to express the comparison of adjectives as illustrated below:

Positive Degree	Comparative Degree	Superlative Degree

Chapter-12: Adjectives

Regular Comparison: Some adjectives with one syllable have the comparative form and the superlative form by suffixing -er and -est to the base/positive form respectively. They are called regular adjectives. For example,:

tall	taller	tallest
short	shorter	shortest
few	fewer	fewest

More/Most Comparison: Adjectives with more than one syllable have the comparative form and the superlative form by adding 'more and most' or 'less and least' respectively before the base/positive form. For example,:

beautiful	more beautiful	most beautiful
dangerous	less dangerous	least dangerous

Irregular Comparison: Some adjectives have irregular (entirely different) comparative form and the superlative form from the base/positive form. They are called irregular adjectives. For example,:

good	better	best
bad	worse	worst
ill	worse	worst
little (amount, uncountable)	less	least
little (size, uncountable)	smaller	smallest
* few (countable)	fewer	fewest
many (countable)	more	most
much (uncountable)	more	most
far (place)	farther	farthest
far (time)	further	furthest
* late (time)	later	latest
late (order)	latter	last
* near (place)	nearer	nearest
near (order)	---	next
* old	older	oldest
old (people)	elder	eldest
---	inner	innermost
---	upper	uppermost
---	outer	outermost

Though regular adjectives, they are also listed here because they are related to the neighbouring irregular adjectives.

Sentence Structures for comparison of adjectives: The verb used in the sentence structures illustrated below is always a Be-Verb / Linking Verb.

1) Sentence Structures for Positive Degree:

a) Subject + Verb +   **as + adjective (positive form) + as** + Subject + Verb.
   independent clause   dependent clause

   She is **as tall as** he is.
   S V   conj.   S V

In the above structure, the expression **'as + adjective + as'** is used as the conjunction of the dependent clause. Besides, the **'as'** before the adjective is an adverb because it modifies the adjective, and the **'as'** after the adjective is a conjunction introducing the dependent clause.

However, the following sentence without verb in the dependent clause is old-fashioned and not used in modern English.

   She is **as tall as** he.   -   old-fashioned
   S V   conj.   S

b) Subject + Verb + **as + adjective (positive form) + as** + Prepositional Object.
                    prepositional expression

   She is **as tall as** him.
   S V   prep.   PO

Note: It is very important to note that the same expression 'as tall as' is used as conjunction in one sentence and preposition in another sentence. The function of the expression is decided by what is followed by the expression. The expression 'as tall as' is a conjunction in the sentence 'She is as tall as he is' because it is followed by the clause 'he is' whereas it is a preposition in the sentence 'She is as tall as him' because it is followed by the pronoun 'him'.

c) Subject + Verb + **as + adjective (positive form) + a/an + noun + as** +
                                                                    Subject + Verb.
   independent clause   dependent clause

   She is **as good a teacher as** he is.
   S V   conj.   S V
   The girls are **as good students as** the boys are.
   S   V   conj.   S   V

In the above structure, the expression **'as + adjective + a/an + noun + as'** can be treated

Chapter-12: Adjectives

as conjunction introducing the dependent clause. The first example can be used with the prepositional object as follows:

    She is **as good a teacher as** him.
    S V   prep.   PO

    d) The comparative adjective expression in each of the above structures can be modified further by placing a suitable *pre-modifier adverb / intensifier* before the first occurrence of 'as' as illustrated below:

    She is *nearly* **as tall as** he is.
    S V   conj.   S V

    She is *not* **as tall as** he is.
    S V   conj.   S V

    She is *only half* **as tall as** him.
    S V   prep.   PO

    She is *certainly* **as good a teacher as** he is.
    S V   conj.   S V

    The girls are *definitely* **as good students as** the boys are.
      S   V   conj.   S   V

    She is *absolutely* **as good a teacher as** him.
    S V   prep.   PO

    2) <u>Sentence Structures for Comparative Degree:</u>

    a) <u>Subject + Verb + **adjective (comparative form)** + **than** + Subject + Verb.</u>
                independent clause   dependent clause

    She is **taller**   **than** he is.
    S   V OC(adj.) conj. S V

In the above structure, **'than'** is used as a conjunction introducing the dependent clause. Another example is given below:

    She is **taller**.   -   a general comparison
    S   V OC (adj.)

b) Subject + Verb + **adjective (comparative form)** + **than** + Prepositional Object.
                                                                        prep.

    She is **taller**   **than** him.
    S   V OC(adj.)   prep. PO

    She is **taller**   **than** he.   -   old-fashioned
    S   V OC(adj.)   conj. S

c) Subject + Verb + **a/an+adjective (comparative form)+noun** + **than** + Subject + Verb.
                    independent clause   dependent clause

    Mala is **a better teacher than** Sona is.
    S   V OC(adj.   n.) conj. S   V

In the above structure, **'than'** is used as a conjunction introducing the dependent clause. The above example is used with the prepositional object as follows:

    Mala is a **better** teacher **than** Balu/him.
    S   V OC(adj.   n.) prep. PO

Another example is given below:

    She is a **better** teacher.   -   a general comparison
    S V   OC(adj.   n.)

d) The comparative adjective expression in each of the above structures can be modified further by placing a suitable *pre-modifier adverb / intensifier* before the comparative form of adjective as illustrated below:

    She is   *not any* **taller than** he is.
    S   V OC(adv.   adj.) conj. S V

    She is   *much* **taller**.
    S V OC(adv. adj.)

    She is   *quite* **taller than** he.   -   old-fashioned
    S V OC(adv. adj.) conj. S

    She is   *no*   **taller than** him.
    S V OC(adv. adj.) prep. PO

    Mala is   *rather a* **better** teacher **than** Sona is.
    S   V OC(adv.   adj.   n.) conj. S   V

    She is   *a bit* **taller**.
    S V OC(adv. adj.)

    Mala is   *a much* **better** teacher **than** Balu/him.
    S   V OC(adv.   adj.   n.) prep. PO

Chapter-12: Adjectives

e) Subject + Verb + **adjective (comparative form) and adjective (comparative form)**.

<u>The tree grew **taller and taller**</u>.
   S   V   OC(adj.)

The above sentence structure is used for <u>double/progressive comparison</u>.

f) Subject + Verb + **more and more / less and less + adjective (positive form)**.

<u>She is becoming **more and more beautiful**</u>.
 S   V   OC(adv.   adj.)
<u>She is becoming **less and less attractive** to him</u>.
 S   V   OC(adv.   adj.)

The above sentence structure is also used for <u>double/progressive comparison.</u>

3) <u>Sentence Structures for Superlative Degree:</u>

Subject + Verb + **the + adjective (superlative form) + of** + all/(quantity) + noun.

<u>He is **the richest of** all the students in the class.</u>
 S V OC(adj.)   Prepositional Phrase)

<u>He is **the richest** man.</u>
 S V OC(adj.)   n.)

<u>He is **the richest**</u>.
 S V OC(adj.)

Pre-modifiers for comparatives and superlatives: When the comparative form or the superlative form of adjectives is to be modified further or to be described even more strongly, we cannot use 'very'. Indeed, we should use pre-modifier adverbs / expressions like **many, much, very much, more, even, far, rather, quite, a lot, lots, a whole lot, a heck, a little, a bit, all the, any, no, by far** and **somewhat**. For example,:

She is <u>a lot</u> **richer than** her husband.
The lady is <u>far</u> **better than** her husband.
She is <u>quite</u> **the most beautiful** person I have ever met.
That is <u>by far</u> **the best** movie.

Comparison of Adjectives of Quantity, namely <u>'Many, Much, Few and Little'</u>: The comparison of these adjectives of quantity needs a special discussion because the verb used in the concerned sentence structures are <u>action verbs</u> with objects. Moreover, some example sentences of this section have a few words given within brackets. It means that they are intentionally left out but grammatically correct. Such sentences are called elliptical sentences and explained in chapter 23 on 'Advanced Sentence Formation'. The comparative forms of these adjectives are given below:

many	more	most
much	more	most
few	fewer	fewest
little	less	least

a) Positive Degree:

<u>He learned   as   *much* English as   (it) was possible.</u>
S   V   O: NP(adv.   adj.   n   ) conj.   S   V   OC(adj.)

Note: **In the above example, the entire object 'as much English' with the following conjunction 'as' can be treated as a conjunction also as illustrated just below:**

<u>She knows **as *many* songs as** he does.</u>
S   V   O: NP / conj.   S   V

<u>She knows **as *many* songs as** him.</u>
S   V   O: NP / prep.   PO   - the object 'as many songs' + 'as' used
                                                                       as a preposition

<u>He has **as *few* brothers as** sisters.</u>
S   V   O: NP / prep.   PO

<u>He learned **as *much* English as** (it was) possible.</u>
S   V   O: NP / conj.   S   V   OC(adj.)

<u>He has   **as *few* as** two dresses.</u>
S   V   O:NP(AdjP   NP   )

<u>He requires   **as *little* as** ₹100.</u>
S   V   O:NP(AdjP   NP)

<u>She knows *twice* **as many songs as** he does.</u>
S   V   O: NP / conj.   S   V

<u>He learned *nearly* **as much English as**   (it) was possible.</u>
S   V   O: NP(adv.   adj.   n   ) conj. S   V   OC(adj.)

<u>She knows *twice* **as many songs as** him.</u>
S   V   O: NP / prep.   PO

Chapter-12: Adjectives

He has ***almost* as few as** two dresses.
S   V   O:NP(AdjP   NP   )

He requires ***just* as little as** ₹100.
S   V   O:NP(AdjP   NP)

b) Comparative Degree:

She knows **more** songs **than** he does.
S   V   O(adj. n.) conj. S V

She knows **more** songs **than** he.   -   old-fashioned
S   V   O(adj. n.) conj. S

She knows **more** songs **than** him.
S   V   O(adj. n.) prep. PO

He has **fewer** brothers.
S   V   O(adj.   n.   )

He has **fewer** brothers **than** sisters.
S   V   O(adj.   n.) prep. PO

He has **fewer (dresses) than** three dresses.
S   V   O(pron.)   prep.   PO

He requires **less (amount) than** ₹100.
S   V   O(pron.)   prep. PO

She knows ***far/many* more** songs **than** he does.
S   V   O(adv.   adj.   n.) conj. S   V

She knows ***far/many* more** songs **than** him.
S   V   O(adv.   adj.   n.) prep. PO

He has ***rather* fewer** brothers.
S   V   O(adv.   adj.   n.)

He has ***even* fewer than** three dresses.
S   V   O(adv. pron.) prep.   PO

He requires ***much* less than** ₹100.
S   V   O(adj. pron.) prep. PO

We need **more** money.
S   V   O(adj.   n.)

We want **less** advice.
S   V   O(adj.   n.)

We want **more and more** money, but **less and less** advice.
S   V   O(adj.   n.) conj. O(adj.   n.)

c) Superlative Degree:

    He got <u>__the most__ points</u>.
    S   V   O(adj.   n.)

    <u>This region has got __the least__ colleges</u>.
    S   V   O(adj.   n.)

Comparison using adjective expressions of '<u>similar to, different from and the same as</u>': The adjectives found in these adjective expressions, namely 'similar, different and same', can be used as normal adjectives also as illustrated below:

    We all have <u>similar</u> problems.
    But, the solutions are <u>different</u>.
    Even the <u>same</u> problems in <u>similar</u> circumstances need <u>different</u> approach.

Now, let us see the sentence structures for comparison using the above expressions.

a) Subject + Verb + **similar to/different from/the same as** + Prepositional Object.

    <u>Your computer is __similar to__ my computer</u>.
          S   V OC(adj.   prep.   PO)

    <u>She looks __different from__ her sister</u>.
    S   V   OC(adj.   prep.   PO)

    <u>My marks are __the same as__ yours</u>.
    S   V OC(pron.   prep. PO)

b) Subject + Verb + **the same** + **noun/expression** + **as** + Prepositional Object.

    <u>Your car has __the same__ colour __as__ mine</u>.
    S   V OC(adj.   n.   PP)

c) The comparative adjective expression in each of the above structures can be modified further by placing a suitable pre-modifier adverb / intensifier before these adjective expressions as illustrated below:

    <u>She looks __slightly different from__ her sister</u>.
    S   V   OC(adv.   adj.   PP)

    <u>My marks are __also almost__ the same __as__ yours</u>.
    S   V OC(adv.   pron.   PP)

    <u>Your car has __nearly__ the same colour __as__ mine</u>.
    S   V OC(adv.   adj.   n.   PP)

Chapter-12: Adjectives

Transformation of Sentences by interchanging degrees of comparison: The same idea/statement, more suitable for superlative degree, can be expressed using different degrees of comparison as illustrated below:

He is **the tallest** boy in the class.
He is **taller than** <u>any other</u> boy in the class.
<u>No other</u> student is **as tall as** he is.
<u>No other</u> student is **as tall as** him.

Usage of 'Different from/to/than': Following are only general guidelines:

She looks <u>different **from**</u> her sister.	-	used before prepositional object
She looks <u>different **to**</u> me.	-	used before prepositional object
She looks <u>different **than**</u> before.	-	used before clause/verb complement

Incomparable Adjectives: Most of the qualities/characteristics vary in intensity under different conditions, and they can be compared. However, some qualities/characteristics always remain the same in all situations and cannot be compared. The adjectives describing such incomparable qualities/characteristics are called incomparable adjectives and are always used in a positive degree only as illustrated below:

The earth is <u>unique</u>. - The earth is said to be unique because only the earth is believed to have life in it whereas no other planet has life and cannot be compared to the earth. As there is no scope for comparison of the earth with other planets in terms of its uniqueness, the adjective 'unique' cannot be compared. Compare it with the following example with a comparable adjective:

The earth is <u>large</u>. - The earth is described to be large in size because its size is large. However, the quality of size is applicable to all other planets also, and the size of the earth can be compared to the size of other planets also. Therefore, the adjective 'large' is comparable as in the sentences 'Earth is <u>larger</u> than Mars' and 'Jupiter is the <u>largest</u> planet in the solar system.'

Some of the incomparable adjectives include 'perfect, unique, universal, mortal, final, vertical, horizontal, right, left, legal, weightless, faultless, etc.'

IV <u>**Adjective Phrase:**</u> A group of words with an adjective as the key/head/main word is called an **adjective phrase**. The key/head/main word will be the last word in the phrase preceded by adverbs of degree. For example,:

The car is <u>very *beautiful*</u>.	-	'beautiful' is the key word
The table is <u>small, long and oval-shaped</u>.	-	group of adjectives used together is also adjective phrase.

Prepositional Phrases as Adjective Phrases called Prepositional Adjective Phrase: A prepositional phrase, i.e., a preposition followed by noun, functioning like an adjective is also called an adjective phrase because it is functionally equivalent to an adjective as illustrated below. In the following examples, the underlined are the prepositional phrases acting as adjective phrases.

Examples | Question Words

A friend <u>of my father</u> met me yesterday.   -   Whose friend?
The girl <u>in the green dress</u> is beautiful.   -   Which girl?

Besides, the prepositional phrases acting as adjective phrases are **post-modifiers**, because, like adjectives, they modify the nouns but are placed after the noun as illustrated below, explaining the difference between the pre-modifier and the post-modifier:

He is a <u>wealthy</u> man.   -   pre-modifier: adjective used before noun
He is a man <u>of wealth</u>.   -   post-modifier: prepositional phrase used after noun

Infinitives as Adjective Phrases called Infinitive Adjective Phrase: Infinitives, a type of verbal, i.e., the base form of verb preceded by 'to', can also function as adjective phrase as illustrated below:

Examples | Question Words

Students have **the duty** <u>to study</u>.   What kind of duty?
The **determination** <u>to win</u> is important in the life.   What kind of determination?

Use of Pre-determiners before Noun Phrases with adjective phrase: Pre-determiners are used before the articles 'a and an' in noun phrases for emphasis as illustrated in the following examples:

It is <u>*such* a beautiful movie</u>.   He has <u>*rather* a good bike</u>.   That was <u>*quite* a nice day</u>.

V **Adjective Clauses:** They are explained in chapter 17 on Clauses and Structural Sentence Types.

VI **Some Common Adjectives:** In the following list of adjectives, regular adjectives are in normal font; *irregular adjectives are in italics*, and **antonyms are in bold**.

Positive Degree	Comparative Degree	Superlative Degree
big	bigger	biggest
little	*less*	*least*
large	larger	largest

Chapter-12: Adjectives

small	**smaller**	**smallest**
short	shorter	shortest
tall	**taller**	**tallest**
long	**longer**	**longest**
fast	faster	fastest
slow	**slower**	**slowest**
hot	hotter	hottest
cold	**colder**	**coldest**
good	*better*	*best*
bad	*worse*	*worst*
old	older	oldest
new	**newer**	**newest**
young	**younger**	**youngest**
pretty	prettier	prettiest
beautiful	*more/less beautiful*	*most/least beautiful*
handsome	*more/less handsome*	*most/least handsome*
ugly	**uglier**	**ugliest**
fat	fatter	fattest
thin	**thinner**	**thinnest**
skinny	**skinnier**	**skinniest**
happy	happier	happiest
sad	**sadder**	**saddest**
full	fuller	fullest
empty	**emptier**	**emptiest**
dark	darker	darkest
bright	**brighter**	**brightest**
heavy	heavier	heaviest
light	**lighter**	**lightest**
funny	funnier	funniest
serious	*more/less serious*	*most/least serious*
interesting	*more/less interesting*	*most/least interesting*
boring	*more/less boring*	*most/least boring*
cheap	cheaper	cheapest
costly	**costlier**	**costliest**
expensive	*more/less expensive*	*most/least expensive*
high	higher	highest
low	**lower**	**lowest**
deep	deeper	deepest
shallow	**shallower**	**shallowest**
healthy	healthier	healthiest
sick	**sicker**	**sickest**
ill	*worse*	*worst*

rich	richer	richest
poor	**poorer**	**poorest**
soft	softer	softest
hard	**harder**	**hardest**
easy	easier	easiest
difficult	*more/less difficult*	*most/least difficult*
tough	**tougher**	**toughest**
clean	cleaner	cleanest
dirty	**dirtier**	**dirtiest**
safe	safer	safest
unsafe	---	---
dangerous	*more/less dangerous*	*most/least dangerous*
same	---	---
different	*more/less different*	*most/least different*
early	earlier	earliest
late	**later**	**latest**
strong	stronger	strongest
weak	**weaker**	**weakest**
great	greater	greatest
mean	**meaner**	**meanest**
friendly	friendlier	friendliest
unfriendly	---	---
hostile	hostiler	hostilest
	more/less hostile	most/least hostile
hungry	hungrier	hungriest
thirsty	thirstier	thirstiest
tired	*more/less tired*	*most/least tired*
busy	busier	busiest
free	**freer**	**freest**
careful	*more/less careful*	*most/least careful*
careless	*more/less careless*	*most/least careless*
troublesome	*more/less troublesome*	*most/least troublesome*
helpful	**more/less helpful**	**most/least helpful**
talkative	*more/less talkative*	*most/least talkative*
favourite	---	---
sweet	sweeter	sweetest
bitter	*more bitter / bitterer*	*most bitter / bitterest*

Chapter 13
Determiners and Articles

Determiners are like adjectives in that they qualify nouns, but they can be <u>used only attributively,</u> and they have <u>no degrees of comparison</u>. Specifically, they determine the scope of nouns or point to the particular nouns while the adjectives tell the quality of nouns.

Question Words: Which (selective), Whose, How many and How much - The answer to these question words in sentences is a determiner.

Examples		Question Words
It is <u>her</u> pen.	-	which/whose (pen)?
<u>That</u> book is mine.	-	which (book)?
I like <u>all</u> the people.	-	which (people)?
<u>A</u> man came yesterday.	-	which (man)?: some man
I saw <u>the</u> man today also.	-	which (man)?: the same man

I <u>Types of determiners:</u> Following are the different types of determiners.

<u>Articles:</u> **(a / an / the):** Articles are used before nouns when we want to limit the scope of the nouns. They should be omitted when nouns are used universally, i.e., without any limited (particular) scope.

<u>Indefinite Articles: (a / an)</u>: They are used to talk about nouns in general, not particular nouns as follows:

> I saw **a** man.
> There is **an** elephant.

'an' is used before nouns beginning with a <u>vowel</u> sound (sounds starting with 'a,e,i,o,u') and **'a'** before nouns beginning with a <u>consonant</u> sound (sounds other than that of vowels).

<u>Definite Article: (the)</u>: Generally, it is used to talk about **the** particular/already-referred nouns as follows:

> He went to **the** park.
> That was **the** first Hindi cinema I have ever seen.
> I saw a man. **The** man was singing.

Specifically, the definite article is used under the following conditions:

1) before the nouns which are unique of their kind; as,

> **The** sun is very bright.
> **The** earth is our planet.

2) when a noun is used to represent the whole class of its kind; as,

> **The** cow is worshipped by Hindus.
> A good teacher would treat **the** children with kindness.

3) with Superlatives; as,

    Mercury is **the** smallest planet.
    This is **the** best grammar book.

4) before proper names of natural places (physical features); as,

    The Indian ocean is to the south of India.
    The Himalayas is to the north of India.

5) before the names of some books which are unique and popular; as,

    The Bible is the holy book of Christians.
    The Ramayana is a very popular epic of India.

6) before an adjective to include all nouns with such quality; as,

    The rich are generally arrogant.
    The beautiful are generally proud.

7) with a proper name qualified by an adjective as well as being unique and popular; as,

    The immortal Thiruvalluvar was a great Tamil poet.
    Alexander **the** great conquered the world.

8) with ordinals; as,

    Everybody wants to be **the** first person to do something.
    The fifth house on this street is mine.

<u>Omission of Articles:</u> Though articles are generally used before nouns, they are omitted under the following conditions. The symbol (---) in the following examples means that the article is omitted.

1) When nouns are used in a general sense, i.e., for telling general truths and facts; as,

    (---) Boys are naughty.
    (---) Discipline is an important virtue.
    (---) Water is good for (---) health.

2) before proper nouns; as,

    (---) Balu is a good boy.
    The capital of Assam is (---) Dispur.

3) before names of relations like father, mother and others; as,

    (---) Mother likes the children.
    (---) Uncle may come tomorrow.

4) before names of institutions used for their primary purpose; as,

    (---) Students go to (---) school.   but   'We live near <u>the</u> school'

Chapter-13: Determiners

5) before names of meals when used in a general sense; as,

(---) Lunch is ready.

6) before names of languages; as,

(---) Tamil is the first classical language of India.

Possessive Adjective Pronouns as determiners: They are used as illustrated below:

It is <u>my</u> pen.   India is <u>our</u> country.
Your shirt is nice.
It is <u>his</u> pen.   We like <u>their</u> town.
It is <u>her</u> pen.
That is <u>its</u> place.

Demonstrative Determiners: Demonstrative determiners point out to some specific nouns as illustrated below:

<u>This</u> pen was given by my friend.   <u>These</u> flowers are for the temple.
<u>That</u> girl is beautiful.   <u>Those</u> girls are more beautiful.
<u>Such</u> occasions are rare.   He did not expect <u>such</u> an excuse.
They had met the <u>other</u> day.   <u>Which</u> way is better?

Quantifiers: They are used to quantify the nouns and to tell how many/how much of these nouns. As illustrated below, some of them are used with countable nouns, some with uncountable nouns and some with both.

I need <u>some</u> rice.   I do not want <u>any</u> food.   I have <u>no</u> money.
I look after <u>some</u> children.   We have <u>enough</u> trees.   They have <u>no</u> children.
He has a <u>few</u> books.   He has <u>fewer</u> books.   He has the <u>fewest</u> books.
She has a <u>little</u> money.   She has <u>less</u> money.   She has the <u>least</u> money.
He has <u>many</u> friends.   He needs <u>more</u> friends.   She has <u>much</u> money.
She needs <u>more</u> money.   <u>All</u> people are not bad.   She loves <u>both</u> her sons.
She has a <u>half</u> share.   I have <u>enough</u> medicines.   He knows <u>several</u> doctors.
He gets <u>twice</u> my salary.   I want <u>five times</u> his salary.   I save <u>one-fifth</u> of my salary.
<u>Each</u> book is valuable.   I know <u>every</u> child in the class. I have <u>one/five</u> pen(s).
You can go to <u>either</u> side.   <u>Neither</u> answer was correct.

Ordinal Determiners: They are used to show the order of nouns as illustrated below:

She likes the <u>first</u> child.   He lives in the <u>fifth</u> lane.
She was the <u>last</u> child.   We can meet <u>next</u> week.
The <u>previous</u> work was fine.   Watch for <u>subsequent</u> developments.

II Position and Order of Determiners: Determiners can be grouped into two types for explaining the position and order of determiners. **Type I** includes the Articles, Possessive Adjective Pronouns and Demonstrative Determiners, and **Type II** includes Quantifiers and Ordinal Determiners, i.e., the determiners related to numbers.

Type I: More than one determiner of this type cannot be used together. For example, we say 'my book, the book', not 'my the book' nor 'the my book.'

Type II: More than one determiner of this type can be used together if it makes sense. For example,:

They can look after <u>some</u> <u>more</u> children.

They can be placed before nouns with or without 'of.' However, when they are combined with pronouns, we have to use 'of' between the determiner and the pronoun as illustrated below:

'all students/all of the students'	not 'all us'	but 'all of us'
'both teachers/both of the teachers'	not 'both them'	but 'both of them'
'some boys/some of the boys'	not 'some you'	but 'some of you'
'neither answer/neither of the answers'	not 'neither them'	but 'neither of them'
'most girls/most of the girls'	not 'most you'	but 'most of you'

As you would have noticed, most of the Type II determiners are indefinite pronouns also. However, some of them cannot be used as indefinite pronouns. Such Type II determiners that cannot be used as indefinite pronouns cannot be used with 'of' as illustrated below:

'no buses'	not 'no of the buses'	nor 'no of them'
'every man'	not 'every of men'	nor 'every of them'

Using this analogy of 'indefinite pronouns/determiners + of + nouns/pronouns', certain <u>noun/pronoun expressions</u> are also used <u>as quantifiers</u> as illustrated below:

He has <u>a couple</u> **of** points.   <u>None</u> <u>of</u> the points are good.
We should know <u>a bit</u> **of** everything.   She knows <u>a great deal</u> **of** music.
He has <u>a lot</u> **of** friends.   You have <u>lots</u> **of** money.
Our country has <u>plenty</u> **of** talent.   We have <u>a lack</u> **of** commitment.

Type II + Type I: When Type II determiner is used before the Type I determiner, we have to use 'of' between them as follows:

I saw <u>some</u> **of** <u>the</u> children.   We know <u>most</u> **of** <u>his</u> friends.
You can follow <u>any</u> **of** <u>these</u> methods.   I like <u>neither</u> **of** <u>these</u> plans.

Type I + Type II: Certain Type I determiner can be used before the Type II determiners. Anyway, no 'of' is required for this combination as illustrated below:

She has <u>a</u> <u>little</u> money.   He knows <u>a</u> <u>few</u> points.

Chapter 14
Adverbs

Adverbs are Describing Words (Modifiers) for Verbs, Adjectives, other Adverbs and Sentences. Abbreviation: **adv**. They describe or give more information about verbs, adjectives and other adverbs. Sometimes, they modify the phrases, the clauses or the whole sentence.

Question Words in general: How, When, Where and Why. The specific form of question words are given below against what the adverb describes - The answer to these questions in sentences is adverb.

Examples	Question Words
Adverbs describing verbs: How / When / Where / Why + Action Verb	
He runs fast.	**How** does he *run*?
I meet him daily.	**How often** do I *meet* him?
He played yesterday.	**When** did he *play*?
We searched everywhere.	**Where** did we *search*?
He lied purposely.	**Why** did he *lie*?
Adverbs describing adjectives and adverbs: How + Adjective / Adverb	
He is a very good boy.	**How** *good* is he?
He runs very fast.	**How** *fast* does he run?
Adverbs modifying the phrases: How + Adverb	
His room is just above our room.	**Where** *exactly* is his room?
I read all through your book.	**How** *thoroughly* did I read the book?
Adverbs modifying the whole sentences/clauses: How / When / Where / Why + Action Verb	
Sometimes, they go out.	**How** often do *they go out*?
Luckily, we won the match.	**How** did *we win the match*?

I Types of Adverbs: Adverbs can be classified according to their meaning as follows:

Adverbs of Manner (showing **How** or in what manner): They include aggressively, softly, **alone**, **together**, badly, **well**, beautifully, bravely, timidly, clearly, carefully, carelessly, correctly, wrongly, eagerly, willingly, grudgingly, unwillingly, easily, **fast, slow**, slowly, greedily, **hard**, loudly, quietly, patiently, impatiently, quickly and rapidly. For example,:

He studied carefully.	He has learned Maths carefully.
The soldiers fought bravely.	She worked hard.
He is living alone.	They are living together.
She has done well.	She has done badly.
They are working willingly.	They are working grudgingly.
Our economy is growing rapidly.	She touched the baby softly.

Adverbs of Time (showing When or at what time): They include before, after, afterwards, already, behind, early, late, soon, daily, today, yesterday, tomorrow, now, then, later, once, sometime, still, yet, long, ago and back. For example,:

    I have seen him <u>before</u>.   He can collect it <u>afterwards</u>.
    She should come <u>early</u>.   The train arrived <u>late</u>.
    The result will be announced <u>soon</u>.   You should go for a walk <u>daily</u>.
    He has come <u>yesterday</u>.   She may come <u>tomorrow</u>.
    The movie is going to start <u>now</u>.   What is wrong <u>then</u>?
    They may meet you <u>sometime</u>.   They will meet you <u>later</u>.
    I have <u>already</u> met him.   I have not met him <u>yet</u>.
    ('yet' is used in negative sentences and questions)
    The story happened <u>long ago</u>.   They met each other <u>long back</u>.

Adverbs of Place/Location (showing Where or in which place): They include ahead, abroad, back, about, across, along, anywhere, everywhere, around, away, behind, by, far, close, near, nearby, backward, forward, down, up, downstairs, upstairs, here, there, high, low, home, in, out, inside, outside, off, on, over, overseas, round, through, under, indoors, outdoors, uphill, downhill, sideways, backwards, forwards, downwards, upwards, inwards, outwards, onwards, northwards, southwards, eastwards and westwards. For example,:

    You should look <u>ahead</u> while driving.   He turned and looked <u>back</u>.
    The beach is <u>away</u> from here.   It is not <u>far</u> to the beach.
    Come <u>here</u>.   Go <u>there</u>.
    We searched for it <u>everywhere</u>.   We could not find it <u>anywhere</u>.
    The exams are drawing <u>near</u>.   My friend is living <u>nearby</u>.
    Move <u>forward/backward</u>.   He has gone <u>downstairs/upstairs</u>.
    She is aiming <u>high/low</u>.   Get <u>in/out</u>.
    You can wait <u>inside/outside</u>.   The ball bounced <u>up and down</u>.

(Please note that 'towards' is a preposition, not an adverb and as such is always followed by a noun or pronoun).

Adverbs of Reason (showing Why or for what): For example,:

She lied <u>purposely</u>.
I was not careful enough. <u>Consequently</u>, I had to suffer.

Adverbs of Definite Frequency (showing How often or at what interval): They include again, daily, monthly, yearly, every month, once, twice and thrice. For example,:

    We will meet <u>again</u>.   He plays football <u>daily</u>.
    This magazine is published <u>monthly</u>.   This magazine is published <u>yearly</u>.
    She goes out <u>every month</u>.   We have met <u>once or twice</u> before.

Chapter-14: Adverbs

Adverbs of Indefinite Frequency (showing How often or at what interval): They include always, often, seldom, never, ever, frequently, sometimes, rarely, generally, still and usually. For example,:

He <u>always</u> plays football.	She <u>never</u> comes in time.
Nobody <u>ever</u> visits her.	We <u>usually</u> go shopping together.
He <u>frequently</u> meets the children.	She <u>rarely</u> goes out.
I do not <u>often</u> go there.	She is <u>still</u> waiting for us.

Adverbs of Indefinite Frequency also include the <u>Negative Adverbs</u> including not, barely, hardly and scarcely. For example,:

I do <u>not</u> like them.	He has <u>not</u> finished the project.
We had <u>scarcely</u> gone out when he entered.	<u>Scarcely</u> had we gone out when he entered.
I <u>hardly</u> see him.	<u>Hardly</u> do I see him.

Adverbs of Certainty/Probability (showing How certain / sure): They include certainly, definitely, probably, undoubtedly, doubtfully and surely. For example,:

He will <u>certainly</u> win.	She <u>definitely</u> went out yesterday.
They are <u>probably</u> in the park.	She <u>doubtfully</u> told that.
<u>Undoubtedly</u>, India is a great country.	He will win <u>undoubtedly</u>.

Adverbs of Attitude/Opinion (showing How / under What feeling/condition the opinion is formed): They include clearly, confidentially, economically, frankly, geographically, honestly, ideally, obviously, officially, personally, seriously, surely, surprisingly, theoretically, practically, ultimately and undoubtedly. For example,:

You will be answered <u>personally</u>.	He was <u>personally</u> punished.
<u>Personally</u>, I would like to support her.	It <u>clearly</u> shows your mind.
<u>Frankly</u>, she is wrong.	She <u>frankly</u> accepted her mistake.
He is <u>obviously</u> the culprit.	<u>Obviously</u>, they do not want it.
<u>Theoretically</u>, you should be punished.	<u>Surprisingly</u>, they won the match.

Adverbs of Degree (showing by How much degree/amount): They are also called <u>intensifiers</u> and include almost, nearly, completely, very, extremely, fairly, quite, just, pretty, enough, too, hardly, scarcely, rather and so. They are generally used before adjectives and adverbs only. For example,:

The theatre is <u>almost</u> full.	The theatre is <u>nearly</u> full.
He ran <u>very</u> fast.	It is <u>extremely</u> cold outside.
They walked <u>quite</u> slowly.	He knows her <u>pretty</u> well.
It is <u>hardly</u> surprising.	There is <u>scarcely</u> a day left.
She fell down <u>rather</u> badly.	He looks <u>so</u> angry.
The door was not thick <u>enough</u> to stop them.	The door was <u>too</u> thick to break.

Connecting Adverbs / Conjunctive Adverbs: They are used to connect/link the ideas expressed by two sentences/clauses. In other words, they connect two sentences/main clauses. They include however, nevertheless, therefore, hence, thus, also, besides, moreover, furthermore, otherwise, consequently, ultimately, etc. For example,:

We can go there. <u>However</u>, we must come back today itself.
It is difficult to complete in time. <u>Nevertheless</u>, you should try.
He had studied very well. <u>Therefore/Hence/Thus</u>, he got good marks.
She is beautiful. <u>Also/Besides/Moreover/Furthermore</u>, she is rich too.
You must study hard. <u>Otherwise</u>, you cannot get good marks.
I was not careful enough. <u>Consequently</u>, I had to suffer.

The connecting adverbs are also called <u>Transitional Expressions</u> and can also include expressions like 'after all', 'at least', 'even so', 'for all that', 'in fact', 'in short', 'in any event', 'of course', 'on the whole' and 'without doubt' because they also relate/link the idea expressed in a sentence with the idea expressed in the previous sentence. For example,:

We should pay our taxes. <u>After all</u>, it is our basic duty.
He may not be rich. <u>At least</u>, he has no debts.
I thought I was late. <u>In fact</u>, I was early.
It is difficult to complete in time. <u>Even so</u>, you should try.

They are dealt with elaborately in chapter 18 on Conjunctions as they function like conjunctions too.

Parallel Adverbs: They are used to refer to (the effect of) the verb/adverb of previous clause/sentence and also to emphasize the meaning of the sentence as illustrated below. In the following examples, words within the brackets are omitted.

She works very hard; <u>as</u> does her friend (work).
I like apples. <u>So</u> does he (like).
I don't like oranges. <u>Neither</u> does she (like). / <u>Nor</u> does she (like).
He does not like apples; <u>nor</u> does he like oranges.
He can't fly. <u>Neither</u> can I (fly). = I can't either.
She is tall; <u>as</u> is her father.

They are also used to emphasize the idea of the sentence as explained more in chapter 20 on Inversion of Subject, Verb and Complement, and also in chapter 23 on Advanced Sentence Formation.

Note: **Adverbs and Be-Verbs / Linking Verbs:** Adverbs are generally used more with action verbs. When they are used with be-verbs, they modify the adjective/adverb (phrase) that follows the be-verb. When used without any following adjective/adverb (phrase), adverbs are placed before the subject to emphasize the meaning of the sentence. For example,:

The theatre is <u>almost</u> *full*. (*adjective*)   They are <u>probably</u> *in the park*. (*adv. phrase*)
<u>There</u> you are. (emphatic sentence)   <u>Here</u> is our best victory. (emphatic sentence)

Chapter-14: Adverbs

When used with linking verbs, they modify the adjective (phrase) that follows as in 'The theatre looks almost *full*'.

II Adverb Phrases:

A group of words with adverb as the key/head/main word is called an **adverb phrase**. The key/head/main word will be the last word in the phrase preceded by adverbs of degree. For example,:

    He completed it very *quickly*.   He knows her pretty *well*.

Prepositional Adverb Phrases: A prepositional phrase, i.e., a preposition followed by noun, functioning like an adverb is also called an adverb phrase because it is functionally equivalent to an adverb as illustrated below. In the following examples, the underlined are the prepositional phrases acting as adverb phrases.

Examples	Question Words
We write with a pen.	**How** do we write?
I play in the evening.	**When** do I play?
A book is on the table.	**Where** is the book?
He plays for fun.	**Why** does he play?

Infinitives as Adverb Phrases called Infinitive Adverb Phrase: Infinitives, a type of verbal, i.e., the base form of verb preceded by 'to', can also function as adverb phrase as illustrated below:

Examples	Question Words
The students are studying hard to get good marks.	**Why** are the students studying hard?
He ran fast to catch the train.	**Why** did he run fast?

These infinitives are also called Adverbs of Purpose (showing **Why** or for what) when they are used as adverb phrases.

III Adverb Clauses:
They are explained in chapter 17 on Clauses and Structural Sentence Types.

IV Additional Functional Types of Adverbs:
Adverbs normally modify words (verb, adjectives and adverb), phrases or even sentences/clauses. Some adverbs, the question words of adverbs such as **'How, When, Where and Why'**, are used to provide additional functions like making questions and making dependent (subordinate) clauses. They are classified according to the additional function provided by them as follows:

Interrogative Adverbs: The above-mentioned question words of adverbs are called interrogative adverbs when they are used in **questions** because the answer for these questions will be adverbs as illustrated below:

<u>How</u> did he study?	-	He studied <u>carefully</u>.
<u>How</u> **many** apples does she have?	-	She has <u>five</u> (many) apples.

(Please note that 'How' modifies the adjective 'many', and therefore it is an adverb. However, the answer is 'five', used as an adjective. It can be viewed as adverb also modifying 'many' as illustrated in the answer for the question. However, 'many' is always omitted and 'five' is used as adjective.)

<u>How</u> **much** money have you got?	-	I have got ₹<u>500</u> (much money).

(It can also be analyzed as above.)

<u>How</u> **old** is your school?	-	My school is <u>100 years</u> old.
<u>How</u> **quickly** can you finish?	-	I can finish it <u>within 10 minutes</u>.
<u>When</u> will the bus come?	-	The bus will come <u>tomorrow</u>.
<u>Where</u> is the key?	-	The key is <u>on the table</u>.
<u>Why</u> do you work very hard?	-	I work very hard <u>to earn more money</u>.

Relative Adverbs: The above mentioned question words are called relative adverbs as described in chapter 17 on Clauses and Structural Sentence Types.

V <u>Position of Adverbs:</u>

Position of Adverbs modifying verbs and sentences/clauses: There are three normal positions for Adverbs, namely **Initial Position, Mid Position and End Position**. Adverbs placed in the **mid** position and in the **end** position modify or describe the verbs while adverbs in the **initial** position modify the whole sentence/clause. These guidelines apply to <u>adverb phrases and adverb clauses</u> also.

End Position: Normally, adverbs are placed in the end position, i.e., at the end of the sentence after the object, if any, or after the verb. Adverbs in the end position modify the verbs. For example,:

She walked off <u>quickly</u>.	-	<u>Adverb of Manner</u> (How)
You can't find him <u>here</u>.	-	<u>Adverb of Place</u> (Where)
We can meet <u>tomorrow</u>.	-	<u>Adverb of Time</u> (When)
We meet <u>daily</u>.	-	<u>Adverb of Definite Frequency</u> (How often)

Order of Adverbs: When many (types of) adverbs are used at the end position in a single sentence, there is a basic order for writing them. The basic order for the adverbs is adverbs of **Manner, Place, Frequency, Time and Purpose (MPFTP)** as illustrated below:

The students study <u>very hard</u> <u>at school</u> <u>every afternoon</u> <u>before evening</u> <u>to get good marks</u>.
                         Manner   Place   Frequency   Time   Purpose

Chapter-14: Adverbs

Nevertheless, if the verb of the sentence is a verb of motion (movement), then the order is **P**lace, **M**anner, **F**requency, **T**ime and **P**urpose **(PMFTP)** as illustrated below:

Students go <u>to school</u> <u>in uniform</u> <u>every morning</u> <u>before 9</u> <u>to attend the prayer</u>.
            Place   Manner   Frequency   Time   Purpose

Mid Position: <u>Adverbs of indefinite frequency **(How often)**</u> are placed in the mid position, i.e., just after the first auxiliary verb if the action verb has auxiliary verb(s). If there is no auxiliary verb, they are placed before the action verb, and if there is Be-Verb, they are placed after the Be-Verb. Adverbs in the mid position modify the verbs. For example,:

    I have <u>never</u> seen the movie.   We had <u>always</u> been playing games.
    She <u>always</u> watches TV.   He does <u>not</u> watch TV.
    I was <u>not</u> in the canteen.   We are <u>usually</u> in the office.

Besides, <u>Adverbs of Certainty/Probability (showing **How certain/sure**)</u> and <u>Adverbs of Attitude/Opinion (showing **How / under What feeling/condition** the opinion is formed)</u> can also be placed in the mid position as illustrated below:

    They are <u>probably</u> in the park.   She <u>doubtfully</u> told that.
    He will <u>certainly</u> win.   He was <u>personally</u> punished.
    She <u>frankly</u> accepted her mistake.   He is <u>obviously</u> the culprit.

Moreover, in negative sentences, the mid-position adverbs are generally placed after the adverb 'not' but placed before the entire complete verb to emphasize the meaning. For e.g.,

    I do not <u>really</u> know him.   I <u>really</u> do not know him. (Emphasized)
    He is not <u>definitely</u> with her.   He <u>definitely</u> is not with her. (Incorrect)

Initial Position: <u>Adverbs of Certainty/Probability (showing **How certain/sure**)</u>, <u>Adverbs of Attitude/Opinion (showing **How / under What feeling/condition** the opinion is formed)</u> and <u>Connecting Adverbs</u> can be placed in the initial position. <u>Adverb Phrases of Purpose</u> are also placed similarly. Adverbs in the initial position modify the whole sentence/clause. For example,:

    <u>Undoubtedly</u>, India is a great country.   <u>Probably</u>, he may win.
    <u>Personally</u>, I would like to support her.   <u>Obviously</u>, they do not want it.
    <u>Theoretically</u>, you should be punished.   <u>Surprisingly</u>, they won the match.
    We can go there. <u>However</u>, we must come back today itself.
    He had studied very well. <u>Therefore/Hence/Thus</u>, he got good marks.
    I was not careful enough. <u>Consequently</u>, I had to suffer.
    <u>To win the match</u>, we have to practise daily.

VII Forms of Adjective-based Adverbs: Many adverbs are closely related to adjectives, and the related adjectives and adverbs have very close forms as explained below:

1) Adverbs formed with the suffix '-ly' added to adjectives: Most adverbs of manner, probability and opinion, and some adverbs of indefinite frequency are closely related to the adjectives and are formed by adding **'-ly'** to the corresponding adjectives as illustrated below:

Adjective		Adverb
quick	-	quickly
slow	-	slowly
bad	-	badly
easy	-	easily
happy	-	happily
probable	-	probably
gentle	-	gently
basic	-	basically
specific	-	specifically
due	-	duly
true	-	truly
normal	-	normally
full	-	fully
dull	-	dully
usual	-	usually

2) Adjectives and adverbs with same form and with similar meaning: Some adjectives and adverbs have the same form with similar meaning. In other words, the same words are used sometimes as adjectives and sometimes as adverbs as illustrated below:

Adjective		Adverb
He is a <u>fast</u> runner.	-	He ran <u>fast</u>.
The sum is <u>hard</u>.	-	He works <u>hard</u> to solve it.
It is my <u>little</u> house.	-	You know <u>little</u> about it.
She always makes a <u>loud</u> noise.	-	Let her not talk <u>loud</u>.
She has <u>much</u> money.	-	She does not spend <u>much</u>.
We have <u>enough</u> food for all.	-	The food is hot <u>enough</u> to eat.
You take the <u>straight</u> road.	-	You go <u>straight</u>.
I live at the <u>far</u> end of the town.	-	We should go <u>far</u> to reach my house.
They have a <u>high</u> opinion about you.	-	You should always aim <u>high</u>.
The flight flies at a <u>low</u> level.	-	The flight flies <u>low</u>.
The exams will be in the <u>near</u> future.	-	The exams are drawing <u>near</u>.
The road is <u>wide</u>.	-	Open your mouth <u>wide</u>.

Chapter-14: Adverbs

Please use the <u>back</u> entrance.	Come <u>back</u> quickly.
He uses the <u>next</u> door.	He lives <u>next</u> to my house.
We go by <u>early</u> train.	We have to get up <u>early</u>.
You can get the <u>first</u> rank.	You can come <u>first</u> in the exam.
We were <u>late</u> for the train.	We came <u>late</u> to the station.
It will probably take a <u>long</u> time.	It will probably take <u>long</u>.
It is a <u>daily</u> train.	You can go <u>daily</u> by this train.
It is a <u>monthly</u> salary.	You will be paid <u>monthly</u>.
<u>Weekly</u> meetings are held regularly.	Reports are published <u>weekly</u>.
We submit <u>yearly</u> income statement.	They will ask us <u>yearly</u>.
He is the <u>only</u> person who can sing.	He can <u>only</u> sing.
She is <u>quick</u> to learn new things.	You can learn <u>quick</u>.

3) Adjective and adverb with different form but with similar meaning: The adjective 'good' has an entirely different form of equivalent adverb though both the adjective and the corresponding adverb have the same meaning as given below:

good   -   well

Another interesting point is that <u>'well' can be used as adjective also</u> predicatively as illustrated below:

He is <u>good</u>.	- 'good' is adjective modifying 'He' and means 'he is a good person'
He is <u>well</u>.	- 'well' is adjective modifying 'He' and means 'he is healthy'
He did <u>well</u>.	- 'well' is adverb modifying the verb 'did' and means 'he did something, say, some work, well'

4) Adverbs with different forms but with similar meaning: Some adverbs have two different forms but with the same meaning as follows:

He cannot speak <u>loud</u>.   =   He cannot speak <u>loudly</u>.

5) Adverbs with two different forms and with different meaning: Some adverbs have two different forms with different meanings:

Adjective	First form of Adverb	Second form of Adverb
hard	hard (with great effort)	hardly (scarcely; almost not)
e.g.,	He works <u>hard</u>.	He <u>hardly</u> works.
high	high (to higher position)	highly (very)
e.g.,	He aims <u>high</u>.	He is <u>highly</u> educated.
late	late (with delay)	lately (recently)
e.g.,	He came <u>late</u>.	He got the job <u>lately</u>.
near	near (in the vicinity)	nearly (almost)
e.g.,	He came <u>near</u>.	He <u>nearly</u> got the job.

Nobody lives <u>there</u>.   -   used as adverb
You can go over <u>there</u>.   -   used as noun because it is the object of the preposition 'over'
She went <u>home</u>.   -   used as adverb. We should not say 'She went to home' because 'home' is used as adverb, not noun, and cannot follow the preposition as only nouns can follow the prepositions
<u>Home</u> is the best place to live.   -   used as noun
She works from <u>home</u>.   -   used as noun because it is the object of the preposition 'from'

2) **'ever'**: It is normally used with the meaning of <u>'at any point of time / by any chance'</u> in negative sentences, questions and if-clauses as illustrated below:

Have you <u>ever</u> been to London?   - 'at any point of time'
If you <u>ever</u> happen to see him, give him some good advice.   - 'by any chance'

'ever' is not normally used to mean 'always', but it means <u>'always'</u> in some expressions like <u>forever, ever since</u> and <u>ever after</u>.

'ever' in <u>affirmative sentences:</u> It is used in affirmative sentences <u>after superlatives</u> as illustrated below:

He is the richest man to <u>ever</u> live here.
She is the only woman <u>ever</u> to fight for her rights.

3) **'else'**: It is used with the meaning of <u>'other than'</u> modifying the adverbs preceding it:

How <u>else</u> can you get it?   We cannot go anywhere <u>else</u>.

4) **'even'**: It is used to express something that is surprising or unexpected as follows:

Freedom fighters had <u>even</u> sacrificed their lives for our country.
<u>Even</u> a fool will appreciate my efforts.   This problem may confuse <u>even</u> the experts.
He is kind <u>even</u> to his enemies.   He is <u>even</u> kind to his enemies.

It is also used to make the comparisons <u>even</u> stronger as illustrated below:

She should try <u>even</u> harder than him.   He is <u>even</u> more intelligent than her.

5) **'also', 'as well' and 'too'**: Though they are all similar with the meaning of 'also', each of them is preferred in different type of sentence/situation as illustrated below:

Chapter-14: Adverbs

He met the minister yesterday, and I have <u>also</u> met the minister today.
- 'also' is more formal and used before the main verb and after be-verb

This book is useful, and interesting <u>too</u>.
They are enjoying the game. I (am) <u>too</u>.
- 'too' is informal and used at the end of the sentence

I have already paid him ₹1000, and I can pay him another ₹100 <u>as well</u>.
- 'as well' is also informal but more formal than 'too'

6) **Nouns as adverbs:** Nouns used after verbs are usually subject complements or object complements. However, nouns can be used sometimes as verb complements also, i.e., adverbs as illustrated below:

You have played <u>two hours</u>.   Vs.   You have played **for** <u>two hours</u>.
- the first sentence uses it as adverb because it immediately follows the action verb 'have played', and the second sentence uses the noun phrase 'two hours' as noun because it follows the preposition 'for'

Which one of the above two sentences is correct? Though both the sentences are correct and mean the same thing, <u>the first sentence is more acceptable</u> because some nouns like 'home' are considered to include an inherent preposition within it and used as adverb directly without any explicit preposition. Similarly, the noun 'two hours' is also used as adverb. A few more examples are:

Walk <u>thirty minutes</u> daily.   Vs.   Walk **for** <u>thirty minutes</u> daily.
We can stay <u>two days</u> at Patna.   Vs.   We can stay **for** <u>two days</u> at Patna.

7) **Adverbs used together:** Some adverbs are used together, combined by conjunctions, to express the meaning of the underlying adverb strongly. Some of them are listed below:

again and again	=	repeatedly
over and over	=	repeatedly
far and near	=	in all directions
far and wide	=	comprehensively
first and foremost	=	first of all
now and then	=	occasionally
on and off	=	intermittently
out and out	=	beyond any comparison
over and above	=	in addition to
to and fro	=	both forward and backward

Such combinations are also called **binomials**. Binomials are formed with nouns also and used as nouns. For example, law and order, pros and cons, odds and ends, hustle and bustle, ups and downs, ins and outs, ifs and buts, etc.

Position of Adverbs modifying adjectives and other adverbs: They are used in the **mid position,** i.e., just before the adjective or the adverb. Adverbs of Degree (showing **by How much** degree/amount), also called intensifiers, are used to modify adjectives and other adverbs. For example,:

    The theatre is almost **full**.   He ran very **fast**.
    It is extremely **cold**.   He knows her pretty **well**.
    The door was too **thick** to break.
    The door was not **thick** enough to stop them. - However, 'enough' is used after the adjective/adverb. It is explained in a later section.

Different Positions for the same adverbs: Sometimes, the same adverb can be treated as different types of adverb and placed in different positions, depending on what it modifies. For example,:

The road was heavily damaged.   -   the adverb 'heavily' modifies the participle/adjective 'damaged', and therefore treated as an adverb of degree.

The rain has damaged the roads heavily.   -   the adverb 'heavily' modifies the verb 'has damaged', and therefore treated as an adverb of manner.

The rain has heavily damaged the roads.   -   this way of using the adverb of manner is also accepted.

Position of Prepositional Adverb Phrases: They occupy the **end position** when they modify the verb and the **initial position** when they modify the whole sentence. For example,:

In the beginning, students would find each other strangers. - modify the whole sentence
They become friends in the end.   - modify the verb

Position of Adverb Clauses: Adverb Clauses, explained in chapter 17 on Clauses and Structural Sentence Types, usually occupy the **end position** or the **initial position**.

Special/Unusual Position of some Adverbs:

1) 'ago' and 'back', adverbs of time, are used after the word (adverb) it modifies as illustrated below:

    The story happened **long** ago.   They met each other **long** back.

    That incidence happened **years** ago.   I saw him **three months** back.
         -      the words 'years' and 'three months' are normally nouns; however, they are used in the sense of adverbs of 'how long'.

2) 'enough' and 'too', adverbs of degree, are used in the mid position but slightly differently as illustrated below:

'enough' as an adverb with the meaning of 'to the necessary degree (positive in meaning)' always goes after adjectives and adverbs as:

Is the teacher **kind** enough?   She worked **hard** enough.

'too' with the meaning of 'more than necessary (negative in meaning)' always goes before adjectives and adverbs as:

It is too **hot**.   She works too **hard**.

'enough' and 'too' are combined with the preposition 'for' and the infinitive as follows:

The dress is **big** enough **for** her.   The drink was too **cold for** me.
The coffee was not **hot** enough **to drink**.   The coffee is too **hot to drink**.

However, 'enough' as adjective is only used before nouns as illustrated below:

We have enough food to serve all.   You will get enough training there.

3) <u>Inversion of Subject and Verb</u> with <u>adverb / adverb phrases / expressions</u> is used for emphasis as illustrated below:

There goes **Balu**. = **Balu** goes there.
Under no circumstances can **we** accept it. = We can't accept it under any circumstances.
Hardly/Scarcely had **I** left when somebody called. = I had hardly/scarcely left …
Only then did **I** understand the situation. = I understood the situation only then.
I like apples. So does **he** (like).
I don't like oranges. Neither does **she** (like). / Nor does **she** (like).

The inversion of subject, verb and other complement is thoroughly discussed in chapter 20 on inversion of subject, verb and complement.

VI <u>Special Uses/Cases of some Adverbs</u>:

1) **Adverbs as nouns: 'here', 'there'** and **'home'**, adverbs of place, can also be used as nouns referring to the <u>places</u> as illustrated below:

Come here.	-	used as adverb
People are working down here.	-	used as noun because it is the object of the preposition 'down'
He will come over here.	-	used as noun because it is the object of the preposition 'over'

pretty	-	pretty (fairly)	prettily (neatly)
	e.g.,	He is <u>pretty</u> young.	He is <u>prettily</u> dressed.
wide	-	wide (of length)	widely (commonly)
	e.g.,	He opened the door <u>wide</u>.	He is <u>widely</u> popular.

6) **Adjectives themselves with '-ly' suffix but with no equivalent adverbs:** Some adjectives have already got '-ly' suffix and have no equivalent adverbs. They include friendly, likely, lively, lonely, silly and ugly. When adverbs with similar meanings as that of these adjectives are required, prepositional adverb phrases with nouns modified by these adjectives can be used as illustrated below:

He was treated <u>in a friendly manner</u>.
The event was organized <u>in a lively way</u>.

VIII Degrees of Comparison: Adverbs can be written in different forms to specify the degree/level by which the intensity of an adverb in one situation differs from the intensity of the same adverb in another situation. This is called the degrees of comparison of adverbs. In other words, it is the comparison of the intensity of the adverbs in different situations. The comparisons are made in the following three ways:

Example	-	Type of comparison and Degrees of Comparison
Bhadhu got up <u>early</u>.	-	no comparison
Bhadhu got up <u>as early as</u> Ram.	-	comparison of <u>equality</u> between two; **positive degree**
Bhadhu got up <u>earlier than</u> Ram.	-	comparison of <u>inequality</u> between two; **comparative degree**
Bhadhu got up <u>earliest</u> of all.	-	comparison of <u>superiority</u> among all; **superlative degree**

At the same time, it is to be noted that <u>some adverbs cannot be compared whereas some can be</u>. Generally speaking, most of the adverbs of manner can be compared while other type of adverbs like adverbs of place and time cannot be compared. However, some of the adverbs of manner that cannot be compared include <u>alone and together</u>, and some of the adverbs of place and time that can be compared include <u>far, close, near, high, low, early, late and soon</u>.

Forms of adverbs for comparison: Three forms of comparison, namely Positive Degree, Comparative Degree and Superlative Degree, are used to express the comparison of adverbs as illustrated below:

Positive Degree	Comparative Degree	Superlative Degree

Chapter-14: Adverbs

Regular Comparison: Some adverbs with one syllable have the comparative form and the superlative form by suffixing -er and -est to the base/positive form respectively. They are called regular adverbs. For example,:

fast	faster	fastest
early	earlier	earliest
close	closer	closest
near	nearer	nearest
high	higher	highest
low	lower	lowest
late	later	latest
soon	sooner	soonest

More/Most Comparison: Adverbs with more than one syllable and ending with mostly '-ly' have the comparative form and the superlative form by adding 'more/less' and 'most/least' respectively before the base/positive form. For example,:

carefully	more/less carefully	most/least carefully
easily	more/less easily	most/least easily

Irregular Comparison: Some adverbs have irregular/entirely different comparative form and the superlative form from the base/positive form. They are called irregular adverbs. For example,:

well	better	best
badly	worse	worst
ill	worse	worst
little	less	least
much	more	most
far (place)	farther	farthest
far (time)	further	furthest

Sentence Structures for comparison of adverbs: The following sentence structures are used for comparison of adverbs as illustrated below:

1) <u>Sentence Structures for Positive Degree:</u>

a) <u>Subject + Verb +</u>   **as + adverb (positive form) + as** + <u>Subject + Verb.</u>
   independent clause   dependent clause

   They run **as fast as** he runs.
    S   V   conj.   S V

II Prepositional Phrase (PP): A preposition along with its (prepositional) object is called a prepositional phrase. Functionally, prepositional phrases have no independent function, and they have to act like **noun phrase** or **adjective phrase** or **adverb phrase**. Use of prepositional phrase as noun phrase is explained in the next section. If a prepositional phrase modifies/describes nouns, then it is an adjective phrase, and if it modifies/describes verbs, adjectives or adverbs, then it is an adverb phrase. They are illustrated with the corresponding questions below wherein the underlined phrases are prepositional phrases.

A book is <u>on the table</u>.   -   The question for the prepositional phrase can be '<u>Where is the book</u>?' wherein the question word 'Where' is a question word of adverb and modifies the verb 'is'. Therefore, it is an <u>adverb phrase</u> of place. Another way of forming the question can be 'On what is the book?' which also means 'Where'.

I saw the book <u>on the table</u>.   -   The question for the prepositional phrase can be '<u>Which book did I see</u>?' wherein the question word 'Which' is a question word of adjective and modifies the noun 'book'. Therefore, it is an <u>adjective phrase</u>. It is to be noted that the same prepositional phrase 'on the table' is used as adverb phrase in the previous example and as adjective phrase in this example.

Besides, the prepositional phrases acting as adjective phrases are called **post-modifiers,** because, like adjectives, they modify the nouns but come after the noun. In the above example, the prepositional phrase 'on the table' modifies the noun 'book' but comes after it. Moreover, it is to be noted that the whole phrase 'the book on the table' is a noun phrase, because the head-word is the noun 'book' modified by the post-modifier 'on the table'.

I play <u>in the evening</u>.   -   The question for the prepositional phrase can be '<u>When do I play?</u>' wherein the question word 'When' is a question word of adverb and modifies the verb 'play'. Therefore, it is an <u>adverb phrase</u>.

Prepositional Phrase as Noun Phrase: Sometimes, prepositional phrase is used as noun phrase also. They are useful for **double prepositions** or **consecutive prepositions**, i.e., when two or more prepositions are used together consecutively as illustrated below:

He shouted <u>from inside the house</u>.   -   The prepositional phrase 'inside the house' has the preposition 'inside' and the noun 'the house' as its object. However, the preposition 'from' has no noun immediately following it. Therefore, the prepositional phrase 'inside the house' is treated as a noun phrase, and the same acts like the object of the preposition 'from'.

Nevertheless, the use of **prepositional phrases as the subject or object** of a sentence/verb is not considered to be good English. For example, the sentence 'During the lunch is a good time for discussion' can be rewritten as 'It is good to discuss during the lunch.'

Chapter-15: Prepositions

Moreover, a prepositional phrase functioning as noun phrase can be called **prepositional noun phrase (PNP)**. Similarly, we have **prepositional adjective phrase (PAdjP)** and **prepositional adverb phrase (PAdvP)**. The prepositional phrases are more specific, more accurate and more precise in meaning than their corresponding basic phrases.

III Types of Prepositions based on their form:

Simple Prepositions: Simple prepositions are single word prepositions, and the common simple prepositions include about, above, over, across, after, before, against, along, among, between, around, at, behind, below, beneath, under, underneath, beside, besides, beyond, but, except, despite, down, up, during, for, by, from, since, to, in, inside, into, on, onto, out, outside, like, near, of, off, past, through, throughout, till, until, towards, upon, with, within and without. They are illustrated below:

1) Simple Prepositions after Verb:

The story is <u>about</u> animals.
A large lamp was hanging <u>over</u> the table.
We can play <u>after</u> our class.
Team A is playing <u>against</u> Team B.
We drove <u>along</u> the highway.
A brave man stood <u>among</u> many animals.
She must be <u>at</u> the college.
Please write <u>below</u> the line.
She rested <u>under</u> the tree.
She sat <u>beside</u> him.
All have come <u>but</u> Ramu.
A stone rolled <u>down</u> the hill.
We enjoyed <u>during</u> the holidays.
We have come <u>from</u> Mumbai.
We may go <u>to</u> Delhi next year.
The children dived <u>into</u> the water.
They were standing <u>outside</u> the school.
Our house is <u>near</u> the junction.
The car went <u>past</u> the cycle.
We studied <u>throughout</u> the night.
You can sit <u>until</u> Madurai.
The decision depends <u>upon</u> you.
We cannot live <u>without</u> water.

The plane is flying <u>above</u> the clouds.
We swam <u>across</u> the river.
We must reach <u>before</u> Tuesday.
Don't stand <u>against</u> the wall.
He had to walk <u>around</u> the lake.
Four is <u>between</u> three and five.
Somebody was standing <u>behind</u> her.
The key was found <u>beneath</u> the clay.
The coin rolled <u>underneath</u> the sofa.
The road goes <u>beyond</u> Srinagar.
All have come <u>except</u> Ramu.
She went <u>up</u> the hills.
The food was prepared <u>for</u> him <u>by</u> her.
We have been living <u>in</u> Chennai <u>since</u> 2000.
They went <u>inside</u> the building.
He ran <u>out</u> the door.
He ran <u>like</u> an arrow.
Somebody has jumped <u>off</u> the train.
Can you see <u>through</u> the wall?
You can wait <u>till</u> 5 pm.
We must go <u>towards</u> our goal.
We should write <u>with</u> pen.
The ticket can be booked <u>within</u> one hour.

3) Sentence Structures for Superlative Degree:

Subject + Verb + **adverb (superlative form) + of** + all/(quantity) + noun.

    He ran **fastest** of all students.
    S V OC(AdvP)

    He ran **fastest**.
    S V OC(adv.)

    Of all the employees, he worked **most carefully**.
    OC   S   V   OC(adv.)

    Of all the employees, he worked **least carefully**.
    OC   S   V   OC(adv.)

Optionally, the superlative form of adverb can be preceded by 'the' as illustrated below:

    He ran **the fastest** of all students.
    Of all the employees, he worked **the most carefully**.

Pre-modifiers / Intensifiers for comparatives and superlatives: When the comparative form or the superlative form of adverbs is to be modified further or to be described even more strongly, we cannot use **'very'**, rather we should use pre-modifiers/intensifiers like **much, very much, more, even, far, rather, quite, a lot, lots, a little, a whole lot, a heck, a bit, all the, any, no, by far and somewhat**. For example,:

    She can look after you even **more carefully** than a doctor.
    Am I any **better**?
    You are much **better** now.
    She drives much **more easily** now.
    She sang by far **the best**.

Transformation of Sentences by interchanging the adverb / adverbial expression: The same idea/statement can be expressed using different adverbial expressions as illustrated below:

    No sooner had he reached the office than his boss left.
    = As soon as he had reached the office, his boss left.
    Scarcely had he reached the office when his boss left.
    = He had scarcely reached the office when his boss left.
    The problem was too difficult to solve.
    The problem was so difficult that it could not be solved.
    We were too late to attend the class.
    We were so late that we could not attend the class.

Chapter 15
Prepositions

Preposition (Position / Relationship Words): Abbreviation: **prep**. They describe the position/relationship of nouns/pronouns in relation to other nouns/pronouns, adjectives and verbs.

Question Words: preposition + What, How, When, Where, Why and Which - The answer to these questions in sentences can be prepositions.

Examples	Relationship	Question Words
There is a **book** <u>on</u> the **table**.	between noun and noun	on what? / where?
I like the **book** <u>on</u> the **table**.	between noun and noun	which (book)?
They are **good** <u>in</u> **dancing**.	between adjective and noun	in what?
I **shall go** <u>in</u> the **morning**	between verb and noun	when?
He can **play** <u>instead of</u> **me**.	between verb and noun	instead of whom?

Most common prepositions: The most common prepositions are **at, in, from, to, for, by, of, on** and **with,** and they are illustrated below:

He is <u>at</u> school now.	He will come back <u>at</u> 5 pm.
The computer is <u>in</u> the hall.	We can use it <u>in</u> the morning.
We have come <u>from</u> Ahmedabad.	We have been here <u>from</u> Monday.
They went <u>to</u> Kanpur.	She has given it <u>to</u> him.
The food is <u>for</u> my grandmother.	It was prepared <u>by</u> my mother.
Please give me a glass <u>of</u> water.	I want a map <u>of</u> France.
There is a book <u>on</u> the table.	They may leave <u>on</u> Monday.
You should write <u>with</u> a pen.	Grandfather is playing <u>with</u> the grandchildren.

Adverbs vs. Prepositions: Adverbs and prepositions are so closely related that some words can be used as both adverb and preposition. The main difference between adverbs and prepositions is that the prepositions are always followed by noun/pronoun whereas the adverbs are not followed by noun/pronoun. It is illustrated below:

We went <u>up</u>.	-	'up' is an adverb because it is not followed by noun
We went <u>up</u> the hill.	-	'up' is a preposition because it is followed by noun

I <u>Prepositional Object (PO):</u> Prepositions are always followed by noun/pronoun which are called prepositional object. For example, look at the following sentence.

There is a book <u>on the table</u>.

In the above sentence, the preposition **'on'** is followed by the noun (phrase) **'the table'**, and so, the noun (phrase) **'the table'** is called the object of the preposition **'on'**.

In the above structure, the expression **'as + adverb + as'** is used as conjunction; the **'as'** before the adverb is also an adverb because it modifies the adverb, and the **'as'** after the adverb is a conjunction introducing the dependent clause.

However, the following sentence without verb in the dependent clause is old-fashioned and not used in modern English.

<u>They run **as fast as** he</u>.   -   old-fashioned
S   V   conj.   S

b) Subject + Verb +   <u>**as + adverb (positive form) + as**</u> + Prepositional Object.
                                prepositional expression

<u>They run **as fast as** him</u>.
S   V   prep.   PO

<u>*Note:*</u> It is very important to note that the same expression 'as fast as' is used as conjunction in one sentence and preposition in another sentence. The function of the expression is decided by what is followed by the expression. The expression 'as fast as' is a conjunction in the sentence 'They run as fast as he runs' because it is followed by the clause 'he runs' whereas it is a preposition in the sentence 'They run as fast as him' because it is followed by the pronoun 'him'.

c) The comparative adverbial expression in each of the above structures can be modified further by placing a suitable <u>*pre-modifier adverb / intensifier*</u> before the first occurrence of 'as' as illustrated below:

<u>They run *nearly* **as fast as** he runs</u>.
S   V   conj.   S V

<u>They run *nearly* **as fast as** him</u>.
S   V   prep.   PO

2) <u>Sentence Structures for Comparative Degree:</u>

a) <u>Subject + Verb + **adverb (comparative form)** + **than** + Subject + Verb.</u>
         independent clause   dependent clause

<u>They run **faster**   **than** he runs</u>.
S   V   OC(adv.) conj. S   V

<u>They run **faster**</u>.   -   a general comparison
S   V   OC(adv.)

In the above structure, **'than'** is used as a conjunction introducing the dependent clause.

b) Subject + Verb + **adverb (comparative form) + than** + Prepositional Object.
　　　　　　　　prepositional expression

　　They run **faster　　than** him.
　　S　　V　　OC(adv.) prep. PO

c) The comparative adverbial expression in each of the above structures can be modified further by placing a suitable *pre-modifier adverb / intensifier* before the comparative form of adverb as illustrated below:

　　They run *twice* **faster　　than** he runs.
　　S　　V　　　　OC(adv.) conj. S　V

　　They run *twice* **faster　　than** him.
　　S　　V　　　　OC(adv.) prep. PO

d) Subject + Verb + **adverb (comparative form) and adverb (comparative form)**.

　　They ran **faster and faster**.
　　S　　V　　OC(adv.)

The above sentence structure is used for double/progressive comparison.

e) Subject + Verb + **more and more / less and less + adverb (positive form)**.

　　They ran **more and more** slowly.
　　S　　V　　OC(adv.)

　　They ran **less and less** fast.
　　S　　V　　OC(adv.)

The above sentence structure is also used for double/progressive comparison.

f) **The + adverb (comparative form)** + Subject + Verb, + **the + adverb (comparative form)** + Subject + Verb.

　　The faster they run, **the sooner** they reach.
　　OC(adv.)　S　V　OC(adv.)　S　V

　　The sooner, the better.　　-　　This sentence has no verb, but it is valid.
　　OC(adv.)　　OC(adv.)

　　The more we want, **the less** we get.
　　OC(adv.)　S　V　OC(adv.)　S　V

The above sentence structure is used for proportionate comparison to show that two things vary or change together proportionately.

2) Simple Prepositions after Noun/Pronoun:

They like cakes besides sweets.
We wear woollen clothes during winter. *
Kerala is a state in India.
He is a player of Team A.
There is a book on the table.
Don't park the car outside our house. *
They have markets throughout the state.
There is a cat under the table.
You wrote the letter with pencil. *

I like him despite his mistakes. *
There is a ball inside the bag.
He pushed the ball into the hole. *
They had gone to an island off the coast.
Shift your dresses onto the second shelf. *
She gave it to me. *
We have class till 5 pm.
You can stay here until 7 pm. *

* These prepositions are actually more related to the verbs.

3) Simple Prepositions after Adjectives:

I am happy about his performance.
He is fond of sweets.
Yours is similar to mine.
He is responsible for arranging the food.
You must be keen on winning the match.
He is popular with the girls.
They are dependent on him.

She is afraid of her boss.
We felt proud of our school.
It is more suitable for children.
She is good at studies.
She is serious about going for a job.
They are opposed to your ideas.
She is interested in reading books.

Complex Prepositions / Phrase Prepositions: They consist of two-word or three-word combinations acting as a single preposition. Some examples are given below:

According to the teacher, you are a good boy.
Apart/Aside from London, I went to Paris also.
The train was cancelled owing to the bad climate.
The day went on well except for one problem.
I want to talk to you prior to the meeting.
The rules for immigrants is same as for the natives.
His ideas were ahead of his time.
Contrary to expectations, he got only poor marks.

It is difficult to go along with him.
He could not walk because of injury.
I got good marks due to my efforts.
He can play instead of me.
We went out regardless of rain.
Keep the medicine out of sight.
Can I sit next to you please?

You should ring the bell in case of fire.
We collect money in aid of poor children.
You can use tomato in place of tamarind.
The stone was broken with the help of an axe.
I want a black pen in addition to the blue pen.
The baby's legs are short in relation to its body.
Balu has signed the paper on behalf of Ramu.
These balls are same with respect to their colour.

The bank is in front of my school.
He is very active in spite of his age.
The stone was broken by means of an axe.
We should work in accordance with the rules.
Change yourself in line with the present world.
She walks slowly on account of her old age.
He gets income from his property on top of his salary.

Chapter-15: Prepositions

    <u>Formation of complex prepositions:</u> Observing the above complex prepositions, it can be noticed that <u>two-word prepositions</u> are formed mostly with adverb + preposition combination, sometimes with preposition + preposition combination (double preposition), sometimes with adjective + preposition combination and rarely with conjunction + preposition combination as in 'because of'. Moreover, <u>three-word prepositions</u> are always formed with the combination of preposition + noun + preposition.

    <u>*Note:*</u> **As prepositions describe the relationship of nouns, adjectives and verbs with other nouns (used as prepositional objects), complex prepositions should not begin with a noun, an adjective or a verb. However, there are some commonly-used exceptions like 'due to', 'prior to', etc. which can also be avoided by using other equivalent prepositions like 'owing to' and 'before' respectively.**

    Complex prepositions are also called **compound prepositions** by some authors whereas some other authors call such prepositions that are formed into compound words like 'into and within' as compound prepositions.

    Marginal Prepositions: Marginal prepositions are not exactly the prepositions in the normal sense of prepositions like 'in, from, to, etc.' On the other hand, they look, sound and function like other parts of speech but can also function like prepositions. Some are illustrated below:

    1) <u>Verbal Marginal Prepositions:</u> They are basically participle form of verbs but functioning as prepositions as illustrated below:

    You can always call me <u>regarding</u> work.   <u>Following</u> the rules, we solved the problem.
    She knows all <u>including</u> computers.   It will cost ₹1000 <u>excluding</u> the lunch.
    She has questions <u>concerning</u> her future.   They are active <u>considering</u> their age.
    They are active <u>given</u> their age.

    2) <u>Other Marginal Prepositions:</u> They include the following:

It is <u>worth</u> ₹1000. ('worth' is normally an adjective or a noun)
You have to pay ₹1000 <u>minus</u> the advance amount. ('minus' can be noun or adjective)
All attended <u>barring</u> one. ('bar' can be noun or verb)

IV <u>**Types of Prepositional Relationships**</u>: Prepositions are used to express many types of relationships as follows:

    1) <u>Position:</u> For example, 'His pen is <u>on</u> the table.'
    2) <u>Place:</u> For example, 'We lived <u>in</u> a small house.'
    3) <u>Time:</u> For example, 'The train leaves <u>at</u> 5 pm.'

4) <u>Manner:</u> For example, 'The soldiers fought <u>with</u> courage.'
5) <u>Means:</u> For example, 'He goes to school <u>by</u> van.' 'He wrote <u>with</u> a pen.'
6) <u>State:</u> For example, 'She is <u>at</u> work.'
7) <u>Purpose:</u> For example, 'We work <u>for</u> money.'
8) <u>Cause/Reason:</u> For example, 'She died <u>of</u> illness.'
9) <u>Measure:</u> For example, 'The prices are up <u>by</u> 5 percent.'
10) <u>Contrast:</u> For example, 'I like him <u>despite</u> his faults.'
11) <u>Inference:</u> For example, 'The meaning can be inferred <u>from</u> the context.'
12) <u>Motive:</u> For example, 'He did it <u>out of</u> gratitude.'
13) <u>Source:</u> For example, 'He gained knowledge <u>from</u> the experience.'

V <u>Consecutive Prepositional Phrases</u>: Sometimes, prepositional phrases are used one after another in the same sentence, each describing the same noun/pronoun or the same verb/adjective/adverb or each complementing each other. It is illustrated below:

I know the person <u>at the corner</u> <u>with an umbrella</u> <u>in his hand</u>.
We had gone <u>to the temple</u> <u>by auto</u>.

VI <u>Usage of common prepositions</u>: Same prepositions can be used in different ways, and different prepositions can be used for the same purpose. They are illustrated below with their correct meaning against each example:

1) <u>About:</u>

The book is <u>about</u> the history of Shimla.	- 'related to/in connection with'
You do not know <u>about</u> him.	- 'anything related to'
He walked <u>about</u> the city.	- 'aimlessly/without any purpose'
They lived somewhere <u>about</u> here.	- 'nearby'
What <u>about</u> your plan?	- 'asking for opinion'
That is a book <u>about</u> Raipur.	- 'with some information only'
This is a book <u>on</u> Cuttack.	- 'serious writing'

2) <u>Above, Over and On:</u>

The fan is <u>above</u> our head.	- 'higher than, but not touching'
The fan is <u>over</u> our head.	- 'higher than, but not touching'
The book is <u>on</u> the table.	- 'above and touching the surface'
We wear the coat <u>over</u> the shirt.	- 'above and touching each other'
She must be <u>over</u> 40 years.	- 'more than'

3) <u>Across and Through:</u>

Can you swim <u>across</u> the river?	- 'from one side to the other side'
My school is <u>across</u> the road.	- 'at the other side'
We can walk <u>across</u> the road.	- 'cross the 2 dimensional space'
We can walk <u>through</u> the subway.	- 'cross the 3 dimensional space'

Chapter-15: Prepositions

4) Across and Along:

Can you swim across the river?	- 'from one side to the other side'
Can you swim along the river?	- 'from one end to the other end'

5) Against:

He is always against our proposal.	- 'opposing'
She hit her head against the door.	- 'on'
The cupboard is against the wall.	- 'touching'

6) Around and About:

We walked around the lake.	- 'move in a circle/curve'
He walked about the town.	- 'aimlessly/without any purpose'
She must be around/about 20 years.	- 'approximately'

7) Below and Under:

He must be under 21.	- 'younger than'
The cat is under the table.	- 'lower than and physically under'
It must be 5 degrees below normal.	- 'lower than and conceptually under'

8) Beside and Besides:

The child sat beside its mother.	- 'by the side of'
I like sweets besides fruits.	- 'in addition to'

9) Down:

She ran down the hill.	- 'from higher part to lower part'
They live down the street.	- 'at the lower/farther part'
We can walk down the road.	- 'along'

10) Of:

This is the house of my friend.	- 'belonging to'
He always thinks of her.	- 'about'
She died of illness.	- 'cause'

11) Off:

He fell off the running train.	- 'from and away'
We should keep off the fire.	- 'away and from'
His house is just off the main road.	- 'near but not on'
She switched off the lights.	- 'not working'

12) On:

The book is <u>on</u> the table.	- 'in the top'
The picture is <u>on</u> the wall.	- 'attached to'
Madurai is <u>on</u> the river Vaigai.	- 'by the side of'
We live <u>on</u> the first floor.	- 'in the particular floor'
He will come <u>on</u> Monday.	- used before days

13) in and on:

He must be <u>on</u> the field.	- 'in the 2 dimensional space'
She is <u>in</u> the house.	- 'in the 3 dimensional space'

14) In, Into and On, Onto:

Students are <u>in</u> the class.	- 'the inside position'
Students ran <u>into</u> the class.	- 'the direction of movement'
The book is <u>on</u> the top shelf.	- 'on the top of something'
We threw old books <u>onto</u> the top shelf.	- 'the direction of movement'

15) Into and Out of:

Students ran <u>into</u> the class.	- 'inside some place'
The hotel was converted <u>into</u> a hostel.	- 'to become'
The boys ran <u>out of</u> the room.	- 'outside some place'

16) <u>In, On and At as prepositions of Place:</u> 'In' is used for larger locations, 'At' for smaller locations and 'On' for exact locations. For example,:

The Dal Lake is <u>at</u> Srinagar <u>in</u> Kashmir.
My school is <u>on</u> 23, Periyar Street <u>at</u> Annanagar <u>in</u> Chennai.

17) <u>In, On and At as prepositions of Time:</u>

'In' is used for longer periods of time and general reference of time: e.g.,
   He will come <u>in</u> 2020 / <u>in</u> June / <u>in</u> the morning / <u>in</u> a minute.
'On' is used for specific days and dates; e.g.,
   He will come <u>on</u> Wednesday / <u>on</u> June 1, 2020.
   He will come on Wednesday evening.
'At' is used for more specific (precise) time; e.g.,
   He will come <u>at</u> 5 pm / <u>at</u> night / <u>at</u> the end of the month.
   (However, we say 'He will be <u>on</u> time.')

Chapter-15: Prepositions

18) From, Since, For and By as prepositions of Time:

You have been on leave since Wednesday / June.	- 'a starting point'
You must come to office from Monday.	- 'beginning of a period'
We have been watching TV since 10 o' clock.	- 'a specific time'
We have been watching TV for 5 hours.	- 'duration'
By tomorrow / 7 p.m., the work will be finished.	- 'not later than / before'

19) By and On as prepositions of Means of Transport:

'By' is used for means of transport generally and 'On' for specific means of transport. For example,:

She goes to school <u>by</u> auto.　　　　He goes to school <u>on</u> his bike / <u>in</u> a taxi.

VII Omission of Prepositions: Prepositions are omitted before the nouns sometimes under the following circumstances. In the following examples, the possible prepositions are given within brackets but should not be used.

1) Before nouns of places when they are used as adverbs, i.e., nouns with an inherent preposition as illustrated below:

She might go (to) there.		Come (to) here.
He went (to) <u>home</u>.	but	He went <u>to</u> the house.

2) Before nouns of time when they are preceded by demonstratives/determiners like **next, last, this, that, one, every, each, some, any and all** as illustrated below:

They meet (on) every Sunday.		We worked (throughout) all night.
We played (on) next day.	but	The meeting was postponed <u>to</u> next day.

3) Before nouns of measurement like **height, weight, length, size, shape, age, colour and number** when they are preceded by Be-Verb as illustrated below:

We are (of) the same age.		They are (of) different height.
The boxes are (of) the same size.		They are (of) different weight.
The bottles are (of) the same shape.	but	I want bottles <u>of</u> same shape.

VIII Ending a sentence with a preposition: It is generally considered wrong to end a sentence with a preposition. However, in modern English, it is permitted with reference to the following:

1) **Question words:** When question word is the object of the preposition:

Whom is this dress for?	=	For whom is this dress? (formal)
Where are you coming from?	=	From where are you coming? (formal)

2) **Relative Clauses** (discussed in chapter 17 on Clauses and Structural Sentence Types): When relative pronoun (discussed in chapter 17 on Clauses and Structural Sentence Types) is the object of the preposition:

    You asked for the same book **that** he told us about.
    =   You asked for the same book about **that** he told us. (formal)

    He was the boy **whom** I used to play with.
    =   He was the boy with **whom** I used to play. (formal)

3) **Passive structures:** Prepositions go with the verbs in passive structures. In fact, the subject is the object of the preposition and need not be repeated:

    We were nicely attended to.   The child likes being pampered with.

4) **Infinitive structures:** Prepositions go with the verbal phrase of infinitive adjective phrase. In fact, the noun before the infinitive is the prepositional object:

    I am looking for a partner to work with.   We urgently need a shelter to live in.

IX Relationship between Adverb and Preposition:

We have already seen that the same word can be used as both adverb and preposition. Besides, we studied that a preposition describes the relationship between a noun/pronoun/adjective/verb and another noun/pronoun. However, some prepositional phrases (i.e., prepositional adverb phrases) can describe the relationship between adverbs and nouns/pronouns. At the same time, when the prepositional phrases modify the adverbs, they can also be treated as adverb phrases modifying the verbs as illustrated below:

    You should come **early** in   **the morning**.
                            adv   prep   NP

    She danced **beautifully** in   **the cultural programme**.
                        adv   prep   NP

In the above two sentences, the prepositional phrases can be used with the verbs alone without the adverbs also.

    He will be **away** from **the work** next week.
               adv   prep   NP

In the above sentence, the adverb 'away' is used in the sense of 'absent', an adjective.

    He runs **fastest** of   **all the students**.
             adv   prep   NP

In the above sentence, the prepositional phrase 'of all the students' modifies the subject 'He' rather than the adverb 'fastest', and the sentence can be rewritten as follows:

    Of **all the students**, he runs **fastest**.

Chapter 16
Phrases and Expressions

As we have already learned, individual words, classified into different parts of speech, are combined together according to the different sentence structures to form valid sentences. Sometimes, a group of words is required as a single unit to act as a part of speech. Such groups of words are called **phrases / expressions** and will not have a complete verb as part of it because the presence of a complete verb would make it a sentence, not a phrase / expression.

I Phrases: Any phrase will be functionally similar to a noun, adjective or adverb. Therefore, a phrase can be defined as a group of words without a complete verb but with some meaning, functioning like a noun, an adjective or an adverb and called noun phrase, adjective phrase and adverb phrase respectively. Noun phrases, adjective phrases and adverb phrases can collectively be called **basic phrases**.

The type of the basic phrase is determined by identifying the **key/head/main word** in the phrase. The key/head/main word will be located as the last word in a phrase. If key/head/main word is a noun, it is a **noun phrase**; if it is an adjective, it is an **adjective phrase**; and if it is an adverb, it is an **adverb phrase**. These three types of phrases are illustrated below where the phrase is underlined and the head word is in *italics*.

Noun Phrase: It is a group of words in which the head word is a noun preceded by adjectives and determiners. For example,:

An old *lady* feeds the birds.

Adjective Phrase: It is a group of words in which the head word is an adjective preceded by adverbs of degree. For example,:

The car is very *beautiful*.

Adverb Phrase / Adverbial Phrase: It is a group of words in which the head word is an adverb preceded by other adverbs of degree. For example,:

He ran very *quickly*.

The noun phrase, adjective phrase and adverb phrase are called the **basic phrases** because even other types of phrases, namely **prepositional phrases** and **verbal phrases,** will also finally function like either noun phrase, adjective phrase or adverb phrase.

Prepositional Phrase: In the prepositional phrase, the head word is a preposition always followed by noun/pronoun called **prepositional object**. It has to function like a noun phrase or an adjective phrase or an adverb phrase. It is described in chapter 15 on Prepositions.

Verbal Phrases: Verbal phrases include gerund, participle and infinitive. Among these verbal phrases, gerunds function like noun (phrase), participles like adjective (phrase) and infinitives like noun (phrase), adjective (phrase) and adverb (phrase). **Absolute Phrase** is a type of participle phrase. They are described in chapter 8 on Verbal Phrases.

Phrases with post-modifiers: Generally, the head word of a phrase is preceded by its modifiers (describing words) like determiners, adjectives and adverbs. Sometimes, the head word can be followed by certain modifiers like prepositional phrase, infinitive phrase or clause which describes the head word. Such modifiers that follow the head word are called **post-modifiers**. Phrases with post-modifiers are illustrated below:

<u>The important</u> **point** <u>of the discussion</u> was sanitation. - noun phrase
pre-modifier (d + adj.)   n   post-modifier (PP)

It is <u>very</u> **important** <u>to behave properly</u>.   - adjective phrase
pre-modifier (adv.)   adj.   post-modifier (inf.)

Verb Phrase: A complete verb in the form of 'auxiliary verb + appropriate verb form' is sometimes called a verb phrase because it is also a group of words as illustrated below:

He <u>has been living</u> here for 10 years.
    verb phrase

<u>*Warning:*</u> **It cannot be treated like a phrase because the presence of a complete verb in a group of words will make the group of words a complete sentence/ clause which cannot be a phrase by definition.**

Use of Phrases: Phrases are generally used to combine many ideas/short sentences into a single long sentence as illustrated below:

The sentences 'A room was in the corner', 'It was damaged and abandoned' and 'It was locked' can be written as a single long sentence with phrases as follows:

<u>Damaged and abandoned</u>, the room <u>in the corner</u> was locked.
participle phrase   prepositional phrase

II Expressions: An expression is also a group of words, but unlike phrases, it not only need function like a noun, adjective or adverb, but also can function like other parts of speech like preposition, conjunction, etc. In a way, phrases can be considered as a kind of expressions. Expressions functioning like other parts of speech are illustrated below:

I want a black pen <u>in addition to</u> the blue pen.   -   expression as preposition
I will finish the work <u>as soon as</u> I can.   -   expression as conjunction

Broadly speaking, expressions include any group of words including phrases, clauses and even sentences with some special/idiomatic meaning.

Chapter 17
Clauses and Structural Sentence Types - Simple, Compound and Complex Sentences

We already know that a **sentence** is a group of words with (a minimum of) subject and finite/complete verb and is complete in meaning, and also that a (more detailed) sentence would have, in addition to the subject and the verb, one or more other structural elements including object, indirect object, other complement, phrase, clause and appositive. Now, we will learn more about the clauses.

A **clause** is a group of words with subject and finite/complete verb and is either complete or incomplete in meaning.

If the clause is complete in meaning, i.e., it can be written as a separate sentence, it is called **independent clause / main clause**. For example,

<u>The room</u> <u>was</u> <u>locked</u>.
   S   V   OC

The above group of words is complete in meaning and, therefore, can be a separate sentence. It also shows that an independent/main clause is a sentence by itself.

If the clause is incomplete in meaning, i.e., it cannot be written as a separate sentence, it is called **dependent clause / subordinate clause**. For example,

When <u>he</u> <u>came back</u>,
    S   V

Please note that it is not a question which should have been 'When did he come back?' The above sentence is not complete in meaning because it only means 'at the time of his coming back' but does not complete it by telling 'what happened?' and, therefore, cannot be a separate sentence because something more should be added to make it complete in meaning. For example, it can be made complete as follows:

<u>When he came back</u>, <u>the room was locked</u>.
dependant clause   independent clause

As it can be seen clearly, the above sentence has two parts, dependant clause as well as independent clause, each having its own subject and finite/complete verb. Therefore, it can be concluded that an independent clause can be written as a separate sentence by itself, but a dependant clause cannot be written as a separate sentence by itself and that a dependant clause should be combined with an independent clause to make it a complete sentence. In other words, the dependant clause **depends** on the independent clause to become complete in meaning.

The above sentence can also be written as follows:

<u>The room was locked</u> <u>when he came back</u>.
independent clause   dependant clause

Please note that a comma is required after the dependant clause when it appears first in the sentence, but the comma is not required when the independent clause comes first.

I **<u>Dependent Clause / Subordinate Clause:</u>** Let us have a closer look at the dependant / subordinate clause with the above example as follows:

When he came back,

First, let us write the above dependent/subordinate clause without the word 'When' and it becomes:

He came back.

Now, it has become a complete sentence, i.e., an independent clause. Therefore, it can be said that a dependent/subordinate clause is formed by adding some words like 'when' to an otherwise independent clause. Such words used to begin dependent/subordinate clauses are all called **Dependent Marker Words** because they are used to make/mark the clause as dependent clause. **Dependent Marker Words** can be <u>subordinating conjunctions</u> (SCn) or <u>relative conjunctions</u> (RCn). **The relative conjunctions include relative pronouns** and **relative adverbs.** These conjunctions are explained below:

Dependent/Subordinate Clauses with Subordinating Conjunctions: Conjunctions used to begin dependent/subordinate clauses are called <u>subordinating conjunctions</u>. The common subordinating conjunctions are **"after, although, as, because, before, if, lest, once, since, than, though, till, unless, until, whereas** and **while"**. They are illustrated below where underlined clauses are dependent/subordinate clauses:

Examples	Question Words
<u>After</u> <u>he comes</u>, you can go.	when
<u>Although / Though</u> <u>we were tired</u>, we finished the work.	in spite of what
<u>As</u> <u>he is a good student</u>, teachers like him.	why
We watched carefully **<u>as / when</u>** <u>the teacher solved the problem</u>.	when
He likes train travel **<u>because</u>** <u>it is comfortable</u>.	why
I studied on my own, <u>not **because** you told me</u>.	why
We had to wait **<u>cos</u>** <u>we arrived early</u>.	why
('**cos**' is an informal form of '**because**')	
I had reached **<u>before</u>** <u>the train left</u>.	when
He is happy **<u>for</u>** <u>he got the first rank</u>.	why
<u>If</u> <u>you study well</u>, you will get good marks.	on what condition
I played carefully **<u>lest</u>** <u>my team lose the match</u>.	why
He will call you **<u>once</u>** <u>it is ready</u>.	when

Chapter-17: Clauses and Structural Sentence Types - Simple, Compound and Complex Sentence

All will be well **providing / provided** you are careful.	on what condition
I have been playing here **since** the sun rose.	from when
Since you are rich, you can help me.	why
Supposing you get a lottery, what will you do?	on what condition
She is taller **than** you are.	how tall
Unless he studies well, he cannot get good marks.	on what condition
He can wait **until / till** I finish my work.	how long
He is tall **whereas** you are short.	when
While it was raining, we played cards.	when
He is very poor **while** his friend is rich.	when
While he is not an expert, he will do his best.	in spite of what

In addition, the following <u>expressions</u> are often used as <u>subordinating conjunctions</u> at the beginning of <u>subordinate clauses</u>.

He talks **as if** he knows everything.	how
As long as we cooperate, we can stay together.	on what condition
He has worked here **as long as** I have known him.	when
Complete the work **as soon as** you can.	when
It looks **as though** it is going to rain.	how
I will talk to her **even if** she does not.	in spite of what
Take an extra pen **in case** you miss one.	on what condition
Please be prepared **or else** you may miss it.	when
I am saving money **so that** I can help my sister.	why

Please note that the question-words for subordinating conjunctions are <u>question-words of adverbs</u>.

Dependent/Subordinate Clauses with Relative Conjunctions, namely Relative Pronouns (RP) and Relative Adverbs (RA): <u>Relative Pronouns</u> are basically question words for nouns and pronouns, but used to begin dependent/subordinate clauses describing the preceding nouns/pronouns. The relative pronouns are **"who, whose, whom, which/ what, that** and **whether"**. Similarly, <u>Relative Adverbs</u> are basically question words for adverbs, but used to begin dependent/subordinate clauses describing the preceding nouns of manner, time, place and reason. The relative adverbs are **"how, when, where** and **why"**. They are illustrated below:

The person **who finished first** got the prize.
              dependent clause

In the above example, the dependent clause is 'who finished first', and the independent clause is 'The person got the prize'. The question word 'who' is called a relative pronoun, because it relates/refers to the preceding noun 'person' in the sentence. <u>Relative pronouns are called so because they relate/refer to some noun or pronoun in a sentence</u>.

He still remembers the day **when** he met her first.
                          dependent clause

In the above example, the dependent clause is 'when he met her first', and the independent clause is 'He still remembers the day'. The question word 'when' is called a relative adverb, because it relates/refers to the preceding noun of time 'day' in the sentence. <u>Relative adverbs are called so because they relate/refer to some noun in a sentence.</u>

Please note that the question-words for relative conjunctions are <u>question-words of adjectives</u> like 'which, what type of, etc.' because they describe the preceding noun / pronoun. The noun or the pronoun related/referred to using relative pronouns or relative adverbs is called **'antecedent'**, and the dependent/subordinate clauses introduced with antecedents are called **Relative Clauses**. More examples are given below:

The man **who** saw us yesterday may come tomorrow.
The man **whom** we saw yesterday may come tomorrow.
The man **whose** hobby is dancing may come tomorrow.
We can meet the man **whom** we saw yesterday.
We can meet the man **who/that** saw us yesterday.
The advertisement messages, **which** are sent by business people, are a nuisance.
I like apple **which** is good for health.
A message **that** is difficult to understand has too many lines.
That is not the way **how** one should behave.
She knows the date **when** he would come back.
He lived in an area **where** only rich people would live.
The shop **where** only costly items are available is not suitable for us.
Nobody can tell the reason **why** he chose such a job.
I do not know (the fact) **whether** he came or not.
   - 'whether' is a relative pronoun because it means '**that or not that**'.

Omission of Antecedent: Antecedents are sometimes omitted because they are implicitly understood. When antecedents are omitted, some relative conjunctions like 'how, when, where, why, that and whether' can be used as subordinating conjunctions also. It is illustrated below where the omitted antecedents are given within brackets:

It is difficult to say (the player) **who** will win the match.
(The player) **Whom** you are going to play today is a tough player.
He listened carefully to (the tips) **what** his coach has said.
Everyone thinks (it) **that** he/she is more important.
He is happy (about the fact) **that** he won the match.
   - Subordinating Conjunction because it answers 'Why (happy)?'
She asked (the possibility) **whether** we know her before.
I will meet her (despite the fact) **whether** you like it or not.
   - Subordinating Conjunction because it answers 'despite What?'
(The place) **Where** the match is held will be announced later.

The question is (the time) **when** the players will reach the stadium.
We watched the plane (at the time) **when** it took off.
   - Subordinating Conjunction because it answers 'When?'
She felt bad for (the way) **how** she behaved in the ground.

Relative Adverbs are prepositional phrases of 'preposition + relative pronouns: The relative adverbs are actually the equivalent of prepositional phrases of 'preposition + relative pronouns'. That is why the clauses introduced with relative adverbs are also called relative clauses. For example,:

Remind me the day <u>when</u> he comes.   = Remind me the day <u>on which</u> he comes.
Remind me the place <u>where</u> he comes. = Remind me the place <u>at which</u> he comes.
Remind me the reason <u>why</u> he comes. = Remind me the reason <u>for which</u> he comes.
Remind me the way <u>how</u> he comes.   = Remind me the way <u>by which</u> he comes.

Who or Whom: The relative pronouns 'who and whom' will relate/refer to some antecedent which, in the form of relative pronoun, will act as the subject or object of the dependent clause. 'Who', the subjective form, should be used for the relative pronoun acting as the subject of the dependent clause and 'Whom', the objective form, for the relative pronoun acting as the object of the dependent clause as illustrated below:

The man **who** was our old leader may come tomorrow.
The man **who** saw us yesterday may come tomorrow.
   - in the above two sentences, the relative pronoun 'who' introduces the dependent clause; it relates / refers to the noun 'man'; moreover, it acts as the <u>subject</u> of the dependent clause.

The man **whom** we saw yesterday may come tomorrow.
   - the relative pronoun 'whom' introduces the dependent clause; it relates / refers to the noun 'man', but it acts as the <u>object</u> of the dependent clause.

That or Which: Unlike the relative pronouns 'who and whom', 'that and which' have no different forms for their use as subject or object, and therefore, the same form (word) is used for both the purposes. However, 'that' is used for a clause that is considered <u>essential / restrictive / defining</u> and without that clause will the sentence be incomplete, and 'which' is used for a clause that is considered <u>non-essential / non-restrictive / non-defining</u> and without that clause also will the sentence be complete. A non-essential clause is set off with commas. For example,:

A message **that** is difficult to understand has too many lines.
   - the relative pronoun 'that' introduces the dependent clause; it relates / refers to the noun 'message'. It is also essential because we want to express that a difficult message has too many lines and not that any message has too many lines.

The advertisement messages, **which** are sent by business people, are a nuisance.
- the relative pronoun 'which' introduces the dependent clause; it relates / refers to the noun 'messages'; however, it is not essential because advertisement messages are sent by business people only and it need not be stated explicitly. Non-essential clauses can be omitted but normally used to give more information.

Dependent/Subordinate Clauses with Compound Relative Pronoun / Compound Relative Adverb: When we add the words 'ever' or 'soever' to the relative pronouns or the relative adverbs, they are called **compound relative pronouns or compound relative adverbs.** The compound relative pronouns are **'whoever, whosoever, whosever, whosesoever, whomever, whomsoever, whichever, whatever and whatsoever'**. The compound relative adverbs are **'however, howsoever, whenever, whensoever, wherever, wheresoever, whyever and whysoever'**. They should be used to relate/refer to plural nouns as illustrated below:

Any three options, **whichever** works fine, can be selected.
Few books, **whatever** costs less than ₹100, would suffice.
Tourist places, **wherever** hotels are available, are easy to visit.
Bus, train and auto, **howsoever** you travel, are all dirty.

Omission of Relative Pronoun/Relative Adverb: Relative Pronouns can be omitted when they are used as objects of verbs or prepositions. For example,:

'The man **whom** we saw yesterday may come tomorrow.' can be written as
The man we saw yesterday may come tomorrow.

'The man **whom** you roamed with may come tomorrow.' can be written as
The man you roamed with may come tomorrow.

Compound Relative Pronoun / Compound Relative Adverb as Subordinating Conjunctions: The compound relative pronouns or the compound relative adverbs can also be used as subordinating conjunctions as illustrated below:

Whatever he does, he does it honestly.

'Whatever' in the clause 'whatever he does' acts as a subordinating conjunction because it is equivalent to saying the following:

Although he does many things, he does all of them honestly.

'Although' is a subordinating conjunction, so is 'Whatever'. Other examples include:
Whoever you are, you should behave properly.   = **Though** you may be anybody, ...
Whenever you meet him, you ask for some money. = **As and when** you meet him, ...
Wherever they go, they are honest.
Whichever you choose, I will like it.

Chapter-17: Clauses and Structural Sentence Types - Simple, Compound and Complex Sentence

Types of dependent/subordinate clauses: The dependent/subordinate clauses can be classified into adverb clauses, adjective clauses and noun clauses depending upon the type of the function performed by the clause in the sentence.

Adverb Clauses: Adverb clauses are the dependent/subordinate clauses which function like adverbs and, therefore, answer the questions of adverbs such as how, when, where, why, on/under what condition / probability / possibility / concession, etc. The adverb clauses are introduced with subordinating conjunctions only. However, it is to be noted that the same words like how, when, where, why, that and whether can be used as both subordinating conjunction and relative conjunction. Clauses introduced by relative conjunctions with antecedents are adjective clauses, and clauses introduced by relative conjunctions without antecedents are noun clauses as explained next. For example,:

He behaves **as if** he is the boss. (Adverb Clause of Manner)
    - adverb clause because it answers how?, a question of adverb.
You can go **when** he comes. (Adverb Clause of Time)
    - adverb clause because it answers when?, a question of adverb.
Keep it back **where** it was. (Adverb Clause of Place)
    - adverb clause because it answers where?, a question of adverb.
You are happy **that/because** she likes you. (Adverb Clause of Reason)
    - adverb clause because it answers why (happy)?, a question of adverb.
She is as tall **as** her husband is. (Adverb Clause of Degree)
    - adverb clause because it answers how (tall)?, a question of adverb.
If you study well, you will get good marks. (Adverb Clause of Condition)
    - adverb clause because it answers on what condition?, a question of adverb.
Although we were tired, we finished the work. (Adverb Clause of Concession)
    - adverb clause because it answers in spite of what?, a question of adverb.
Whichever you choose, I will like it. (Adverb Clause of Concession)
    - adverb clause because it answers in spite of what?, a question of adverb.
The shop **where** only costly items are available is not suitable for us.
    - not adverb clause but adjective clause because it answers which shop?, a question of adjective and also because 'where' is used as a relative conjunction / adverb with the antecedent 'shop'.
When the match is held will be announced later.
    - not adverb clause but noun clause because it answers what is the time of the match?, a question of noun and also because 'when' is used as a relative conjunction / adverb without any antecedent.
Find out **whether** she likes or not.
    - noun clause because it answers what?, a question of noun and also because 'whether' is used as a relative conjunction / pronoun without any antecedent.

Adjective Clauses: Adjective clauses are the dependent/subordinate clauses which function like adjectives and, therefore, answer the questions of adjectives such as which, what kind of, etc. <u>The adjective clauses are introduced with relative conjunctions with antecedents</u>, i.e., only such clauses where the relative conjunctions relate/refer to some preceding noun or pronoun are adjective clauses. Clauses where the relative conjunctions do not relate to some preceding noun or pronoun can be noun clauses or adverb clauses depending on their function. Adjective clauses are also called **post-modifiers** because they modify the preceding nouns. For example,:

The man **who** saw us yesterday may come tomorrow.
- adjective clause because it answers <u>which man</u>?, a question of adjective and also because '<u>who</u>' is a relative conjunction / pronoun with the antecedent 'man'.

The shop **where** only costly items are available is not suitable for us.
- adjective clause because it answers <u>what type of shop</u>?, a question of adjective and also because '<u>where</u>' is a relative conjunction / adverb with the antecedent 'shop'.

Few books, **whatever** costs less than ₹100, would suffice.
- adjective clause because it answers <u>what type of books</u>?, a question of adjective and also because '<u>whatever</u>' is a relative conjunction / pronoun with the antecedent 'books'.

It is difficult to say **who** will win the match.
- not adjective clause but noun clause because it answers only <u>who</u>?, a question of noun and also because '<u>who</u>' is used as a relative conjunction / pronoun without any antecedent.

Whichever you choose, I will like it.
- not adjective clause but adverb clause because it answers <u>in spite of what condition</u>?, a question of adverb and also because '<u>whichever</u>' is used without any antecedent and also as a subordinating conjunction.

<u>Note</u>: Sometimes, <u>an apparently adjective clause</u> can refer to and modify the whole sentence, rather than a particular word, thus functioning as an adverb clause. Though it is accepted mostly, it will not be accepted in a very formal context.

For example,:

<u>He has run away from the spot of the crime,</u> **which** <u>shows that he is guilty</u>.
      independent clause   adverb clause

This sentence should formally be written as follows:

<u>He has run away from the spot of the crime, and it shows that he is guilty</u>.
      independent clause   independent clause

Chapter-17: Clauses and Structural Sentence Types - Simple, Compound and Complex Sentence

Noun Clauses: Noun clauses are the dependent/subordinate clauses which function like nouns and, therefore, answer the questions of nouns such as what, who, whom, etc. The noun clauses are introduced with relative conjunctions without antecedents, i.e., only such clauses in which the relative conjunctions do not relate/refer to some preceding noun or pronoun but work (stand on their own) as noun itself are noun clauses. On the other hand, if a relative conjunction in a clause relates to some preceding noun or pronoun, it is an adjective clause, and if it is used as a subordinating conjunction without any antecedent, it is an adverb clause. For example,:

It is difficult to say **who will win the match**.
- noun clause used as object because it answers who?, a question of noun and also because 'who' is used as a relative conjunction / pronoun without any antecedent.

I do not know **where the match is held**.
- noun clause used as object because it answers what is the place of the match?, a question of noun and also because 'where' is used as a relative conjunction / adverb without any antecedent.

I always knew **that he would win the match**.
- noun clause used as object because it answers what?, a question of noun and also because 'that' is used as a relative conjunction / pronoun without any antecedent.

Whether you can win the match depends on **how you practice**.
- first underlined clause is a noun clause used as subject because it answers what?, a question of noun and also because 'whether' is used like 'that or not that', a relative conjunction/pronoun, without any antecedent.
- second underlined clause is also a noun clause used as the object of the preposition 'on' because it answers on what?, a question of noun and also because 'how' is used as a relative conjunction / adverb without any antecedent.

The question is **when the players will reach the stadium**.
- noun clause used as subject complement because it answers what?, a question of noun and also because 'when' is used as a relative conjunction / adverb without any antecedent.

I like fruits **which are good for my health**.
- not noun clause but adjective clause because it answers only what type of?, a question of adjective and also because 'which' is used as a relative conjunction / pronoun with the antecedent 'fruits'.

He is finally happy **that he won the match**.
- not noun clause but adverb clause because it modifies the adjective 'happy' and answers only how happy / why?, a question of adverb and also because that' is used as a subordinating conjunction.

Adverb Clause or Adjective Clause or Noun Clause?: It is very important to know that a dependent/subordinate clause is considered to be an adverb clause, an adjective clause or a noun clause mainly depending on the type of its function in the sentence, not on the word (conjunction) introducing the clause because the very same dependent/subordinate clause can be used as an adverb clause or an adjective clause or a noun clause in different sentences as illustrated below:

<u>Wherever you go</u>, you should come home before 10 pm.   - adverb clause
Important places <u>wherever you go</u> should be known to us.   - adjective clause
You should tell us <u>wherever you go</u>.   - noun clause

I will go <u>when he comes</u>.   - adverb clause
Many may not know the date <u>when he comes</u>.   - adjective clause
<u>When he comes</u> is a secret.   - noun clause

Elliptical Clause: Elliptical Clause is a clause in which some words have been left out, but the missing parts of the clause can be guessed easily from the context. Strictly speaking, an elliptical clause may seem incorrect, but it is generally accepted and used because it is more concise and elegant as illustrated below with the underlined parts dropped.

After (<u>we had gone to</u>) London, we went to Paris.
Though (<u>she is</u>) beautiful, she is very humble.
While / Though (<u>he is</u>) welcoming the new proposal, he expresses some reservations.
You can buy a new pen if / when (<u>it is</u>) really required.

II <u>Joining/Combination of Clauses (Structural Sentence Types)</u>: As we have just learned, dependant clauses are combined with independent clauses to make it a valid sentence. Even otherwise, the clauses can be combined to make longer sentences that can convey more complete meaning than the shorter sentences. Based on the combination of clauses, the sentences can be classified structurally into simple sentences, compound sentences and complex sentences that are explained below with examples:

Simple Sentence (SmpS): If a sentence has only one independent clause and no other clauses, it is a simple sentence.

<u>The room was locked</u>.
   independent clause

It can be observed from the above example that an independent clause is a (simple) sentence by itself. Moreover, the above example is an example of a <u>short simple sentence</u> without phrases. Short simple sentences cannot express more meaningful thoughts. A <u>long simple sentence</u> is written <u>with phrases</u> to give more information as illustrated below:

Chapter-17: Clauses and Structural Sentence Types - Simple, Compound and Complex Sentence

The old and useless room was locked. — noun phrase

The room, old and useless, was locked. — adjective phrase used in apposition

The damaged and abandoned room was locked. — noun phrase

Damaged and abandoned, the room was locked. — participle phrase

The room, damaged and abandoned, was locked. — participle phrase used in apposition

Having been damaged and abandoned, the room was locked. — participle phrase

The room in the corner was locked. — prepositional phrase used as adjective phrase

Damaged and abandoned, the room in the corner was locked. — participle phrase; and prepositional phrase used as adjective phrase

On his arrival, the room was locked. — prepositional phrase used as adverb phrase

In spite of the room being locked, he tried to enter the room. — prepositional phrase used as adverb phrase; and infinitive phrase

Entering the locked room was not possible. — gerund phrase

The room being locked, he could not enter the room. — participle phrase used as absolute phrase

Only after breaking the lock, he entered the room. — prepositional adverb phrase

Sentence Structure and Punctuation for simple sentences: The sentence structure for simple sentences is same as the basic sentence structure with phrases in the initial position, mid position and/or end position.

Compound Sentence (CpdS): If a sentence has two or more independent clauses joined together, it is a compound sentence. The independent clauses can be joined by coordinating conjunctions, connecting (conjunctive) adverbs or, sometimes, semicolon alone. Even after the independent clauses are joined together, they would still remain as independent clauses. Different ways of joining the independent clauses are explained below:

Compounding (Joining) with coordinating conjunctions: Coordinating conjunctions join the elements of a sentence like words, phrases or clauses of equal importance, and they include **'for, and, nor, but, or, yet** and **so'** which can be remembered easily with the acronym **'FANBOYS'** which is formed with the first letter of these coordinating conjunctions. Examples for compound sentences with coordinating conjunctions are given below:

He had studied well, **and** he got good marks.
  independent clause   independent clause

She is rich, **but** she is simple.

I like cricket, **yet** my favourite game is football.
We can go shopping, **or** we can watch TV.
He wanted to buy a computer, **so** he had saved some money.
I did not see it, **nor** did they.
He rushed, **for** it was late. (the use of 'for' as a coordinating conjunction is limited or old-fashioned, **for** it has the connotation of 'because', a subordinating conjunction)

Compounding (Joining) with connecting (conjunctive) adverbs: Similar to coordinating conjunctions, connecting adverbs can also be used to combine independent clauses to make compound sentences. Connecting adverbs include however, nevertheless, therefore, hence, thus, also, besides, moreover, furthermore, otherwise, consequently, ultimately, etc. For example,:

I like cricket; **however**, my favourite game is football.
independent clause   independent clause

It is difficult to complete in time; **nevertheless**, you should try.
He had studied very well; **therefore/hence/thus**, he got good marks.
She is beautiful; **also/besides/moreover/furthermore**, she is rich.
You must study hard; **otherwise**, you cannot get good marks.
I was not careful enough; **consequently**, I had to suffer.

The connecting adverbs can also include expressions like 'after all', 'at least', 'even so', 'for all that', 'in fact', 'in short', 'in any event', 'of course', 'on the whole', 'without doubt', etc. because they also relate/link the idea expressed in an independent clause with the idea expressed in the previous independent clause. For example,:

We should pay our taxes; **after all**, it is our basic duty.
He may not be rich; **at least**, he has no debts at all.
I thought I was late; **in fact**, I was early.
It is difficult to complete in time; **even so**, you should try.

Connecting (Conjunctive) adverbs are explained elaborately in chapter 18.

Compounding (Joining) with semicolon: Though rare, a semicolon can also be used to combine independent clauses to make compound sentences. For example,:

I like cinema; he likes sports.

Chapter-17: Clauses and Structural Sentence Types - Simple, Compound and Complex Sentence

Sentence Structure and Punctuation for compound sentences: Compound sentences can be punctuated in the following ways:

1) independent-clause, **coordinating-conjunction** independent-clause. For example,:
   I like cinema, but he likes sports.
2) independent-clause; **connecting-adverb**, independent-clause. For example,:
   I like cinema; however, he likes sports.
3) independent-clause; independent-clause. For example,:
   I like cinema; he likes sports.

Common Punctuation Errors in compound sentences: They are illustrated below:

a) Fused Sentence: It means no punctuation between independent clauses as in 'I like cinema he likes sports.'; it should be 'I like cinema; he likes sports.'

b) Comma Splices: It means using comma (,) instead of semicolon (;) as in 'I like cinema, he likes sports.'; it should be 'I like cinema; he likes sports.'

c) Run-on Sentence: It means using a coordinating conjunction without the preceding punctuation of comma (,) between independent clauses as in 'I like cinema but he likes sports.', but it should be 'I like cinema, but he likes sports.'

It can also mean using a connecting adverb without the preceding punctuation of semicolon (;) and/or the following comma(,) between independent clauses as in 'I like cinema however he likes sports.'; however, it should be 'I like cinema; however, he likes sports.'

Complex Sentence (ClxS): If a sentence has one independent clause joined with one or more dependent/subordinate clauses, it is a complex sentence. Fox example,:

<u>If you study well</u>, <u>you will get good marks</u>.
dependent clause   independent clause

He likes train travel **because** it is comfortable.
Although we were tired, we finished the work.
She is taller **than** you are.
The man **whose** hobby is dancing *may come tomorrow.*
He lived in an area **where** only rich people would live.
A message **that** *is difficult to understand has too many lines.*
The shop **where** *only costly items are available is not suitable for us.*
He will support **whoever** wins the match.
Whoever you are, you should behave properly.

Examples with more than one dependent clause/subordinate clause:

When he entered the class, all students shouted **that** he got the first rank.
   adverb clause   independent clause   noun clause
- even without the adverb clause, the sentence is a complex sentence.

Whether you can win the match or not depends on **how** you practice.
- it has two dependent clauses, and the first dependent clause is the subject of the verb of the main clause 'depends on'.

<u>Sentence Structure and Punctuation for complex sentences:</u> Complex sentences can be punctuated in the following ways:

1) dependent-clause, independent-clause. e.g., While he likes sports, I like cinema.
2) independent-clause dependent-clause. e.g., I like cinema while he likes sports.
3) part-of-independent-clause **essential-dependent-clause** part-of-independent-clause.
   e.g., The teacher who teaches 6th standard is very kind.
4) part-of-independent-clause, **nonessential-dependent-clause**, part-of-independent-clause.
   e.g., Ms. Mala, who teaches 6th standard, is very kind.

<u>Cleft Sentence/Emphatic Sentence:</u> Cleft sentence is explained in chapter 1. Structurally speaking, cleft sentence is a simple sentence written as a complex sentence in order to emphasize/focus a particular part like subject, object, verb, etc. of the original simple sentence. For example,:

I wrote this book.	It is I who wrote this book.
He studied in Oxford University.	It was Oxford University where he studied.
He studied in Oxford University.	The university where he studied was Oxford.
She worked throughout the day.	All/What she did was work throughout the day.

Compound-Complex Sentence: If a compound sentence, i.e., a sentence with two or more independent clauses, is joined with one or more dependent/subordinate clauses, it is a compound-complex sentence. For example,:

She was watching TV, **and** her brother was playing **when** their parents came back.
 independent clause   independent clause   adverb clause
           compound sentence   adverb clause
                  complex sentence

Whenever they go shopping, she buys dresses **but** he buys game CDs.

Simple or Compound or Complex Sentence?: The same facts/ideas can be expressed/written using any of the simple, compound or complex sentences as illustrated below:

The facts/ideas to be expressed for our example are as follows:
   1) She invited him.
   2) He did not want to go.

They are written below using different types of structural sentences:

<u>She invited him</u>.   <u>He did not want to go</u>.   - two **simple sentences**
independent clause   independent clause

<u>In spite of being invited by her,</u>   <u>he did not want to go</u>. - **simple sentence**
prepositional phrase as adverb phrase   independent clause
  - though it looks complicated, it is only a simple sentence because it has only one clause, i.e., the independent clause with the subject of 'he' and the finite verb of 'did not want'. Also, the other part of the sentence is only a prepositional phrase because the expression 'in spite of' is a complex preposition with the prepositional object 'being invited' which is only a gerund phrase, not a finite verb.

<u>She had invited him</u>, **but** <u>he did not want to go</u>.   - **compound sentence**
independent clause   independent clause

<u>Although she had invited him,</u> <u>he did not want to go</u>. - **complex sentence**
dependent clause   independent clause

Rewriting two or more simple sentences into a single sentence is called **Synthesis of Sentences**. The rewritten single sentence can be a simple sentence or compound sentence or complex sentence.

<u>What type of sentence should we use?</u>: The facts/ideas can be expressed using any type of sentence, but what type of sentence should we use? Generally, we should not use too many short and simple sentences; otherwise it will be monotonous for the readers, often reminding of their primary school stuff. We should try to use a variety of sentences, sprinkled with various structural elements such as appositives, phrases, clauses, idioms, etc., to make our writing more interesting and lively. The variety of sentences include not only the structural sentence types of simple, compound and complex sentences but also other types including functional types of declarative sentences, interrogative sentences, imperative sentences and exclamatory sentences; positive and negative sentences; sentences of active voice and passive voice; long, medium and short sentences; and comparison sentences of various degrees of comparison such as positive, comparative and superlative. In short, it should be a mixture of all types of sentences including short and simple sentences in right proportion.

It is true that sentences with phrases and clauses rather than those with simple words give more space/room for the writer to express an idea. However, we should not think that using only long simple sentences with phrases, compound sentences and complex sentences is good English and that using short simple sentences is bad English. It depends on the particular idea to be expressed.

III Transformation of Structural Sentences into each other: One type of structural sentence can be rewritten into another type using different structural elements like appositives, phrases, clauses, etc. in such a way that does not change the original meaning. However, all facts/ideas may not be suitable for all types of sentences.

Guidelines for Transformation of Structural Sentences:

1) *Elements of Structural Sentences:*

Short simple sentence = one main clause only **but no phrases or no subordinate clauses**
Long simple sentence = one main clause with phrases **but no subordinate clauses**
Compound sentence = two or more main clauses with(out) phrases **but no subordinate clauses**
Complex sentence = one main clause with(out) phrases **and subordinate clauses**

2) *Phrases*, in this regard, generally refer to the verbal phrases of gerunds, participles, infinitives. However, nouns / noun phrases, adjectives / adjective phrases, adverbs / adverb phrases and prepositional phrases are also used in this way. When the phrases other than the verbal phrases are used, they are used with the generally-omitted participle of 'being' and, therefore, they are also equivalent to the verbal phrase of participles as illustrated below:

They could not do anything, not sure about what would happen next.
                                    adjective phrase

It is equivalent to:

They could not do anything, being not sure about what would happen next.
                                    participle

3) *Method of transformations:* Going by the elements of the structural sentences as given just above in *elements of structural sentences*, it can be said that one type of sentence can be converted into another by changing either phrase to main clause or subordinate clause; the main clause to phrase or subordinate clause; or subordinate clause to phrase or main clause. It can be represented as follows also:

    Long Simple Sentence : Phrase   + main clause.
    Compound Sentence   : Main clause + coordinating conjunction + main clause.
    Complex Sentence   : Subordinate clause   + main clause.

The guidelines for conversion of the structural sentences into each other can be given from two points of views, namely the clauses and phrases and the structural sentence types. Any of them can be used because both are guidelines for doing the same thing. They are given below one by one.

Chapter-17: Clauses and Structural Sentence Types - Simple, Compound and Complex Sentence

I <u>Guidelines based on Clauses and Phrases</u>:

1) **Independent Clause to Dependent Clause**: It is used for converting:

a) <u>two simple sentences into complex sentence (a synthesis)</u>

   A man saw us yesterday. He may come tomorrow.
       = The man **who** <u>saw us yesterday</u> may come tomorrow.

b) <u>compound sentence into complex sentence</u>

   <u>You study well</u>, **and** <u>you will get good marks</u>.
       = **If** <u>you study well</u>, you will get good marks.

2) **Dependent Clause to Independent Clause**: It is used for converting:

a) <u>complex sentence into two simple sentences</u>

   The man **who** <u>saw us yesterday</u> may come tomorrow.
       = A man saw us yesterday. He may come tomorrow.

b) <u>complex sentence into compound sentence</u>

   If <u>you study well</u>, you will get good marks.
       = <u>You study well</u>, **and** <u>you will get good marks</u>.

Additional examples are given below in such a way that the first line has independent clauses; the second line has dependent clause along with the other independent clause; and they illustrate the above two guidelines mutually.

   <u>He had studied well</u>. <u>He got good marks</u>.
       = **As** <u>he had studied well</u>, he got good marks.
   <u>He had studied well</u>, **and** <u>he got good marks</u>.
       = **As** <u>he had studied well</u>, he got good marks.
   <u>She is rich</u>, **but** <u>she is simple</u>.
       = **Though** <u>she is rich</u>, she is simple.
   <u>I like cricket</u>, **yet** <u>my favourite game is football</u>.
       = **Although** <u>I like cricket</u>, my favourite game is football.
   <u>We should cook now</u>, **or** <u>we cannot eat</u>.
       = **Unless** <u>we cook now</u>, we cannot eat.

He wanted to buy a computer, **so** he had saved some money.
  = He had saved some money **so that** he could buy a computer.
The train journey is comfortable, **so** everybody likes it.
  = Everybody likes train journey **because** it is comfortable.
You are rich, **but** your friend is poor.
  = You are rich **whereas** your friend is poor.
He has to play the toughest player today. He is worried about it.
  = He is worried **that** he has to play the toughest player today.
He won the match, **and** he is finally happy.
  = He is finally happy **that** he won the match.
He would win the match, **and** I always know that.
  = I always know **that** he would win the match.
Was the match played? I do not know.
  = I do not know **whether** the match was played.
We saw a man yesterday. He may come tomorrow.
  = The man **whom** we saw yesterday may come tomorrow.
A message is difficult to understand, **and** it has too many lines.
  = A message **that** is difficult to understand has too many lines.
Apple is good for health. I like it.
  = I like apple **which** is good for health.
His coach has said something. He listened carefully.
  = He listened carefully to **what** his coach has said.
She behaved badly in the ground. She felt bad for that.
  = She felt bad for **how** she behaved in the ground.
He would come back. Only she knows the date.
  = Only she knows the date **when** he would come back.
Only rich people would live there, **yet** he lives there.
  = He lives **where** only rich people would live.
That shop has only costly items. It is not suitable for us.
  = The shop **where** only costly items are available is not suitable for us.
Where is the match held? It will be announced later.
  = The venue **where** the match is held will be announced later.
He chose that job, **but** nobody knows the reason.
  = Nobody knows the reason **why** he chose that job.
Can you win the match? It depends on your practice.
  = **Whether** you can win the match depends on **how** you practise.

Chapter-17: Clauses and Structural Sentence Types - Simple, Compound and Complex Sentence

3) Independent Clause to Phrase (Verbal Phrases of gerund, participle and infinitive; Prepositional Phrase; Basic Phrases of noun phrase, adjective phrase and adverb phrase)

It is used for converting:

a) <u>two simple sentences into one long simple sentence (a synthesis)</u>

He finished the work yesterday. He may come today.
= <u>Having finished the work yesterday</u>, he may come today.
          participle
I went to the Railway Station. I wanted to book tickets.
= I went to the Railway Station <u>to book tickets</u>.
                      infinitive
You can use the Internet to book tickets. It is easy.
= <u>Using the Internet</u> to book tickets is easy.
          gerund
That shop has only costly items. It is not suitable for us.
= The shop <u>with only costly items</u> is not suitable for us.
          prepositional phrase
Where is the match held? It will be announced later.
= <u>The venue to hold the match</u> will be announced later.
      noun phrase

b) <u>compound sentence into one long simple sentence</u>

He had studied well, **and** <u>he got good marks</u>.
= <u>Having studied well</u>, he got good marks.
      participle
<u>She is rich</u>, **but** <u>she is simple</u>.
= <u>In spite of being rich</u>, she is simple.
   prepositional phrase with gerund

4) Phrase to Independent Clause: It is used for converting

a) <u>one long simple sentence into two simple sentences</u>

<u>Having finished the work yesterday</u>, he may come today.
= He finished the work yesterday. He may come today.

b) <u>one long simple sentence to compound sentence</u>

<u>Having studied well</u>, he got good marks.
= <u>He had studied well</u>, **and** <u>he got good marks</u>.

Examples are given below in such a way that the first line has independent clauses; the second line has the phrase for one of the independent clauses along with the other independent clause; and they illustrate the above two guidelines mutually.

He studies well. He will get good marks.
= <u>Studying well</u>, he will get good marks.
He has studied well, **so** <u>he can get good marks</u>.
= <u>Having studied well</u>, he can get good marks.
He has been studying well for many years. He will definitely get admission.
= <u>Studying well for many years</u>, he will definitely get admission.
<u>He studied well</u>, **so** <u>he got good marks</u>.
= <u>Having studied well</u>, he got good marks.
He was not studying well yesterday. He cannot answer the question.
= <u>Not studying well yesterday</u>, he cannot answer the question.
He will study well. He will get good marks.
= <u>Going to study well</u>, he will get good marks.
<u>Her son won the match</u>, **and** <u>she is happy</u>.
= <u>Her son having won the match</u>, she is happy.
<u>She invited him</u>, **and** <u>he went to the party</u>.
= <u>She having invited him</u>, he went to the party.
= <u>Having been invited by her</u>, he went to the party.
<u>She invited him</u>, **but** <u>he did not go to the party</u>.
= <u>In spite of her having invited him</u>, he did not go to the party.
= <u>Despite her having invited him</u>, he did not go to the party.
= <u>Despite her invitation</u>, he did not go to the party.
= <u>In spite of having been invited by her</u>, he did not go to the party.
<u>He was not invited</u>, **but** <u>he went to the party</u>.
= <u>In spite of not having been invited</u>, he went to the party.
= <u>Despite no invitation</u>, he went to the party.
<u>He is a student</u>, **so** <u>he must study</u>.
= <u>Being a student</u>, he must study.
<u>His mother was not a student</u>, **so** <u>she needed not study</u>.
= <u>Not being a student</u>, his mother needed not study.
She has been to London. Her parents are proud of that.
= <u>She having been to London</u>, her parents are proud.
<u>She will be a teacher from tomorrow</u>, **and** <u>her parents are happy</u>.
= <u>She going to be a teacher from tomorrow</u>, her parents are happy.
Apple is good for health. I like it.
= <u>Apple being good for health</u>, I like it.
<u>Only rich people would live there</u>, **yet** <u>he lives there</u>.
= He lives in the area <u>only rich people living</u>.
<u>Study well</u>, **and** <u>you will get good marks</u>.
= <u>In the event of your studying well</u>, you will get good marks.

Chapter-17: Clauses and Structural Sentence Types - Simple, Compound and Complex Sentence 169

I like cricket, **yet** my favourite game is football.
 = In spite of my liking cricket, my favourite game is football.
We should cook now, **or** we cannot eat.
 = In the event of our not cooking now, we cannot eat.
We saw a man yesterday. He may come tomorrow.
 = The man having been seen by us yesterday may come tomorrow.
 = The man seen by us yesterday may come tomorrow.
A message is difficult to understand, **and** it has too many lines.
 = A message being difficult to understand has too many lines.
That shop has only costly items. It is not suitable for us.
 = The shop having only costly items is not suitable for us.
 = The shop with only costly items is not suitable for us.
He wanted to buy a computer, **so** he had saved some money.
 = He had saved some money in order to buy a computer.
 = In order to buy a computer, he had saved some money.
All students should study well. Our teacher expects it.
 = Our teacher expects all students to study well.
He practices very hard. His aim is to win the match.
 = He practices very hard to win the match.
 = To win the match, he practices very hard.
He has won the match, **so** he is happy.
 = He is happy to have won the match / for having won the match.
 = Having won the match, he is happy.
Her child was loved by all. She was very satisfied.
 = She was very satisfied for her child to have been loved by all.
She is a teacher, **and** she is happy.
 = She is happy to be a teacher. / Being a teacher, she is happy.
She was a teacher, **and** she is happy about it.
 = She is happy about to have been a teacher.
 = Having been a teacher, she is happy.
The tea was very hot. It was difficult to drink.
 = The tea was too hot to drink.
He may come back, **but** it is doubtful.
 = His coming back is doubtful.
Can you win the match? It depends on your practice.
 = Your winning the match or not depends on your practice.
I teach English grammar also. It is my hobby.
 = Teaching English grammar is my hobby.
 = My hobby is teaching English grammar.
Yours friends appreciate your knowledge, **and** I like it.
 = I like your friends appreciating your knowledge.
 = I like your knowledge being appreciated by your friends.

They served in the military. It was great for them.
   = It was great for them <u>to have served in the military</u>.
   = <u>Having served in the military</u> was great for them.
<u>They were tortured by the enemies,</u> **but** <u>they accepted it happily for the country</u>.
   = They accepted <u>having been tortured by the enemies</u> happily for the country.
He would come back. Only she knows the date.
   = Only she knows <u>the date of his coming back</u>.
He has to play the toughest player today. He is worried about it.
   = He is worried <u>about having to play the toughest player today</u>.
   = <u>Having to play the toughest player today</u>, he is worried.
His coach said something. He listened carefully.
   = He listened carefully <u>to the words of his coach</u>.
She behaved badly in the ground. She felt bad for that.
   = She felt bad <u>for having behaved badly in the ground</u>.
   = She felt bad <u>for her bad behaviour in the ground</u>.
   = <u>Having behaved badly in the ground</u>, she felt bad.
Meeting our leader is our dream. We are looking forward for that.
   = We are looking forward <u>to meeting our leader</u>.
<u>He won the match,</u> **and** <u>he is finally happy</u>.
   = He is finally happy <u>for having won the match</u> / <u>to have won the match</u>.
   = <u>Having won the match</u>, he is finally happy.

5) Dependent Clause to Phrase (Verbal Phrases of gerund, participle and infinitive; Prepositional Phrase; Basic Phrases of noun phrase, adjective phrase and adverb phrase)

It is used for converting <u>complex sentence into one long simple sentence</u>.

She knows the date **when** he would come back.
    = She knows the date <u>of his coming back</u>.
                prepositional phrase with gerund
The shop **where** only costly items are available is not suitable for us.
    = The shop <u>having only costly items</u> is not suitable for us.
          participle
I am saving money **so that** I can help my sister.
    = I am saving money <u>to help my sister</u>.
          infinitive
The shop **where** only costly items are available is not suitable for us.
    = The shop <u>with only costly items</u> is not suitable for us.
       prepositional phrase
She is so tired **that** she could not stand.
    = <u>(Being) So tired</u>, she could not stand.
       adjective phrase

Chapter-17: Clauses and Structural Sentence Types - Simple, Compound and Complex Sentence

Where the match is held will be announced later.
= The venue of the match will be announced later.
   noun phrase

6) Phrase to Dependent Clause

It is used for converting one long simple sentence into complex sentence.

After completing the work, you can go.
= **After** you complete the work, you can go.

Examples are given below in such a way that the first line has dependent clauses with the independent clause; the second line has the phrases for the dependent clauses along with the independent clause; and they illustrate the above two guidelines mutually.

Although he worked hard, he could not finish the work.
= In spite of his working hard, he could not finish the work.
= In spite of his hard work, he could not finish the work.
= Despite his working hard, he could not finish the work.
If you study well, you will get good marks.
= In the event of your studying well, you will get good marks.
Unless you study well, you will not get good marks.
= In the event of your not studying well, you will not get good marks.
= You will not get good marks without studying well.
As he is a good student, teachers like him.
= He being a good student, teachers like him.
You prepare bread toast **before** I finish the homework.
= You prepare bread toast before my finishing the homework.
We watched **when** the plane took off.
= We watched the plane taking off.
We had to wait **because** we arrived early.
= Having arrived early, we had to wait.
For the car was smashed and damaged, it looked vandalized.
= Smashed and damaged, the car looked vandalized.
He is happy **for** he got the first rank.
= Having got the first rank, he is happy.
He trained her carefully **lest** she lose the match.
= In order to avoid her losing the match, he trained her carefully.
= For the fear of her losing the match, he trained her carefully.
= For the purpose of her not losing the match, he trained her carefully.
I have been playing here **since** the sun rose.
= I have been playing here since/from the time of the sun having risen.
= I have been playing here since/from the time of the sunrise.
Since you are rich, you can help me.
= Being rich, you can help me.

He can wait **until** I finish my work.
> = He can wait till the time of finishing my work.

He is tall **whereas** you are short.
> = At the same time of your being short, he is tall.
> = In spite of your being short, he is tall.

He is very poor **while** his friend is rich.
> = At the time of his friend being rich, he is poor.
> = Despite his friend being rich, he is poor.

While it was raining, we played cards.
> = At the time of raining, we played cards.

While he is not an expert, he will do his best.
> = In spite of not being an expert, he will do his best.

Whatever they do, they should abide by the law.
> = In spite of doing anything, they should abide by the law.

The man **who** is our leader may come tomorrow.
> = The man, our leader, may come tomorrow.

The man **who** was our old leader may come tomorrow.
> = The man having been our leader may come tomorrow.

The man **who** saw us yesterday may come tomorrow.
> = The man having seen us yesterday may come tomorrow.

The man **whom** we saw yesterday may come tomorrow.
> = The man seen by us yesterday may come tomorrow.

The man **whose** hobby is dancing may come tomorrow.
> = The man with the hobby of dancing may come tomorrow.

A message **that** is difficult to understand has too many lines.
> = A message being difficult to understand has too many lines.
> = A message difficult to understand has too many lines.

The messages, **which** are sent by business people, are a nuisance.
> = The messages sent by business people are a nuisance.

He lived in an area **where** only rich people would live.
> = He lived in an area the rich people living.

The shop **where** only costly items are available is not suitable for us.
> = The shop having only costly items is not suitable for us.
> = The shop with only costly items is not suitable for us.

Nobody can tell the reason **why** he chose such a job.
> = Nobody can tell the reason for his choosing such a job.

That is not the way **how** one should behave.
> = That is not the way for one to behave.

I always know **that** he would win the match.
> = I always know about his winning the match.

It is difficult to say **who** will win the match.
> = It is difficult to predict the winner of the match.

He will support **whoever** wins the match.
    = He will support <u>anybody winning the match</u>.
I do not know **where** the match is held.
    = I do not know <u>the venue of the match</u>.
Whether <u>you can win the match or not</u> depends on <u>how you practise</u>.
    = <u>Your winning the match or not</u> depends on <u>your practice</u>.
Whom <u>you are going to play today</u> is a tough player.
    = <u>The person going to play with you today</u> is a tough player.
He is worried **that** <u>he has to play the toughest player today</u>.
    = He is worried <u>about having to play the toughest player today</u>.
He listened carefully to **what** <u>his coach said</u>.
    = He listened carefully to <u>the words of his coach</u>.
She felt bad for **how** <u>she behaved in the ground</u>.
    = She felt bad for <u>her behaviour in the ground</u>.
    = She felt bad for <u>having behaved badly in the ground</u>.
    = <u>Having behaved badly in the ground</u>, she felt bad.
He is finally happy **that** <u>he won the match</u>.
    = He is finally happy <u>about having won the match</u> / <u>to have won the match</u>.
    = <u>Having won the match</u>, he is happy.
I like apple **which** <u>is good for health</u>.
    = <u>Apple being good for health</u>, I like it.

II <u>Guidelines based on Structural Sentence Types:</u>

1. <u>Simple Sentences to Compound Sentences:</u>

1 a) *Two simple sentences into a compound sentence (a synthesis):* Two simple sentences can be joined into a compound sentence using one of the coordinating conjunctions of 'FANBOYS' as illustrated below:

<u>She invited him</u>.   <u>He could not go</u>.   - **simple sentences**
independent clause   independent clause

    <u>She invited him</u>, **but** <u>he could not go</u>.   - **compound sentence**
    independent clause   independent clause

1 b) *One long simple sentence with phrase to a compound sentence:* The phrase in the simple sentence should be converted into an independent clause and combined to the original independent clause using a coordinating conjunction as illustrated below:

<u>She practised very hard</u> <u>for the success</u>.   - **simple sentence**
independent clause   prepositional phrase

    <u>She practised very hard</u>, **and** <u>she was successful</u>.- **compound sentence**
    independent clause   independent clause

In spite of being invited by her, he did not want to go. - **simple sentence**
prepositional phrase   independent clause

She invited him, **but** he did not want to go. - **compound sentence**
independent clause   independent clause

2. Simple Sentences to Complex Sentences:

2 a) *Two simple sentences to a complex sentence (a synthesis)*: One of the simple sentences should be converted into a dependent/subordinate clause as illustrated below:

You are rich.   You can help me.   - **simple sentences**
independent clause   independent clause

Since you are rich, you can help me.   - **complex sentence**
dependent clause   independent clause

He gave a movie CD.   It was very good.   - **simple sentences**
independent clause   independent clause

The movie CD **that** he gave   was very good. - **complex sentence**
independent   (dependent clause)   clause

2 b) *One long simple sentence with phrase to a complex sentence*: The phrase in the simple sentence should be converted into dependent clause as illustrated below:

He admitted his mistake of copying in the test.   - **simple sentence**
independent clause   prepositional phrase

He admitted his mistake **that** he had copied in the test. - **complex sentence**
independent clause   dependent clause

Having copied in the exam, he was barred.   - **simple sentence**
participle phrase   independent clause

As he had copied in the exam, he was barred.   - **complex sentence**
dependent clause   independent clause

The coffee was too hot for us   to drink.   - **simple sentence**
independent clause   infinitive phrase

The coffee was so hot **that** we could not drink. - **complex sentence**
independent clause   dependent clause

Chapter-17: Clauses and Structural Sentence Types - Simple, Compound and Complex Sentence

3. <u>Two short Simple Sentences to one long Simple Sentence with phrase (a synthesis):</u>
One of the simple sentences should be converted into a phrase as illustrated below:

    He plays football regularly.   It is his hobby.   - two **simple sentences**
    independent clause   independent clause

        Playing football regularly *is his hobby*.   - one **long simple sentence**
        (gerund phrase)   independent clause   with gerund phrase as subject

    He was listening to the radio.   He read a story.   - two **simple sentences**
    independent clause   independent clause

        Listening to the radio, he read a story.   - one long **simple sentence**
        participle phrase   independent clause

    We must solve the problems. There are still few more problems.- two **simple sentences**
    independent clause   independent clause

        We still have few more problems to solve.   - one long **simple sentence**
        independent clause   infinitive phrase

4. <u>Compound Sentences to Simple Sentences</u>: One of the independent clauses should be converted into a phrase as illustrated below:

    He was the youngest boy, **but** he won the match.   - **compound sentence**
    independent clause   independent clause

        Despite being the youngest boy, he won the match.   - **simple sentence**
        prepositional phrase   independent clause

    She studied very well, **and** she got the first rank.   - **compound sentence**
    independent clause   independent clause

        Having studied very well, she got the first rank.   - **simple sentence**
        participle phrase   independent clause

    You must work hard, **or** you cannot finish the work.   - **compound sentence**
    independent clause   independent clause

        You must work hard to finish the work.   - **simple sentence**
        independent clause   infinitive phrase

5. <u>Compound Sentences to Complex Sentences</u>: One of the independent clauses should be converted into a dependent/subordinate clause as illustrated below:

    He knew the difficulty, **yet** he tried it.   - **compound sentence**
    independent clause   independent clause

        Although he knew the difficulty, he tried it.   - **complex sentence**
        dependent clause   independent clause

You must study hard; **otherwise**, you cannot get good marks. - **compound sentence**
independent clause   independent clause

Unless you study hard, you cannot get good marks.   - **complex sentence**
dependent clause   independent clause

She wanted to get good marks, **so** she studied well.   - **compound sentence**
independent clause   independent clause

She studied well   **so that** she could get good marks. - **complex sentence**
independent clause   dependent clause

6. <u>Complex Sentences to Simple Sentences:</u> The dependent clause should be converted into a phrase as illustrated below:

I do not know   **when** I shall finish the work.   - **complex sentence**
independent clause   dependent clause

I do not know   the time of my finishing the work. - **simple sentence**
independent clause   noun phrase with prepositional phrase

The place   **where** the criminal is hiding *is unknown*.   - **complex sentence**
independent   dependent clause   clause

The place of criminal's hiding   *is unknown*. - **simple sentence**
(noun phrase with prepositional phrase) independent clause.
The criminal's hideout is unknown.   - **simple sentence**
(noun phrase)   independent clause
The hideout of the criminal   *is unknown*. - **simple sentence**
(noun phrase with prepositional phrase) independent clause.

(The above **simple sentences** have noun phrases as the subject.)

Note: As illustrated above, we can use noun (phrase) in the place of verbal phrases. Similarly, adjective (phrase) and adverb (phrase) can also be used in the place of verbal phrases as illustrated just below.

Though she was not sure about it, she attempted.   - **complex sentence**
dependent clause   independent clause

Not even sure about it,   she attempted.   - **simple sentence**
(AdjP with prepositional phrase)   independent clause
Without being sure about it,   she attempted.   - **simple sentence**
(prepositional phrase with gerund) independent clause
In spite of not being sure about it, she attempted.   - **simple sentence**
(prepositional phrase with gerund) independent clause

Chapter-17: Clauses and Structural Sentence Types - Simple, Compound and Complex Sentence

<u>**Though** she made a mistake,</u> <u>she did not know it</u>. - **complex sentence**
 dependent clause   independent clause

<u>Unknowingly, she made a mistake</u>. - **simple sentence**
 adverb   independent clause

<u>Without knowing about it,</u>   <u>she made a mistake</u>. - **simple sentence**
 (prepositional phrase with gerund) independent clause

<u>In spite of making a mistake,</u>   <u>she did not know it</u>. - **simple sentence**
 (prepositional phrase with gerund)   independent clause

The movie CD **that** *he gave*   *was very good*. - **complex sentence**
 independent   dependent clause   clause

<u>The movie CD **given by him**</u>   <u>was very good</u>. - **simple sentence**
 independent   (participle phrase)   clause

7. <u>Complex Sentences to Compound Sentences</u>: The dependent clause should be converted into an independent clause and joined with the original independent clause using a coordinating conjunction as illustrated below:

<u>I did not know</u>   **that** <u>you had done it</u>.   - **complex sentence**
 independent clause   dependent clause

<u>You had done it</u>, **but** <u>I did not know</u>.   - **compound sentence**
 independent clause   independent clause

<u>**Unless** you study well,</u> <u>you will not get good marks</u>. - **complex sentence**
 dependent clause   independent clause

<u>You study well</u>, **or** <u>you will not get good marks</u>. - **compound sentence**
 independent clause   independent clause

<u>**Although** we knew the result,</u> <u>we did not tell them.</u> - **complex sentence**
 dependent clause   independent clause

<u>We knew the result</u>, **yet** <u>we did not tell them</u>. - **compound sentence**
 independent clause   independent clause

IV <u>**Mutually Dependent Clauses**</u>: Two dependent clauses can be written in such a way that each of them is dependent on each other. However, none of them can be written separately as a separate sentence. They are used with the <u>negative / restrictive adverbs</u> as follows:

<u>Hardly</u> had **I** left <u>when</u> somebody called. = I had <u>hardly</u> left <u>when</u> somebody called.
<u>Scarcely</u> had **we** begun, <u>when</u> the doorbell rang. = We had <u>scarcely</u> begun, <u>when</u> …
<u>No sooner</u> had **she** finished her work <u>than</u> she was assigned a new work.
   = <u>As soon as</u> she had finished her work, she was assigned a new work.

Chapter 18
Conjunctions

As we have already learned, conjunctions are joining words used to join words, phrases and clauses in a sentence. The types of conjunctions are given below.

I Coordinating Conjunctions (CCn): **Coordinating conjunctions** join the elements of a sentence like words, phrases or clauses of equal importance, and they include **'for, and, nor, but, or, yet** and **so'** which can be remembered easily with the acronym 'FANBOYS' which is formed with the first letter of these coordinating conjunctions. <u>Coordinating conjunctions should be used to join similar grammatical constructions only like noun with noun, word with word, phrase with phrase, clause with clause etc., not noun with adjective, phrase with clause, etc</u>. The meaning of these conjunctions is as follows and as illustrated:

for	-	for the reason of
and	-	in addition to
nor	-	and not (and neither)
but	-	however, on the other hand
or	-	alternatively
yet	-	however, on the other hand, nevertheless
so	-	therefore

I bought a bat **and** ball.	-	joining words
Madurai is famous for the old big Meenakshi Temple **and** the beautiful river, 'Vaigai'.	-	joining phrases
He had studied well, **and** he got good marks.	-	joining ind. clauses
She is rich, **but** she is simple.	-	joining ind. clauses
Did you go to the cinema **or** watch TV?	-	joining phrases
I did not finish it, **nor** did she.	-	joining ind. clauses
It is cloudy, **yet** it is hot.	-	joining ind. clauses
She is beautiful, **so** I like her.	-	joining ind. clauses
He rushed, **for** it was late.	-	joining ind. clauses

(the use of **'for'** as a coordinating conjunction is limited or old-fashioned, **for** it has the connotation of **'because'**, a subordinating conjunction)

II Subordinating Conjunctions (SCn): A subordinating conjunction introduces a dependent clause. The common subordinating conjunctions are **"after, although, as, because, before, if, lest, once, since, than, that, though, till, unless, until, whereas, whether and while"**. They are illustrated below with their meaning on the right:

Chapter-18: Conjunctions

After he comes, you can go.	(later in time)
Although / Though we were tired, we finished the work.	(in spite of the fact that)
As he is a good student, teachers like him.	(for the reason that)
We watched carefully **as** the teacher solved the problem.	(at the time when)
He likes train travel **because** it is comfortable.	(for the reason that)
I studied on my own, not **because** you told me.	(not for the reason that)
We had to wait **cos** we arrived early.	(for the reason that)

('**cos**' is an informal form of '**because**')

I had reached **before** the train left.	(earlier than)
He is happy **for** he got the first rank.	(for the reason that)
If you study well, you will get good marks.	(on the condition that)
I played carefully **lest** my team lose the match.	(for the fear that)
He will call you **once** it is ready.	(at the time when)
All will be well **providing / provided** you are careful.	(on the condition that)
I have been playing here **since** the sun rose.	(from the past time when)
Since you are rich, you can help me.	(for the reason that)
Supposing you get a lottery, what will you do?	(on the condition that)
She is taller **than** you are.	(in comparison to)
He is happy **that** he won the match.	(for the reason that)
Unless he studies well, he cannot get good marks.	(on the condition that)
He can wait **until / till** I finish my work.	(up to the time when)
He is tall **whereas** you are short.	(on the other hand)
I will meet her **whether** you like it or not.	(despite that or not that)
While it was raining, we played cards.	(at the time when)
He is very poor **while** his friend is rich.	(on the other hand)
While he is not an expert, he will do his best.	(despite the fact that)

In addition, the following <u>expressions</u> are often used as <u>subordinating conjunctions</u> at the beginning of <u>subordinate clauses</u>.

He talks **as if** he knows everything.	(in a similar way)
As long as we cooperate, we can stay together.	(on the condition that)
He has worked here **as long as** I have known him.	(during the period)
Complete the work **as soon as** you can.	(immediately after)
It looks **as though** it is going to rain.	(in a similar way)
I will talk to her **even if** she does not.	(in spite of a possibility)
Take an extra pen **in case** you miss one.	(for the possibility)
Please be prepared **or else** you may miss it.	(otherwise)
I am saving money **so that** I can help my sister.	(for the purpose of)

<u>*Note:*</u> Dependent clauses introduced with subordinating conjunctions are adverb clauses.

Sub-types of Subordinating Conjunctions: Subordinating Conjunctions can be classified according to their meaning also as follows:

1) <u>Time</u>: For example, 'I arrived **before** the office was open.'
2) <u>Purpose</u>: For example, 'I was very careful **lest** I make a mistake.'
3) <u>Cause/Reason</u>: For example, 'I had to wait, **because** I arrived early.'
4) <u>Result</u>: For example, 'I am saving money **so that** I can help my sister.'
5) <u>Condition</u>: For example, '**If** you study well, you will get good marks.'
6) <u>Concession</u>: For example, '**Although** he was poor, he was very honest.'
7) <u>Comparison</u>: For example, 'She is taller **than** you are.'
8) <u>Emphasis</u>: For example,:
   a) '**so** + adj./adv. + **that**' as in 'She is **so** good **that** all like her' and 'He runs **so** fast **that** he can overtake a car'.
   b) '**such** +(adj.+noun)+ **that**' as in 'She is **such** a good girl **that** all like her' and 'He is **such** a fast runner **that** he can overtake a car'.

III **Relative Conjunctions (RCn):** <u>Relative Pronouns</u>, namely "**who, whose, whom, which/what, that** and **whether**", and <u>Relative Adverbs</u>, namely "**how, when, where** and **why**", are also used to combine clauses. Therefore, they can be called relative conjunctions. For example,:

The person **who** finished first got the prize.
He still remembers the day **when** he met her first.

Relative conjunctions are explained elaborately in chapter 17 on 'Clauses and Structural Sentence Types'.

IV **Correlative Conjunctions:** Correlative conjunctions are used in pairs to show the relationship between the similar grammatical parts of the sentence joined by the correlative conjunction. They are illustrated below:

1) The first group of conjunctions (with the second word of the correlative conjunction being similar to coordinating conjunction) can be used to join any type of equivalent constructs like words, phrases, clauses, etc.

both ... and	She is **both** intelligent **and** beautiful.
either ... or	I shall **either** do the work **or** read a book.
	Either you write a letter **or** you send an e-mail.
neither ... nor	He is **neither** poor **nor** sick.
	Neither can he support us **nor** can he neglect us.
whether ... or	I do not know **whether** she will come **or** not?
not only ... but also	The boy is **not only** smart **but also** hard-working.
	Not only is the boy smart **but also** he is hard-working.
rather ... than	I would **rather** stay at home **than** go to the library.
more ... than	**More** people came **than** had been invited.
just as ... so too	**Just as** we love our country, **so too** do others.
what with ... and	**What with** all her relatives **and** friends, she suffered alone.

Chapter-18: Conjunctions

2) The second group of conjunctions can be used to join only clauses, both main clause and subordinate clause, resulting in complex sentences.

if ... then	**If** that is true, **then** you are right.
hardly ... when	**Hardly** had he arrived home, **when** the phone rang.
	He had **hardly** arrived home, **when** the phone rang.
scarcely ... when	**Scarcely** had we gone to bed, **when** the door was knocked.
	We had **scarcely** gone to bed, **when** the door was knocked.
no sooner ... than	**No sooner** had I left the office, **than** she came.
	I had **no sooner** left the office, **when** she came.

V **Parallel Construction**: Combining similar constructs/ideas is referred to as parallel construction. It is achieved with correlative conjunctions. However, it should be noted that only similar constructs can be combined, not dissimilar/different constructs as illustrated below:

The car turned **either** left **or** to the right. - **Incorrect** because 'either' is followed by the adverb, 'left', and 'or' is followed by the prepositional phrase 'to the right', i.e., different types of constructs.

The car turned **either** left **or** right.   - **Correct** because both 'either' and 'or' are followed by adverbs, namely 'left' and 'right', i.e., same types of constructs.

The car turned **either** to the left **or** to the right.- **Correct** because both 'either' and 'or' are followed by prepositional phrases, namely 'to the left' and 'to the right', i.e., same types of constructs.

VI **Connecting Adverbs / Conjunctive Adverbs**: They are used to connect/link the ideas expressed by two sentences/clauses. In other words, they connect two sentences/ main clauses and are similar to coordinating conjunctions. Connecting adverbs include 'however, nevertheless, therefore, hence, thus, also, besides, moreover, furthermore, otherwise, consequently and ultimately'. For example,:

I like cricket; **however**, my favourite game is football.
independent clause   independent clause

It is difficult to complete in time; **nevertheless**, you should try.
He had studied very well; **therefore/hence/thus**, he got good marks.
She is beautiful; **also/besides/moreover/furthermore**, she is rich too.
You must study hard; **otherwise**, you cannot get good marks.
I was not careful enough; **consequently**, I had to suffer.

The above examples are written with the punctuation mark semi-colon (;). However, the clauses can also be terminated with full stop (.) also as illustrated below:

He had studied very well. **Therefore**, he got good marks.
You must study hard. **Otherwise**, you cannot get good marks.

The connecting adverbs can also include expressions like 'after all', 'at least', 'even so', 'for all that', 'in fact', 'in short', 'it seems', 'in any event', 'I think', 'I suppose', 'I hope', 'of course', 'on the whole' and 'without doubt' because they also relate/link the idea expressed in a sentence with the idea expressed in the previous sentence. For example,:

We should pay our taxes. **After all**, it is our basic duty.
He may not be rich. **At least**, he has no debts at all.
It is difficult to complete in time; **even so**, you should try.
She is very rich and beautiful; **for all that**, she is humble.
I thought I was late; **in fact**, I was early.
She has many cars, bungalows, and many more; **in short** she is rich.
He looks very tired; **it seems** he is not well.
You may not have enough money; **in any event** you should buy it.
He looks very happy today; **I think** he has some good news.
He helped his sister to get a job; **of course** he should.
She has many cars, bungalows, and many more; **on the whole** she is rich.
India will win more Olympic medals one day. **Without doubt**, that will be great.

VII <u>**Transitional Expressions**</u>**:** Connecting (Conjunctive) adverbs are also called transitional expressions because they are not only used to just relate/link ideas, clauses and sentences but also used to move from one idea to another idea. On the whole, they add a <u>sense of coherence</u> to the writing. These expressions are summarized below according to the type of transition:

Addition	:	additionally, in addition, also, alternatively, and, besides, equally important, furthermore, finally, then
Repetition/Restatement	:	in other words, that is (i.e.)
Comparison (Similarity)	:	similarly, likewise, also, in the same manner/way
Comparison (Contrast)	:	but, yet, still, however, on the other hand, nevertheless, nonetheless, notwithstanding, at the same time, conversely, in contrast, on the contrary, instead
Concession	:	of course, possibly, perhaps, granted (accepted)

Chapter-18: Conjunctions

Emphasis	:	of course, indeed, in fact, truly, above all
Sequence and Time	:	first, firstly, first of all, second, secondly, third, thirdly, ... next, then, finally, lastly, at last, last but not the least, initially, later, currently, recently, simultaneously, meanwhile, immediately, subsequently, eventually, soon, afterwards
Place	:	in the background, in the back, in the foreground, in the front, behind the scene
Example	:	for example, e.g., for instance, namely, as an illustration, to illustrate, specifically
Cause	:	for this reason
Effect/Result	:	therefore, hence, so, accordingly, consequently, as a consequence, thus, as a result, clearly then
Summary/Conclusion	:	finally, in conclusion, in brief, in short, in the end, on the whole, therefore, at last, to conclude/summarize, thus

Chapter 19
Direct Speech and Indirect (Reported) Speech

Direct Speech and Indirect Speech are two different ways of writing/telling to others at a later point of time what somebody (i.e., anybody including others and ourselves) has told earlier.

I Direct Speech: In direct speech, the original speaker's words are exactly reproduced without any change. The <u>sentence structure</u> for direct speech has two parts, namely <u>Reported Clause</u> and <u>Reporting Clause</u>. Reported Clause has the original speaker's words exactly reproduced without any change within quotation marks. Then, the Reported Clause is preceded or followed by the Reporting Clause in the form of 'Speaker said/asked/ordered/ requested/exclaimed etc.' as illustrated below:

<u>He said,</u>   <u>"I have played football."</u>
Reporting Clause   Reported Clause

<u>"I have played football,"</u> <u>he said</u>.
Reported Clause   Reporting Clause

II Indirect Speech / Reported Speech: In the <u>sentence structure</u> of indirect speech, the speaker's words (i.e., the reported clause) are expressed after converting them into as if it is told by the listener to a third person. Besides, the words of present tense in the speaker's words are converted into words of past tense. Reporting clause is also changed suitably. For example,

<u>He told me that</u>   <u>he had played football.</u>
words of listener   converted words of speaker
Reporting Clause   Reported Clause

III Punctuation for Direct Speech: Punctuation of sentences in direct speech should be done carefully as given below:

Declarative Sentence: If the reporting clause precedes the reported clause, the comma should be put just after the reporting clause; the period (full stop) at the end of the reported clause should be within the quotation mark; and no punctuation should be used after the quotation mark. If the reporting clause follows the reported clause, the comma should be put just before the final quotation marks with the period at the end of the reporting clause. For example,:

He said, "I have played football."   "I have played football," he said.

Interrogative/Imperative/Exclamatory Sentences: The punctuation of these sentences in direct speech is also similar to that of the declarative sentences except that the punctuation marks, namely question mark, period / comma and exclamation mark, would be used respectively to end the reported clause. For example,:

He said, "Did he do his duty first?"   "What did he do first?" He said.
He said, "Close the door."   "Please open the door," He said.
He said, "How beautiful she is!"   "What a car!" He said.

Chapter-19: Direct Speech and Indirect (Reported) Speech

IV <u>**Change of words in Direct Speech to Indirect Speech:**</u> As illustrated above, some words in direct speech are modified in indirect speech. For example, the present perfect tense 'have played' is changed to past perfect tense 'had played' because when the listener reports what the first person has told, it was finished in the past and it is only reported by the listener to a third person. Like tense, other words in the direct speech are also modified suitably to convey the Past Tense. For example, today becomes that day, now becomes then, etc. Following is the list of such changes to be made:

	Direct Speech	Indirect Speech
Tenses (Action Verb)	Simple Present Present Continuous Present Perfect Present Perfect Continuous Simple Past Past Continuous Past Perfect Past Perfect Continuous	Simple Past Past Continuous Past Perfect Past Perfect Continuous Past Perfect Past Perfect Continuous *No Change* *No Change*
Tenses (Be-Verb)	Present Past	Past *No Change*
Modal Verbs (including future tense auxiliaries)	shall will can may must	should would could might had to
	(There is no change to should, would, could, might and ought to)	
Time / Place Words	today tomorrow yesterday last week now ago here thus	that day the next day the day before the week before then before there so
Pronoun	I my me we our us	he/she/it his/her/its him/her/it they their them
	(There is no change for other pronouns)	

You can skip the following changes if you do not follow it immediately, because they are described elaborately in the next section.

	Direct Speech	Indirect Speech
Reporting Verb of Declarative Sentence	said	told/said+(that) told+pronoun+(that) said to+pronoun+(that)
Reporting Verb of Yes/No Interrogative Sentence	said/asked	asked+if/whether+ Declarative Sentence of Interrogative Sentence
Reporting Verb of Question-Word Interrogative Sentence	said/asked	asked + Question-Word + Declarative Sentence of Interrogative Sentence
Reporting Verb of Imperative Sentence	said/asked/ requested/ordered	asked/requested/ordered (pronoun)+infinitive+ other component
Reporting Verb of Exclamatory Sentence	said/exclaimed/ wondered	exclaimed/wondered+(that) +Declarative Sentence of Exclamatory Sentence

V Indirect Speech of different Types of Sentences: Guidelines for converting different types of sentences in Direct Speech to Indirect Speech are explained and illustrated below:

Declarative Sentence: The reporting verb (i.e., the verb of the reporting clause) 'said' should be changed to 'told/said that' or 'told + pronoun + that' or 'said to + pronoun + that' followed by the declarative sentence in the reported clause with the suitably changed words of tense, time and pronoun.

Direct Speech	:	He said, "I have played football today."
Indirect Speech	:	He said that he had played football that day.
Indirect Speech	:	He said he had played football that day. - 'that' is omitted
Direct Speech	:	She said, "I shall come tomorrow."
Indirect Speech	:	She told that she should come the next day.
Direct Speech	:	Balu said, "I am hungry."
Indirect Speech	:	Balu said to me that he was hungry.

Chapter-19: Direct Speech and Indirect (Reported) Speech

Direct Speech : Balu said, "I could not finish yesterday."
Indirect Speech : Balu told me that he could not finish the day before.
Indirect Speech : Balu told me he could not finish the day before. - 'that' is omitted

If the reported clause has a <u>long simple sentence with phrases, compound sentence or complex sentence</u>, it should be modified carefully as illustrated below:

Direct Speech : He said, "Talking to my friend on my mobile, I had crossed the road and met with a minor accident."
Indirect Speech : He said that talking to his friend on his mobile, he had crossed the road and met with a minor accident.

Direct Speech : He said, "I am lucky that I got this job."
Indirect Speech : He said that he was lucky that he had got that job.

Direct Speech : He said, "I had gone to Madurai, <u>and</u> I met my friend."
Indirect Speech : He said that he had gone to Madurai <u>and</u> that he met his friend.

Direct Speech : He said, "I had gone to Madurai <u>and</u> met my friend."
Indirect Speech : He said that he had gone to Madurai <u>and</u> met his friend.

Direct Speech : He said, "I had gone to Madurai, <u>but</u> I did not meet my friend."
Indirect Speech : He said that he had gone to Madurai <u>but</u> did not meet his friend.

Direct Speech : He said, "When I went to Madurai, I met my friend."
Indirect Speech : He said that when he had gone to Madurai, he met his friend.

Direct Speech : He said, "If I go to Madurai again, I shall meet my friend."
Indirect Speech : He said that if he went to Madurai again, he would meet his friend.

Yes/No Interrogative Sentence: The reporting verb (the verb of the reporting clause) 'asked/said' should be changed to 'asked if' or 'asked whether' followed by the declarative sentence form of the question in the reported clause with the suitably changed words of tenses, time and pronoun.

Direct Speech : He said, "Has Ramu played football today?"
Indirect Speech : He asked if Ramu had played football that day.

Direct Speech : The child asked, "Is the food ready?"
Indirect Speech : The child asked whether the food was ready.

Question-Word Interrogative Sentence: The reporting verb (the verb of the reporting clause) 'asked/said' should be changed to 'asked + Question-Word' followed by the declarative sentence form of the question in the reported clause with the suitably changed words of tenses, time and pronoun.

Direct Speech	:	He said, "Why did Ramu play football today?"
Indirect Speech	:	He asked why Ramu had played football that day.
Direct Speech	:	Balu asked, "When did you write the letter?"
Indirect Speech	:	Balu asked when I had written the letter.
Direct Speech	:	She asked, "What flower is it?"
Indirect Speech	:	She asked what flower it was.
Direct Speech	:	The teacher asked, "What do you think is the correct answer?"
Indirect Speech	:	The teacher asked us what we thought was the correct answer.
Direct Speech	:	The teacher asked, "When did he say (that) he would return?"
Indirect Speech	:	The teacher asked when he had said (that) he would return.

Imperative Sentence: The reporting verb (the verb of the reporting clause) 'said/asked/requested/ordered' should be changed to 'asked/requested/ordered/advised + pronoun (if any)' followed by the infinitive of the verb of the imperative sentence in the reported clause with the suitably changed words of tenses, time and pronoun.

Direct Speech	:	He said, "Please attend the party tomorrow."
Indirect Speech	:	He requested me to attend the party the next day.
Direct Speech	:	The boss said, "Don't leave the office now."
Indirect Speech	:	The boss ordered me not to leave the office at that time.
Direct Speech	:	The teacher said, "Aim very high and work hard for that."
Indirect Speech	:	The teacher advised us to aim very high and work hard for that.

The following example of imperative sentence is important because the suggested action is to be done both by the speaker and the listener and as such it should be changed carefully into indirect speech as illustrated below:

Direct Speech	:	My friend said, "Let's go for a movie."
Indirect Speech	:	My friend suggested that we should/would go for a movie.

Chapter-19: Direct Speech and Indirect (Reported) Speech

Indirect Speech of imperative sentences can be written using 'that clause' with modal verb as in declarative sentences as illustrated below:

Direct Speech : He said, "Please attend the party tomorrow."
Indirect Speech : He requested me that I might/would attend the party the next day.

Direct Speech : The boss said, "Don't leave the office now."
Indirect Speech : The boss ordered me that I should not leave the office at that time.

Exclamatory Sentence: The reporting verb (the verb of the reporting clause) 'said/ exclaimed/wondered' should be changed to 'exclaimed/wondered + (that)' or 'exclaimed/ wondered to + pronoun + (that)' followed by the equivalent declarative sentence form of the exclamatory sentence in the reported clause with the suitably changed words of tenses, time and pronoun.

Direct Speech : He said, "What a beautiful girl she is!"
Indirect Speech : He exclaimed that she was a very beautiful girl.

Direct Speech : She exclaimed, "How bravely he has fought!"
Indirect Speech : She exclaimed that he had fought very bravely.

Subjunctive Sentence: Subjunctive sentences are mostly like declarative sentences in form and sometimes like imperative and exclamatory sentences. We have just learned that imperative and exclamatory sentences can be written in indirect speech using their equivalent declarative sentence forms. Therefore, subjunctive sentences can be written in indirect speech using the same guidelines as that of declarative sentences except that the tense of the verb in subjunctive mood should not be changed as illustrated below:

Direct Speech : She said, "He suggests that she attend the meeting."
Indirect Speech : She said he suggested that she attend the meeting.

Direct Speech : He said, "If I were rich, I would buy a car."
Indirect Speech : He said that if he were rich he would buy a car.

Direct Speech : He said, "God bless you!"
Indirect Speech : He blessed that God bless me.

Direct Speech : He said, "Long live our King!"
Indirect Speech : He wished that our King live long(er).

VI Exception of guidelines/rules:

1) Though the tense is generally changed in the indirect speech, it is not necessary to change the tense if what is reported in the reported clause is always/still true as illustrated below:

Direct Speech	:	He said, "Only God is the greatest."
Indirect Speech	:	He said that only God is the greatest.
Direct Speech	:	He said, "His mother is very kind."
Indirect Speech	:	He said that his mother is very kind.

2) If the reporting verb is in present tense/future tense, we should not change the tense in both the reporting clause and the reported clause as illustrated below:

Direct Speech	:	He says/will say, "I know English well."
Indirect Speech	:	He says/will say that he knows English well.

VII Divided Direct Speech:
In direct speech, the reporting clause usually comes in the beginning or at the end of the sentence as illustrated in all the above examples. However, the reporting clause can come in the middle also as illustrated below:

Direct Speech	:	"Balu," shouted his boss, "Get out."
Indirect Speech	:	His boss shouted at Balu to get out.
Direct Speech	:	"As Veeran is brave," said his grandmother, "he has fought with the tiger."
Indirect Speech	:	His grandmother told that as Veeran was brave, he had fought with the tiger.
Direct Speech	:	"Why are you worried?" his mother said. "I can help you do the homework. Bring your note book."
Indirect Speech	:	His mother asked why he was worried; told that she could help him do the homework and asked him to bring his notebook.

Chapter 20
Inversion of Subject, Verb and Complement

Normally, declarative sentences begin with Subject followed by Verb which is again followed by Object and Other Complement. However, sometimes, subject and verb (or subject + verb and complement) are inverted in forming declarative sentences to emphasize the idea of the sentence. Let's see the types of inversions:

1) Inversion of Subject and Complete Verb (both Action Verb and Be-Verb) is used for emphasis with Adverbs of Place/Time as follows:

1 a) When the subject is noun, the following sentence structure is followed:

Adverb of Place/Time + Complete Verb + **Subject**; e.g.,

Here comes **the bus**.	=	**The bus** comes here.
There is **Balu**.	=	**Balu** is there.
Under a tree was standing **my friend**.	=	**My friend** was standing under a tree.

In the park near the school were sitting **the children with their parents**.
= **The children with their parents** were sitting in the park near the school.
First came **the fire alarm**, then came **the fire engine**.

Using the above sentence structure, the adverb **'there'** can also be used as introductory subject/word in sentences with Be-Verb / Linking Verb, and the actual subject will follow the verb as illustrated below:

> There **is** a book on the table.   There **are** some books on the table.
> - please note the use of the verbs. Singular verb 'is' is used for singular subject 'a book', and plural verb 'are' is used for plural subject 'some books'.

1 b) When the subject is pronoun, the following sentence structure is followed:

Adverb of Place/Time + **Subject** + Complete Verb; e.g.,

There **you** are.	-	Subject is **'you'**
Up the hill **they** went.	-	Subject is **'they'**

2) Inversion of Subject and Auxiliary Verb of Action Verb is used with Negative/Restrictive Adverbs or Parallel Adverbs for emphasis using the following sentence structures as follows:

2 a) with Negative/Restrictive Adverbs:

Negative/Restrictive Adverb + Auxiliary + **Subject** + Main Verb; e.g.,

Under no circumstances can **we** accept it. = We can't accept it under any circumstances.

<u>Only then</u> did **I** understand the situation. = I understood the situation <u>only then</u>.
<u>Seldom</u> have **I** seen such a film. = I have <u>seldom</u> seen such a film.
<u>Rarely</u> could **she** have made a mistake. = She could <u>rarely</u> have made a mistake.
<u>Never</u> have **I** felt better. = I have <u>never</u> felt better.

2 b) <u>mutually dependent clauses with Negative/Restrictive Adverbs</u>:

<u>Negative/Restrictive Adverb</u> + Auxiliary + **Subject** + Main Verb
 + Other Complement + the Subordinate Clause; e.g.,

<u>Hardly</u> had **I** left <u>when</u> somebody called. = I had <u>hardly</u> left <u>when</u> somebody called.
<u>Scarcely</u> had **we** begun <u>when</u> the doorbell rang. = We had <u>scarcely</u> begun, <u>when</u> ...
<u>No sooner</u> has **she** finished her work <u>than</u> she was assigned a new work.
   = <u>As soon as</u> she has finished her work, she was assigned a new work.

2 c) Conditional Sentences with impossible conditions in which the Restrictive Adverb 'Only' can be omitted:

(<u>Only</u>) + Auxiliary + **Subject** + Main Verb + Other Complement + the Subordinate Clause; e.g.,

(<u>Only</u>) Had **I** known it, I would not have gone there. = If I had known it, I would ...
(<u>Only</u>) Were **he** rich, he would buy everything. = If he were rich, he would ...

This structure is also used for specifying what should be done on occurrence of a stated condition. For example,

Should **you** meet him, ask for his new address and phone number.

2 d) with <u>Parallel Adverbs referring to the action (verb) of previous clause/sentence</u>:

Independent Clause; <u>Parallel Adverb</u> + Auxiliary + **Subject** + Main Verb; e.g.,

In the following examples, words within brackets are omitted.

She works very hard; <u>as</u> do **her friends** (work).
I like apples. <u>So</u> does **he** (like).
I don't like oranges. <u>Neither</u> does **she** (like). / <u>Nor</u> does **she** (like).
He can't fly. <u>Neither</u> can **I** (fly). = I can't either.
He does not like apples; <u>nor</u> does **he** like oranges.

3) **Inversion of Subject and Be-Verb** is used with <u>Negative/Restrictive Adverbs</u> or <u>Parallel Adverbs</u> for emphasis using the following <u>sentence structures</u>:

3 a) <u>Negative/Restrictive Adverb</u> + Be-Verb + **Subject**; e.g.,

<u>Never</u> were **we** selfish.
<u>Rarely</u> can be **a theft** in this area.

Chapter-20: Inversion of Subject and Verb / Subject + Verb and Complement

3 b) Independent Clause; <u>Parallel Adverb</u> + Be-Verb + **Subject**; e.g.,

She is tall; <u>as</u> is **her mother**.
He can be a successful industrialist; <u>as</u> was **his father**.
Balu was not a teacher; <u>nor</u> was **his mother or father**.
I have been to Bengaluru; <u>so</u> have been **my friends**.

4) **Inversion of Subject and Be-Verb** with <u>Adjective Phrase / Noun Phrase</u>: It is used to emphasize the <u>subject complement</u> by placing it before the inverted Be-Verb and subject using the following <u>sentence structure</u>:

4 a) <u>Comparative Adjective Phrase</u> + Be-Verb + **Subject**; e.g.,

<u>Even more important</u> was **your behaviour** at the party.
= more emphatic than '**Your behaviour** at the party was <u>even more important</u>.'

4 b) <u>Adjective Phrase / Participle Phrase</u> + Be-Verb + **Subject**; e.g.,

<u>Safely hidden under the rock</u> was **the treasure**.
<u>Always coming first</u> is **our Boss**.
<u>Very happy with their performance recently</u> were **the Indian athletes**.
<u>Blessed</u> are **the ones** who love others.

4 c) <u>Adjective phrase with 'so' [+ Noun/Adjective Phrase]</u> + Be-Verb + **Subject** + that-clause; e.g.,

<u>So beautiful</u> is **she** that everyone would love her.
<u>So strong a man / A man so strong</u> is **he** that everyone would admire him.

5) **Inversion of Subject and Reporting Verbs:** It is used for reporting by somebody, say, a story writer / journalist, what was told/asked by other people as illustrated below:

"What do you know?" <u>asked</u> **Balu**.   "He wanted to inform you," <u>said</u> **Balu**.
"Please come here," <u>requested</u> **Balu**.   "What a wonderful day!" <u>exclaimed</u> **Balu**.

6) **Inversion of the order of modifiers in a noun phrase** for emphasis**:**

His love for <u>so wild a</u> friend is shocking. = His love for <u>a very wild</u> friend is shocking.

Chapter 21
Interrogative Sentences (Questions) - Advanced

We have already seen, in chapter 6, how to form questions for the sentences with basic sentence structures. In this chapter, we are going to see how to form questions for sentences with advanced sentence structures. The basic rules for forming the questions are same for the advanced questions also. However, the additional elements in the sentences such as verbal phrases, clauses, etc. are to be dealt with properly. The additional elements to be handled properly are underlined in the following discussion to highlight how they are handled.

1. Questions for sentences with action-like Linking Verb: Though what follows a linking verb is a subject complement, the question-words for verb complement may also have to be used as illustrated below:

  She will become a doctor.
    -   What will she become?
  The food smells good.
    -   How does the food smell?
  She has become beautiful.
    -   How/What has she become?

2. Question for sentences with Causative Verb: e.g.,

  I shall have the mechanic repair the bike.
    -   What shall I have the mechanic do?
    -   How shall I repair the bike?
  I shall have the bike repaired by the mechanic.
    -   What shall I have the bike being done?

3. Question for sentences with Perception Verb: e.g.,

  She saw him play/playing.
    -   What did she see him do?

4. Question for sentences with Thinking Verb: e.g.,

  We want them to serve the nation.
    -   What do we want them to do?

5. Questions for sentences with Prepositional Adjective Phrase: e.g.,

  I saw the book with a cover.
    -   Which book did I see?

Chapter-21: Interrogative Sentences (Questions) - Advanced

6. Questions for sentences with Prepositional Adverb Phrase: e.g.,

  A book is on the table.
  - Where / On what is the book?
  I play in the evening.
  - When do I play?

7. Questions for sentences with Prepositional Noun Phrase: e.g.,

  He shouted from inside the house.
  - Where did he shout from?

8. Questions for sentences with Gerund: These questions are same as for subject, object and subject complement because gerunds are functionally nouns.

9. Questions for sentences with Participle:

  a. <u>Participle used attributively:</u> These questions are same as for adjectives because such participles are functionally adjectives.

  b. <u>Participle used predicatively:</u> These questions are similar to the questions for adverbs. For example,:

  Playing well in the season, he scored many goals till now.
  - How did he score many goals till now?
  Walking along the beach, I saw her.
  - When did I see her?

10. Questions for sentences with Infinitive Noun Phrase: These questions are same as for subject, object and subject complement because infinitive noun phrases are functionally nouns.

11. Questions for sentences with Infinitive Adjective Phrase: These questions are same as for adjectives.

12. Questions for sentences with Infinitive Adverb Phrase: These questions are similar to the questions for adverbs. For example,

  We should study to get good marks.
  - Why should we study?

13. Questions for sentences with Noun Clause: e.g.,

  I believe that he is the best student.
  - Who believes that he is the best student?
  I believe that he is the best student.
  - What do I believe?
  I believe that he is the best student.
  - Who do I believe is the best student?

I believe that he is the best student.
- What do I believe that he is?
- What do I believe about him?

That he is the best student is well known.
- What is well known?

She knew that he would win the match.
- Who did she know would win the match?

She knew that he would win the match.
- What did she know he would win?

She predicted last month itself that he would win the match.
- When did she predict (that) he would win the match?

He is proud of how he played.
- What is he proud of?

14. Questions for sentences with Adjective Clause: e.g.,

A player who is very young will play this year.
- What kind of player will play this year?

A few tournaments, whichever are popular, are suitable for him.
- Which tournaments are suitable for him?

15. Questions for sentences with Adverb Clause: e.g.,

He will be happy when she wins the match.
- When will he be happy?

She will win the match if she prepares well.
- How will she win the match?

She plays continuously because she likes it.
- Why does she play continuously?

He will be happy if she wins the match.
- Who has to win the match if he is to be happy?

He will be happy if she wins the tournament this year itself.
- Who has to win and when should that person win if he is to be happy?

16. Questions for Degrees of Comparison of Adjectives/Adverbs: e.g.,

He is tall.
He is as tall as his friend is.
He is taller than his friend.
He is the tallest of all in the class.
- How tall is he?

He runs fast.
He runs as fast as his friend.
He runs faster than his friend.
He runs fastest of all in the class.
- How fast does he run?

Chapter 22
Punctuation

Punctuation is a set of symbols used to mark the different parts of sentences like beginning of the sentence, end of the sentence, order of words, etc. and also to change the stress/rhythm of reading the sentences. Common punctuation marks/symbols include the following:

comma (,)	period (full stop) (.)
question mark (?)	exclamation mark (!)
apostrophe (')	quotation mark (" ", ' ')
bracket ( )	dash (—)
hyphen (-)	ellipsis (…)
colon (:)	semicolon (;)

The uses of the punctuation marks are explained below:

I Terminating a sentence:

a) The period (.) is used to terminate the declarative sentences and the imperative sentences as illustrated below:

    We are learning punctuation now.
    Do not write without proper punctuation.

b) The question mark (?) is used to terminate the interrogative sentences as illustrated below:

    What do you think about punctuation?

c) The exclamation mark (!) is used to terminate the exclamatory sentences as illustrated below:

    How important the punctuation is!

II Separating units of a sentence:

a) The comma (,) is used to separate the items in a list; however, comma should not be used after the item which is just before the word 'and' as illustrated below:

    I like apple, orange, chocolate and cake.

b) The comma (,) is also used to separate the independent clauses in a compound sentence as illustrated below:

I wanted to eat cake, but it was sold out.

c) The comma (,) is also used to separate the Reporting Clause and the Reported Clause in Direct Speech as illustrated below:

He said, "I like apple, orange, chocolate and cake."

d) The double quotation mark (" ") is used to mark the Reported Clause in Direct Speech as illustrated below:

He said, "I like apple, orange, chocolate and cake."

e) The double quotation mark (" ") is also used to set off the words which are referred to or quoted but not used as a regular part of speech as illustrated below:

The name of the book is "How to cook delicious food."

f) The single quotation mark (' ') can also be used like the double quotation mark. However, it is generally used when something is to be quoted within another already quoted words as illustrated below:

They exclaimed, "He is the 'Super Star' today."

g) The semicolon (;) is also used to separate the independent clauses in a compound sentence as illustrated below:

It is difficult to get cake now; nevertheless, you should try.

h) The semicolon (;) and the comma (,) are used together to separate groups of items in a list as illustrated below:

I like many types of eatables: apple, orange and some more fruits; cake, bread and biscuit; cool drinks, ice-cream and milk-shakes and finally boiled items.

i) The colon (:) is used to introduce a list of items as illustrated just below:

There are so many places to enjoy: cinemas, parks, beach, hotels, play-ground, etc.

Chapter-22: Punctuation

j) The colon (:) is also used to separate the independent clauses in a compound sentence when the second independent clause is a summation of what is told in the first independent clause as illustrated below:

It was very late, and I thought I would miss the train: Eh! I got it.

k) The colon (:) is also used to separate the hour and the minutes in time expressions as illustrated below:

It was 1:13 PM.

l) The dash (—) is used to separate and emphasize some additional information in a sentence as illustrated below:

Her cooking — improvised by her imagination — is very good.

m) The parenthesis ( ) is used to give some additional information in a sentence as illustrated below:

Her cooking (except for a very few latest dishes) is very good.

n) The slash/oblique (/) is used to separate alternative words or phrases as illustrated in the subject of this sentence itself.

III Combining units of words:

a) The hyphen (-) is used to join compound words as illustrated below:

She cooks mouth-watering dishes for us.

b) The apostrophe (') is used to express the possessive case of nouns and the contractions as illustrated below:

I like my mother's cooking.
I couldn't resist her dishes.

IV Omission of words/phrases:

a) The ellipsis (…) is used to indicate the intentional omission of words because it is too long and/or can be understood from the context as illustrated below:

I had eaten all the items like cake, chocolate, … before my parents came.

b) The ellipsis (...) is also used to omit a part of the sentence quoted from some other writing as illustrated below:

Adelle Davis quoted that "Eat breakfast like a king ...a pauper."

In the above example, the actual quotation is "Eat breakfast like a king, lunch like a prince and dinner like a pauper."

c) Besides, the ellipsis (...) is used to indicate a deliberate silence or pause also as illustrated below:

I had eaten ... some fruits.   -   In this example, the ellipsis indicates a deliberate silence or pause because the speaker would possibly have hidden something.

V Capitalization: Capital letters are used in the following cases as illustrated with each rule below:

a) To begin a sentence:

An apple a day keeps the doctor away.

b) To begin the proper nouns and the adjectives derived from the proper nouns:

Many Tamil people have the name Murugan.

c) To begin the nouns and the pronouns which indicate the deity:

A Tamil said "Lord Murugan is our deity, and He always graces us."

d) Capitalization of governmental words such as government, department, office, bureau, secretariate, directorate, collectorate, federal, etc.: These words are to be capitalized when they are used specifically or officially but not generically.

The Government of India is a democratic government. (specific; generic)
The Department of Socail Welfare has announced new welfare schemes, and the Department will implement them within this year. (specific; official)
Some government offices are located in remote places. (generic)

e) Capitalization of job titles: The rule is similar to the above point. Besides, capitalize the titles if used before names but without comma.

The President of India addressed the presidents of other countries. (specific; generic)
The director of the board, Rajan, met Chairman Pradeep. (used before name with comma; used before name without comma)
We will try to meet director Steven Spielberg. (profession, not a title)

Chapter 23
Advanced Sentence Formation

I Using Absolute Phrases / Participle Phrases: Absolute phrases, explained in chapter 8 on Verbal Phrases, modify the whole sentence rather than a word like subject/object. In the following examples, the words/expression given within brackets are usually omitted:

> The mobile always ringing, he switched it off during the meeting.
> The meeting (being/having been) over, he switched on the mobile again.
> Having decided to expand their market, he tried to contact more dealers.
> He had to use the landline, his mobile's charge drained.
> He sent even e-mails, some dealers not answering.
> Finally, he went home, his work (being) completely over, his mind relaxing, his face (being) happy and his thought (being) full of his family.

II Loose Sentence: It is a long sentence with a number of details (phrases/clauses) attached to it *at the end of the sentence*. For example,:

> Finally, he went home, his work (being) completely over, his mind relaxing, his face (being) happy and his thought (being) full of his family.
>
> After the exams, students would plan to enjoy the holidays, playing outdoor, indoor and computer games, watching movies and TV, visiting relatives and friends and touring hill stations and sanctuaries.
>
> We can write to the local Government, appreciating some of their services, requesting to improve the infrastructure and even complaining about some problems.
>
> That was a good departmental store, spacious, clean, cheap and attentive.
>
> That was a good departmental store, all items available, all attendants neatly dressed, credit cards accepted and home delivery arranged.
>
> We met our old school teacher after we had enquired many people, after we had gone around many places, but, fortunately, just before he was about to leave the country.

III Periodic Sentence: It is a long sentence with a number of details (phrases/clauses) placed *at the beginning of the sentence*. For example,:

> Finally, his work (being) completely over, his mind relaxing, his face (being) happy and his thought (being) full of his family, he went home.
>
> Having worked very hard, travelled a long distance and studied a lot, he was very tired.
>
> If you study well, if you work hard, if you practice well and if you persevere, you will get the first rank.
>
> After you finish your work, after you eat and after you become totally free, you can come to my house to help me.

IV Using Appositives: Using appositives result in concise and precise sentences as illustrated below:

Balu, <u>intelligent and systematic</u>, studies regularly.
= (Being) intelligent and systematic, Balu studies regularly.
= Balu who is intelligent and systematic studies regularly.

Teachers like those students, <u>intelligent and systematic</u>.
= Teachers like those students, (being) intelligent and systematic.
= Teachers like those students who are intelligent and systematic.

Teachers trained some students, <u>less intelligent and unsystematic</u>, to improve them in their studies.
= Teachers trained some students, (being) <u>less intelligent and unsystematic</u>, to improve them in their studies.
= Teachers trained some students who are <u>less intelligent and unsystematic</u>, to improve them in their studies.

Appositive, <u>just introduced in chapter 1</u>, is illustrated more here.
= Appositive, which is introduced in chapter 1, is illustrated more here.

V Parallel Structure: The main requirement of the parallel structure is the use of same type of constructs (word/phrase/expression/clause) for related ideas in the same sentence. For example, if we use infinitive for one action, we should use the same for other actions too, but we should not use infinitive for one action and gerund for another action as illustrated below:

I want to <u>play</u>, <u>ride</u>, <u>dance</u> and <u>enjoy</u>.	- parallel and correct
I want to <u>play</u>, <u>ride</u>, **dancing** and <u>enjoy</u>.	- not parallel and incorrect
He is <u>tall</u>, <u>handsome</u> and <u>intelligent</u>.	- parallel and correct
He is <u>tall</u>, <u>handsome</u> and **an intelligent boy**.	- not parallel and incorrect
<u>Playing games</u> like football is better than <u>watching TV</u>.	- parallel and correct
<u>Playing games</u> like football is better than **to watch TV**.	- not parallel and incorrect
Children like those who <u>love</u>, <u>care</u> and <u>pamper</u>.	- parallel and correct
Children like those <u>who love</u>, <u>who care</u> and <u>who pamper</u>.	- parallel and correct
Children like those <u>who love</u>, <u>care</u> and **who pamper**.	- not parallel and incorrect

The teacher advised the students <u>that they should attend the classes regularly</u>, <u>that they should listen carefully</u>, <u>that they should not talk among them during the class</u> and <u>that they should try to get good marks in all the subjects</u>. - parallel and correct

The teacher advised the students <u>that they should attend the classes regularly</u>, <u>that they should listen carefully</u>, <u>that they should not talk among them during the class</u> and **to try to get good marks in all the subjects.** - not parallel and incorrect

Chapter-23: Advanced Sentence Formation 203

I like her <u>beauty</u>, <u>character</u>, <u>quality</u> and <u>ability</u>.	- parallel and correct
I like her <u>beauty</u>, <u>character</u>, <u>quality</u> and **her ability.**	- not parallel and incorrect
Either <u>I like her</u> or <u>I don't (like her)</u>.	- parallel and correct
Either <u>I like her</u> or **not**.	- not parallel and incorrect
I like her not only <u>for her beauty</u> but also <u>for her intelligence</u>.	- parallel and correct
I like her not only <u>for her beauty</u> but also **that she is intelligent**.	- not parallel ...
I like her not only <u>for her beauty</u> but also **for intelligence**.	- not parallel ...
He has neither <u>the money</u> nor <u>the ability</u> to finish the work.	- parallel and correct
He has neither <u>the money</u> nor **is he able** to finish the work.	- not parallel ...
She <u>was studying</u> well and <u>will study</u> well.	- parallel and correct
She **was** and <u>will study</u> well. - incorrect because 'was' cannot be combined with 'study'	

VI <u>Fragments</u>: A group of words used as a sentence is called a fragment if there is no finite/complete verb or if a subordinate/dependent clause is used without a main/independent clause. We should not use the fragments generally as illustrated below:

<u>The ability to finish in time</u>.	-	a phrase and a fragment; incorrect as a sentence
He has <u>the ability to finish in time</u>.	-	a phrase and a part of a complete (correct) sentence
<u>When I met her</u>.	-	a subordinate/dependent clause and a fragment; incorrect as a sentence
<u>When I met her</u>, she was playing.	-	a subordinate/dependent clause and a part of a complete (correct) sentence

However, they can be used for very limited and specific purposes as illustrated below:

a) <u>Answering a question</u>:

   At what time are you going to finish?   Five o' clock. (accepted as a sentence)
   Who won the match?   India. (accepted as a sentence)

b) <u>Answering a question emphatically</u>:

What is his speciality? <u>The ability to finish on time</u>. / <u>Punctuality</u>. / <u>Devotion to the work</u>.
  - The above underlined words are fragments; however, they are accepted as sentences.

c) <u>In exclamation</u>:   An award winning movie! (accepted as a sentence)
                                  Not really! (accepted as a sentence)

d) <u>As a transitional element</u>:   At last, the result. (accepted as a sentence)

VII Elliptical Sentences: In elliptical sentences, some words are deliberately left out because they can be guessed. Functionally, the words are omitted simply because they can be guessed from the context or because the repetition of the same words can be avoided. Strictly speaking, an elliptical sentence may seem incorrect, but it is generally accepted and used because it is more concise and elegant as (it is) illustrated below with the underlined parts dropped:

After (<u>we had gone to</u>) London, we went to Paris.   - contextual guessing
Though (<u>she is</u>) beautiful, she is very humble.   - avoiding repetition
He can speak English, but his friend can't (<u>speak English</u>).   - avoiding repetition
She is more beautiful than Miss World (<u>is</u>).   - avoiding repetition
There are many books, but I need just one (<u>book</u>).   - avoiding repetition
They have some strategy; however, I don't know what
              (<u>strategy they have</u>).   - contextual guessing
You can call me whenever (<u>you are</u>) free.   - contextual guessing
At last, the results having been announced;
    Rama got first rank, Sona (<u>got</u>) second rank
    and Kala (<u>got</u>) third (<u>rank</u>).   - avoiding repetition
If you study biology, you can become a doctor, and if
    (<u>you study</u>) Maths, (<u>you can become</u>) an engineer.   - avoiding repetition

Some patterns for Elliptical Sentences: Structurally, the elliptical sentences can be formed with the following patterns as illustrated with each pattern below:

a) Omitting main verb after auxiliary verb:

"She asked you to phone her." "I will (<u>phone her</u>)."

"You must study now." "Yes, I am (<u>studying now</u>)."

b) Using only first word of the auxiliary verb when the auxiliary verb has more than one word:

"He would not have finished the work." "Yes, He would (<u>have finished</u>)." Or
              "No, He would not (<u>have finished</u>)."

c) Using the verb 'do' instead of repeating the main verb:

"She finished the work." "I *did* as well." (= <u>I also finished the work</u>).

d) Omitting main verb after 'to' in infinitives:

"She asked you to phone her." "Of course, I have to (<u>phone her</u>)."
"You must study now." "No, I don't have to (<u>study now</u>)."

Chapter-23: Advanced Sentence Formation

e) Tag questions (explained in Chapter 6 on Interrogative Sentences - Questions):

You are a student, aren't you (<u>a student</u>)?
You are not a teacher, are you (<u>a teacher</u>)?

f) Omitting the noun after adjective:

"Which dress do you want?" "I want the red (<u>dress/one</u>)."

g) Omitting the participle 'being' before adjective:

(<u>Being</u>) Beautiful and rich, she is proud.
(<u>Being</u>) True to his parents, he always obeys them.

h) Omitting the gerund 'being' before adjective:

Their statement is accepted as (<u>being</u>) true.

i) Single word substitution:

"Can you finish the work?" "I think *so*." (= <u>I think that I can finish the work</u>).
"What kind of invitation do you expect?" "A formal *one*." (= <u>A formal invitation</u>).

j) Single word substitution with inversion of subject and auxiliary verb / main verb:

He has finished the work. *So* has she. (= <u>She has also finished the work</u>).
He has not finished the work. *Neither* has she. (= <u>She has not also finished the work</u>).
She is tall; *as* is her mother. (= <u>She is also tall like her mother</u>).

k) Omission of the expression 'Let (it)' in standard expressions:

(<u>Let it</u>) Come what may, I will face it.   (<u>Let/May</u>) God bless you!

l) Omission of the expression 'Let noun/pronoun' for emphasis:

(<u>Let her</u>) Try as she might (<u>do</u>), (<u>but</u>) she cannot finish it.

m) Omission of the introductory subject 'it' and its be-verb:

As (<u>it is</u>) always, she did the talking.
The problem can be solved as (<u>it was</u>) done earlier.

n) With some coordinating conjunctions, namely and, but & or:

I studied and (<u>I</u>) wrote the poem.   They are my friends and (<u>my</u>) relatives.
She is beautiful but (<u>she is</u>) simple.   You must study or (<u>you must</u>) sleep now.

o) After certain subordinating conjunctions like though, while, etc.:

After (<u>we had gone to</u>) London, we went to Paris.
Though (<u>she is</u>) beautiful, she is very humble.
While / Though (<u>he is</u>) welcoming the new proposal, he expresses some reservations.
You can buy a new pen if / when (<u>it is</u>) really required.

Informal Elliptical Sentences: Some structures of the elliptical sentences can be used only informally and are considered incorrect/wrong formally. For example,:

(She) Wonders what to do.		(I) Hope to see you again.
(It) Won't work.		(I) May see you tomorrow.
(I) Haven't seen him.	but not	(I) Have seen him.
(He is) Coming tomorrow.	but not	He (is) coming tomorrow.
You (are) ready?		Ready?
(Have you) Got a pen?		(Does) Anybody want more?

Incorrect Elliptical Sentences: Though some words can be omitted in elliptical sentences, the omission of words should not result in either a grammatically incorrect sentence or a semantically (i.e., by meaning) incorrect sentence. As a specific example, be-verb should not be used alone without subject as illustrated below:

Though (she) is beautiful, she is very humble.	-	incorrect
Though (she is) beautiful, she is very humble.	-	correct
You can call me whenever (you) are free.	-	incorrect
You can call me whenever (you are) free.	-	correct
The problem can be solved as (it) was done earlier.	-	correct*

* though verb is used without the subject, it is still correct because the subject 'it' is only an introductory subject.

The problem can be solved as (it was) done earlier.	-	correct
More students passed than (the number of students) failed.	-	correct*

* though verb 'failed' is used without the subject, it is still correct because the conjunction 'than' joins both the verbs 'passed' and 'failed.'

VIII <u>**Other topics on Advanced Sentences:**</u> Other topics related to advanced sentence formation would include the inversion of subject, verb and complement as explained in chapter 20, the figures of speech as explained in chapter 29, the use of appropriate pre-modifiers in degrees of comparison of adjectives and adverbs as explained in chapter 12 and chapter 14 respectively, the correct use of conditional sentences, subjunctive sentences, causative verbs, perception verbs, thinking verbs and verbs of opinion/knowledge as explained in chapter 7 and the appropriate use of idioms, proverbs and quotations as explained in chapter 27.

Chapter 24
Same Words - Different Parts of Speech

Same words can be used as different parts of speech as illustrated below:

He has a <u>fast</u> car. (Adjective)   He can run <u>fast</u>. (Adverb)
Some people <u>fast</u> for festivals. (Verb)   They end the <u>fast</u> the next day. (Noun)

Some of the common differently used words are illustrated below:

about	- preposition	-	related to: He knows everything <u>about</u> her.
	- adverb	-	approximately, nearly: The entry fees is <u>about</u> ₹500.
		-	aimlessly: They roamed <u>about</u> in the market.
above	- preposition	-	at a higher place/position; more than: Her salary is <u>above</u> his salary.
	- adverb	-	at/to a higher place/position: She lives just <u>above</u>.
	- adjective	-	at a higher place/position: Answer the <u>above</u> questions.
below	- preposition	-	at a lower place/position; less than: His salary is <u>below</u> her salary.
	- adverb	-	at/to a lower place/position: She lives just <u>below</u>.
left	- adverb	-	towards left: You have to turn <u>left</u> now.
	- adjective	-	of the left: Raise your <u>left</u> hand.
	- noun	-	the left side: He lives in the first <u>left</u>.
right			(it can also be used just like 'left')
after	- preposition	-	at a later time/place/position: We can meet <u>after</u> lunch.
	- adverb	-	afterwards: She realized soon <u>after</u>.
	- conjunction	-	at a time later than something: Marks will be given <u>after</u> papers are corrected.
before	- preposition	-	at an earlier time/place/position: We must meet <u>before</u> lunch.
	- adverb	-	in the past, not now: We had met <u>before</u>.
	- conjunction	-	at a time earlier than something: Papers are to be corrected <u>before</u> the marks are given.
next	- adverb	-	afterwards: We can meet <u>next</u>.
	- adjective	-	coming immediately after: The <u>next</u> train to Madurai is at 12:30 pm.

near	- preposition	-	at a short distance/time away from something: We live <u>near</u> the market.
	- adjective	-	at a short distance/time away: The venue of the meeting is just <u>near</u>.
	- adverb	-	at a short distance/time away: The exams are drawing <u>near</u>.
	- verb	-	get closer: The book is <u>nearing</u> completion.
far	- adverb	-	at a long distance away: We have to go <u>far</u>.
	- adjective	-	at a long distance away: Our house is at the <u>far</u> end of the road.
all	- adverb	-	completely, very much: He was <u>all</u> excited about the journey.
	- determiner	-	the whole lot/number of: He himself ate <u>all</u> the cake.
	- pronoun	-	all people/things: <u>All</u> are welcome.
any	- adverb	-	used as emphasizing pre-modifier in negative sentences: He was not <u>any</u> better.
	- determiner	-	the nothing of (used in negative sentences): He did not eat <u>any</u> cake.
	- pronoun	-	nothing (used in negative sentences): We did not get <u>any</u> of the medals.
some	- adverb	-	approximately (used before numbers): <u>Some</u> ten applications came.
	- determiner	-	some number of: We could scrutinize <u>some</u> applications only.
	- pronoun	-	some people/things: <u>Some</u> came for the interview.
few	- determiner	-	two or some more in number (countable): We could scrutinize a <u>few</u> applications only.
	- pronoun	-	two or some more people/things (countable): <u>Few</u> came for the interview.
many	- determiner	-	a lot more in number (countable): We could scrutinize <u>many</u> applications today.
	- pronoun	-	a lot more people/things (countable): <u>Many</u> came for the interview.
little	- adverb	-	slightly: She slept only <u>little</u> last night.
	- determiner/ adjective	-	some (uncountable): We got <u>little</u> appreciation only for our hard work.
	- noun	-	some (uncountable): We got a <u>little</u> only.

Chapter-24: Same Words - Different Parts of Speech

much	- adverb	-	to a great degree: She is <u>much</u> better now.
	- determiner/ adjective	-	a lot of (uncountable): We got <u>much</u> appreciation for our little work.
	- pronoun	-	lot (uncountable): <u>Much</u> is unknown even today.
enough	- adverb	-	adequately (used after adjectives/adverbs): This place is not good <u>enough</u> to live in.
	- determiner	-	adequate: There is not <u>enough</u> food.
	- pronoun	-	adequate amount/more than what is acceptable: I had <u>enough</u> of this.
like	- preposition	-	similar to somebody/something: He treated me <u>like</u> a friend.
	- adjective	-	similar: 2/4 and 3/4 are <u>like</u> fractions.
	- conjunction	-	in the same way: He plays well, <u>like</u> he studies hard.
	- verb	-	want/enjoy something because it is attractive: She will certainly <u>like</u> you.
as	- preposition	-	like somebody/something: He treated me <u>as</u> a friend.
	- adverb	-	(used for comparison): She is <u>as</u> beautiful as her sister.
	- conjunction	-	for the reason of: He will get good marks <u>as</u> he studies hard.
	- relative pronoun	-	like: She will select the same dress <u>as</u> I do.
but	- preposition	-	other than something: He did everything <u>but</u> one.
	- conjunction	-	however: They worked hard, <u>but</u> they could not complete.
except	- preposition	-	other than something: He did everything <u>except</u> one.
	- conjunction	-	unless: I will not pay him <u>except</u> he completes the work.
down	- preposition	-	from a higher point to a lower point: A stone rolled <u>down</u> the hill.
	- adverb	-	from a higher point to a lower point: Prices may go <u>down</u>.
	- adjective	-	coming into; not functioning: The <u>down</u> train is at 7 pm. The computer is <u>down</u>.
	- noun	-	lower point/position: There are <u>ups</u> and <u>downs</u> in the life.
	- verb	-	bring down to stop (informal): The pilot had to <u>down</u> the plane suddenly.

up	- preposition	-	from a lower point to a higher point: They went <u>up</u> the hill.
	- adverb	-	from a lower point to a higher point: Prices may go <u>up</u>.
	- adjective	-	going out; functioning: The <u>up</u> train is at 7 pm. The computer is <u>up</u>.
	- noun	-	higher point/position: There are <u>ups</u> and <u>downs</u> in the life.
	- verb	-	raise: The brokers <u>upped</u> the prices of the lands.
either	- determiner	-	one or the other of two: You can give <u>either</u> book.
	- adverb	-	refers to a similar situation in a negative sentence: He cannot go. I cannot <u>either</u>.
	- conjunction	-	this or that: He is <u>either</u> an Indian <u>or</u> a Pakistani.
	- pronoun	-	one or the other of the two: "Which one do you want?" "<u>Either</u> is OK."
neither	- determiner	-	none of the two: You gave <u>neither</u> book.
	- adverb	-	refers to a similar situation in a negative sentence: He cannot go. <u>Neither</u> can I.
	- conjunction	-	not this and also not that: He is <u>neither</u> an Indian <u>nor</u> a Pakistani.
	- pronoun	-	none of the two: "Which one do you want?" "<u>Neither</u> is OK."
else	- adverb	-	some other; any other; different: She cannot go anywhere <u>else</u>.
	- adjective	-	some other; any other; different: Do you want anything <u>else</u>?
	- conjunction	-	if not; otherwise: Study well, <u>else</u> it is difficult to get good marks.
even	- adverb	-	pre-modifier to express surprise or to express something strongly: You cannot go there <u>even</u> now.
	- adjective	-	smooth; same phase; equal: We need <u>even</u> surface to play.
	- verb	-	smoothen; equal: They will <u>even</u> the surface. Try to <u>even</u> the score.
for	- preposition	-	related to; concerning: We need books <u>for</u> children.
	- conjunction	-	because: He danced well <u>for</u> he practiced a lot.

Chapter-24: Same Words - Different Parts of Speech

need(s)	- verb	-	requires: He <u>needs</u> books for children.
	- modal verb	-	required to: He <u>need</u> not come now.
	- noun	-	requirements: His <u>needs</u> are just a few.
no	- determiner	-	not any: <u>No</u> candidate is stronger.
	- adverb	-	answer for a question: "Are you coming?" "<u>No</u>, I am not."
		-	not: He is <u>no</u> longer living here.
	- noun	-	the answer 'no': I did not expect a <u>no</u> from you.
yes	- adverb	-	answer for a question: "Are you coming?" "<u>Yes</u>, I am."
	- noun	-	the answer 'yes': I just want an <u>yes</u> from you.
one	- determiner	-	some: We shall meet <u>one</u> day.
	- noun/pronoun	-	anything/anybody: <u>One</u> may be surprised.
once	- adverb	-	one time: We have met <u>once</u>.
	- conjunction	-	as soon as; when: <u>Once</u> you reach the station, please call me.
only	- adverb	-	restricted to: <u>Only</u> three persons are allowed in an auto.
	- adjective	-	restricted to: Is she the <u>only</u> female in the group?
	- conjunction	-	except that; but: I would come, <u>only</u> I have work.
round	- preposition	-	in a roundabout motion: The earth moves <u>round</u> the sun.
		-	on the other side of something: His house is just <u>round</u> the market.
	- adverb	-	in a circular way: He has to turn <u>round</u> to reach his house.
	- adjective	-	circular: The earth is <u>round</u>.
	- noun	-	a stage of a series of events: She won the first <u>round</u> of the tournament easily.
	- verb	-	go around something: We <u>rounded</u> the market many times.
		-	approximate a number: We have to <u>round</u> our total income to the next tens.
since	- preposition	-	from: We have been living here <u>since</u> 2000.
	- adverb	-	from some time in the past: They did not meet ever <u>since</u>.
	- conjunction	-	till now; because: It is ten years <u>since</u> I met him last. I invited him <u>since</u> he was my friend.
so	- adverb	-	very much: He was <u>so</u> happy to meet her.
	- conjunction	-	therefore: I could not meet him, <u>so</u> I phoned him.

still	- adverb	-	until now: He <u>still</u> loves her.
	- adjective	-	not moving: The water is <u>still</u> here.
	- noun	-	photo; calmness:
			It is a <u>still</u> from the new cinema.
			We can feel the <u>still</u> of the night.
	- verb	-	become/make calm and quiet:
			She tried to <u>still</u> her frightened child.
such	- determiner	-	of some type:
			I never faced <u>such</u> a situation.
	- pronoun	-	: <u>Such</u> was her happiness.
that	- determiner	-	referring to somebody/something not near:
			I saw <u>that</u> movie yesterday.
	- pronoun	-	referring to somebody/something not near:
			<u>That</u> is the right answer.
	- adverb	-	pre-modifier for adjectives/adverbs:
			It was not <u>that</u> easy to meet the minister.
	- relative pronoun	-	referring to the antecedent:
			I got back the pen <u>that</u> was lost.
	- conjunction	-	introducing a noun clause:
			He told <u>that</u> he had gone to cinema yesterday.
till	- preposition	-	until: We cannot stop <u>till</u> 6 pm.
	- conjunction	-	until: We cannot stop <u>till</u> it is over.
well	- adverb	-	: She studied <u>well</u>.
	- adjective	-	: He is/feels <u>well</u> now.
	- interjection	-	used to introduce something we say; used as a mark of our feeling/opinion not expressed explicitly:
			<u>Well</u>, as I told earlier …
			<u>Well</u>, I am not sure.
			<u>Well</u>, I think you start now.
	- noun	-	a hole in the ground for water/oil:
			We have a <u>well</u> in our house.
while	- conjunction	-	used to contrast two things; during the same time:
			<u>While</u> I like biscuit, he likes chocolate.
			He was studying <u>while</u> his mother was cooking.
	- noun	-	a period of time:
			We have not spoken for a <u>while</u>.
	- verb	-	spend the time lazily:
			Do not <u>while</u> away the useful time.
yet	- adverb	-	still; even now; even up to this time:
			He has not <u>yet</u> replied.
	- conjunction	-	nevertheless:
			It is cloudy, <u>yet</u> it is hot.

Chapter 25
Compound Words, Compound Adjectives and Compound Adverbs

I Compound words: The words formed by combining two words together as a single word are called compound words. Some are illustrated below:

news	+	paper	=	newspaper
bed	+	room	=	bedroom
hand	+	some	=	handsome

Compound words can be any parts of speech. There are thousands of such compound words available in English. A good dictionary or a vocabulary book will help you to learn such words. However, some of the commonly used first word of compound words are given below, and they can be used to form compound words using a good dictionary.

air	as in	aircraft	back	as in	background
bed	as in	bedroom	black	as in	blacksmith
butter	as in	butterfly	copy	as in	copyright
counter	as in	counterfoil	cross	as in	crossbar
cut	as in	cut-out	day	as in	daylight
door	as in	doormat	down	as in	downstairs
earth	as in	earthquake	end	as in	endpoint
eye	as in	eyewash	fire	as in	fireman
foot	as in	footboard	fore	as in	forenoon
free	as in	freedom	grand	as in	grandmother
hair	as in	haircut	hand	as in	handbag
hard	as in	hardship	head	as in	headache
high	as in	highland	home	as in	homeland
house	as in	housewife	ice	as in	iceberg
in	as in	income	key	as in	keyboard
king	as in	kingdom	land	as in	landmark
life	as in	lifetime	light	as in	lighthouse
low	as in	lowland	main	as in	mainland
man	as in	mankind	master	as in	mastermind
middle	as in	middleman	news	as in	news-stand
night	as in	nightclub	off	as in	offshore
out	as in	outgoing	over	as in	overact
pass	as in	password	pay	as in	payroll
pin	as in	pinpoint	play	as in	playground
rain	as in	rainwater	run	as in	runway
sand	as in	sandbox	school	as in	schoolbag
sea	as in	seacoast	ship	as in	shipyard

213

short	as in	shortcoming	show	as in	showcase
side	as in	sideline	sky	as in	skyscraper
snow	as in	snowfall	some	as in	somebody
step	as in	stepsister	stop	as in	stopgap
sun	as in	sunflower	super	as in	superman
sweet	as in	sweetbread	table	as in	tablecloth
thumb	as in	thumbnail	thunder	as in	thunderstorm
time	as in	timetable	top	as in	topmost
turn	as in	turnover	type	as in	typewriter
under	as in	underarm	up	as in	upstairs
wall	as in	wallpaper	war	as in	warpath
wash	as in	washout	water	as in	waterfall
wind	as in	windmill	with	as in	within
wood	as in	woodcutter	yard	as in	yardstick

If you refer to a good dictionary for these first words, you can find many other compound words for them.

Some compound words have got <u>very formal or legal or official</u> uses and are not commonly used. Moreover, their meanings are also not very straightforward. They are illustrated below. The following list includes a few commonly used other words also.

whereabouts		-	the place where somebody/something is in: e.g.,
	- noun	-	<u>Whereabouts</u> of the missing person is not yet known.
whereas		-	used to compare two unrelated/contrasting facts: e.g.,
	- conjunction	-	He is a tennis player <u>whereas</u> his sister is a singer.
whereby		-	by which; because of which: e.g.,
	- adverb	-	We have a scheme <u>whereby</u> you can easily pay the debt.
wherein		-	exactly in which place/position: e.g.,
	- adverb	-	<u>Wherein</u> have we gone wrong in our plan?
	- conjunction	-	I can tell <u>wherein</u> we have gone wrong.
whereof		-	of/about what or of/about which: e.g.,
	- conjunction	-	She does not really know <u>whereof</u> she speaks.
whereupon		-	as a result of this; therefore: e.g.,
	- conjunction	-	They accused each other, <u>whereupon</u> the problem started.
wherever		-	in any place; 'where' with surprise: e.g.,
	- conjunction	-	He becomes popular <u>wherever</u> he goes.
	- adverb	-	<u>Wherever</u> has he gone? ('where' with surprise)
wherewithal		-	requirements like money, things, skill, power, etc.: e.g.,
	- noun	-	They lack the <u>wherewithal</u> to complete the work.
thereabouts		-	near some place or roughly: e.g.,
	- noun	-	They have come from Nellai or <u>thereabouts</u>.

Chapter-25: Compounds Words, Compound Adjectives and Compound Adverbs

thereafter		-	after that time: e.g.,
	- adverb	-	He joined the army and did not return <u>thereafter</u>.
thereby		-	through which; as a result of which: e.g.,
	- adverb	-	We teach the poor children, <u>thereby</u> helping them to learn.
therefore		-	due to which; as a result of which: e.g.,
	- adverb	-	She had studied very hard; <u>therefore</u>, she got good marks.
therefrom		-	from that point/thing/place: e.g.,
	- adverb	-	They studied the problem and other issues arising <u>therefrom</u>.
therein		-	in/within that thing: e.g.,
	- adverb	-	We will repair the engine and anything contained <u>therein.</u>
thereof		-	of the thing mentioned there: e.g.,
	- adverb	-	Police seized all documents and any paper <u>thereof</u>.
thereon		-	on/about the thing mentioned there: e.g.,
	- adverb	-	The meeting will discuss that point and any reports <u>thereon.</u>
thereto		-	to the thing mentioned there: e.g.,
	- adverb	-	He has to hand over the house and the land attached <u>thereto.</u>
thereunder		-	under the thing mentioned there: e.g.,
	- adverb	-	You got the benefits under the plan and any schemes <u>thereunder.</u>
thereupon		-	immediately after that: e.g.,
	- adverb	-	I got a medal, and my friends <u>thereupon</u> cheered me up.
therewith		-	with the thing mentioned there: e.g.,
	- adverb	-	You will get everything mentioned <u>therewith</u>.
hereabouts		-	near/around this place: e.g.,
	- noun	-	They must have come from <u>hereabouts</u>.
hereafter		-	after this place/point: e.g.,
	- adverb	-	<u>Hereafter,</u> he would be referred to as the benefactor.
hereby		-	through this; as a result of this: e.g.,
	- adverb	-	We <u>hereby</u> declare our innocence.
herein		-	in/within this thing: e.g.,
	- adverb	-	Nobody wants to see reason now, and <u>herein</u> lies the problem.
hereof		-	of the thing mentioned here: e.g.,
	- adverb	-	Finish the work before the date mentioned <u>hereof</u>.
hereupon		-	immediately after this: e.g.,
	- adverb	-	You can expect people to make a beeline <u>hereupon</u>.

herewith	-	with the thing mentioned here; with this: e.g.,
- adverb	-	I <u>herewith</u> attach the necessary documents.
henceforth	-	from some particular time and thereafter fully: e.g.,
- adverb	-	He got the first rank once, and <u>henceforth</u> he did not turn back.
halfway	-	in the middle between two places/times/positions: e.g.,
- adverb	-	It is just <u>halfway</u> between Chennai and Tirunelveli.

The following words are also compound words; however, the root/base words of these words are so merged/synthesized together that they do not look like compound words any longer. Besides, they are not commonly used now.

thither (to + there)
whence (from + where)
thence (from + there/that place/position)

II <u>**Compound-Adjectives:**</u> Two or more words are combined with hyphens to form adjectives specifically, and such words are called compound adjectives as illustrated below:

Mumbai is a <u>thickly-populated</u> city.
               compound adjective

Forms of Compound-Adjectives: Compound adjectives are formed in the following ways:

1) Adverb + present/past Participle:

Mumbai is a <u>densely-populated</u> city.
Mumbai has <u>brightly-lit</u> streets.
Mumbai's traffic is a <u>never-ending</u> story.

The adverb + participle combination is hyphenated and used as a single adjective only when they are used attributively as illustrated above. However, they are not combined together but used as adverb and participle (adjective) separately when they are used predicatively as illustrated below:

Mumbai is <u>densely populated</u>.
Mumbai's streets are <u>brightly lit</u>.

Chapter-25: Compounds Words, Compound Adjectives and Compound Adverbs

2) Adjective + present/past Participle:

Open-minded Mumbaikars are fashion-conscious.
They are broad-minded, not narrow-minded.
Are Mumbaikars kind-hearted and well-behaved?
Visiting Mumbai may have long-lasting and far-reaching effects.

3) Noun + present/past Participle:

The record-breaking hotels of Mumbai have mouth-watering dishes.
Yet, Mumbaikars' home-made dishes are more delicious.
Are Mumbaikars money-minded, and do they believe in market-driven economy?

4) Other combinations:

a) **noun + noun:** Mumbai is popular for its road-side dishes.

b) **noun + adjective:** Mumbai is world-famous, but is it trouble-free?

c) **adjective + noun:** What do we like to dress up, full-length or half-length mirror?

d) **number + noun:** I have a four-storey building in Mumbai.

III Compound-Adverbs: Like compound adjectives, compound adverbs are also formed specifically. However, they are not as common as compound adjectives. They are illustrated below:

The culprits got off scot-free at the end.
You can pay your loan interest-free now.
Do not drive catty-cornered across the road.

Chapter 26
Collocation and Patterns for words

Generally, words are combined together to make meaningful phrases and sentences according to the rules of the parts of speech and the sentence structures. However, all words are not combined with other words just according to the rules alone even if they are grammatically correct. In English, there is a tendency to use certain words with certain other words only and to use certain words in some specific verb/sentence patterns only. Such use of the words is the topic of this chapter.

I Collocation: If particular words tend to occur or belong together, it is called a collocation. For example, we always say 'beautiful girl' to describe a good-looking girl and 'handsome boy' to describe a good-looking boy, but we don't say 'beautiful boy' or 'handsome girl' though they would also mean the same thing and are grammatically correct. Therefore, 'beautiful girl' and 'handsome boy' are examples of collocation because they always tend to occur together.

How to form collocation: Unfortunately, there is no fixed rule for forming collocations, and they are formed just out of experience and observation over a period of time, because such collocations have been in use for a long period since the past. However, we have to know that most of the collocations are formed in the following combination of words:

1) adjectives and nouns	as in	'beautiful girl' but 'handsome boy'
2) verbs and nouns	as in	'do the work' but 'make a progress'
3) verbs and adjectives	as in	'feel happy' but 'get angry'
4) verbs and adverbs	as in	'go ahead' and 'come back'
5) adverbs and adjectives	as in	'extremely painful' and 'absolutely terrible'
6) adverbs and verbs	as in	'categorically deny' but 'honestly believe'
7) complex prepositions	as in	'with respect to' and 'in spite of'

A good dictionary can help you to form the correct collocations if you know one of the words, preferably the key word, to be combined. Some common collocations are given below:

Chapter-26: Collocation and Patterns for Words

1) adjective and noun collocations:

   <u>rotten</u> egg, fish
   <u>stale</u> bread, biscuits
   <u>sour</u> milk, cream
   <u>big</u> asset, house, picture, problem, question, mistake, surprise, brother, eater, dreamer
   <u>great</u> effect, extent, idea, impact, fun, pleasure, joy, pride, strength, skill
   <u>large</u> majority, population, quantity, scale, number
       (<u>big</u> is used for item, happenings and persons, <u>great</u> for feelings and qualities
         and <u>large</u> for number and measurements)
   <u>grand</u> event, opera, success, tour
   <u>heavy</u> suitcase, smoker, meals, cold, week, causalities, rain
   <u>light</u> suitcase, meals, week, causalities
   <u>slight</u> cold, chance, accent, damage, shortage
   <u>strong</u> influence, views, support, case, chance, accent
   <u>weak</u> influence, case, subject
   <u>severe</u> weather, shortage, pressure, penalties
   <u>mild</u> weather
   <u>lenient</u> penalty
   <u>hard/difficult</u> exam, question, day, life, times
   <u>easy</u> exam, question, day, life, times
   <u>deep</u> sleep, feeling, devotion, depression
   <u>high/low</u> cost, density, energy, expectation, opinion, pressure, price, quality, speed
   <u>absolute</u> agony, despair
   <u>utter</u> loathing, fury, catastrophe
   <u>total</u> ecstasy, bliss, madness
   <u>complete</u> astonishment
   <u>heartfelt</u> wishes, condolences

2) <u>verb and noun collocations:</u>

   <u>have</u> breakfast, dinner, a drink, a tea, a walk, a bath, a test
   <u>have</u> a holiday, a relationship, time, a haircut, a headache, a problem
   <u>do</u> some exercise, a job/work, homework, the housework, an examination, cleaning
   <u>do</u> a favour, business, nothing, the shopping, the cooking, one's best
   <u>make</u> dinner, bed, a mess, trouble, peace, some tea, a change, a decision, an effort
   <u>make</u> a noise, furniture, money, mistake
       (<u>do</u> is generally used for daily activities/work and general ideas, and
         <u>make</u> is used for constructing or creating something that we can touch and see)
   <u>break</u> ice, his/her heart, a leg, a news, a habit, the rule/law, a promise, a record
   <u>get</u> a job, the sack, home, a surprise, permission, the message

catch a mouse, fire, a ball, a bus, a flight, a cold, a thief, someone's attention
keep a diary, a promise, someone's place, the change, control
keep an appointment, a secret, a pet
pay a visit, cash, a salary, interest, attention, the price, the bill
find a cure, the answer, a way, a solution, the money, happiness, time
find a partner, a replacement, space
save space, energy, time, electricity, money, someone's seat, oneself trouble
take a break, a chance, a seat, notes, a taxi, a look, an exam, rest
miss a goal, somebody, a point, a chance/opportunity, a flight, an appointment, a lesson

3) verb and adjective collocations:

get ready, wet, angry, burnt, divorced, married, started, worried, lost, frightened
feel proud, disappointed, free, comfortable, sleepy, happy, hurt, old, nervous, tense
keep quiet, calm
go quiet, wild, dark, crazy, bad, missing, white, mad, sour

4) verb and adverb/preposition collocations:

come direct, complete with, prepared, close, right back, first, last, early, late
catch by surprise
pay by cheque
go ahead, abroad, overseas

5) adverb and adjective collocations:

terribly sorry, wrong
well/fully aware
vitally important
fast asleep
wide awake
widely read
brutally murdered
bitterly disappointed, ashamed
heavily damaged
utterly stupid, ridiculous
richly decorated
highly qualified
completely successful, different
awfully nice, pretty, good, drunk

Chapter-26: Collocation and Patterns for Words

6) adverb and verb collocations:

categorically deny	= deny wholeheartedly without any reservation
deeply regret	= regret strongly with much feeling
enthusiastically endorse	= endorse with great joy
freely enjoy	= enjoy without any restriction/hesitation
fully recognize	= recognize completely without any doubt
honestly believe	= believe truly
positively encourage	= encourage without any doubt
readily agree	= agree without hesitation
sincerely hope	= hope with best wishes
strongly recommend	= recommend with full belief
totally reject	= reject without any doubt
utterly refuse	= refuse without any doubt

7) complex prepositions:

All complex prepositions are collocations only because they are fixed expressions.

II Patterns for words: Similar to collocation, some words tend to occur in particular verb/sentence pattern to express the correct meaning. For example,

One should have the **luck** to live in this area.

In the above sentence, 'have the **luck** to do something' is a pattern for the word 'luck' more frequently used to express that 'one should be lucky enough to do something'. However, it is odd to say 'One should possess the luck to do something.'

Another example is that we say **'get to your feet'** to mean 'get up after sitting' but not 'make/stand to your feet'.

As already pointed out, collocations and patterns can only be improved by experience and observation. One has to continuously try to learn them by reading books/magazines, watching English channels on TV, listening to others conversing in English and more importantly, by using them whenever possible.

Chapter 27
Idioms, Proverbs and Quotations

I Idiom: An idiom is a group of words whose meaning as a group/single unit is different from the literal meanings of the individual words. For example, the group of words 'have a ball' is an idiom with the meaning of 'have a lot of fun/enjoyment' which is different from its literal meaning of 'having a ball in our hand physically'. It is illustrated below:

The party was great. We <u>had a ball</u>.

Phrasal verbs are also sometimes described as idioms. However, strictly speaking, idioms are much more than phrasal verbs because idioms are formed using different types of phrases, expressions or even clauses. Some common idioms are given below:

Idiom	Meaning
ace (up the sleeves)	secret advantage/trick/weapon
acid test	real test which will proves one's capacity
get the act together	organize one's efforts more systematically
add fuel to the flames	do/say something to make the situation worse
much ado about nothing	unnecessary worry/fuss about something
all ears	listening very attentively: e.g., Tell me. I am <u>all ears</u>.
all hell broke loose	react suddenly very angrily and, sometimes, violently: e.g., <u>All hell broke loose</u> when the results were announced.
upset the applecart	spoil a satisfactory plan/process
up in arms	be very angry
have an axe to grind	have personal reasons/interest in something common
on the back burner	not considered important any longer
back to square one	be back to the original position
set the ball rolling	initiate/start an activity which others would follow
the ball is in your court	it is your turn to act
jump on the bandwagon	join an activity/organization because it is successful
bare one's heart	empty one's feeling to others
bear the brunt of something	suffers the (bad) effect of something
below the belt	attack/criticize others unfairly
benefit of doubt	unable to prove one's guilt due to the absence of the evidence: e.g., The accused was released on the <u>benefit of doubt</u>.
best of both worlds	advantages of two different (opposite) things
think better of something	stop doing something: e.g., I <u>thought better of</u> smoking.
between the devil and the deep blue sea	only two bad/worse choices are available: e.g., He has to either borrow or sell the property. He is between …

Chapter-27: Idioms, Proverbs and Quotations

Idiom	Meaning
beyond redemption	no hope of improvement / recovery
a bitter pill to swallow	something very difficult/unpleasant to accept
in black and white	something (agreement) in writing, not just in words
black market	illegal buying and selling
black sheep	odd man out; somebody different from others
blank cheque	allow somebody to take as much as he/she wants
a blessing in disguise	thought to be unpleasant but turned to be advantageous
in the blink of an eye	instantaneously with no time to notice
make the blood boil	make angry
blow up in somebody's face	somebody's plan fails and make the things difficult
blue-chip company	a very sound company financially and performancewise
out of the blue	happening suddenly and unexpectedly
bone of contention	matter of disagreement
make no bones about something	speak out frankly even if it is embarrassing
in somebody's good/bad books	in somebody's good/bad opinion
get too big for his boots	behave immodestly
nip something in the bud	stop something in the beginning itself
take the bull by horns	face a problem directly and decisively
burn your fingers	suffer financially
don't beat around the bush	ask somebody to tell directly
butter someone up	praise somebody unduly and try to get something
have the cake and eat it too	try to have the advantages of two alternative situations
sell like hot cakes	sell very quickly in large number
call someone's bluff	challenge somebody to do what they threaten to
call it quits/a day	stop/end doing something
call a spade a spade	speak the truth frankly
play the cards right	do the things correctly in order to succeed
carrot and stick policy	a policy to reward the achievers and punish the defaulters
put the cart before the horse	do the things in wrong order
carve out a niche	develop a market/audience for something
case in point	a very good example
cash cow	something that brings income (money) regularly
let the cat out of the bag	reveal a secret
catch somebody's eye	attract
catch somebody red-handed	catch somebody on doing something wrong
throw caution to the wind	ignore the caution and proceed
change of heart	changed opinion
old chestnut	something very old and not interesting
clean slate	without any remarks
clinch a deal	succeed in getting an agreement through
clip someone's wings	limit somebody's freedom
close to home	take something intimately

not have a clue	not knowing anything about
come clean	tell the truth
come in handy	be useful sometime
come rain or shine	do the things regularly without regard to anything
come to the crunch	reach a difficult/critical situation
come to senses	be able to think clearly
come to grip with something	understand something and deal with it properly
come what may	to tell that anything may happen, but be normal / firm
corridors of power	top level of government administration
couch potato	a lazy person always lying down without doing anything
crack the whip	use authority to control others
crack down on something	take severe action on something
crocodile tears	shed false tears
far cry from something	tell that something is entirely different from the required one
a cut above	a higher quality
cut the ground from under somebody's feet	weaken somebody
cut out for something	fit for doing something
cutting edge	advanced/advantageous level/position
in the dark	not informed/told
dead end	the last/end point beyond which nothing is there
dead set against something	completely opposed to
a raw deal	unfair treatment
deliver the goods	finish the work as promised
dig one's own grave	do the things that cause one's own downfall/failure
do somebody's dirty work	doing one's own unpleasant work like domestic chores
donkey work	unpleasant boring work
dog's life	a very unpleasant position/situation to be in
go to the dogs	become unsuccessful / less successful
let sleeping dogs lie	not to disturb/instigate something that would cause trouble
in the doldrums	in a gloomy situation
doubting Thomas	a person who will not believe anything without proof
down to earth	sensible, practical and friendly
draw a blank	get no desired result despite the efforts
draw a line	to stop at some point beyond which it is unacceptable
drop a bombshell	say something that will greatly affect/change something
a drop in the ocean	a very small amount
hit the dust	humorous way of referring to death
dwell on something	always think/talk about something
lend an ear	listen carefully
turn a deaf ear	refuse to listen / pay attention
music to your ears	a good news

Chapter-27: Idioms, Proverbs and Quotations

easy as pie	easy to do
eat one's own words	admit that what one has told was wrong
on the edge of one's seat	be very interested and excited
have all eggs in one basket	depend on just one source / invest all in one item
at the eleventh hour	just at the end/last possible moment
make ends meet	difficult to pay for even day-to-day expenses
every nook and cranny (corner)	everywhere
every Tom, Tick and Harry	everybody / somebody very ordinary
explore all avenues	try all the possibilities to find a solution
eyes in the back	very observant and watch everything happening around
more to it than meets the eye	something more than what we could see directly
see eye to eye	agree with someone
turn a blind eye	ignore something/somebody intentionally
do not bat an eyelid	showing no emotion
face value	the value of something just from its appearance
keep a straight face	look serious
fall on the deaf ears	be ignored
fall from grace	loose respect because of some wrongdoing
fall into one's lap	get something without any effort
false move	a wrong/risky/dangerous move/action
fast-track something	give high priority to something
to a fault	to a very great extent; excessively
a feather in one's cap	a great achievement
feel the pinch	suffer from lack of money
back on the feet	completely recovered after an accident/illness
drag one's feet	delaying a decision
on the fence	unable to take a decision
fever pitch	becoming very intense and exciting
fiddling while Rome burns	doing unimportant things when there is a serious problem
field day	doing something brilliantly and easily
fight a losing battle	continue to do something though it is likely to fail
fight tooth and nail	fight/do something with all the energy
fight shy of something	be reluctant/shy to do something
a figment of one's imagination	something not real but an imagination
fine tuning	make small final changes to something to improve it
fish in troubled waters	try to gain something from a troubled/disturbed condition
fish out of water	somebody/something out of their place
have other fish to fry	have some other important work to do
fit the bill	be suitable for a requirement
fling oneself into something	do something with lot of involvement and enthusiasm
with flying colours	do something successfully and remarkably
flying start	do something successfully in the beginning itself

follow suit	do the same thing that somebody else has done
food for thought	something that makes us to think over seriously
fool's paradise	in a state of false contentment
put one's foot down	oppose something strongly
free-for-all	a situation wherein anybody can do anything
a free hand	have complete permission to do something
<u>There is no such thing as free lunch</u>.	to say that nothing is free including love
free ride	get something easily without any effort
of one's own free will	voluntarily, not compulsorily
gather dust	some plan or project not getting attention for some time
get cracking	do something immediately
get the hand dirty	get involved and do something personally
get rid of	free oneself from something bad
get a second bite	get a second chance
get the sack	loose a job
get off the hook	escape without punishment for wrongdoing
get the better of somebody	defeat somebody
get to the bottom of something	solve a problem by finding out the true cause
get something off the ground	put something into operation
get wise to something	learn something not known before
give as good as you get	treat people as badly/well as they treat you
give the game away	reveal a secret and loose something finally
give somebody a run for their money	give strong competition
give somebody the slip	manage to hide from somebody
give up the ghost	die / stop working
go all out	do something with full effort and all resources
go down in history	get recorded in the history because it is important
go down well	easily and readily accepted
go the extra mile	do more than what is expected
go haywire	become out of control
go off on a tangent	do/say something not connected to the main topic
go out of the way	take special/extraordinary care to do something
go the whole hog	do something thoroughly and completely
go great guns	doing very well
go to great length	do everything possible to succeed
go places	showing talent and ability to be successful
golden opportunity	a very favourable chance not to be missed
golden handshake	a large sum of money given on retirement
<u>Good riddance!</u>	to say that some unwanted person/thing is gone forever
grease somebody's palm	bribe somebody
green with envy	very jealous/envious
grey area	unclear and therefore difficult to understand/deal with

Chapter-27: Idioms, Proverbs and Quotations

grin and bear it	accept without complaining though not satisfactory
grin from ear to ear	look very satisfied
groan inwardly	feel bad about something but not expressing out
prepare the ground	make it easier for a future action to happen
nurse/bear a grudge	have a feeling of resentment or ill-will towards others
through the grapevine	(hear/learn casually) through informal sources like friends
guinea pig	somebody used for testing something new like medical treatment
by a hair's breadth	just manage to escape from a danger
split hairs	pay too much attention to differences that are not important
hammer some point home	make the point understood clearly
hand in glove	do something in collusion or in secret understanding/association
upper hand	take control over others
have one's hand tied	prevent somebody from doing something by rule/situation
wash the hands off something	refuse to be involved any more
get the hang of something	get to know how to do it
hard as nails	tough and showing no sympathy
hard and fast rule	strict rule
have a hangover	suffer from unpleasant after-effects
have a stab at something	try something new
bury the hatchet	forget the differences/quarrel and become friends again
bury one's head in the sand	refuse to face the unpleasant truth
head over heels	completely/deeply
your heart misses a beat	you have a sudden feeling of fear or excitement
hell-bent on something	recklessly determined to do something without caring about others or the consequences
hidden agenda	hidden interests or ulterior motives
high and dry	(left in) a difficult situation without help
hold your breath	wait excitedly and anxiously for a result of something
holier-than-thou	thinking that oneself is more virtuous than others
by hook or crook	through any means, even if it is dishonest
hope against hope	continue to be hopeful when the situation is very bad
a dark horse	somebody secretive
beat a dead horse	waste time and energy to achieve something impossible
hot potato	sensitive and controversial matter
household name	someone/something very familiar
hue and cry	loud opposition
icing on the cake	extra benefit that makes the situation even better

in safe hands	reliable person, and we need not worry when we leave/hand over something with the person
ins and outs	all details of something/some place
add insult to injury	make a situation worse
iron fist/hand in the velvet glove	actually inflexible and determined but gentle-looking
jack of all trades	one who knows many things but is not a master at any
juggling act	doing different things simultaneously and satisfactorily
just around the corner	likely to happen very soon
keep your fingers crossed	hope that something will be successful
keep a low profile	be quiet so that nobody notices you
keep your options open	delay the decision so that you can choose from many possibilities
keep someone posted	continuously update someone with the latest news
get a kick out of something	get a feeling of enjoyment out of something
kickback	illegal money/bribe paid to gain some advantage
kill two birds with one stone	succeed in doing two things at the same time
on its knees/brought to knees	in a very weak situation
know which side your bread is buttered	know where your interests lie
knuckle down to something	start working on something very seriously
lame excuse	a weak and unconvincing explanation
last resort	the last option/thing to do because all other options failed
That's is the last straw!	to say that you are already annoyed with what has happened/been told and that you cannot tolerate any more
laugh up your sleeves	secretly laugh/be amused at somebody else's suffering
laughing stock	a person others laugh at because he/she has done something stupid and ridiculous
in leaps and bounds	very rapid and spectacular progress or growth
learn the hard way	learn through your own experience without guidance
learning curve	time taken to learn something
leave no stone unturned	try all the possibilities
pull somebody's leg	tease somebody
Let the cat out of the bag!	to say that somebody has revealed the secret unintentionally
to the letter	follow the rule/instruction strictly
like a headless chicken	become very excited and behave in a disorderly way
bottom line	the most important point
cross the line	do something unacceptable and beyond the limits
read between lines	add/discover a new meaning in something that is not really told
lion's den	be in the strong opponent's place and face him/her
lion's share	major part/share of something
live high off the hog	be rich and wealthy and lead such a life

Chapter-27: Idioms, Proverbs and Quotations

lock horns	fight/argue with somebody
lock, stock and barrel	everything
at loggerheads	disagree very strongly with somebody else
lose touch	not doing something for long and almost forget that
at a loss	not knowing what to do/tell in a difficult/tight situation
the lull before the storm	unusual calmness before a time/period of violent activity
a lump in the throat	a sudden sad and shocking feeling
in the lurch	in a difficult/embarrassing situation
make a beeline for something	hurry towards something
make fun of	joke about others in an unkind way
make or break	very critical situation which will cause total success or ruin
cannot make head or tail of it	not able to understand something at all
make headway	make progress
make a mountain out of molehill	exaggerate something
make your mouth water	feel like eating something as it looks and smells good
make someone see reason	persuade someone to be sensible
mean business	be very serious about something
method in one's madness	not as irrational as it seems
burn the midnight oil	stay very late at night to study/finish some work
The mind boggles!	to say that something is very difficult to understand
mind your P's and Q's	be careful about how you behave and what you say
miss the boat	miss a good opportunity
mixed blessing	something pleasant but with some disadvantages
once in blue moon	rarely
a moot point	a subject/point giving rise to argument/debate
a pain in the neck	somebody very irritating and annoying
neck and neck	in a very close competition
a needle in a haystack	something impossible to find/locate
next to nothing	very little or almost nothing
new lease of life	get a chance to live longer after a serious illness or to live a better life
in the nick of time	at the last moment
nitty-gritty	finer details
no great shakes	useless, ineffective or not very good
no hard feelings	no resentment or bitterness
no smoke without fire	something must be true though it is not explicit/open
nothing doing	refuse completely
Nothing succeeds like success!.	to say that success leads to more successes
nothing to write home about	nothing great to notice/comment
null and void	legally invalid
go nuts	become completely foolish/eccentric/mad

nuts and bolts	detailed facts
in a nutshell	in short/briefly
at odds	disagree
odds and ends	small articles/items of all sorts
off the record	say something privately, not officially/publicly
in the offing	likely to happen/come soon
hold out an olive branch	end a disagreement and make peace
on ice/in the cold storage	postponed indefinitely
on the cards	likely to happen soon
one-upmanship	quality/wish to have a control over others
open the floodgates	release something which was under tight control
other side of the coin	the unknown aspect of somebody/something
out of circulation	unavailable in the market
out of the picture	somebody/something no longer relevant to a situation
out of question	something impossible
over my dead body	absolutely refuse to allow someone to do something
paint the town red	go out, roam around and enjoy immensely
pass the buck	do not take the responsibility but pass it to others
pay dividends	get the benefits
pillar to post	to go from place to place to get/finish something
tickled pink	very pleased about something
in the pipeline	under progress or being organized at the moment
play with fire	take unnecessary risks
play havoc	cause disorder and confusion
play into somebody's hand	fall prey to somebody else's (opponent's) harmful plan
play second fiddle	accept and be at a lower position to somebody else
pour cold water on something	discourage something
press something home	insist on something
prolong the agony	make an unpleasant situation last longer
proud as peacock	extremely proud
pull a fast one	gain an advantage over others
pull the plug	end something / provide no more support
pull through	recover from a serious illness
put one's foot in other's mouth	say/do something that offends/embarrass others
put up/on a brave face	try to look cheerful when confronted with difficulties
put a spanner in the works	cause problems and prevent something from happening
put somebody on the spot	ask embarrassing questions to somebody
in a quandary	very difficult to decide what to do next
no quick fix	no simple solution
quick/short temper	tendency to get angry easily
a race against time	a situation when we have to work very quickly
from rags to riches	become very rich after having been very poor

Chapter-27: Idioms, Proverbs and Quotations

raise eyebrows	show surprise/disapproval
take the rap	accept the blame or punishment even if you have not done it
smell a rat	suspect that something is wrong
recipe for disaster	a plan likely to produce disaster
set the records straight	to correct a misunderstanding / mistake
refresh someone's memory	remind someone of facts seemingly forgotten by them
roll out the red carpet	give a special warm treatment to somebody
red tape	official rules and bureaucratic paperwork preventing work from being done quickly
take someone for ride	cheat/deceive someone
ripple effect	an effect that produces some other effect and so on
rise to the occasion	manage to do something in a difficult situation
hit the road	start a journey / introduce a new product in the market
roaring trade/practice	excellent business or practice by a professional, say, a doctor
Rob Peter to pay Paul.	pay one debt with money borrowed from somewhere else
rock the boat	do something that will upset a situation/cause problems
no rocket science	not a very difficult one to understand
roll up your sleeves	get ready for hard work
learn the ropes	learn how to do a particular work
rub shoulders	have an opportunity to meet and talk with important people
rule the roost	be important and powerful to decide the important things
safe bet	a safe proposition without any risks
sail close to the winds	do some dangerous things but within the limits
sail through something	succeed without difficulty
with a pinch of salt	accept/take something with a bit of doubt
in the same boat	in a similar unpleasant/difficult situation
by the same token	in a similar way
save your breath	do not waste your energy advising/speaking to someone
scare somebody out of their wits	frighten someone very badly
go scot-free	escape without punishment for some wrongdoing
sell someone down the river	betray someone who trusts you
sell your soul	do something wrong/illegal
set in stone	permanent and cannot be changed
set the stage	create a situation that facilitate some event to occur
settle a score	take revenge
in bad shape	in poor physical condition
come out of one's shell	become less shy and more talkative and outgoing
shoot oneself in the foot	do/say something against your own interest
shopping spree	enjoy shopping/outing usually spending much money
window shopping	look at things in a shop without buying
show one's true colours	show one's real nature/character

shrug something off	dismiss something as unimportant
sign on the dotted line	sign an official document
born with a silver spoon	be born in a rich and privileged family
sit on the fence	avoid taking decisions
by the skin of somebody's teeth	almost failed but just managed to do it
the sky is the limit	no limit for something like success
sleeping/silent partner	an investor in a business but not actively participating
sling mud	damage somebody's reputation
it slipped the mind	forgot
on the sly	do something secretly
smooth waters	something making regular and easy progress
a snake in the grass	someone who pretends to be a friend
pull up one's socks	work harder to achieve something
speak the same language	have similar tastes and ideas
speak volumes	expresses very clearly even without words
spin a yarn	tell an unbelievable story, but as if it has happened
spread like wildfire	some news spread very fast
spur of the moment	suddenly without planning
stand on your feet	be independent and need no help from others
stand one's ground	maintain your position and refuse to yield
stand the test of time	continue to be useful/popular for a very long time
state of the art	most advanced with latest technology
steal someone's thunder	take somebody else's ideas/plans and show as if these are our own
steal the show	get more attention or praise than other participants
stick to one's guns	show strong determination when faced with opposition
sticky fingers	the tendency to steal
on a sticky wicket	a difficult situation
stir up a hornet's nest	do something causing commotion
a storm in a teacup	make an unnecessary fuss/excitement
by no stretch of imagination	however hard you may imagine/try to believe
as stubborn as a mule	very obstinate
stumbling block	an obstacle / a big problem to do something
sugar the pill	make an unpleasant news more acceptable
swallow your words	admit that you have done something wrong
a swollen head	somebody proud and conceited
swim with/against the tide	agree with/oppose the ideas most people have
in full swing	happening with full force without any disturbance
the tail wagging the dog	reversal of roles with smaller part controlling the main part
take a back seat	allow somebody else to take the important role
take care of	watch one's health; make arrangements
take one's life in one's hand	take a risk that involves even the risk of life

Chapter-27: Idioms, Proverbs and Quotations

take matters into your own hands	take action yourself without waiting for others
take a nosedive	decreases in value very rapidly
take something in your stride	deal with the situation calmly without any tension
take stock of a situation	assess all the aspects of a problem/situation
take the words out of somebody's mouth	say exactly what somebody else will say
a tall story	unbelievable story/statement
tech savvy	having sufficient knowledge and skill to handle technical / electronic gadgets
on tenterhooks	be anxious and excited while waiting for something
There was not a soul.	nobody is present
a thin line	difference between two feelings/situations is almost nil
a thing of the past	something no longer used
think outside the box	be innovative
a thorn in your side	somebody continuously irritating/annoying you
throw caution to the wind	take risks without worrying about the danger
tie the knot	get married
tight spot	difficult situation
time is ripe	right moment to do something
tip of the iceberg	a very small part of actually a much larger problem
tit for tat	something bad given in return for the one received earlier
keep someone on toes	make someone stay very alert
bite your tongue	say something not really intended
tongue-tied	be nervous and not able to speak clearly
on the tip of the tongue	you know it but not able to remember it at the moment
train of thought	a sequence of related/connected thoughts
tricks of the trade	a clever way of doing things
tried and tested	already successfully tested and used, and can be trusted
turn on the heat	put pressure on somebody
take a turn for the worse	getting worse than before
turn over a new leaf	change the behaviour and lead a better life
in the twinkling of an eye	instantaneously with no time to notice
twist somebody's arm	force somebody to do something
Two is company; three is a crowd.	to say that only two people, particularly lovers, can have privacy
put two and two together	reach the correct conclusion with the available information
two-faced	deceitful and insincere; untrustworthy; unbelievable
in two minds	having difficulty in deciding what to do
you cannot unring a bell	you cannot undo what has been done
on the up and up	becoming increasingly successful
up in the air	not yet decided/settled
up to the mark/par	meeting the required standard

up and running	started and functioning successfully
uphill task/battle	very difficult task to finish
vanish into thin air	disappear completely in a mysterious way
vote with one's feet	leave without voting to show the disapproval
wait for the cat to jump	delay an action until we see how events turn out
waiting game	delaying an action until we see how events turn out
waiting in the wings	waiting for an opportunity to grasp it immediately
walk a tightrope	be in a difficult/delicate situation where one should be careful
walking/mobile encyclopedia	very knowledgeable person
watch one's step	to be very careful
on the same frequency/wavelength	two persons sharing the common interests
pull your weight	work hard as everyone else in a team
a wet blanket	boring and unenthusiastic person
have a whale of a time	enjoy very much
while the going is good	when the situation is favourable
white lie	harmless small lie to avoid hurting somebody
whiz-kid	young but very talented
win-win	favourable for all concerned
get wind of something	get to know about something secret/private
wing it	improvise or to deal with a situation unexpectedly but cleverly
at your wits end	not knowing what to do
a wolf in sheep's clothing	a bad person in the disguise of a good/nice person
out of woodwork	out of nowhere (suddenly out of somewhere)
word of mouth	not through official announcement but by means of telling others
worlds apart	completely different
worth one's salt	somebody working well in good conscience (honestly)
Xerox copy	not original
Your guess is as good as mine.	to say that neither knows the answer

II Proverb: A proverb is an expression or sentence, formed as a result of experience and observation, which conveys some general truth or advice that guides us to lead our life carefully, practically and satisfactorily. For example,

'Face is the index of the mind' is a proverb that tells us that the face reflects one's mind and that we can read it to know the state of his/her mind.

Chapter-27: Idioms, Proverbs and Quotations

Some common proverbs are given below with the explanation/meaning:

Absence/Distance makes the heart grow fonder.
= When someone we love is away, we feel for them more.
Actions speak louder than words.
= What we do is more important than what we speak.
All that glitters is not gold. = Appearance can be deceptive.
All things are difficult before they are easy.
= Unless we try something, it will always be difficult.
An apple a day keeps the doctor away.
= If you take a fruit (an apple) daily, you will be healthy.
= A small preventive treatment wards off serious problems.
An idle mind/brain is the devil's workshop.
= If we are busy doing some work, we will not get bad thoughts in our mind.
Any time is no time.
= If the date and time is not fixed, something may never happen.
A bad workman blames his tools.
= Somebody not good at work would try to find fault with other things.
A bird in hand is worth two in a bush.
= It's better to keep what you have than to risk losing it by searching for something better.
A burnt child dreads the fire.
= A bad experience will make people more cautious thereafter.
A chain is no stronger than its weakest link.
= Even a small weakness may cause the whole thing to fail.
A friend in need is a friend indeed.
= Someone who helps you when you are in trouble is a real friend.
A friend to all is a friend to none. = You cannot be a friend of everybody.
A known devil is better than an unknown angel.
= It is better to deal with a known difficult person than to try to have an unknown person who could be even worse.
Beauty is only skin deep.
= One's mind/character is more important than one's appearance.
Beauty is in eye of the beholder.
= What is beauty differs from person to person.
Beggars can't be choosers.
= When we have no choice, we have to accept something.
Better late than never.
= It is better to do something even if it is late.
= It is better to do something slowly than not to do it all.
Birds of a feather flock together. = Like-minded people will get together.
Blood is thicker than water.
= Family relationship is stronger than the relationship with others.

Charity begins at home. = One should care for his/her family first.
Cleanliness is next to godliness.
  = It is important to keep the body and the surroundings clean.
Diamond cuts diamond.
  = Two people are equally matching in wits/cunning.
  = A bad thing has to be removed/compensated with another bad thing only.
Diligence is the mother of good fortune. = Hard work brings rewards.
Don't bark if you cannot bite.
  = Don't complain if you cannot win / enforce your point of view.
Don't count your chickens before they are hatched.
  = Don't rely on something that is likely to happen but not yet.
  = Don't be too confident that something will be successful.
Don't judge a book by its cover.
  = Don't judge by appearances.
  = Don't comment on a book without reading it.
Easier said than done. = It is easy to advise others but difficult to follow/do.
Empty vessels make the most noise.
  = The least intelligent people talk more, thinking that they are more intelligent.
Every dog has its day. = Everybody succeeds sometime in the life.
Every man has his price.
  = Everybody has a weakness which can be exploited by others to their advantage.
Every Why has a Wherefore. = There is an explanation for everything.
Experience is the father of wisdom. = Knowledge/Wisdom comes of experience only.
Facts speak louder than words.
  = The truth is more important than what one claims in words.
Familiarity breeds contempt.
  = Getting too close to someone causes not only lack of respect for him/her,
    but also more expectation from him/her that may, in turn, cause contempt
    for each other.
Give someone an inch, and they will take a mile.
  = If you help other people giving your things, they will try to occupy the whole thing.
  = Some people are never satisfied, always asking for more.
God helps those who help themselves.
  = One (You) should not be idle just praying to God, but do what is required.
Great minds think alike.
  = People of high calibre and intelligence tend to form similar ideas.
Haste makes waste.
  = Something hurriedly done without much thought/care will be a waste.
He who wills the end will the means.
  = If you are determined to do something, you will find a way.
He laughs best who laughs last. = We should not express our joy too soon.
Home is where the heart is. = Home is the place where the people we love are there.

Chapter-27: Idioms, Proverbs and Quotations

Honesty is the best policy. = Whatever we do, we should be honest first.
If a camel gets his nose in a tent, his body will follow.
    = If you allow somebody intrusive to enter into your life, your life will be difficult.
If you chase two rabbits, you will not catch either one.
    = If you do two things simultaneously, you may not succeed.
If you want a friend, be a friend first. = Be friendly to others first.
If wishes were horses, then beggars would ride.
    = One should work hard to achieve/get things.
Ignorance is bliss. = We need not worry about things we really do not know.
It is always darkest before the dawn. = Every problem has a solution.
It never rains, but it pours. = Bad things happen one after another.
It's no use crying over spilt milk.
    = There is no use worrying about something which has already happened.
Justice delayed is justice denied.
    = The inordinate delay of justice is almost the denial of justice.
Knowledge is power. = Knowledge is more powerful than the money and the physical power.
Kill the goose that lays the gólden egg. = Don't be too greedy.
Kindness begets kindness. = If you are kind to others, others will also be kind to you.
Learn to walk before you run. = Don't do anything without knowing about it.
Let bygones be bygones. = Let's forgive and forget the past quarrels.
Lightening never strikes in the same place twice.
    = No two situations are exactly the same.
Like father, like son. = A son will resemble his father in character also.
Look before you leap. = Consider possible consequences before taking action.
Love is blind. = A person in love does not see the faults of the person he/she loves.
Make hay while the sun shines.
    = Take advantage of a good situation that may not last longer.
Man proposes, God disposes.
    = We may wish/do things, but only God/destiny decides the outcome.
Manners make the man. = You are judged by your manners and behaviours.
Men make houses, women make homes.
    = Men just earn, but women creates the loving environment in our homes.
Money begets money. = If somebody has money, he/she will make more money.
Money doesn't grow on trees. = We should not spend money lavishly.
Necessity is the mother of invention.
    = The need for something forces the people to find a way of obtaining it.
Never say die. = Never give up.
Nobody is perfect. = Don't blame others unnecessarily and too much.
No man can serve two masters. = You cannot work for/satisfy two different people.
No news is good news. = If we don't know the news/result, we can assume all is well.

No smoke without fire. = If there is a rumour, there could be some truth behind it.
Once bitten, twice shy. = People tend to be careful after some unpleasant experience.
One of these days is none of these days.
    = If you try to do something one of these days without doing it today, it may never happen.
One today is worth two tomorrow.
    = What we have is better than what we may have latter.
One man's meat is another man's poison. = People like different things.
Opportunity seldom knocks twice. = One should grasp an opportunity immediately.
Penny wise, pound foolish. = We should be careful about all we spend/do.
People living in glass houses should not throw stones.
    = One should not criticize others for faults similar to one's own.
Practice what you preach. = We should follow our own advice first.
Prevention is better than cure.
    = We should prevent a problem rather than trying to solve it.
Rome was not built in a day. = We cannot achieve things so easily.
Saying is one thing, doing is another. = We should follow our own words.
Snug as a bug in a rug. = Feeling very comfortable.
Spare the rod and spoil the child.
    = Unless we scold/punish a child for small mistakes, we will spoil the child's character.
Still waters run deep. = A quiet person can have a lot of knowledge and wisdom.
A stitch in time saves nine. = It is better to act when the problem is still smaller.
Stolen fruit is the sweetest. = What is forbidden is the most tempting.
The early bird catches the worm. = Do it as early as you can.
The end justifies the means.
    = If the end result or the intention is good, even unfair methods can be used.
The first step is the hardest. = To begin something is the hardest, not doing it.
The more haste, the less speed. = You can only do the things slower if you hurry up.
The more you have; the more you want. = Having more cannot satisfy anybody.
The pen is mightier than the sword.
    = You can achieve more by writing than by fighting.
The tongue wounds more than a lance.
    = Wordy insults can be more hurtful than physical injuries.
To err is human, to forgive is divine.
    = It is natural to make mistakes, so we should forgive.
Too many cooks spoil the food/broth.
    = If too many people are involved in something, it will not be done properly.
Truth is stranger than fiction.
    = Sometimes, events in real life are stranger than the events in the stories.
Two wrongs don't make a right. = Taking revenge is not correct.

Chapter-27: Idioms, Proverbs and Quotations

Union is strength. = We should not fight with each other.
Virtue is its own reward.
    . = We should not expect others to praise us for doing things in the right way.
Walls have ears. = Be careful while talking because others may overhear.
Waste not, want not. = If you do not waste, you will have enough for later.
When the cat is away, the mice play. = People have a lot of fun when the boss is out.
When in Rome, do as the Romans do.
    = One should follow the local customs of a place where you are.
Where there is a will, there's a way.
    = If you are serious and determined to do something, you can do it.
Wisdom is better than strength.
    = Knowledge is more powerful than the money and the physical power.
You scratch my back, and I will scratch yours.
    = If you help others, others will also help you.

III Quotation: A quotation is also like a proverb and is an expression, phrase or sentence conveying some general truth or advice that guides us to lead our life carefully, practically and satisfactorily. The main differences between the quotation and the proverb are that quotations are more direct in meaning and that the author of the quotation is usually known. Moreover, the quotations can be on any topic/subject, not just on virtues and truths. Some examples of quotations are given below:

    Knowledge is Power.   - Sir Francis Bacon
    A pessimist sees the difficulty in every opportunity;
        an optimist sees the opportunity in every difficulty. - Winston Churchill
    Respect yourself and others will respect you.   - Confucius
    Anyone who has never made a mistake
        has never tried anything new.   - Albert Einstein

Chapter 28
Other Word Groups/Types

We have already learned that words are classified into different parts of speech, namely noun, pronoun, verb, etc., according to the similarity in their function in sentences. Words can be classified into other groups also based on some other similarities. Such groups of words are discussed below.

I Affix (Prefix/Suffix): A letter or group of letters added to the beginning or the end of a word called root/stem word is called an affix, and it changes the meaning of the root word when added. If the affix is added to the beginning of a word, it is called a **prefix,** and if added to the end of a word, it is called a **suffix**. Such words are called affixes because they are added to other words and the similarity among these words is their position in the words. Prefix and suffix are illustrated below:

<u>care</u>ful, care<u>less</u> - 'ful' and 'less' are suffixes, because they are added to the end of the word 'care'.

<u>re</u>do, <u>un</u>do - 're' and 'un' are prefixes, because they are added to the beginning of the word 'do'.

Common **prefixes** include the following:

prefix	meaning	example
a, an	not	amoral, anarchy
ante	before	antenatal
anti	against/opposite	anti-cricket, anticlimax
arch	chief	archbishop
be	make	befriend
bi	two	bilingual
co	together	co-author, co-existence
counter	against/opposite	counterattack
cross	across/between	cross-border
cyber	computer technology	cyberspace
de	reverse/undo	defrost
demi	half	demigod
dis	opposite/reverse	dishonest, disconnect
down	to a lower level	downgrade, downstairs
e	electronic	e-mail, e-commerce
ex	former	ex-president
extra	outside	extracurricular
fore	before/front	forewarn, forearm
in, il, im, ir	not	incredible, illegal, immoral, irrational

Chapter-28: Other Word Groups/Types

inter	between	inter-school competition
intra	within	intra-school competition
mal	badly	malfunction
mid	middle	midsummer
mini	small	minicomputer
non	not/opposite	non-violence, non-vegetarian
out	longer than / outside	outgrow, outcast
over	too much / across	overpopulated, overseas
post	after	postdated
pre	before	prefix, prehistoric
pro	in favour of	pro-cricket
quasi	partly	quasigovernment
re	again	rewrite
semi	half/partially	semifinal, semiliterate
step	by remarriage	stepmother, stepsister
sub	under/below	submarine, substandard
super	above/greater	supersonic, superman
trans	across	transcontinental, transform, translate, transfer
tri	three	trilingual
ultra	extremely/beyond	ultramodern, ultrasonic
un	not/reverse	unhappy, uncomfortable, undo, undress
under	below/less	underclothes, underestimate
up	to a higher level	upgrade, upstairs
vice	deputy	vice-president

Common **suffixes** include the following:

suffix	meaning / purpose	example
able	can be done	eatable, washable
acy	to form noun from adjectives ending in 'ate'	accuracy, literacy
age	to form noun from other nouns	drainage, mileage
aholic	to form adjective meaning 'addicted'	workaholic
al	to form adjective meaning 'of'	national, political
	to form noun meaning 'action'	approval, arrival
an	to form adjective meaning 'of'	Indian
ance	to form noun meaning 'action'	performance
ancy	to form noun meaning 'a state'	pregnancy
ant	to form adjectives meaning 'with quality'	brilliant, relevant
	to form noun meaning 'doing something'	assistant
ar,er,r	to form noun meaning 'someone doing'	beggar, winner
arian	to form noun meaning 'somebody'	vegetarian

Suffix	Function	Example
ary	to form adjective meaning 'of'	planetary
ate	to form adjective meaning 'with quality'	affectionate
	to form verb meaning 'to become'	activate, motivate
	to form noun meaning 'group'	electorate
	to form noun meaning 'office of some officer'	collectorate
ation	to form noun from verbs	examination
ative	to form adjective meaning 'with quality'	talkative
dom	to form noun meaning 'area of', 'a state'	kingdom, freedom
ed	to form past tense and past participle	asked, played
	to form descriptive adjectives	bad-tempered
ee	to form noun meaning 'someone doing'	absentee, trainee
eer	to form noun meaning 'someone doing'	engineer
en	to form past participle	eaten, given
	to form verb meaning 'to become'	strengthen, widen
	to form adjective meaning 'made of'	golden, woollen
	to form plural of some nouns	children, oxen
ence	to form noun meaning 'a state'	existence
ency	to form noun meaning 'a state'	dependency
ent	to form adjectives meaning 'state'	apparent, different
	to form noun meaning 'somebody doing something'	student, resident
ery	to form noun meaning 'a state/collection'	slavery, machinery
ese	to form noun meaning 'nationality/language'	Chinese, Japanese
ess	to form female gender	poetess, actress
est	to form superlative adjectives	longest, tallest
fold	to form adjective meaning 'times'	twofold
ful	to form adjective meaning 'full of'	beautiful, painful
	to form noun meaning 'equal to'	handful, mouthful
hood	to form noun meaning 'a state'	childhood, likelihood
ial	to form adjective meaning 'of'	financial
ian	to form nouns meaning 'of'	Indian, musician
ic, ical	to form adjective meaning 'of'	historic, historical
ice	to form noun meaning 'a state'	justice
ics	to form noun meaning 'a study'	mathematics
ie	to form noun used to/by young children	auntie, doggie
ify	to form verb meaning 'make something happen'	simplify, pacify
ing	to form present participle	going, eating
ion	to form noun from verbs	creation, discussion
ise	to form noun meaning 'state/knowledge of'	expertise
ish	to form adjective meaning 'like'	childish, foolish
ism	to form noun meaning 'belief/attitude/illness'	Hinduism, heroism
ist	to form noun meaning 'of some belief'	communist, racist
itude	to form noun meaning 'a state'	aptitude, magnitude

Chapter-28: Other Word Groups/Types

ity	to form nouns from adjectives	regularity, validity
ive	to form noun meaning 'someone doing'	detective, explosive
	to form adjective meaning 'of quality'	aggressive
ize/ise	to form verb	criticize, modernize
like	to form adjective meaning 'of quality'	childlike
less	to form adjective meaning 'without'	endless, pointless
let	to form noun meaning 'very small'	droplet, booklet
ling	to form noun meaning 'young'	duckling, nestling
long	to form adjective meaning 'in that way'	headlong, sidelong
ly	to form adverb	slowly, yearly
	to form adjective meaning 'with a character'	friendly, godly
ment	to form nouns from verbs	development
monger	to form noun meaning 'someone doing'	rumour-monger
most	to form adjective meaning 'nearest to'	innermost, utmost
ness	to form noun meaning 'the state of being'	happiness
ock	to form noun meaning 'little'	bullock, hillock
or	to form noun meaning 'someone doing something'	conductor, sailor
ous	to form adjective meaning 'with a characteristic'	dangerous
ship	to form noun meaning state/skill	friendship, craftsmanship
	to form a position meaning 'position'	professorship
some	to form adjective meaning 'with a characteristic'	troublesome
ster	to form noun meaning 'someone who is'	youngster, gangster
th	to form noun meaning 'a state'	warmth, growth
	to form adjective from numbers	fifth, thousandth
ty	to form noun meaning 'the state of being'	certainty, safety
ual	to form adjective meaning 'of'	habitual, sexual
uble	to form adjective meaning 'able to'	soluble
ure	to form noun meaning 'some action'	closure, failure
ward/wards	to form adjective/adverb meaning 'in the direction'	backward
wise	to form adjective/adverb meaning 'in the direction'	clockwise, lengthwise
y	to form certain nouns	expiry, jealousy
	to form noun used to/by young children	mummy, daddy
y, ey	to form adjectives meaning 'like/with something'	snowy, feathery

II '-nym' words like Synonym, Antonym, etc.: Words are classified into another set of groups based on the similarity in the properties exhibited by them. Such groups of words can be called '-nym' words because the name of such groups of words end with the suffix '-nym'.

Synonym: Synonyms are the words with same or similar meaning. For example, the word 'give' has the synonyms of 'award, bestow/confer, contribute, deliver, donate, hand over, lend, present, provide, supply and yield'. Though the synonyms are same or similar in meaning, all such words cannot be used in all places as if they have exactly the same meaning. While one word is appropriate for a given context, another synonym will be more appropriate for another context as illustrated below:

'We <u>give</u> pocket money to children, but we <u>contribute</u> to education fund, <u>donate</u> to an orphanage, <u>lend</u> money or a household item to friends, <u>present</u> a birthday gift, <u>hand over</u> our responsibility to others, <u>deliver</u> a speech in functions, <u>provide</u> a shelter to the homeless people and <u>supply</u> water from our well to others.'

'All speakers <u>bestowed</u> high praise on the humble scientist, and the minister <u>awarded</u> him a cash prize of one crore rupees because his research <u>has yielded</u> remarkable results in energy conservation.'

Antonym: Antonyms are the words which are opposite in meaning. For example, the word 'give' has the antonyms of 'get, receive, take, keep, retain and withhold'.

Like dictionary giving the meaning of words, **thesaurus** is a book which lists the synonyms and antonyms for the words.

Hyponym: Hyponyms are the words which represent elements/members of a particular category/group or belong to a particular category/group. For example, the words 'apple, orange, banana and grapes' are hyponyms of 'fruit' while 'mother, father, son, daughter, brother, sister, grandmother, grandfather, grandson, granddaughter, husband and wife' are hyponyms of 'family'. The words representing the categories like 'fruit and family' are called **hypernyms**.

Holonym: Holonyms are the words which represent the parts of a whole thing. For example, the words 'eye, nose and mouth' are holonyms of 'face' which, a whole thing, is called **meronym**.

Homonym: Homonyms are the words which are alike in spelling and sound but different in meaning. For example, the word 'bat' can refer to a cricket bat or to a bird-like animal which flies in the night.

The other two groups of words based on the spelling, sound and meaning are given below:

Chapter-28: Other Word Groups/Types

Homograph: Homographs are the words which are alike in spelling but different in sound and meaning. For example, the word 'wound' as a noun refers to an injury with the pronunciation of 'woond', and as the past participle of verb 'wind' can mean 'wrap/move in a circular movement'.

Homophone: Homophones are the words which are alike in sound but different in spelling and meaning. For example, the words 'year and ear' are homophones because they sound alike but are different in spelling and meaning.

III Other Word Types: Some more types of words are also identified based on a specific property exhibited by them as follows:

Anagram: It is a word created by rearranging the letters of another word. For example, 'but and tub', 'tip and pit' and 'listen and silent' are anagrams of each other.

Alphagram: It is a word, mostly meaningless, formed by rearranging the letters of another word simply in alphabetical order. For example, 'dorw' is the alphagram of 'word'.

Palindrome: A palindrome is a word which will be the same word when the letters of the word are written in the reverse order. In other words, words that read the same both forward and backward are called palindromes. For example, 'madam' and 'Malayalam' are palindromes.

Chapter 29
Figures of Speech

Figures of speech refer to the style of using words in sentences in such a way that it means something different than what it would normally / literally mean and that the reader has to figure out the intended meaning. In short, when a sentence has a figurative meaning, it is said to be written with figures of speech. For example,

She is like a rose.

If we take the literal meaning of the sentence, it would mean a girl and a rose look exactly the same with either the girl having petal-like feature or the rose having a face, hands and legs of a human being. On the other hand, the above sentence is written with a figure of speech because it compares/likens a girl with a rose because the girl may be as beautiful as a rose. The intended meaning is to make the reader feel that the girl is so beautiful that she can be compared to a rose. Sometimes, even a group of sentences can form a figure of speech together.

I Use of figures of speech: Figures of speech are used to add beauty, variety, emotion, intensity, emphasis and clarity to the writing so that it kindles the interest and the imagination of the readers and makes the reading more enjoyable.

II Types of figures of speech: There are so many types of figures of speech. Some of the common figures of speech are given below:

Simile: It is a way of comparing and likening something with something else because the first thing shows a property of the second thing as in 'She is like a rose' wherein a girl is compared to a rose because she may be as beautiful or colourful as a rose.

In a simile, the words 'like' and 'as' are used to show the comparison. Some commonly used similes are given below:

fit like a glove	run like a deer	chatter like a monkey
sleep like a log	eat like a pig	swim like a fish
eyes like a hawk	sing like a bird	shine like the sun
as cold as ice	as white as snow	as blue as the sky
as dark as night	as quiet as a mouse	as proud as a peacock
as bright as day	as light as a feather	as timid as a doe
as deep as the ocean	as blind as a bat	as regular as the sun

Metaphor: It is also a way of comparing two things, but here one thing is equated to another thing because they are similar or exhibit almost the same property/behaviour as in 'Her heart is a stone' wherein a girl's heart is compared/equated to a stone because her heart is also feeling-less like a stone. Few more examples are given below:

Chapter-29: Figures of Speech

Life is a <u>boat</u> which should sail smoothly. (life = boat)
The winner stole the <u>spotlight</u> in the beginning itself. (spotlight = attention)
He was given a <u>yellow-card</u> in the school. (yellow-card = warning)
The boss is a <u>rock</u>. (boss = rock)
He would always <u>spin</u> yarn. (spin yarn = lie)

Hyperbole: It is used to emphasize or express an emotion very strongly by means of exaggeration. For example,

I have told you a <u>million</u> times to write the homework.

The word 'million' is a hyperbole because it exaggerates the number of times as it is not possible to tell something so many times, but it expresses the emotion of speaker that in spite of being told really so many times, the listener has not completed the homework. Other examples could be:

My grandfather has <u>tons of money</u>. (tons of money means 'lot of money')
I am <u>starving</u> now. (starving means 'feeling very hungry')

Euphemism: It refers to the indirect/polished/more acceptable way of telling unpleasant things or harsh truths. For example,:

She <u>passed away</u>. (passed away means 'die')
He is in the <u>restroom</u>. (restroom means 'toilet')

Personification: Treating non-human things like animals, objects, ideas, etc. as human beings or with human qualities is called personification. For example,:

<u>Experience</u> is the best <u>teacher</u>.
<u>Necessity</u> is the <u>mother</u> of invention.

Irony: Using words with opposite meaning in a sarcastic way to mean exactly the opposite meaning is called irony. For example,:

Yes, he will help you, by making your purse lighter frequently.
Don't worry. The teacher will do the homework for you.
Is she beautiful? I think her grandmother is very beautiful.

Interrogation: It involves asking questions to put across a point more effectively, not for getting an answer. For example,:

Is it not my right to have a share in my ancestor's property?
= I have all the rights over my ancestor's property.
Am I your servant?
= You cannot ask/order me to do your work.

Synecdoche: (pronounced as 'sinekdiki') In synecdoche, a part is used to represent the whole or a whole to represent a part. For example,:

This <u>finger</u> deserves a gold ring.   (finger represents a person)
<u>India</u> won the world cup.   (India represents its team)

Metonymy: In metonymy, one related word, not exactly the accurate word, is used to represent something. For example,:

The <u>house</u> passed the new law.   (house represents members of the parliament)
The <u>bench</u> reserved the judgment.   (the bench represents the judges)

Antithesis: In antithesis two contrasting but related ideas are expressed in the same sentence. For example,:

Man proposes; God disposes.
To err is human; to forgive is divine.

Oxymoron: It is a way of using two contradictory words to emphasize the meaning of one of the words. For example,:

A <u>deafening silence</u> followed after the news broke out.
Her <u>absence</u> was <u>conspicuous</u>.

Climax: It is a way of writing in which ideas/properties are arranged in the increasing order of importance. For example,:

One should learn to love <u>himself, his family, his country and finally God</u>.
He <u>got up, got ready, kicked his bike and sped away</u>.
Matha, Pitha, Guru and Deivam.   means 'Mother, Father, Teacher and God.'
    -     an Indian proverb stating the way to salvation.

Anticlimax: Anticlimax is the opposite of Climax and is a way of writing in which ideas/properties are arranged in the decreasing order of importance for expressing ridicule or satire. For example,:

Not only does he <u>dance, sing and drink,</u> but also he <u>vomits</u> at the end.
Man <u>builds castles and palaces, lives in rooms, lies in even smaller beds and finally ends up within the soil</u>.

The above being the last example of the book, does it sound anticlimax for this book? Not really! Actually this anticlimax is the Climax of the book because <u>we started the grammar with parts of speech, went on to different sentence structures and further on to different types of words and peaked it with the figures of speech</u>. Is this conclusion a **Paradox**, another figure of speech? Best of luck.

Part II

Grammar Exercises

1. Exercise for Chapter 2: Nouns

a) **Identify the <u>nouns</u> in the following sentences:**

1. Schools and Colleges are the important places in the life of people.
2. Knowledge is power.
3. We cannot live in this world without knowledge.
4. Unless we have enough knowledge, other people may cheat and deprive us of our valuable things in our life like money, jewels, our rights, etc.
5. Teachers are the backbone of the schools and colleges.
6. Teachers make our schooling memorable in many ways.
7. It is the educational institutions where we get the basic knowledge that would lead us, our children, our relatives and even our country in the right direction in the future.
8. Our great leaders of the past like Nehruji and Kamaraj had realized this basic fact and contributed very much for education through schools and colleges.
9. It is our responsibility not only to educate ourselves, but also to help as many children/people to have a proper education; thereby illuminating the life of all the people of our mother country, India.
10. At the same time, we should realize that learning does not stop at schools and colleges, but it continues throughout our life in other forms because our own experience is the best teacher.

b) **Identify the <u>common nouns</u> and the <u>proper nouns</u> in the following sentences:**

1. Chennai is the capital of an Indian state called Tamil Nadu.
2. The city of Chennai is located along the south eastern coast of the Bay of Bengal.
3. This city is very popular for the Marina Beach, the second longest beach in the world.
4. The old name of Chennai was Madras.
5. Earlier the home of the entire south Indian film industry and now, the home of mainly the Tamil film industry, Chennai has many cinema studios like AVM studios.
6. The city also has popular educational institutions like IIT, Anna University, Madras Medical College, etc.
7. It is also well known for its commercial centres like T.Nagar, Purasawalkam, Parris Corner, etc.
8. Unlike many modern cities, Chennai is also popular for its cultural art forms like Bharatanatyam, a classical south Indian dance, and the music season during the month of December, a golden period for the lovers of the traditional music, especially the Carnatic Music.
9. This book, English Grammar (Simple, Practical and Comprehensive), written by V P Kannan, is fortunate to be published from this great city.

Grammar Exercises

c) **Write the abstract nouns from the following words:**

serve, long, infant, true, good, owner, pirate, child, cruel, live, short, flatter, humble, great, brave, free, believe, broad, advise, brother, defend, sane, dark, hero, hate, friend, judge, king, sell, succeed, act, wide, bitter, high, man, deep, think, strong, agent, punish, die, young, occupy, sweet, choose, know, poor, priest, quick, discover, persevere, expect, Hindu, move, rich, pilgrim, wise, obey, ignorant, captain

d) **Identify the collective nouns in the following:**

1. The fleet is ready for the proposed operations.
2. The jury would pass the judgement today.
3. The President asked the army to be on alert.
4. The police tried to disperse the agitating crowd.
5. The mob tried to attack the cricket team.
6. The parliament set up a committee to look into the urgent needs of the nation.
7. He was surprised to see his family in the temple.

e) Some collective nouns cannot be used independently and should be used with the prepositional phrase of 'of + plural noun' only. **In the following exercise, fill in the blanks with the suitable collective noun from the list given below:**

album, band, batch, bed, board, body, bunch, bundle, catalogue, chain, chest, class, cloud, cluster, collection, colony, constellation, crew, flight, flock, galaxy, gang, glossary, group, grove, heap, herd, hive, host, pack, pair, patrol, plague, range, ream, reel, regiment, roll, row, series, shoal, shower, stack, string, suite, swarm, troop, troupe, wreath, zoo

1. a _troop_ of dancers
2. a _____ of events
3. a _____ of sticks
4. a _wreath_ of flowers
5. a _____ of stars
6. a _____ of wild animals
7. a _gang_ of rowdies
8. a _____ of monkeys
9. a _____ of soldiers
10. a _crew_ of sailors
11. a _____ of rooms
12. a _____ of old stamps
13. a _string_ of beads
14. a _____ of film stars
15. a _____ of students
16. a _pack_ of cards
17. a _____ of insects
18. a _____ of musicians
19. a _flock_ of sheep
20. a _____ of buffaloes
21. a _____ of words
22. a _bed_ of oysters
23. a _____ of bees
24. a _____ of directors
25. a _colony_ of ants
26. a _____ of shops
27. a _____ of tools
28. a _row_ of houses
29. a _____ of leaders
30. a _____ of paper
31. a _shoal_ of fish
32. a _____ of film
33. a _____ of shoes
34. a _reel_ of cloth
35. a _____ of policemen
36. a _____ of arms
37. a _heap_ of rubbish
38. a _____ of possibilities
39. a _____ of grapes
40. an _album_ of photos
41. a _____ of trees
42. a _____ of drawers
43. a _range_ of mountains
44. a _____ of planes
45. a _____ of items
46. a _cloud_ of flies
47. a _____ of keys
48. a _____ of friends
49. a _shower_ of rain
50. a _____ of rats
51. a _____ of trainees

f) Identify the nouns in the following sentences and classify them into <u>countable nouns and uncountable nouns</u>:

1. Home is the best place for everybody.
2. Though our house may not have all facilities, we like it.
3. One gets the basic needs like food, love and affection in the home.
4. However, we need some minimum facilities in our houses.
5. Water is very important.
6. Supply of milk and newspaper at our doorstep adds to our convenience.
7. Fortunately, even grocery items like rice, wheat, sugar, salt, oil, egg, butter, vegetables, bun, cookie, etc. are delivered at our doorstep.
8. The proximity to the school is very important for the children.
9. Availability of other services like hospital, market, bus stop, etc. nearby really helps.
10. In spite of all the comforts and facilities of the home, sometimes, we like to visit places like beach, cinema hall, park, hotel, etc. for a change of environment and enjoyment.
11. Even after all the fun and enjoyment outside our home, we cannot help thinking about the popular proverb 'East or west, home is best.'

g) Write the <u>plural</u> for the following nouns:

crisis, jeans, wife, cat, life, boy, box, lady, game, radius, fish, computer, grown-up, girl, knife, man, mango, foot, thief, tooth, child, people, family, ferry, prize, man-of-war, logo, roof, pen, brother-in-law, kilo, mouth, class, aircraft, cattle, shelf, flower, potato, cow, scissors, mathematics, city, branch, desk, house, sheep, owl, half

h) Write the <u>other gender</u> for the following nouns. If a noun has no other gender, identify if it is a common gender or a neuter gender:

mother, parent, uncle, sister, grandfather, aunt, cousin, child, son, niece, granddaughter, man, girl, husband, queen, lord, nun, gentleman, madam, author, hostess, poet, manager, priestess, actor, conductress, emperor, princess, hero, washer-man, master, milkman, saleswoman, widow, bridegroom, client, driver, pilot, waiter, witch, giant, heir, baby, servant

cow, hen, bird, tiger, animal, lion, horse, table, peacock, goose, fish, stallion, deer, dog, bull, goat, bee, ewe, pen, computer

i) Write the <u>possessive case</u> for the following nouns:

mothers, father, Balu, uncle, aunties, box, boxes, class, classes, boy, boys, parents, boss, bosses, houses, man, men, poet, poets, poetess, poetesses, tiger, tigress, table, tables, brother, sisters, city, cities, river, rivers, love, feeling, feelings

Grammar Exercises

2. Exercise for Chapter 3: Pronouns

a) Identify the pronouns in the following sentences, their type and case:

1. We, three friends working in the same office, had gone to Andaman on tour with our families.
2. My father had also come with us.
3. It was an exciting first air journey for my son because he always wanted me to take him on a flight somewhere.
4. Our children made friends with each other, and they enjoyed themselves.
5. My son had enjoyed the beaches along with his mother because she got a relief for herself also from her office schedule.
6. All shared their feelings with one another.
7. Jarawa people are one of the indigenous people of Andaman, and they are still living in their own world. We met them on our way to another island.
8. Such was our enjoyment that this will remain in everybody's memory, and none would forget it.
9. After all, who can forget it? Even you cannot if your family had also visited with you.
10. Everybody enjoyed everything there that nobody disliked anything though many may not appreciate it.
11. Anybody's experience, mine, ours, yours, his, hers, its or theirs is a good experience, and so was ours.
12. Though the expenditure was about ₹20,000/- each, we ourselves would like to amuse ourselves once again.
13. Whom should we thank for? It is God whose mercy made it happen to all of us.

b) Write the correct form of the personal pronoun in the following sentences using the pronouns given within brackets, if any:

1. __I__ (I/my/me) am a boy, and __She__ (she/her) is a tall beautiful girl.
2. __We__ (we/us) do not know each other before.
3. Yet, __her__ (she/her) face looked familiar to __me__ (I/my/me).
4. __My__ (I/my/me) friend came suddenly to invite for __his__ (he/his/him) birthday, and __he__ (he/his/him) introduced __her__ (she/her) to __me__ (I/my/me).
5. __He__ (he/his/him) wanted everybody known to __him__ (he/his/him) to attend __his__ (he/his/him) birthday party.
6. Suddenly, __she__ (she/her) remained __me__ (I/my/me) of __our__ (we/our/us) childhood when __their__ (they/their/them) family was __our__ (we/our/us) neighbours.
7. Yes, __they__ (they/their/them) lived in __our__ (we/our/us) neighbourhood earlier, and __we__ (we/our/us) helped __them__ (they/their/them) once.

8. There was a puppy in **her** (she/her) house, and **it** (it/its) would always play with **us** (we/our/us).
9. **We** (we/our/us) liked **it** (it/its/it) very much as **its** (it/its) colour was attractive.
10. **You** (you/your) would also like **it** (it/its) if **your** (you/your) family were with **us** (we/our/us) because **it** (it/its) would have played with **you** (you/your) also.
11. The puppy was **hers** (she/her/hers); however, **it** (it/its) became all **ours** (we/our/us/ours) soon.
12. Finally, **we** (we/our/us) all went back home with the childhood memories, **mine** (I/my/me/mine), **his** (he/his/him), and **hers** (she/her/hers).

c) Write the suitable **reflexive pronoun, emphatic pronoun or reciprocal pronoun** in the following sentences and identify its type correctly:

1. I **myself** learned drawing.
2. I taught **myself** drawing.
3. I learned drawing **myself**.
4. He cooked the dinner **himself**.
5. They patted **each other** on their back for a little success.
6. The monkey is scratching **itself**.
7. We **ourselves** had to take a decision.
8. She blamed **herself** for her poor condition.
9. One should defend **oneself** against the bullies.
10. You should behave **yourself**.
11. Parents should love **each other**.
12. All family members should love **one another**.

d) Write the suitable **demonstrative pronoun, indefinite pronoun or distributive pronoun** in the following sentences using the given pronouns and identify **its type** correctly:

all, anybody, each, either, everybody, everything, few, many, neither, nobody, none, nothing, one, somebody, such, that, these, this, those

1. _____ was her devotion for her studies.
2. Hey you two! _____ can play, but _____ can leave now.
3. Hey you two! _____ of you can play, but _____ of you can leave now.
4. _____ wants love and affection.
5. _____ are in this table, and _____ are in that table.
6. You should not give it to _____.
7. _____ is the gift given by my friend.

Grammar Exercises

8. Though it is good, only _____ will appreciate, but _____ will oppose.
9. There is _____ coming; _____ should leave now.
10. _____ can succeed except _____.
11. I want to meet _____ and give them _____ a gift.
12. We will take care of _____; there is _____ to worry about.
13. _____ were invited, but only _____ came.
14. I want to meet _____ of them and give _____ of them a gift.
15. Our guest will meet _____ _____ at a time.

3. Exercise for Chapter 4: Verbs - Basics & Chapter 5: Negative Sentences

a) **Classify the <u>Verbs</u> into <u>Be-Verbs</u> and <u>Action Verbs</u> and for Action Verbs, pick out the <u>auxiliary verb</u> and the <u>main verb form</u> from their <u>complete verbs</u>:**

b) **Identify the <u>Verbs,</u> their <u>Tenses</u> and the <u>Voice</u>:**

1. The car stopped suddenly.
2. I think you cannot finish your work.
3. She must be playing with the kids now.
4. We shall be the winners in the tournament.
5. They have been living here since 2000.
6. Don't dream all the day.
7. What a beautiful girl she is!
8. Thirukural was composed by Thiruvalluvar.
9. The train had not left when I reached the station.
10. I shall have finished my work by tomorrow.
11. The sky looks cloudy today.
12. The school bell is ringing loudly.
13. They are going to Madurai.
14. He may not be punished for his mistakes.
15. I have been in this room for the last one year.
16. Nowadays, computers are used in every office.
17. We were just inside the room the whole day.
18. The boys were playing yesterday between 4 pm to 6 pm.
19. You have seen the latest movie of your favourite actor.
20. The book was being written for many months.
21. We shall be watching the movie this time tomorrow.
22. We are Indians.
23. They had been living here for 10 years, and we shall have been here for 20 years.
24. We have been known to him for a long time.
25. He will have been honoured for his charity.

c) **Write some verbs like 'play, go, etc.' in all tenses and aspects under active and passive voices.**

d) **Fill in the blanks with the <u>correct tense of the verbs</u> (given within brackets) based on the context of their usage in the following sentences:**

1. Students _____ (finish) the classwork just now.
2. He _____ (go) to school daily.
3. We _____ (travel) by train tomorrow at this time.
4. She _____ (be) a student last year.

Grammar Exercises

5. We _____ (be) boys.
6. Yesterday, the meeting _____ (start) before we _____ (reach).
7. I _____ (be) a student till last year.
8. The trains _____ (run) late for almost a month.
9. We _____ (watch) a movie between 11 AM to 2 PM tomorrow.
10. I _____ (be) a doctor next year.
11. They _____ (construct) the bridge for many years before its inauguration.
12. She _____ (live) here for 10 years by next year.
13. My father _____ (come) tomorrow.
14. I _____ (meet) my old friend yesterday.
15. They _____ (be) students last year.
16. They _____ (be) to London next year.
17. He _____ (be) a doctor next year.
18. The traffic _____ (move) slowly now.
19. We _____ (be) to London. (after it was over in the past)
20. She _____ (be) a teacher.
21. We _____ (go) to celebrate our sports day next month.
22. It _____ (eat) the food already.
23. I _____ (be) a boy.
24. You _____ (become) a doctor by June next year.
25. We _____ (play) here daily.

e) Write the sentences obtained by answering the above questions of (d) in **passive voice** wherever applicable.

f) Write the sentences obtained by answering the above questions of (d) and (e) as **negative sentences**.

g) **Fill in the blanks with the correct modal verbs in the following sentences:**

1. He _____ visit his native place. (obligation/compulsion)
2. _____ you help me please? (request)
3. _____ I help you please? (offer)
4. We _____ to be punctual for the class. (being bound)
5. I _____ come tomorrow to your place. (future)
6. His mother _____ help him do the homework. (possibility)
7. The situation was such that our team _____ win the match. (past chance)
8. I _____ go now. (necessity)
9. We _____ help him because of his poverty. (obligation)
10. Our team _____ win the match. (chance)
11. She _____ sing and dance when she was a child. (past habit)
12. _____ I come in please? (permission)
13. He _____ drive very fast. (daring)
14. You _____ help him do the homework. (ability)
15. He _____ come day-after-tomorrow. (future)

4. Exercise for Chapter 6: Interrogative Sentences & Chapter 7: Verbs - Advanced

a) Identify the **structural elements** of subject, verb, object, indirect object and other complement (subject complement, verb complement and object complement) and also their corresponding **parts of speech**:

b) Identify the **type of the verb** as transitive verb, intransitive verb or linking verb and also the **causative verbs/perception verbs**:

c) Write the **Yes/No question** and the **Question-Word question** for each structural element:

1. His statements sound more logical now.
2. The plane was believed to have been hijacked by the militants.
3. The old actor was very popular.
4. I consider him to be an expert.
5. The young player has been to many countries even before.
6. My mother wrote a letter.
7. The old man was walking slowly along the road.
8. He would always be in the library.
9. You should make him work sincerely.
10. We can go shopping today and fishing tomorrow.
11. His capacity to sing and dance made him popular in the village.
12. One should always keep trying.
13. We should study the lessons daily very carefully.
14. She is our class teacher.
15. The ball was lost by a tall boy.
16. I gave him a ball.
17. We can get the house painted by him.
18. The police found the missing child playing in a distant park.

d) Identify the **mood** of the sentence:

1. Please attend the meeting without fail.
2. The chairman will not attend the meeting.
3. God bless you!
4. If you were here, he would not attend the meeting.
5. The manager suggests that you attend the meeting.
6. God blesses you.
7. It is vital that we discuss that point in the meeting.
8. Be quite in the meeting.

Grammar Exercises

9. Long live our beloved MD!
10. When will the meeting take place?
11. I wish I were the Managing Director.
12. Will the Managing Director attend the meeting?
13. Outsiders should not attend the meeting.
14. He behaves as if he were the Managing Director.
15. The manger will attend the meeting.

e) Fill in the blanks with the correct <u>extended modal verbs</u> in the following sentences:

1. He _____ to the married life slowly. (future adoption)
2. You _____ visit your native place. (suggestion)
3. He _____ finish the work today itself. (compulsion)
4. She _____ attend the interview. (obligation - (use be-verb as modal))
5. Our team _____ win the match. (implied future)
6. I _____ to leave the office when he came. (imminence - (use adjective expression))
7. You _____ study hard in the future. (obligation)
8. I _____ read many books. (past habit)
9. I _____ study than play. (preference)
10. The manager _____ fix the meeting yesterday itself. (past compulsion)

f) Use the correct <u>particle</u> with the given base verb to form the appropriate <u>phrasal verb</u> in the following sentences:

1. The news will cheer you ____.
2. Don't go _____ your wishes as it will not take you anywhere.
3. He gets _____ with many people simultaneously.
4. They let us _____ finally.
5. It is difficult to put ___ ____ these naughty children.
6. We made ___ a story to avoid the punishment.
7. Take ____ your shoes after coming ____.
8. She might drop _____ any day this week.
9. The bus broke _____ on its way to Chennai.
10. You must keep ____ your good efforts.
11. It is easy to sort _____ your problem.
12. Some rich people will back ____ our development programmes.
13. Students should hand _____ the home work in time.
14. Children grow ____ _____ their dresses quickly.
15. The car would run ____ of petrol any time.
16. A bomb blew ____ from an old vehicle.

17. Give ___ smoking.
18. Our flight may take ____ any time.
19. The manager may call ____ you anytime.
20. Pick ____ the correct answer.
21. We should set ___ a meeting before tomorrow.
22. The result of our hard work may wear ____.
23. They fell _____ due to many differences between them.
24. A baby sitter looks _____ the child.
25. They decided to go _____ with their plans.
26. We may come ____ animals on the way.
27. It is difficult to figure _____ the meaning of the writing.
28. Thieves may break ____ to steal.
29. He has handed _____ his bag to his friend.
30. One should do _____ the bad habits.
31. We must warm ____ before exercising.
32. I ran ____ my old friend unexpectedly.
33. Please hold ___ for 5 minutes.
34. They turned _____ our offer.
35. She tries to show _____ much in front of others.
36. He has not yet turned ____ for the meeting.
37. You may use the petrol ____ in the car.
38. You should stick ____ the diet.
39. The meeting is put ____ till next week.
40. She caught ____ soon with the other students.
41. Students get _____ early in the morning to study.
42. He has to pay ____ his mistakes.
43. A stranger cut ____ during the meeting.
44. We should not look _____ the poor people.
45. He has to wake ____ early every Monday.
46. You may hang ____ at the park.
47. We should check _____ at the hotel before 8 AM.
48. Our plan will work ____ finally.
49. An young man came _____ to help the poor people.
50. My friend may call _____ after some time.
51. He decided to hang ____ for some more time.
52. Kind people brought an orphan child ____ in an orphanage.
53. He may find ____ the answer for that difficult problem.
54. I easily get mixed ____ in this area.
55. We can work ____ the total cost beforehand.

5. Exercise for Chapter 8: Verbal Phrases - Gerund, Participle and Infinitive

a) **Identify the <u>type of the verbal phrase</u> as <u>gerund</u>, <u>participle</u> and <u>infinitive</u>:**

b) Also, identify their <u>corresponding functional type of the basic phrases,</u> namely noun phrase, adjective phrase and adverb phrase:

1. Gandhiji is accepted to have been one of the greatest leaders of the world.
2. One could see the many coastal villages devastated by the Tsunami.
3. We need more people to serve the poor people.
4. We can see them play in the ground.
5. We should not be afraid to tell the truth.
6. What you should do is just listen in the class.
7. She was about to leave the office.
8. Eating too much ruins our health.
9. He needs a lot of practice to win the match.
10. Everybody likes being loved.
11. We should allow the children to enjoy also.
12. She looks excited.
13. Swimming is a good exercise.
14. Having walked a long distance, he was tired.
15. He must be lucky to have been invited for the party.
16. I saw my friend walking along the road.
17. The making of the future is in our hand also.
18. He can help you prepare for the exam.
19. One of the main reasons for pollution is cutting of trees.
20. He came running.
21. The weather being fine, I went out for walking.
22. People are happy about the improving economic condition.
23. I will make him pay his debts to you soon.
24. He was tired after having walked a long distance.
25. To play football daily is his love.
26. They want to play football now.
27. Having been delayed by the torrential rains, the train came very late.
28. Let us play.
29. Many a scenery is there to been seen.
30. Walking along the beach, I saw my old friend.
31. It is very important to help each other in difficulties.
32. He was very proud to have served in the military.
33. We must practice to win the match.
34. A letter describing the problems of the teachers was sent to the management.
35. The manager will tell you where to go for marketing.
36. To finish the work in time, we had to struggle very much.

c) **Fill in the blanks with the correct form of verbal phrase using the verb given within brackets:**
1. _____ (love) by grandmother during the childhood was a happy experience.
2. I look forward to _____ (see) you next week.
3. _____ (laugh) heartily, we went out to play.
4. _____ (work) the whole day, I was very tired.
5. You cannot see her _____ (talk) to him.
6. You must work hard _____ (finish) the work in time.
7. Although _____ (obsess) with his singing, she did not even talk to him.
8. We are sorry _____ (hear) the bad news.
9. He is quick in _____ (understand) the new things.
10. He has to give up _____ (smoke).
11. He does not want _____ (play) with strangers.
12. You should avoid _____ (make) silly mistakes in the exam.
13. _____ (keep) him _____ (work) the whole day is very difficult.
14. We were disappointed at the officer _____ (behave) rudely to ladies.
15. Tourists were sorry _____ (treat) badly by the local people.
16. You should have the power _____ (do) any work.
17. _____ (understand) new things quickly, he learned many things.
18. She must have come _____ (meet) you.
19. The train _____ (come) late, the passengers were tired.
20. The old man, _____ (be) a teacher, wants to read more books.
21. He is quick _____ (understand) the new things.
22. He prefers _____ (play) football to _____ (study) his lessons.
23. He may be punished for _____ (make) the mistake deliberately.
24. I had to come _____ (run) very fast _____ (meet) you.
25. She loves _____ (love).
26. So as _____ (make) her happy, he bought her many dresses.
27. Can you see the car _____ (come) fast towards us?
28. Not _____ (use) to the new place, I had to search for his house.
29. There is nothing _____ (lose) for them.
30. You must be ashamed not _____ (tell) the truth.
31. We were tired of _____ (wait) in the long queue.
32. The old woman _____ (be) a patient for a long time succumbed finally.
33. _____ (laugh) loudly will relax our mind.
34. The dictator _____ (kill) in the accident, the people heaved a sigh of relief.
35. It is strange _____ (see) her at this time.
36. The buildings _____ (damage) by the earthquake should be demolished.
37. They are happy _____ (help) many poor children last year alone.
38. I was fond of _____ (swim) during the childhood.
39. The girl, _____ (dance) to the new tune, was fascinating.
40. _____ (fascinate) by his _____ (sing), she followed him everywhere.

6. Exercise for Chapter 12: Adjectives & Chapter 13: Determiners and Articles

a) Identify the adjectives and determiners:

1. I like this pen.
2. Her son has grown taller now.
3. She remains young even after many years.
4. Today is hot.
5. He often becomes angry.
6. An apple daily is good for your health.
7. She looks beautiful in the new dress.
8. All students can wear whatever dress they like.
9. Either book is good for every child.
10. An elephant has taken my bag.
11. She likes her first son very much.
12. Those days are memorable in my life.
13. Neither book was good.
14. Some people do not want any money though they have no money.
15. Hercules was very strong.
16. Our child may get the first prize.
17. He is the most intelligent student in the class.
18. We may never get to meet such people.
19. One should buy few books every year.
20. A strange man had come yesterday.
21. Their habits are strange to us.
22. Cat licks its paw.
23. Give him an egg daily.
24. The milk went bad yesterday.
25. The weather turned cold suddenly.

b) Write the correct form of comparison of adjectives:

1. He has as _____ (many) brothers as sisters.
2. He is _____ (tall - use with a pre-modifier) than she is.
3. He is _____ (tall) his brother was 2 years back.
4. Her sister is _____ (short) _____ her brother.
5. My problem is _____ (same) _____ your problem.
6. Our school is _____ (good) than their school.
7. Our town has the _____ (same) issues _____ yours.
8. She has even _____ (few) than three dresses.

9. She is _____ (fill with a pre-modifier) as tall as her husband.
10. She is _____ (fill with a pre-modifier) the most beautiful actress.
11. She is as tall as _____ (he/him).
12. She looks _____ (different) ____ me.
13. She looks _____ (beautiful) than her sister.
14. She looks _____ (different) _____ before.
15. The _____ (rich) man is not the _____ (intelligent) man.
16. The tree grew _____ and _____ (tall).
17. Their houses are _____ (similar) _____ each other.
18. These twins look _____ (different) _____ each other.
19. This is the _____ (small) car I have ever seen.
20. Today's weather is _____ (bad) than yesterday's.
21. You are as _____ (good) a teacher as he is.
22. You are becoming _____ and _____ (beautiful).

c) **Fill in the blanks with correct article. If no article is required, write '(no article)':**

1. He is _____ champion of _____ school.
2. _____ umbrellas are useful on rainy days.
3. _____ sun gives energy to all its ___ planets.
4. We can spend _____ hour in the park.
5. He is _____ tall boy.
6. We have to go to _____ university for higher studies.
7. _____ Mahatma Gandhi is ___ father of ___ India.
8. _____ dog is _____ pet animal.
9. _____ egg is good for health.
10. We are studying _____ English, and it is ___ language of _____ English people.
11. _____ honesty is _____ best policy.
12. Children should go to _____ school.
13. _____ poor always suffer.
14. _____ children like ___ mother very much.
15. Take _____ umbrella to school.
16. She is _____ tallest girl in _____ class.
17. I want _____ one-rupee note.
18. My mother has _____ egg.
19. _____ great Caesar was an emperor.
20. _____ Ganga is ___ holy river.

Grammar Exercises 265

7. Exercise for Chapter 14: Adverbs

a) **Identify the adverbs and their types as adverbs of manner, adverbs of place, adverbs of time, adverbs of definite frequency, adverbs of indefinite frequency, adverbs of probability, adverbs of opinion, adverbs of degree, parallel adverbs and connecting adverbs:**

1. Those people may never visit this town.
2. They had to travel all alone.
3. Ladies used to go out rarely in the past.
4. She is seldom dressed beautifully.
5. We have to study carefully.
6. The show was almost full.
7. They were going there.
8. We often play cricket with our friends.
9. Personally, I was surprised to know the facts.
10. Please go backward to make more space.
11. They really worked hard. So did we.
12. Students should study daily.
13. Parents always love their children.
14. He could hardly complete the work.
15. She looks pretty cool.
16. I usually get up early.
17. The temperature went up fast yesterday.
18. It was very difficult. Nevertheless, he tried.
19. We do not like baseball. Nor do our friends.
20. He was actually late. However, the event was yet to start.
21. She went out angrily.
22. We can meet later, not now.
23. You can pay afterwards.
24. She is obviously the right person.
25. He wanted to search everywhere.

b) **Write the adverbs and adverb phrases given within brackets in the correct position:**

1. You can meet him. (now)
2. He became a popular singer. (thus)
3. We are bound to learn English. (obviously)
4. The story is good. (pretty)
5. My mother watches TV. (hardly)
6. I would talk to him. (over phone, sometimes)
7. I have seen her. (before, never)

8. They vacated the house. (last year)
9. He ran. (fast, very)
10. We took a pledge to work. (in the office, very hard, throughout the year, daily, to finish the project)
11. They have not met. (recently)
12. The lock was not difficult to break for the thief. (enough)
13. The bedroom is. (upstairs)
14. The theatre is full. (almost)
15. We had met long. (ago/back)
16. The children were playing. (happily)
17. There is a solution for this vexed problem. (theoretically)
18. We should play. (one hour, daily)
19. He would have gone. (home)
20. Have you met him? (ever, during the last 5 years)
21. He must be. (only, here)
22. We can meet. (around 4 PM, outside)
23. The box is difficult to carry. (too)
24. She is kind to her enemies. (even)
25. He can speak English. (well)
26. Some people are hurt. (in the accident, badly)
27. We do not go. (there, often)
28. He may not be available. (after 3 PM, tomorrow)
29. It is extremely hot. (in summer)
30. She watches TV. (in the evening, always)

c) **Write the <u>correct form of comparison of adverbs:</u>**

1. The _____ (fast) you walk, the _____ (soon) you reach.
2. You should drive _____ (fast) to win the race.
3. Can you run _____ (fast) than him?
4. No _____ (soon) had he left than his friend came.
5. You should do it _____ and _____ slowly. (use double comparison)
6. She drives as fast as _____ (he/him).
7. They ran _____ and _____ (fast - use double comparison) near the end.
8. Can he write _____ (clearly) than before?
9. _____ (soon) he had left, his friend came.
10. You can also try to drive _____ (fast - use with a pre-modifier) than he would.
11. He drives _____ (fast) than a champion would drive.
12. We played _____ (good) of all.
13. The boss behaved _____ (politely) than many others.
14. She danced _____ (gracefully) of all participants.
15. She can speak French _____ (fluently) English.

Grammar Exercises

8. Exercise for Chapter 15: Prepositions

a) Identify the prepositions, the type of preposition as simple or complex, prepositional objects and prepositional phrases:

b) Classify the types of prepositional phrases as prepositional adverb phrase, prepositional adjective phrase or prepositional noun phrase based on their function as adverb, adjective or noun respectively:

1. The flight was flying just above the city before landing.
2. A boy went up the hill.
3. Write with pen but without seeing others.
4. He has come from Delhi and will go to Mumbai on Monday.
5. Kamaraj led a simple life for the sake of the common people.
6. We can wait for you till 5 pm.
7. Kamaraj opened many schools in order to spread the literacy in Tamil Nadu.
8. The driver jumped off the car.
9. My grandmother was very fond of me.
10. He had to work hard until late night.
11. The opposition party walked out of the Assembly.
12. In course of time, he felt sorry for the behaviour.
13. He has really worked hard in comparison to his old age.
14. We have to play against the local team.
15. Apart from Tamil Nadu, I toured the whole South India.
16. She suffered in the life in spite of being rich.
17. Some people go to the Ayappan temple along with family.
18. For a short period, I went to school with my father.
19. I was walking along the road all alone.
20. The headmaster is standing in front of the school.
21. By virtue of being the headmaster, he tried to enforce discipline among the students.
22. We should live in line with the modern world.
23. The child was sitting beside mother.
24. We are same with respect to the salary.
25. The school children are running across the road.
26. We have been living in Chennai since 2000.
27. Actors act according to the guidance of the directors.
28. He entered the politics with an eye to becoming a minister.
29. I walk around the park daily.
30. Move your dresses onto the top shelf.
31. The hostel was behind the college.
32. He behaves like a rich man in the bank near the post office.
33. She loved her sons despite her sufferings.

34. The payment was already made with reference to his claims.
35. The people of Andaman travel by means of ships daily.
36. I found my pen beneath the papers.
37. He misused his official power in favour of his family.
38. The team played below the standard.
39. There was a big crowd inside and outside the hall.
40. The officer came inside from his chamber.

c) **Fill in the blanks with <u>appropriate preposition</u> or the part of complex preposition:**

1. The ball was _____ the table.
2. I will return your money _____ a month.
3. He spoke _____ behalf _____ all employees.
4. Contrary _____ the expectation, I enjoyed the tour very much.
5. There is a book _____ the table.
6. He was born _____ two sisters.
7. I want to write _____ a pen of knowledge, not gold.
8. We should not wish _____ our capacity.
9. Many people went _____ the closed shop.
10. All are present _____ him.
11. She could not walk fast _____ account _____ the pain in the legs.
12. The work was cancelled owing _____ some problems.
13. We have to work on Saturday _____ lieu _____ the holiday for the Onam.
14. The birds fly _____ the bridge.
15. We deposited the amount _____ accordance _____ the rule.
16. Their responsibility _____ regard to the failure of the system is not defined.
17. He was very tall _____ his friends.
18. In the event _____ a hung parliament, a coalition government may be formed.
19. The government has many welfare schemes _____ aid of poor people.
20. He has to look after nephews also _____ his children.
21. We should work carefully _____ our goal.
22. We have to finish the work in compliance _____ the agreement.
23. There is a temple _____ top of the hill.
24. The cricket fans rushed _____ the stadium.
25. It is difficult to walk _____ the crowded streets.
26. He told me _____ his adventure _____ the holiday.
27. Gandhiji followed non-violence _____ his life.
28. We live _____ Annanagar _____ Chennai.
29. I shall solve the problem _____ the help of my friend.
30. The result will depend _____ her.
31. I have bought a gift _____ my son, and it will be given _____ him _____ his mother.

Grammar Exercises

32. He decided to walk _____ the street.
33. He bought a black shoe in addition _____ the brown one.
34. The food was very good except _____ the price.
35. He used milk powder in place _____ milk.
36. We can buy many things in our life _____ money.
37. They walked _____ of using the car.
38. We have to buy vegetables regardless _____ their prices.
39. The fan is _____ the dining table.
40. She has died _____ consequence of the fracture _____ the leg.
41. Our school was _____ Chennai and would start _____ 8 AM daily.
42. They expressed their displeasure by way _____ writing to their boss.
43. Every man would be rich or poor in relation _____ others.

9. Exercise for Chapter 16: Phrases and Expressions

a) **Identify the basic phrases and their types; prepositional phrases and their functional types; and verbal phrases, their types and their functional types**:

1. I still have my old school books.
2. He has a problem to solve immediately.
3. The problem is about to be solved now.
4. They went out of the room.
5. Climbing up the tree, she slipped down.
6. We heard a sound from inside his room.
7. He scored a goal almost surprisingly in the last minute.
8. We played daily with an old ball.
9. She is really very beautiful.
10. The kings wore clothes made of silk with lines of golden threads.
11. The problem may be difficult to solve immediately.
12. He always longed to fly by air.
13. The flight having landed safely after a technical snag, everybody heaved a sigh of relief.
14. She walked in a beautiful style.
15. We should not board the running train.
16. We can go swimming in the sea next week.
17. The teacher will not allow you to write the test today.
18. Reading books is a very good habit.
19. My parents have advised me to study well.
20. Being deaf and dumb, she could not hear nor speak.
21. To keep cool is the most difficult.
22. We play daily in the evening.
23. He worked very hard and sincerely.
24. She got the first prize definitely unexpectedly.
25. A very tall boy has joined our class today.
26. Completely destroyed by Tsunami, the village looks deserted.
27. We pray to get the blessings of God.
28. He felt very sorry for his mistakes.
29. We were very happy at their treating us with respect.
30. That was a village without any facility.
31. Children like playing in the park.
32. A book of that author is published today.
33. The old man walks with a walking stick.
34. Walking is good for health.
35. My teacher is very kind and sincere.
36. She seems to be very reasonable in her demands.
37. Everybody needs somebody else to share their feelings.
38. He lives happily in his own house.
39. I want the ball on the loft.
40. The day was spoiled by the heavy torrential rains.

Grammar Exercises

10. Exercise for Chapter 17: Clauses and Structural Sentence Types - Simple Sentence, Compound Sentence and Complex Sentence & Chapter 18: Conjunctions

a) Identify the Conjunctions, if any, and their types as Coordinating Conjunction (CCn), Subordinating Conjunction (SCn) and Relative Conjunction (i.e., Relative Pronoun (RP) or Relative Adverb (RA)):

b) Identify the Subordinate/Dependant Clause (if any) and their types as Noun Clause (NCls), Adjective Clause (AdjCls) and Adverb Clause (AdvCls):

1. I know that he would get first mark in the school.
2. Do you know which is the main cause of ragging among the students?
3. She was such an intelligent person that she could answer all questions.
4. You have to follow these rules as long as you stay here.
5. If you work hard and sincerely, you will achieve your goal.
6. Though he has less money, he is satisfied in the life.
7. This is the house where I have been living for many years.
8. She was crying and running as if someone chased her to kill.
9. My classmate who is also my colleague has invited me to his house.
10. You can go when he comes.
11. Please let me know in case he troubles you.
12. Nobody can understand how such criminal activities developed in colleges.
13. When he comes is important.
14. Where his life is leading him is a mystery.
15. Everybody liked her because she was kind and polite.
16. I could not remember where I lost my keys.
17. Whatever you do, you should be honest.
18. No scientist is able to tell how the universe will end.
19. The doctor whom we consulted has asked us to come the next day.
20. He has taken me to a shop where we can buy almost anything.
21. She is taller than he is.
22. Who will win the match is a million dollar question.
23. He was very careful lest he should make some mistake.
24. I do not know the time when he comes.
25. We reached the theatre before the show was started.

c) Identify the type of sentences as Simple Sentence (SmpS), Compound Sentence (CpdS) and Complex Sentence (ClxS):

d) Identify the verbal phrases, if any, and their types as Noun Phrase (NP), Adjective Phrase (AdjP), and Adverb Phrase (AdvP) if it is a simple sentence:

e) **Identify <u>the main clauses</u> if it is a compound sentence:**

f) **Identify <u>the subordinate clauses and their types</u> as <u>Noun Clause (NCls), Adjective Clause (AdjCls) and Adverb Clause (AdvCls)</u> if it is a complex sentence:**

1. If you believe God sincerely, all your problems will be solved easily.
2. Although she had helped all her friends, nobody helped her in her need.
3. Our success depends on how all of us work sincerely.
4. It was very costly; otherwise, I would have bought it.
5. The country which we are going to visit is vulnerable to terrorism.
6. A lady had come yesterday, and she gave this parcel for you.
7. Either you can read a book or watch TV.
8. Whether we will win or they will lose is not the problem now.
9. My teacher is very helpful, so she would help you also.
10. Being a foreigner, one should be more careful.
11. Playing joyfully in the park, the children sang and danced.
12. We all know that he would quit one day.
13. Neither could she cook well nor could she teach the children.
14. She is rich, yet she is simple.
15. He must reach the station in time, or he would miss the train.
16. They worked very hard; however, they could not finish the work.
17. You may meet him tomorrow when he returns from abroad.
18. After finishing the home work, you can go out to play.
19. She is neither intelligent nor beautiful.
20. Rich and powerful, he could do many things easily.
21. The problem would have been difficult; even so, you should have tried.
22. Not only does she sing but also she dances.
23. He has planned to pursue his higher studies abroad.
24. The messenger did not come yesterday, nor did he call.
25. Students should listen carefully to what is being taught in the class.
26. I really liked the sweet he had given yesterday.
27. The knowledge of grammar is essential in any language.
28. We searched thoroughly, but the book could not be found.
29. Driving in the crowded city is very difficult.
30. We should not give the students the exercises that are too difficult to solve.
31. Beaten up and punished wrongly by the police, he felt shattered.
32. You are sincere, and you will get the benefit.
33. Hardly had we closed the door when somebody rang the calling bell.
34. He will get into trouble unless he corrects himself now itself.
35. Having finished the work earlier, he relaxed for some time.

Grammar Exercises

g) Transform/Rewrite the following <u>simple sentences into compound sentences</u>. If there are two simple sentences in a single question, combine them into a compound sentence:

h) Transform/Rewrite the following <u>simple sentences into complex sentences</u>. If there are two simple sentences in a single question, combine them into a complex sentence:

1. Having spent many years abroad, he finally decided to come home.
2. He has dedicated his life for the country. He was honoured by the Government.
3. I wanted to attend the meeting. I could not attend.
4. Heavily damaged by the recent rains, the roads are in a bad condition.
5. Her husband's income was not sufficient for the family. She also went to work.
6. The actor had to struggle a lot earlier to achieve the present popularity.
7. Winning in the Olympics was a dream from his childhood.
8. He has always followed the teachings of Thiruvalluvar.
9. While eating, she would watch TV.
10. I have an ambition to become a leader with vision for the country.

i) Transform/Rewrite the following <u>compound sentences into simple sentences</u>. If required, the simple sentences can be written as two separate sentences:

j) Transform/Rewrite the following <u>compound sentences into complex sentences</u>:

1. She was poor in Mathematics, so she wanted to go for tuition.
2. The train was coming fast, but the young man tried to cross the track.
3. We have somehow finished the project, yet we had a tough time then.
4. We have to closely watch the children, or they may behave mischievously.
5. She is a good cook, but she is slow.
6. Follow the steps carefully, or you cannot understand the sum.
7. The hunter had hidden himself behind the bushes, and he waited for the deer.
8. We must work sincerely; after all, we get salary.
9. We did not have enough amount; nevertheless, we decided to buy a land with loan.
10. He is the richest man in the town, yet he does not discriminate among the people.
11. He sings, plays music, dances and acts; in short, he is a versatile actor.
12. He could not look after their parents well, nor could his brother.

k) **Transform/Rewrite the following <u>complex sentences into simple sentences</u>. If required, the simple sentences can be written as two separate sentences:**

l) **Transform/Rewrite the following <u>complex sentences into compound sentences</u>:**

1. The person who finishes first will get a complement from me.
2. We must finish the work before the boss comes next week.
3. If you cannot do some work, do not take it up.
4. The thief has hidden behind the wall so that nobody could see him.
5. The army started their operation as soon as they got the ammunitions.
6. You can eat as much as you like.
7. Tell me the reason why you behaved like that.
8. I was worried when my friend behaved like that.
9. Although she tried to listen to class, she could not do so.
10. He gave a treat because he got a promotion.

m) **Fill in the blanks with suitable <u>conjunctions</u>:**

1. _____ you work hard, you cannot succeed.
2. _____ he was playful, he got very good marks.
3. _____ does he teach the students _____ does he help them.
4. I want a bat _____ a ball.
5. He practiced very hard; _____, he won the match.
6. _____ she is poor, her friends are rich.
7. He could touch the roof _____ he was very tall.
8. _____ you work hard, you will succeed.
9. You may go _____ he comes.
10. A boy drove the car _____ he is well experienced.
11. _____ had he finished the work _____ the boss gave another work.
12. You should not drive very slow; _____, we cannot go there in time.

11. Exercise for Chapter 19: Direct Speech and Indirect Speech

a) **Rewrite the sentences of direct speech into indirect speech and the sentences of indirect speech into direct speech:**

1. My colleague asked, "Are you coming for tea?"
2. Our constitution says, "All are equal."
3. Her younger son asked her whether she would buy a new toy.
4. Our neighbour said, "We have been living here for 20 years."
5. His colleague said, "Running along the road, a girl fell down suddenly."
6. My boss asked if I had finished the work.
7. The teacher told that Brahmaputra is the longest river in India.
8. My colleague asked, "Will you come to the office or go to the site tomorrow?"
9. My friend asked, "Who is your favourite hero here?"
10. She told me that she had gone to her native place and met her sister.
11. The chief guest said that we would have finished 100 years after independence in 2047.
12. The boss shouted, "Get out."
13. The parents asked the boy why he had gone to the shop the day before.
14. The boss ordered that I should not go out then.
15. The child asked, "Mummy, When did father say he would come?"
16. My friend said, "Please attend my birthday party."
17. My colleague requested that I attend the meeting that day.
18. "When can you finish the work?" asked my boss.
19. He said, "I shall finish the work tomorrow."
20. We told him to be nice to others.
21. "We should always be ready to sacrifice for the country," the PM said.
22. My grandma started, "There lived a king a thousand years ago."
23. Our colleague suggested, "Let us go for tea as we are tired."
24. The teacher asked, "Have you sacrificed anything for others today?"
25. She said to me that she had tried to finish the work before her boss came.
26. I told my friends, "Today is my birthday."
27. The priest blessed him that he live longer.
28. She said, "How intelligent my son is!"
29. My colleague said, "How fast you are driving!"
30. The teacher said, "Go to the library now."
31. "If I find a suitable job for you, I will let you know," my friend said.
32. The priest said, "God is great and helps us."
33. He said, "If I were you, I would not go there."
34. My friend said that he had gone to cinema the day before.
35. Mother said, "Don't go out to play because it is raining."
36. The auto driver asked where the passenger wanted to go.
37. The foreigner said, "What a beautiful country it is!"
38. The fans exclaimed that their hero had made the stunts in the movie brilliantly.
39. The members suggested that we would have a get-together with family.
40. The teacher advised the students to study well for the examination.

12. Exercise for Chapter 20: Inversion of Subject, Verb and Complement

a) Rewrite the sentences without inversion into sentences with inversion and vice versa:

1. If he had known her, he would have spoken to her.
2. My father was a teacher; so was my uncle.
3. I do not like coffee. Nor does my friend.
4. Were I poor, I would not have purchased a car.
5. The convoy comes here.
6. He should have done it under some very difficult situation.
7. He works very hard. His wife also works very hard.
8. If I were rich, I would buy a luxury car.
9. No sooner had he reached home than his boss called.
10. We were playing under the banyan tree.
11. More important was your attitude towards life.
12. Barely had we entered the room, when the room-boy knocked the door.
13. Should I buy a new car, it would be a luxury car.
14. Under the sun all are equal.
15. She would rarely have visited a village.
16. So poor were they that they could not afford to have even a rented house.
17. Very intelligent is she to learn many languages easily.
18. Shocked was he that he lost his investment in shares.
19. There he goes.
20. Only then would he have realized his mistakes.
21. Down the road went the cattle.
22. Seldom have I gone to his house.
23. Benefits of the new schemes had scarcely reached the people when the prices shot up.
24. My friend is not tall. His father or his mother is also not tall.
25. As soon as he had finished the work, he left immediately.
26. She was so happy that she could not suppress it.
27. A man so strong was he that everybody admired him. / So strong a man was he that everybody admired him.
28. He does not like coffee. He does not like tea also.
29. The boss had hardly left when some visitor entered.
30. I have never seen her.

13. Exercise for Chapter 29: Figures of Speech

a) **Identify the figures of speech**:

1. Let the mouth of these words speak more and more.
2. From a hill top, the lights of the city looked like bright stars.
3. He earns; his son spends.
4. That was a happy death for her.
5. Are we not equal partners in the business?
6. The boss was in his restroom.
7. He just entered the room, cracked some jokes, amused everybody and disappeared suddenly.
8. He might even eat the food of 100 people.
9. The boy threw a stone like an arrow.
10. The king's face was as bright as a sun.
11. The office enjoyed the promotion of the boss.
12. Security systems of modern offices have become the controlling authority of staff.
13. Despite the poverty, she finished school, college and even a doctoral degree from a university.
14. The day during the eclipse seemed as dark as night.
15. He finally escaped from the punishment with a true lie.
16. The young man was sent to a Correction Centre.
17. Crores? no!, lakhs? no! thousands? no!, hundreds? no!, but only tens was his salary in.
18. Did not he work sincerely for you so long?
19. The public school won the 100 metres race.
20. She looked as beautiful as a rose and weighed as light as a feather.
21. Chimpanzee should be more beautiful than his sister.
22. The city life is a hell for the rural people.
23. The pen is mightier than the sword.
24. The village welcomed the minister with warmth.
25. The two groups had fought first, then discussed, met many times to negotiate, but finally nothing came of it.
26. That luxury car was like a super deluxe apartment.
27. Loyalty is a good virtue; but disloyalty is rewarded more sometimes.
28. She would have cursed him a million times.
29. He must certainly be a real teacher to have taught you bad things.
30. Experience teaches us many lessons in our life.

Part III

Key to Grammar Exercises

Key to Grammar Exercises

1. Exercise for Chapter 2: Nouns

Note: In the following answers, nouns used as a different part of speech is not treated as nouns. For example, in the phrase 'Tamil film industry', the nouns 'Tamil' and 'film' are used as adjectives and therefore not identified as nouns.

a) Identify the nouns in the following sentences:

1. schools, colleges, places, life, people 2. knowledge, power 3. world, knowledge 4. knowledge, people, things, life, money, jewels, rights 5. teachers, backbone, schools, colleges 6. teachers, schooling, ways 7. institutions, knowledge, children, relatives, country, direction, future 8. leaders, past, Nehruji, Kamaraj, fact, education, schools, colleges 9. responsibility, children, people, education, life, people, country, India 10. time, learning, schools, colleges, life, forms, experience, teacher

b) Identify the common nouns and the proper nouns in the following sentences:

1. common: capital, state; proper: Chennai, Tamil Nadu 2. common: city, coast; proper: Chennai, Bay of Bengal 3. common: city, beach, world; proper: Marina Beach 4. common: name; proper: Chennai, Madras 5. common: home, industry, studios; proper: Chennai, AVM studios 6. common: city, institutions; proper: IIT, Anna University, Madras Medical College 7. common: centres; proper: T.Nagar, Purasawalkam, Parris Corner 8. common: cities, forms, dance, season, month, period, lovers, music; proper: Chennai, Bharatanatyam, December, Carnatic Music 9. common: book, city; proper: English Grammar (Simple, Practical yet Comprehensive), V P Kannan

c) Write the abstract nouns from the following words:

serve - service; long - length; infant - infancy; true - truth; good - goodness; owner - ownership; pirate - piracy; child - childhood; cruel - cruelty; live - livelihood; short - shortness; flatter - flattery; humble - humbleness, humility; great - greatness; brave - bravery; free - freedom; believe - belief; broad - breadth; advise - advice; brother - brotherhood; defend - defence; sane - sanity; dark - darkness; hero - heroism; hate - hatred; friend - friendship; judge - judgement; king - kingdom; sell - sales; succeed - success; act - action; wide - width; bitter - bitterness; high - height; man - manhood; deep - depth; think - thought; strong - strength; agent - agency; punish - punishment; die - death; young - youth; occupy - occupation; sweet - sweetness; choose - choice; know - knowledge; poor - poverty; priest - priesthood; quick - quickness; discover - discovery; persevere - perseverance; expect - expectation; Hindu - Hinduism; move - movement; rich - richness; pilgrim - pilgrimage; wise - wisdom; obey - obedience; ignorant - ignorance; captain - captaincy

d) **Identify the collective nouns in the following:**

1. fleet 2. jury 3. army 4. police, crowd 5. mob, team 6. parliament, committee, nation 7. family

e) Some collective nouns cannot be used independently and should be used with the prepositional phrase of 'of + plural noun' only. **In the following exercise, fill in the blanks with the suitable collective noun from the list given below:**

1. a troupe of dancers
2. a series of events
3. a bundle of sticks
4. a wreath of flowers
5. a constellation of stars
6. a zoo of wild animals
7. a gang of rowdies
8. a troop of monkeys
9. a regiment of soldiers
10. a crew of sailors
11. a suite of rooms
12. a collection of old stamps
13. a string of beads
14. a galaxy of film stars
15. a class of students
16. a pack of cards
17. a swarm of insects
18. a band of musicians
19. a flock of sheep
20. a herd of buffaloes
21. a glossary of words
22. a bed of oysters
23. a hive of bees
24. a board of directors
25. a colony of ants
26. a chain of shops
27. a chest of tools
28. a row of houses
29. a body of leaders
30. a ream of paper
31. a shoal of fish
32. a roll of film
33. a pair of shoes
34. a reel of cloth
35. a patrol of policemen
36. a cluster of arms
37. a heap of rubbish
38. a host of possibilities
39. a bunch of grapes
40. an album of photos
41. a grove of trees
42. a stack of drawers
43. a range of mountains
44. a flight of planes
45. a catalogue of items
46. a cloud of flies
47. a chain of keys
48. a group of friends
49. a shower of rain
50. a plague of rats
51. a batch of trainees

f) **Identify the nouns in the following sentences and classify them into countable nouns and uncountable nouns:**

1. countable: home, place; uncountable: everybody 2. countable: house, facilities; uncountable: 3. countable: needs, home; uncountable: food, love, affection 4. countable: facilities, houses; uncountable: 5. countable: ; uncountable: water 6. countable: supply, newspaper, doorstep; uncountable: milk, convenience 7. countable: items, egg, vegetables, bun, cookie, doorstep; uncountable: rice, wheat, sugar, salt, oil, butter 8. countable: school, children; uncountable: proximity 9. countable: services, hospital, market, bus stop; uncountable: availability 10. countable: comforts, facilities, home, places, beach, cinema hall, park, hotel; uncountable: change, environment, enjoyment 11. countable: home, proverb; uncountable: fun, enjoyment, east, west

Key to Grammar Exercises 281

g) **Write the <u>plural</u> for the following nouns:**

crisis - crises, jeans - (only plural), wife - wives, cat - cats, life - lives, boy - boys, box - boxes, lady - ladies, game - games, radius - radii, fish - fish/fishes, computer - computers, grown-up - grown-ups, girl - girls, knife - knives, man - men, mango - mangoes, foot - feet, thief - thieves, tooth - teeth, child - children, people - (already plural) / peoples, family - families, ferry - ferries, prize - prizes, man-of-war - men-of-war, logo - logos, roof - roofs, pen - pens, brother-in-law - brothers-in-law, kilo - kilos, mouth - mouths, class - classes, aircraft - aircrafts, cattle - (only plural), shelf - shelves, flower - flowers, potato - potatoes, cow - cows, scissors - (plural only), mathematics - (uncountable), city - cities, branch - branches, desk - desks, house - houses, sheep - sheep, owl - owls, half - halves

h) **Write the <u>other gender</u> for the following nouns. If a noun has no other gender, identify if it is a common gender or a neuter gender:**

mother - father, parent - (common gender), uncle - aunt, sister - brother, grandfather - grandmother, aunt - uncle, cousin - (common gender), child - (common gender), son - daughter, niece - nephew, granddaughter - grandson, man - woman, girl - boy, husband - wife, queen - king, lord - lady, nun - monk, gentleman - lady, madam - sir, author - authoress, hostess - host, poet - poetess, manager - manageress, priestess - priest, actor - actress, conductress - conductor, emperor - empress, princess - prince, hero - heroine, washer-man - washer-woman, master - mistress, milkman - milkwoman, saleswoman - salesman, widow - widower, bridegroom - bride, client - (common gender), driver - (common gender), pilot - (common gender), waiter - waitress, witch - wizard, giant - giantess, heir - heiress, baby - (common gender), servant - maid

cow - bullock, hen - cock, bird - (common gender), tiger - tigress, animal - (common gender), lion - lioness, horse - (common gender), table - (neuter gender), peacock - peahen, goose - gander, fish - (common gender), stallion - mare, deer - (common gender), dog - bitch, bull - cow, goat - nanny goat, bee - (common gender), ewe - ram, pen - (neuter gender), computer - (neuter gender)

i) **Write the <u>possessive case</u> for the following nouns:**

mothers - mothers', father - father's, Balu - Balu's, uncle - uncle's, aunties - aunties', box - box's, boxes - boxes', class - class's, classes - classes', boy - boy's, boys - boys', parents - parents', boss - boss's, bosses - bosses', houses - houses', man - man's, men - men's, poet - poet's, poets - poets', poetess - poetess's, poetesses - poetesses', tiger - tiger's, tigress - tigress's, table - table's, tables - tables', brother - brother's, sisters - sisters', city - city's, cities - cities', river - river's, rivers - rivers', love - love's, feeling - feeling's, feelings - feelings'

2. Exercise for Chapter 3: Pronouns

a) **Identify the pronouns in the following sentences, their type and case:**

1. we - personal and nominative; our - personal and possessive
2. my - personal and possessive; us - personal and accusative
3. it - personal and nominative; my - personal and possessive; he - personal and nominative; me - personal and accusative; him- personal and accusative
4. our - personal and possessive; each other - reciprocal and accusative; they - personal and nominative; themselves - reflexive and accusative
5. my - personal and possessive; his - personal and possessive; she - personal and nominative; her - personal and accusative; her - personal and possessive
6. all - indefinite and nominative; their - personal and possessive; one another - reciprocal and accusative
7. they - personal and nominative; their - personal and possessive; we - personal and nominative; them - personal and accusative; our - personal and possessive
8. such - demonstrative and nominative; our - personal and possessive; this - demonstrative and nominative; everybody's - indefinite and possessive; none - indefinite and nominative; it - personal and accusative
9. who - interrogative and nominative; it - personal and accusative; you - personal and nominative; your - personal and possessive; you - personal and accusative
10. everybody - indefinite and nominative; everything - indefinite and accusative; nobody - indefinite and nominative; anything - indefinite and accusative; many - indefinite and nominative; it - personal and accusative
11. anybody's - indefinite and possessive; mine, ours, yours, his, hers, its, theirs - personal and genitive
12. each - distributive and accusative; we - personal and nominative; ourselves - emphatic and nominative; ourselves - reflexive and accusative
13. whom - interrogative and accusative; we - personal and nominative; it - personal and nominative; whose - relative and possessive; it - personal and accusative; all - indefinite and accusative; us - personal and accusative

b) **Write the correct form of the personal pronoun in the following sentences using the pronouns given within brackets, if any:**

1. I, she 2. we 3. her, me 4. my, his, he, her, me 5. he, him, his 6. she, me, our, their, our 7. they, our, we, them 8. her, it, us 9. we, it, its 10. you, it, your, us, it, you 11. hers, it, ours. 12. we, mine, his, hers

Key to Grammar Exercises

c) **Write the suitable <u>reflexive pronoun, emphatic pronoun or reciprocal pronoun</u> in the following sentences and identify its type correctly:**

1. myself - emphatic 2. myself - reflexive 3. myself - emphatic 4. himself - emphatic 5. themselves - reflexive 6. itself - reflexive 7. ourselves - emphatic 8. herself - reflexive 9. oneself - reflexive 10. yourself - emphatic 11. each other - reciprocal 12. one another - reciprocal

d) **Write the suitable <u>demonstrative pronoun, indefinite pronoun or distributive pronoun</u> in the following sentences using the given pronouns and identify <u>its type</u> correctly:**

1. such - demonstrative 2. anybody - indefinite, nobody - indefinite 3. either - indefinite, none - indefinite 4. everybody - indefinite 5. these - demonstrative, those - demonstrative 6. anybody - indefinite 7. this - demonstrative 8. few - indefinite, many - indefinite 9. somebody - indefinite, nobody - indefinite 10. nobody - indefinite, one - demonstrative 11. all - indefinite, each - distributive 12. everything - indefinite, nothing - indefinite 13. many - indefinite, few - indefinite 14. all - demonstrative, each - demonstrative 15. all - indefinite, one - distributive

3. Exercise for <u>Chapter 4: Verbs - Basics & Chapter 5: Negative Sentences</u>

a) **Classify the <u>Verbs</u> into <u>Be-Verbs</u> and <u>Action Verbs</u> and for Action Verbs, pick out the <u>auxiliary verb</u> and the <u>main verb form</u> from their <u>complete verbs</u>:**

1. stopped - action and no aux. 2. think - action and no aux.; cannot + finish 3. must be + playing 4. shall be - be 5. have been + living 6. don't + dream 7. is - be 8. was + composed 9. had not + left; reached - action and no aux. 10. shall have + finished 11. looks - action and no aux. 12. is + ringing 13. are + going 14. may not be + punished 15. have been - be 16. are + used 17. were - be 18. were + playing 19. have + seen 20. was being + written 21. shall be + watching 22. are - be 23. had been + living; shall have been - be 24. have been + known 25. will have been + honoured

b) **Identify the <u>Verbs</u>, their <u>Tenses</u> and the <u>Voice</u>:**

1. stopped - simple past and active 2. think - simple present and active; cannot finish - modal and active 3. must be playing - modal and active 4. shall be - simple future and no voice 5. have been living - present perfect continues and active 6. don't dream - no tense (infinitive) and active 7. is - simple present and no voice 8. was composed - simple past and passive 9. had not left - past perfect and active; reached - past and active 10. shall have finished - future perfect and active 11. looks - simple present and

active 12. is ringing - present continuous and active 13. are going - present continuous and active 14. may not be punished - modal and passive 15. have been - present perfect and no voice 16. are used - simple present and passive 17. were - simple past and no voice 18. were playing - past continuous and active 19. have seen - present perfect and active 20. was being written - past continuous and passive 21. shall be watching - future continuous and active 22. are - simple present and no voice 23. had been living - past perfect continuous and active; shall have been - future perfect and no voice 24. have been known - present perfect and passive 25. will have been honoured - future perfect and passive

d) **Fill in the blanks with the <u>correct tense of the verbs</u>** (given within brackets) **based on the context of their usage in the following sentences:**

1. Students <u>have finished</u> the class work just now. 2. He <u>goes</u> to school daily. 3. We <u>shall be travelling</u> by train tomorrow at this time. 4. She <u>was</u> a student last year. 5. We <u>are</u> boys. 6. Yesterday, the meeting <u>had started</u> before we <u>reached</u>. 7. I <u>had been</u> a student till last year. 8. The trains <u>have been running</u> late for almost a month. 9. We <u>shall be watching</u> a movie between 11 AM to 2 PM tomorrow. 10. I <u>shall be</u> a doctor next year. 11. They <u>had been constructing</u> the bridge for many years before its inauguration. 12. She <u>will have been living</u> here for 10 years by next year. 13. My father <u>will come</u> tomorrow. 14. I <u>met</u> my old friend yesterday. 15. They <u>were</u> students last year. 16. They <u>will have been</u> to London next year. 17. He <u>will be</u> a doctor next year. 18. The traffic <u>is moving</u> slowly now. 19. We <u>have been</u> to London. 20. She <u>is</u> a teacher. 21. We <u>are going</u> to celebrate our sports day next month. 22. It <u>has eaten</u> the food already. 23. I <u>am</u> a boy. 24. You <u>will have become</u> a doctor by June next year. 25. We <u>play</u> here daily.

e) **Write the sentences obtained by answering the above questions of (d) in <u>passive voice</u> wherever applicable.**

1. The class work has been finished by the students just now. 2. No passive 3. No passive 4. No passive 5. No passive 6. No passive 7. No passive 8. No passive 9. No passive 10. No passive 11. No passive 12. No passive 13. No passive 14. My old friend was met by me yesterday. 15. No passive 16. No passive 17. No passive 18. No passive 19. No passive 20. No passive 21. Our sports day is going to be celebrated by us next month. 22. The food has been eaten by it already. 23. No passive 24. No passive 25. No passive

f) **Write the sentences obtained by answering the above questions of (d) and (e) as negative sentences.**

Negative sentences for the answers of (d):

1. Students have not finished the class work just now. 2. He does not go to school daily. 3. We shall not be travelling by train tomorrow at this time. 4. She was not a student last year. 5. We are not boys. 6. Yesterday, the meeting had not started before we did not reach. 7. I had not been a student till last year. 8. The trains have not been running late for almost a month. 9. We shall not be watching a movie between 11 AM to 2 PM tomorrow. 10. I shall not be a doctor next year. 11. They had not been constructing the bridge for many years before its inauguration. 12. She will not have been living here for 10 years by next year. 13. My father will not come tomorrow. 14. I did not meet my old friend yesterday. 15. They were not students last year. 16. They will not have been to London next year. 17. He will not be a doctor next year. 18. The traffic is not moving slowly now. 19. We have not been to London. 20. She is not a teacher. 21. We are not going to celebrate our sports day next month. 22. It has not eaten the food already. 23. I am not a boy. 24. You will not have become a doctor by June next year. 25. We do not play here daily.

Negative sentences for the answers of (e):

1. The class work has not been finished by the students just now. 2. No passive 3. No passive 4. No passive 5. No passive 6. No passive 7. No passive 8. No passive 9. No passive 10. No passive 11. No passive 12. No passive 13. No passive 14. My old friend was not met by me yesterday. 15. No passive 16. No passive 17. No passive 18. No passive 19. No passive 20. No passive 21. Our sports day is not going to be celebrated by us next month. 22. The food has not been eaten by it already. 23. No passive 24. No passive 25. No passive

g) **Fill in the blanks with the correct modal verbs in the following sentences:**

1. He should visit his native place. (obligation/compulsion) 2. Could you help me please? (request) 3. May I help you please? (offer) 4. We ought to be punctual for the class. (being bound) 5. I shall come tomorrow to your place. (future) 6. His mother may help him do the homework. (possibility) 7. The situation was such that our team might win the match. (past chance) 8. I must go now. (necessity) 9. We must help him because of his poverty. (obligation) 10. Our team may win the match. (chance) 11. She would sing and dance when she was a child. (past habit) 12. May I come in please? (permission) 13. He dare drive very fast. (daring) 14. You can help him do the homework. (ability) 15. He will come day-after-tomorrow. (future)

4. Exercise for Chapter 6: Interrogative Sentences & Chapter 7: Verbs - Advanced

a) Identify the <u>structural elements</u> of subject, verb, object, indirect object and other complement (subject complement, verb complement and object complement) and also their corresponding <u>parts of speech</u>:

b) Identify the <u>type of the verb</u> as transitive verb, intransitive verb or linking verb and also the <u>causative verbs/perception verbs</u>:

c) Write the <u>Yes/No question</u> and the <u>Question-Word question</u> for each structural element:

```
          d    n         v          adv   adj    adv
          --- ----------  -------    ----- ------ ------
   1.    His statements sound      more logical now.
           S      V(linking)          SC       VC
```

    Do his statements sound more logical now?   - yes/no
    What sounds more logical now?   - subject
    How/What do his statements sound now?   - SC
    When do his statements sound more logical?   - VC

```
          d    n       v              inf             prep  d    n
          --- -----  ---------------  --------------------- ---  ---  ---------
   2.    The plane was believed   to have been hijacked  by   the militants.
             S      V(intransitive)    ObjC(INP)        : OC(PAdvP) of inf
```

    Was the plane believed to have been hijacked by the militants?   - yes/no
    What was believed to have been hijacked by the militants?   - subject
    What was the plane believed to be?   - ObjC
    By whom was the plane believed to have been hijacked?   - OC(PAdvP) of inf

```
          d    adj   n      v        adv   adj
          --- ----  -----  ----      ----- --------
   3.    The old  actor  was       very popular.
              S          V(linking)    SC
```

    Was the old actor very popular?   - yes/no
    Who was very popular?   - subject
    How/What was the old actor?   - SC

Key to Grammar Exercises

```
           pron    v                        pron   inf    d    n
           ----   ---------                 ----   -----  ---  ------
    4.      I     consider                  him    to be an   expert.
            S     V(transitive & perception) O            ObjC
```

Do I consider him to be an expert?	- yes/no
Who considers him to be an expert?	- subject
Whom do I consider to be an expert?	- object
How/Whom/What do I consider him?	- ObjC

```
          d    adj      n      v        prep adj    n       adv    adv
          ---  -------  -----  -------- ---- ------ ------- -----  -------
    5.    The  young    player has been  to  many  countries even  before.
                   S          V(linking)               VC
```

Has the young player been to many countries even before?	- yes/no
Who has been to many countries even before?	- subject
Where has the young player been to even before?	- VC
When has the young player been to many countries?	- VC

```
          d    n        v        d    n
          ---  -------  -----    --   ------
    6.    My   mother   wrote    a    letter.
                 S      V(transitive)   O
```

Did my mother write a letter?	- yes/no
Who wrote a letter?	- subject
What did my mother write?	- object

```
          d    adj  n    v               adv    prep   d    n
          ---  ---  ---- --------------- -----  -----  ---  -----
    7.    The  old  man  was walking     slowly along  the  road.
                  S       V(intransitive)           VC
```

Was the old man walking slowly along the road?	- yes/no
Who was walking slowly along the road?	- subject
How was the old man walking along the road?	- VC
Where was the old man walking slowly?	- VC

```
       pron    A     adv    v            prep   d     n
       ----   ------ ------ --           ----  ---   --------
8.     He     would  always be           in    the   library.
       S      A      VC     V(linking)         VC
```

Would he always be in the library?   - yes/no
Who would always be in the library?   - subject
When would he be in the library?   - VC
Where would he always be?   - VC

```
       pron   v                        pron   inf    adv
       ----  ----------------          ----  ------  ---------
9.     You   should make               him   work    sincerely.
       S     V(transitive & causative) O     ObjC
```

Should you make him work sincerely?   - yes/no
Who should make him work sincerely?   - subject
Whom should you make work sincerely?   - object
What should you make him (to do)?   - ObjC

```
       pron   v                gerund   adv    conj   gerund    adv
       ----  ------            -------- ------ ----   -------   ---------
10.    We    can go            shopping today  and    fishing   tomorrow.
       S     V(intransitive)   VC: PO                 : PO
```

Can we go shopping today and fishing tomorrow?   - yes/no
Who can go shopping today and fishing tomorrow? - subject
What can we go (for) today and tomorrow?   - PO
When can we go shopping and fishing?   - VC

```
       d    n        inf  conj  inf    v            pron  adj      prep  d    n
       ---  -------- ---- ----  ------ ------       ----  -------- ----  ---  ------
11.    His  capacity to sing and dance made         him   popular  in    the  village.
                      S                 V(transitive O     ObjC    (PAdvP)
                                        & causative)
```

Did his capacity to sing and dance make him popular in the village? - yes/no
What made him popular in the village?   - subject
What did his capacity to sing and dance make him in the village?   - ObjC
Where did his capacity to sing and dance make him popular?   - PAdvP

Key to Grammar Exercises 289

```
         pron    A      adv    v              gerund
         ----  ------- ------ -----          ------
    12.  One   should  always keep           trying.
          S      A       VC   V(transitive)    O
```

Should one always keep trying?   - yes/no
Who should always keep trying?   - subject
When should one keep trying?   - VC
What should one keep on (doing)?   - object

```
         pron  v              d     n       adv   adv   adv
         ---  -------------  ---  --------  ----- ----- ---------
    13.  We   should study  the   lessons   daily very  carefully.
          S   V(transitive)        O                    VC
```

Should we study the lessons daily very carefully?   - yes/no
Who should study the lessons daily very carefully?   - subject
What should we study daily very carefully?   - object
When should we study the lessons very carefully?   - VC
How should we study the lessons daily?   - VC

```
         pron  v           d    adj    n
         ---  ---         ---  -----  --------
    14.  She  is          our  class  teacher.
          S   V(linking)         SC
```

Is she our class teacher?   - yes/no
Who is our class teacher?   - subject
What/Who is she?   - SC

```
         d    n    v              prep  d    adj    n
         ---  ---- ---------      ----  ---  ----  ----
    15.  The  ball was lost       by    a    tall  boy.
           S  V(intransitive)            VC(PAdvP)
```

Was the ball lost by a tall boy?   - yes/no
What was lost by a tall boy?   - subject
By whom was the ball lost?   - VC(PAdvP)

```
      pron    v              pron    d    n
      ----   -----            ----   ---- -----
 16.  I      gave             him    a    ball.
      S      V(transitive)    IO     O
```

Did I give him a ball?　　　　　　　　　　　　　　- yes/no
Who gave him a ball?　　　　　　　　　　　　　　 - subject
What did I give him?　　　　　　　　　　　　　　 - object
Whom did I give a ball?　　　　　　　　　　　　　- IO

```
      pron    v                            d    n        prt       prep  pron
      ----  ------                         ---  ------   --------  ----  ----
 17.  We    can get                        the  house    painted   by    him.
      S     V(transitive & causative verb)      O        ObjC  :VC(PAdvP)
```

Can we get the house painted by him?　　　　　　　　- yes/no
Who can get the house painted by him?　　　　　　　- subject
What can we get painted by him?　　　　　　　　　　- object
What can we get the house done by him?　　　　　　　- ObjC
By whom can we get the house painted?　　　　　　　 - VC(PAdvP)

```
      d    n       v             d     prt        n      prt    prep  d    adj       n
      ---  ------  ------        ---   --------   -----  ------ ----  --   -------   -----
 18.  The  police  found         the   missing    child  playing in   a    distant   park.
      S            V(transitive)       O                 ObjC :  VC(PAdvP)
```

Did the police find the missing child playing in a distant park?　- yes/no
Who found the missing child playing in a distant park?　　　　　　- subject
Whom did the police find playing in a distant park?　　　　　　　 - object
What did the police find the missing child doing?　　　　　　　　 - ObjC
Where did the police find the missing child playing?　　　　　　　- VC(PAdvP)

d) **Identify the <u>mood</u> of the sentence:**

1. imperative 2. indicative 3. subjunctive 4. subjunctive 5. subjunctive 6. indicative
7. subjunctive 8. imperative 9. subjunctive 10. indicative 11. subjunctive 12. indicative
13. indicative 14. subjunctive 15. indicative

e) **Fill in the blanks with the correct <u>extended modal verbs</u> in the following sentences:**

1. will get used (to) 2. had better 3. has to 4. is to 5. is about to 6. was required (to)
7. have got to 8. used to 9. would rather 10. had to

Key to Grammar Exercises

f) Use the correct <u>particle</u> with the given base verb to form the appropriate <u>phrasal verb</u> in the following sentences:

1. up 2. after 3. along 4. down 5. up, with 6. up 7. off, back 8. in 9. down 10. up 11. out 12. up 13. in 14. out, of 15. out 16. up 17. up 18. off 19. on 20. out 21. up 22. out 23. apart 24. after 25. ahead 26. across 27. out 28. in 29. over 30. away, with 31. up 32. into 33. on 34. down 35. off 36. up 37. up 38. to 39. off 40. up 41. up 42. for 43. in 44. down, upon 45. up 46. on 47. in 48. out 49. up 50. in 51. on 52. up 53. out 54. up 55. out

5. Exercise for <u>Chapter 8: Verbal Phrases - Gerund, Participle and Infinitive</u>

a) Identify the <u>type of the verbal phrase</u> as <u>gerund</u>, <u>participle</u> and <u>infinitive</u>:

b) Also, identify their <u>corresponding functional type of the basic phrases</u>, namely noun phrase, adjective phrase and adverb phrase:

1. to have been one of the greatest leaders of the world - infinitive; noun phrase 2. devastated by the Tsunami - participle; adjective phrase 3. to serve the poor people - infinitive; adjective phrase 4. play in the ground - bare infinitive; adjective phrase 5. to tell the truth - infinitive; adverb phrase 6. listen in the class - bare infinitive; noun phrase 7. to leave the office - infinitive; noun phrase 8. eating too much - gerund; noun phrase 9. to win the match - infinitive; adjective phrase 10. being loved - gerund; noun phrase 11. to enjoy also - infinitive; noun phrase 12. excited - participle; adjective phrase 13. swimming - gerund; noun phrase 14. Having walked a long distance - participle; adjective phrase 15. to have been invited for the party - infinitive; adverb phrase 16. walking along the road - participle; adjective phrase 17. making of the future - gerund; noun phrase 18. prepare for the exam - bare infinitive; noun phrase 19. cutting of trees - gerund; noun phrase 20. running - participle; adverb phrase 21. the weather being fine - participle; absolute phrase & adverb phrase: walking - gerund; noun phrase 22. improving economic condition - gerund; noun phrase 23. pay his debts to you soon - bare infinitive; noun phrase 24. tired - participle; adjective phrase: having walked a long distance - gerund; noun phrase 25. to play football daily - infinitive; noun phrase 26. to play football now - infinitive; noun phrase 27. having been delayed by the torrential rains - participle; adjective/adverb phrase 28. play - bare infinitive; noun phrase 29. to be seen - infinitive; adjective phrase 30. walking along the beach - participle; adjective/adverb phrase 31. to help each other in difficulties - infinitive; adverb phrase 32. to have served in the military - infinitive; adverb phrase 33. to win the match - infinitive; adverb phrase 34. describing the problems of the teachers - participle; adjective phrase 35. to go for marketing - infinitive; adjective phrase: marketing - gerund; noun phrase 36. to finish the work in time - infinitive; adverb phrase: to struggle very much - infinitive; noun phrase

c) **Fill in the blanks with the <u>correct form of verbal phrase</u> using the verb given within brackets:**

1. being loved 2. seeing 3. laughing 4. having worked 5. talk 6. to finish 7. obsessed 8. to hear 9. understanding 10. smoking 11. to play 12. making 13. keeping, work 14. behaving 15. to have been treated 16. to do 17. understanding 18. to meet 19. having come 20. being 21. to understand 22. playing, studying 23. making 24. running, to meet 25. being loved 26. to make 27. coming 28. used   29. to lose 30. to tell 31. waiting 32. being 33. laughing 34. having been killed 35. to see 36. damaged 37. to have helped 38. swimming 39. dancing 40. fascinated, singing

6. Exercise for <u>Chapter 12: Adjectives & Chapter 13: Determiners and Articles</u>

a) **Identify the <u>adjectives and determiners</u>:**

1. this - determiner 2. her - determiner; taller - adjective 3. young, many - adjectives 4. hot - adjective   5. angry - adjective 6. an, your - determiners; good - adjective 7. beautiful, new - adjectives; the - determiner 8. all, whatever - determiners 9. either, every - determiners; good - adjective 10. an, my - determiners 11. her, first - determiners 12. those, my - determiners; memorable - adjective 13. neither - determiner; good - adjective 14. some, any, no - determiners 15. strong - adjective 16. our, the, first - determiners 17. the - determiner; most intelligent - adjective 18. such - determiner 19. few - adjective; every - determiner 20. a - determiner; strange - adjective 21. their - determiner; strange - adjective 22. its - determiner 23. an - determiner 24. the - determiner; bad - adjective 25. the - determiner; cold - adjective

b) **Write the correct form of <u>comparison of adjectives</u>:**

1. many 2. quite taller 3. as tall as 4. shorter than 5. same as 6. better 7. same, as 8. fewer 9. nearly 10. by far 11. him 12. different to 13. more beautiful 14. different than 15. richest, most intelligent 16. taller and taller 17. similar to 18. different from 19. smallest 20. worse 21. good 22. more and more beautiful

c) **Fill in the blanks with <u>correct article</u>. If no article is required, write 'no article':**

1. the, the 2. no article 3. the, no article 4. an 5. a 6. no article / the 7. no article, the, no article 8. no article, a 9. no article 10. no article, the, the 11. no article, the 12. no article 13. the 14. no article, no article 15. an 16. the, the 17. a 18. an 19. the 20. the, a

Key to Grammar Exercises   293

7. Exercise for Chapter 14: Adverbs

a) **Identify the <u>adverbs</u> and <u>their types</u> as adverbs of manner, adverbs of place, adverbs of time, adverbs of definite frequency, adverbs of indefinite frequency, adverbs of probability, adverbs of opinion, adverbs of degree, parallel adverbs and connecting adverbs:**

1. never - indefinite frequency 2. all - degree; alone - manner 3. rarely - indefinite frequency 4. seldom - indefinite frequency; beautifully - manner 5. carefully - manner 6. almost - degree 7. there - place 8. often - indefinite frequency 9. personally - opinion 10. backward - place 11. really - degree; hard - manner; so - parallel adverb 12. daily - definite frequency 13. always - indefinite frequency 14. hardly - manner 15. pretty - degree 16. usually - indefinite frequency; early - time 17. fast - manner; yesterday - time 18. very - degree; nevertheless - connecting adverb 19. not - negation; nor - parallel adverb 20. actually - manner; however - connecting adverb; yet - time 21. angrily - manner 22. later - time; not - negation; now - time 23. afterwards - time 24. obviously - probability 25. everywhere - place

b) **Write the adverbs and adverb phrases given within brackets in the <u>correct position</u>:**

1. You can meet him <u>now</u>. 2. <u>Thus</u>, he became a popular singer. 3. <u>Obviously</u>, we are bound to learn English. 4. The story is <u>pretty</u> good. 5. My mother <u>hardly</u> watches TV. 6. I would talk to him <u>over phone</u> <u>sometimes</u>. 7. I have <u>never</u> seen her <u>before</u>. 8. They vacated the house <u>last year</u>. 9. He ran <u>very fast</u>. 10. We took a pledge to work <u>very hard</u> <u>in the office</u> <u>daily</u> <u>throughout the year</u> <u>to finish the project</u>. 11. They have not met <u>recently</u>. 12. The lock was not difficult <u>enough</u> to break for the thief. 13. The bedroom is <u>upstairs</u>. 14. The theatre is <u>almost</u> full. 15. We had met long <u>back</u>. 16. The children were playing <u>happily</u>. 17. <u>Theoretically</u>, there is a solution for this vexed problem. 18. We should play <u>one hour daily</u>. 19. He would have gone <u>home</u>. 20. Have you <u>ever</u> met him <u>during the last 5 years</u>? 21. He must be <u>only</u> <u>here</u>. 22. We can meet <u>outside around 4 PM</u>. 23. The box is <u>too</u> difficult to carry. 24. She is kind <u>even</u> to her enemies. 25. He can speak English <u>well</u>. 26. Some people are hurt <u>badly</u> <u>in the accident</u>. 27. We do not <u>often</u> go <u>there</u>. 28. He may not be available <u>after 3 PM</u> <u>tomorrow</u>. 29. It is extremely hot <u>in summer</u>. 30. She <u>always</u> watches TV <u>in the evening</u>.

c) **Write the <u>correct form of comparison of adverbs</u>:**

1. faster, sooner 2. fastest 3. faster 4. sooner 5. more and more 6. him 7. faster and faster 8. more clearly 9. as soon as 10. much faster 11. faster 12. best 13. more politely 14. most gracefully 15. as fluently as

8. Exercise for Chapter 15: Prepositions

a) **Identify the prepositions, the type of preposition as simple or complex, prepositional objects** and **prepositional phrases**:

b) **Classify the types of prepositional phrases** as **prepositional adverb phrase, prepositional adjective phrase** or **prepositional noun phrase** based on their function as adverb, adjective or noun respectively:

1. above - simple; PO - the city; PP - above the city (PAdvP): before - simple; PO - landing; PP - before landing (PAdvP)
2. up - simple; PO - the hill; PP - up the hill (PAdvP)
3. with - simple; PO - pen; PP - with pen (PAdvP): without - simple; PO - seeing others; PP - without seeing others (PAdvP)
4. from - simple; PO - Delhi; PP - from Delhi (PAdvP): to - simple; PO - Mumbai; PP - to Mumbai (PAdvP): on - simple; PO - Monday; PP - on Monday (PAdvP)
5. for the sake of - complex; PO - the common people; PP - for the sake of the common people (PAdvP)
6. for - simple; PO - you; PP - for you (PAdvP): till - simple; PO - 5 pm; PP - till 5 pm (PAdvP)
7. in order to - complex; PO - spread (bare infinitive); PP - in order to spread (PAdvP): in - simple; PO - Tamil Nadu; PP - in Tamil Nadu (PAdvP)
8. off - simple; PO - the car; PP - off the car (PAdvP)
9. of - simple; PO - me; PP - of me (PAdvP)
10. until - simple; PO - late night; PP - until late night (PAdvP)
11. out of - complex; PO - the Assembly; PP - out of the Assembly (PAdvP)
12. in course of - complex; PO - time; PP - in course of time (PAdvP): for - simple; PO - the behaviour; PP - for the behaviour (PAdvP)
13. in comparison to - complex; PO - his old age; PP - in comparison to his old age (PAdvP)
14. against - simple; PO - the local team; PP - against the local team (PAdvP)
15. apart from - complex; PO - Tamil Nadu; PP - apart from Tamil Nadu (PAdvP)
16. in - simple; PO - the life; PP - in the life (PAdvP): in spite of - complex; PO - being rich; PP - in spite of being rich (PAdvP)
17. to - simple; PO - the Ayappan temple; PP - to the Ayappan temple (PAdvP): along with - complex; PO - family; PP - along with family (PAdvP)
18. for - simple; PO - a short period; PP - for a short period (PAdvP): to - simple; PO - school; PP - to school (PAdvP): with - simple; PO - my father; PP - with my father (PAdvP)
19. along - simple; PO - the road; PP - along the road (PAdvP)
20. in front of - complex; PO - the school; PP - in front of the school (PAdvP)
21. by virtue of - complex; PO - being the headmaster; PP - by virtue of being the headmaster (PAdjP): among - simple; PO - the students; PP - among the students (PAdvP)

Key to Grammar Exercises 295

22. in line with - complex; PO - the modern world; PP - in line with the modern world (PAdvP)
23. beside - simple; PO - mother; PP - beside mother (PAdvP)
24. with respect to - complex; PO - the salary; PP - with respect to the salary (PAdvP)
25. across - simple; PO - the road; PP - across the road (PAdvP)
26. in - simple; PO - Chennai; PP - in Chennai (PAdvP): since - simple; PO - 2000; PP - since 2000 (PAdvP)
27. according to - complex; PO - the guidance of the directors; PP - according to the guidance of the directors (PAdvP): of - simple; PO - the directors; PP - of the directors (PAdjP)
28. with - simple; PO - an eye; PP - with an eye (PAdvP): to - simple; PO - becoming a minister; PP - to becoming a minister (PAdvP)
29. around - simple; PO - the park; PP - around the park (PAdvP)
30. onto - simple; PO - the top shelf; PP - onto the top shelf (PAdvP)
31. behind - simple; PO - the college; PP - behind the college (PAdvP)
32. like - simple; PO - a rich man; PP - like a rich man (PAdvP): in - simple; PO - the bank; PP - in the bank (PAdvP): near - simple; PO - the post office; PP - near the post office (PAdvP)
33. despite - simple; PO - her sufferings; PP - despite her sufferings (PAdvP)
34. with reference to - complex; PO - his claims; PP - with reference to his claims (PAdvP)
35. by means of - complex; PO - ships; PP - by means of ships (PAdvP)
36. beneath - simple; PO - the papers; PP - beneath the papers (PAdvP)
37. in favour of - complex; PO - his family; PP - in favour of his family (PAdvP)
38. below - simple; PO - the standard; PP - below the standard (PAdvP)
39. inside and outside - compound; PO - the hall; PP - inside and outside the hall (PAdvP)
40. inside - simple; PO - from his chamber; PP - inside from his chamber (PAdvP): from - simple; PO - his chamber; PP - from his chamber (PNP)

c) **Fill in the blanks with appropriate preposition or the part of complex preposition:**

1. on 2. within 3. on, of 4. to 5. on 6. with 7. with 8. beyond 9. past 10. except 11. on, of 12. to 13. in, of 14. across 15. in, with 16. with 17. in comparison with 18. of 19. in 20. in addition to 21. towards 22. with 23. on 24. into 25. in 26. about, during 27. in 28. at, in 29. with 30. on 31. for, to, by 32. along 33. to 34. for 35. of 36. with 37. instead 38. of 39. above 40. in, in 41. in, at 42. of 43. to

9. Exercise for Chapter 16: Phrases and Expressions

a) **Identify the basic phrases and their types; prepositional phrases and their functional types; and verbal phrases, their types and their functional types:**

Abbreviations used: noun phrase (NP), adjective phrase (AdjP), adverb phrase (AdvP), prepositional phrase (PP), prepositional noun phrase (PNP), prepositional adjective phrase (PAdjP), prepositional adverb phrase (PAdvP), participle (prt), infinitive (inf), infinitive noun phrase (INP), infinitive adjective phrase (IAdjP) and infinitive adverb phrase (IAdvP)

1. my old school books - NP
2. a problem - NP: to solve immediately - inf; IAdjP
3. the problem - NP: about to be solved now - PP; PAdjP: to be solved now - inf; INP
4. out of the room - PP; PAdvP: of the room - PP; PNP: the room - NP
5. climbing up the tree - prt; PAdjP: up the tree - PP; PAdvP: the tree - NP
6. a sound - NP: from inside his room - PP; PAdjP: inside his room - PP; PNP: his room - NP
7. a goal - NP: almost surprisingly - AdvP: in the last minute - PP; PAdvP: the last minute - NP
8. with an old ball - PP; PAdvP: an old ball - NP
9. really very beautiful - AdjP
10. the kings - NP: made of silk - prt; AdjP: of silk - PP; PAdvP: with lines -PP; PAdjP: of golden threads - PP; PAdjP: golden threads - NP
11. the problem - NP: to solve immediately - inf; IAdvP
12. to fly by air - inf; INP: by air - PP; PAdvP
13. the flight - NP: the flight having landed safely after a technical snag - absolute phrase; adverb phrase: after a technical snag - PP; PAdvP: a technical snag - NP: a sigh of relief - NP: of relief - PP; PAdjP
14. in a beautiful style - PP; PAdvP: a beautiful style - NP
15. the running train - NP
16. swimming - gerund: in the sea - PP; PAdvP: the sea - NP: next week - NP used as adverb
17. the teacher - NP: to write the test today - inf; INP: the test - NP
18. reading books - gerund; NP: a very good habit - NP
19. my parents - NP: to study well - inf; INP
20. being deaf and dumb - prt; AdjP
21. to keep cool - inf; INP: the most difficult - AdjP
22. in the evening - PP; PAdvP
23. very hard and sincerely - AdvP
24. the first prize - NP: definitely unexpectedly - AdvP
25. a very tall boy - NP: our class - NP
26. completely destroyed by Tsunami - prt; AdjP: by Tsunami - PP; PAdvP: the village - NP: deserted - prt; AdjP
27. to get the blessings of God - inf; IAdvP: the blessings of God - NP: of God - PP; PAdjP
28. very sorry - AdjP: for his mistakes - PP; PAdvP: his mistakes - NP

Key to Grammar Exercises 297

29. very happy - AdjP: at their treating us with respect - PP; PAdvP: their treating us with respect - gerund; NP: with respect - PP; PAdvP
30. a village without any facility - NP: without any facility - PP; PAdjP: any facility - NP
31. playing in the park - gerund; NP: in the park - PP; PAdvP: the park - NP
32. a book of that author - NP: of that author - PP; PAdjP: that author - NP
33. the old man - NP: with a walking stick - PP; PAdvP: a walking stick - NP
34. walking - gerund; NP: for health - PP; PAdvP
35. my teacher - NP: very kind and sincere - AdjP
36. to be very reasonable in her demands - inf; IAdjP: very reasonable - AdjP: in her demands - PP; PAdvP: her demands - NP
37. to share their feelings - inf; IAdvP: their feelings - NP
38. in his own house - PP; PAdvP: his own house - NP
39. the ball on the loft - NP: on the loft - PP; PAdjP: the loft - NP
40. the day - NP: by the heavy torrential rains - PP; PAdvP: the heavy torrential rains - NP

10. Exercise for **Chapter 17: Clauses and Structural Sentence Types - Simple Sentence, Compound Sentence and Complex Sentence & Chapter 18: Conjunctions**

a) Identify the **Conjunctions**, if any, and **their types** as **Coordinating Conjunction (CCn)**, **Subordinating Conjunction (SCn)** and **Relative Conjunction (i.e., Relative Pronoun (RP) or Relative Adverb (RA))**:

b) Identify the **Subordinate/Dependant Clause** (if any) and their types as **Noun Clause (NCls), Adjective Clause (AdjCls) and Adverb Clause (AdvCls)**:

1. that - RP: that he would get first mark in the school - NCls
2. which - RP: which is the main cause of ragging among the students - NCls
3. such ... that - SCn: that she could answer all questions - AdvCls
4. as long as - SCn: as long as you stay here - AdvCls
5. If - SCn: if you work hard and sincerely - AdvCls
6. though - SCn: though he has less money - AdvCls
7. where - RA: where I have been living for many years - AdjCls
8. as if - SCn: as if someone chased her to kill - AdvCls
9. who - RP: who is also my colleague - AdjCls
10. when - SCn: when he comes - AdvCls
11. in case - SCn: in case he troubles you - AdvCls
12. how - RA: how such criminal activities developed in colleges - NCls
13. when - RA: when he comes - NCls
14. where - RA: where his life is leading him - NCls
15. because - SCn: because she was kind and polite - AdvCls
16. where - RA: where I lost my keys - NCls
17. whatever - SCn: whatever you do - AdvCls
18. how - RA: how the universe will end - NCls

19. whom - RP: whom we consulted - AdjCls
20. where - RA: where we can buy almost anything - AdjCls
21. than - SCn: than he is - AdvCls
22. who - RP: who will win the match - NCls
23. lest - SCn: lest he should make some mistake - AdvCls
24. when - RA: when he comes - AdjCls
25. before - SCn: before the show was started - AdvCls

c) **Identify the type of sentences as <u>Simple Sentence (SmpS), Compound Sentence (CpdS) and Complex Sentence (ClxS)</u>:**

d) **Identify <u>the verbal phrases</u>, if any, and <u>their types</u> as <u>Noun Phrase (NP), Adjective Phrase (AdjP), and Adverb Phrase (AdvP)</u> if it is a simple sentence:**

e) **Identify <u>the main clauses</u> if it is a compound sentence:**

f) **Identify <u>the subordinate clauses and their types</u> as <u>Noun Clause (NCls), Adjective Clause (AdjCls) and Adverb Clause (AdvCls)</u> if it is a complex sentence:**

1. ClxS: if you believe God sincerely - AdvCls
2. ClxS: although she had helped all her friends - AdvCls
3. ClxS: how all of us work sincerely - NCls
4. CpdS: it was very costly; I would have bought it - main clauses
5. ClxS: which we are going to visit - AdjCls
6. CpdS: a lady had come yesterday; she gave this parcel for you - main clauses
7. CpdS: you can read a book; you can watch TV - main clauses
8. ClxS: whether we will win or they will lose - NCls
9. CpdS: my teacher is very helpful; she would help you also - main clauses
10. SmpS: being a foreigner - AdjP
11. SmpS: playing joyfully in the park - AdjP
12. ClxS: that he would quit one day - NCls
13. CpdS: she could not cook well; she could not teach the children - main clauses
14. CpdS: she is rich; she is simple - main clauses
15. CpdS: he must reach the station in time; he would miss the train - main clauses
16. CpdS: they worked very hard; they could not finish the work - main clauses
17. ClxS: when he returns from abroad - AdvCls
18. SmpS: after finishing the home work - AdvP
19. SmpS:
20. SmpS: (Being) rich and powerful - AdjP
21. CpdS: the problem would have been difficult; you should have tried - main clauses
22. CpdS: she sings; she dances - main clauses
23. SmpS: to pursue his higher studies abroad - inf; NP
24. CpdS: the messenger did not come yesterday; he did not call - main clauses

Key to Grammar Exercises

25. ClxS: what is being taught in the class - NCls
26. ClxS: (that) he had given yesterday - AdjCls
27. SmpS
28. CpdS: we searched thoroughly; the book could not be found - main clauses
29. SmpS: driving in the crowded city - gerund; NP
30. ClxS: that are too difficult to solve - AdjCls
31. SmpS: beaten up and punished wrongly by the police - AdjP
32. CpdS: you are sincere; you will get the benefit - main clauses
33. ClxS with mutually dependent clauses: hardly had we closed the door - AdvCls; when somebody rang the calling bell - AdvCls
34. ClxS: unless he corrects himself now itself - AdvCls
35. SmpS: having finished the work earlier - participle; AdjP

g) Transform/Rewrite the following <u>simple sentences into compound sentences</u>. If there are two simple sentences in a single question, combine them into a compound sentence:

1. He had spent many years abroad, and he finally decided to come home.
2. He has dedicated his life for the country, and he was honoured by the Government.
3. I wanted to attend the meeting, but I could not attend.
4. The roads were heavily damaged by the recent rains; therefore, they are in a bad condition.
5. Her husband's income was not sufficient for the family; therefore, she also went to work.
6. The actor struggled a lot earlier, and he could achieve the present popularity.
7. Winning in the Olympics was a dream for him, and he had it from his childhood.
8. <u>It will not be a meaningful transformation.</u>
9. She would eat and would watch TV.
10. I have an ambition, and it is to become a leader with vision for the country.

h) Transform/Rewrite the following <u>simple sentences into complex sentences</u>. If there are two simple sentences in a single question, combine them into a complex sentence:

1. After he had spent many years abroad, he finally decided to come home.
2. As he has dedicated his life for the country, he was honoured by the Government.
3. Though I wanted to attend the meeting, I could not attend.
4. Because the roads were heavily damaged by the recent rains, they are in a bad condition.
5. As her husband's income was not sufficient for the family, she also went to work.
6. The actor had to struggle a lot earlier so that he could achieve the present popularity.
7. <u>It will not be a meaningful transformation.</u>
8. He has always followed the teachings Thiruvalluvar had taught.
9. She would watch TV when she eats.
10. I have an ambition that I would become a leader with vision for the country.

i) Transform/Rewrite the following <u>compound sentences into simple sentences</u>. If required, the simple sentences can be written as two separate sentences:

1. She was poor in Mathematics. She wanted to go for tuition.
2. The train was coming fast. The young man tried to cross the track.
3. We have somehow finished the project. We had a tough time even then.
4. We have to closely watch the children. They may behave mischievously.
5. She is a good cook. She is slow.
6. Follow the steps carefully. Otherwise, you cannot understand the sum.
7. The hunter had hidden himself behind the bushes. He waited for the deer.
8. We must work sincerely. After all, we get salary.
9. We did not have enough amount. Nevertheless, we decided to buy a land with loan.
10. He is the richest man in the town. Yet, he does not discriminate among the people.
11. He sings, plays music, dances and acts. In short, he is a versatile actor.
12. He could not look after their parents well. His brother also could not.

j) Transform/Rewrite the following <u>compound sentences into complex sentences</u>:

1. As she was poor in Mathematics, she wanted to go for tuition.
2. Though the train was coming fast, the young man tried to cross the track.
3. Though we have somehow finished the project, we had a tough time then.
4. We have to closely watch the children lest they behave mischievously.
5. Even though she is a good cook, she is slow.
6. Unless you follow the steps carefully, you cannot understand the sum.
7. The hunter had hidden himself behind the bushes when he waited for the deer.
8. We must work sincerely because we get salary.
9. Though we did not have enough amount, we decided to buy a land with loan.
10. Though he is the richest man in the town, he does not discriminate among the people.
11. As he sings, plays music, dances and acts, he is a versatile actor.
12. Just as he could not look after their parents well, his brother also could not.

k) Transform/Rewrite the following <u>complex sentences into simple sentences</u>. If required, the simple sentences can be written as two separate sentences:

1. You finish first. You will get a complement from me.
2. The boss comes next week. We must finish the work before that.
3. Do not take up some work not possible for you to do.
4. The thief has hidden behind the wall. Nobody could see him.
5. The army got the ammunitions. Immediately, they started their operation.
6. <u>It will not be a meaningful transformation</u>.
7. You behaved like that. Tell me the reason.
8. My friend behaved like that. I was worried.
9. She tried to listen to class. She could not do so.
10. He got a promotion. He gave a treat.

Key to Grammar Exercises

l) Transform/Rewrite the following <u>complex sentences into compound sentences</u>:

1. You finish first, and you will get a complement from me.
2. The boss comes next week, and we must finish the work before that.
3. <u>It will not be a meaningful transformation.</u>
4. The thief has hidden behind the wall, and nobody could see him.
5. The army got the ammunitions, and immediately, they started their operation.
6. <u>It will not be a meaningful transformation.</u>
7. You behaved like that, so tell me the reason.
8. My friend behaved like that; therefore, I was worried.
9. She tried to listen to class, but she could not do so.
10. He got a promotion, and he gave a treat.

m) **Fill in the blanks with suitable <u>conjunctions</u>:**

1. unless 2. though 3. neither, nor 4. and 5. therefore 6. while 7. because 8. if 9. when 10. as if 11. hardly, when 12. otherwise

11. Exercise for <u>Chapter 19: Direct Speech and Indirect Speech</u>

a) **Rewrite the sentences of <u>direct speech into indirect speech</u> and the sentences of <u>indirect speech into direct speech</u>:**

1. My colleague asked whether I was coming for tea.
2. Our constitution says that all are equal.
3. Her younger son asked her, "Will you buy a new toy?"
4. Our neighbour said that they have been living there for 20 years.
5. His colleague told that running along the road, a girl had fallen down suddenly.
6. My boss said, "Have you finished the work?"
7. The teacher said, "Brahmaputra is the longest river in India."
8. My colleague asked whether I would come to the office or go to the site the next day.
9. My friend asked who my favourite hero was there.
10. She said to me, "I had gone to my native place and met my sister."
11. The chief guest said, "We will have finished 100 years after independence in 2047."
12. The boss shouted at us to get out. / The boss shouted that we should get out.
13. The parents asked the boy, "Why did you go to the shop yesterday?"
14. The boss said, "Do not go out now."
15. The child asked her mummy when father said he would come.
16. My friend requested me to attend his birthday party.
17. My colleague said, "Please attend the meeting today."
18. My boss asked when I could finish the work.
19. He said that he should finish the work the next day.

20. We told him, "Be nice to others."
21. The PM said that we should always be ready to sacrifice for the country.
22. My grandma started the story that there had lived a king a thousand years before.
23. Our colleague suggested that we would go for tea as we were tired.
24. The teacher asked if we had sacrificed anything for others that day.
25. She said, "I tried to finish the work before my boss came."
26. I told my friends that that day was my birthday.
27. The priest blessed him, "Long live my boy."
28. She exclaimed that her son was very intelligent.
29. My colleague exclaimed that I was driving very fast.
30. The teacher asked us to go to the library then. / The teacher told that we should go to the library then.
31. My friend said to me that if he found a suitable job for me, he would let me know.
32. The priest said that God is great and helps us.
33. He told that if he were me, he would not go there.
34. My friend said, "I went to cinema yesterday."
35. Mother told us not to go out to play because it was raining.
36. The auto driver asked the passenger, "Where do you want to go?"
37. The foreigner exclaimed that it is a very beautiful country.
38. The fans said, "How brilliantly our hero made the stunts!"
39. The members said, "Let us have a get-together with family."
40. The teacher said, "Study well for the examination."

12. Exercise for <u>Chapter 20: Inversion of Subject, Verb and Complement</u>

a) **Rewrite the sentences without inversion into sentences with inversion and vice versa:**

1. *Had he known her, he would have spoken to her.*
2. My father was a teacher, and my uncle was also a teacher.
3. I do not like coffee, and my friend also does not like coffee.
4. If I were poor, I would not have purchased a car.
5. *Here comes the convoy.*
6. *Only under some very difficult situation should have he done it.*
7. *He works very hard; so does his wife.*
8. *Were I rich, I would buy a luxury car.*
9. As soon as he had reached home, his boss called.
10. *Under the banyan tree we were playing.*
11. Your attitude towards life was more important.
12. We had barely entered the room, when the room-boy knocked the door.
13. If I buy a new car, it would be a luxury car.
14. All are equal under the sun.
15. *Rarely would she have visited a village.*

Key to Grammar Exercises

16. They were so poor that they could not afford to have even a rented house.
17. She is very intelligent to learn many languages easily.
18. He was shocked that he lost his investment in shares.
19. He goes there.
20. He would have realized his mistakes only then.
21. The cattle went down the road.
22. I have seldom gone to his house.
23. *Scarcely had the benefits of the new schemes reached the people when the prices shot up.*
24. *My friend is not tall; nor is his father or mother.*
25. *No sooner had he finished the work than he left immediately.*
26. *So happy was she that she could not suppress it.*
27. He was such a strong man that everybody admired him.
28. *He does not like coffee. Neither does he like tea.*
29. *Hardly had the boss left when some visitor entered.*
30. *Never have I seen her.*

13. Exercise for <u>Chapter 29: Figures of Speech</u>

a) **Identify the figures of speech:**

1. synecdoche 2. simile 3. antithesis 4. oxymoron 5. interrogation 6. euphemism 7. climax 8. hyperbole 9. simile 10. simile 11. metonymy 12. synecdoche 13. climax 14. simile 15. oxymoron 16. euphemism 17. anticlimax 18. interrogation 19. metonymy 20. simile 21. irony 22. metaphor 23. metonymy 24. metonymy 25. anticlimax 26. simile 27. antithesis 28. hyperbole 29. irony 30. personification.

Part IV

Appendices

1. Index

A

absolute phrase: 83, 148, 201
abstract noun: 19
accusative case: 21, 22
action verb: 3, 26, 27, 35, 39 - 41,
 53 - 59, 65, 81 - 85, 107, 119, 185, 191
action verb cum auxiliary verb: 41
action verb cum be-verb: 39
action verb cum modal verb: 40
active voice: 27, 29, 33, 56, 58, 59, 81,
 82, 85, 90
actor: 57, 86, 87
adjective: 3, 49, 67, 82, 85, 100 - 114,
 116, 117, 130, 131, 219
adjective clause (adjectival clause): 13, 156,
 158, 196
adjective phrase (adjectival phrase): 10, 11,
 13, 86, 111, 112, 138, 139,
 147, 164 - 177, 193 - 195
adjectives of quantity: 100, 107
adjunct: 101
advanced sentence formation: 201
adverb: 4, 84, 85, 87, 105, 119 - 137, 146,
 191 - 193, 220, 221
adverb/adverbial clause: 13, 155, 158, 196
adverb/adverbial phrase: 10, 11, 86, 123,
 138, 139, 147, 164 - 177, 195
adverbial: 9, 134 - 136
adverbs of attitude: 121, 125
adverbs of certainty: 121, 125
adverbs of definite frequency: 120
adverbs of degree: 111, 121, 123, 126, 147
adverbs of indefinite frequency: 121, 125
adverbs of manner: 119, 124, 130, 132
adverbs of opinion: 121, 125, 130
adverbs of place/location: 120, 127, 132, 191
adverbs of probability: 121, 125, 130
adverbs of time: 120, 126
affix: 240
agent: 56 - 59, 87
alphabet: 1
alphagram: 245
anagram: 245
antecedent: 152, 153, 155 - 157
anticlimax: 248
antithesis: 248
antonym: 17, 244
apostrophe: 21, 92, 197, 199
appositive: 12, 202
article: 3, 115 - 117
aspect of verb: 27
aspects of noun: 20
assertive sentence: 15
auxiliary verb: 27-29, 31, 36 - 38, 40, 41, 46,
 92, 125, 191, 204, 205

B

bare infinitive: 88
base form of verb: 11, 14, 27, 29, 46, 67, 85
basic phrases: 10, 147
being verb (be-verb): see be-verb
be-verb: 3, 26, 37 - 40, 46, 57, 59, 66, 81,
 82, 84, 85, 89, 91, 122, 185, 191 - 193, 205
binomials: 129

C

capitalization: 200
case: 21, 22
causative sentence: 56, 86, 87

causative verb: 56-59, 86 - 89, 194
clause: 12 - 14, 53, 149-177, 184 - 190, 192 - 196, 198
cleft sentence: 15, 88, 162
climax: 248
collective noun: 20
collocation: 17, 218
colon: 198, 199
comma: 197, 198
comma splice: 161
common gender: 21
common noun: 19
comparative degree: 102, 105, 109, 112, 132, 134
comparison of adjective: 102 - 111, 196
comparison of adverb: 132 - 136
complementary words for tenses: 35, 36
complete verb: 27, 28, 148, 191, 203
complex preposition: 5, 140, 141
complex sentence: 14, 149, 161 - 163, 164 - 177, 181, 187
compound adjective: 16, 213, 216
compound adverb: 16, 213, 217
compound gerund: 81
compound preposition: 141
compound relative adverb: 154
compound relative pronoun: 154
compound sentence: 14, 159 - 163, 164 - 177, 187, 198, 199
compound word: 16, 199, 213 - 217
compound-complex sentence: 162
conditional sentence: 53, 64, 192
conjugation of verb: 90
conjunction: 5, 13, 14, 148, 150 - 161, 173, 177, 178 - 183
conjunctive adverbs: 122, 160, 181, 182
connecting adverbs: 122, 125, 160, 181, 182

consecutive prepositional phrases: 142
consonant: 1, 20, 115
continuous tense: 27, 28, 30-39, 56, 66, 81-85
contraction of verbs: 51, 92 - 97, 199
coordinating conjunction: 159, 161, 173, 177, 178, 181, 205
copula verb: 54
correlative conjunction: 180, 181
countable noun: 20, 24, 117

D

dangling modifier: 84
dangling phrase: 84
dash: 199
declarative sentence: 15, 62, 63, 184, 186, 189, 191, 197
definite article: 115
degrees of comparison: 102, 111, 132, 196
demonstrative determiner: 117
demonstrative pronoun: 24
dependent clause: 12, 149, 150, 151, 161, 164 - 177, 192
dependent marker word: 150
determiner: 3, 48, 49, 102, 115 - 118, 145, 147
direct speech: 16, 184 - 190, 198
distributive pronoun: 25
double quotation mark: 198
dynamic verb: 56

E

elements of structural sentences: 164
ellipsis: 199, 200
elliptical clause: 158
elliptical sentence: 204 - 206
emphatic pronoun: 23
emphatic sentence: 15, 162

ending a sentence with a preposition: 145
essential clause: 153, 162
euphemism: 247
exclamatory sentence: 15, 63, 184, 186, 189, 197
expression: 12, 88, 147, 148, 182
extended modal verb: 65 - 67

F

FANBOYS: 159, 173, 178
feminine: 21
figures of speech: 17, 246 - 248
finish + present participle: 54
finite verb: 27, 29, 31
first conditional sentence: 53
first person: 22, 26, 37
first person plural: 26
first person singular: 26
forms of adverbs: 130 - 133
fragments: 203
functional sentence type: 15
fused sentence: 161
future continuous: 27 - 41, 85, 91
future perfect: 27 - 41, 85, 91
future perfect continuous: 27 - 41, 85, 91
future tense: 27 - 41, 85, 94

G

gender: 21
genitive case: 22
gerund: 11, 81, 82, 89, 91, 164 - 177, 195
gerund phrase: see gerund
go + present participle: 53

H

holonym: 244

homograph: 245
homonym: 244
homophone: 245
hyphen: 199, 216
hyperbole: 247
hypernym: 244
hyponym: 244

I

idiom: 14, 222
imperative mood: 27, 63
imperative sentence: 15, 63, 64, 188, 189, 197
incomplete verb: 29
indefinite article: 115
indefinite pronoun: 24, 101, 118
independent clause: 12, 149, 158 - 162, 164 - 177, 192, 193, 198, 199
indicative mood: 27, 62 - 64
indirect object: 7 - 9
indirect speech: 16, 184 - 190
infinite verb: 29
infinitive: 12, 81, 85 - 89, 91, 112, 123, 164 - 177, 186, 188, 195, 204
infinitive adjective phrase: 86, 112, 146, 195
infinitive adverb phrase: 86, 123, 195
infinitive noun phrase: 86, 195
infinitive phrase: 12, 81, 85 - 89, 91, 164 - 177
informal contraction: 97
inseparable phrasal verb: 68
intensifier: 105, 106, 110, 121, 126, 134 - 136
intensive pronoun: 23
interjection: 5
interrogation: 247
interrogative adverb: 124
interrogative pronoun: 23, 25
interrogative sentence: 15, 47 - 52, 62, 186 - 188, 194 - 196, 197
intransitive verb: 54

introductory subject: 98, 99, 191, 205, 206
inversion of subject + verb
       and complement: 191 - 193
inversion of subject and verb: 127,
       191 - 193, 205
irony: 247
irregular comparison: 103, 133
irregular verb: 27, 42

K

keep + present participle: 54

L

learning verb: 88
linking verb: 54, 55, 122, 191, 194
long simple sentence: 158, 164 - 177, 187
loose sentence: 201

M

main clause: see independent clause
main verb form: 27 - 29, 46 - 48
marginal preposition: 141
masculine: 21
meronym: 244
metaphor: 17, 246
metonymy: 248
modal auxiliary verb: see modal verb
modal verb: 36 - 40, 65 - 67, 94, 185:
    see extended modal verb also
modifier: 13, 100, 119, 193
mood: 27, 62 - 64
mutually dependent clauses: 177, 192

N

negative sentence: 46, 48
neuter gender: 21
nominative case: 21, 22
non-causative: 87
non-essential clause: 153, 154
non-finite verb: 29
noun: 2, 19 - 21
noun adjunct: 101
noun clause: 13, 157, 158, 195
noun phrase: 10, 11, 13, 86, 138, 139, 147,
       164-177, 193, 195
number: 20, 26
number of subject: 26

O

object: 6 - 9, 21 - 23, 29, 31, 37, 46 - 49,
       54 - 62, 68, 137, 147, 194, 195
object complement: 7, 10, 50, 55, 58, 61
object form: 22, 23
objective case: 21 - 23
oblique: see slash
omission of antecedent: 152
omission of article: 116
omission of preposition: 145
omission of relative adverb: 154
omission of relative pronoun: 154
order of adjective: 102
order of adverb: 124
order of determiner: 117
ordinal determiner: 117
other complement: 6, 7, 9, 49, 60, 61, 191-193
oxymoron: 248

Index

P

palindrome: 245
paradox: 248
parallel adverbs: 122, 191 - 193
parallel construction: 181
parallel structure: 202
parenthesis: 199
participle: 12, 82 - 84, 89, 91, 101, 164 - 177, 193, 195, 201, 216, 217
participle phrase: see participle
particle: 68, 69
parts of speech: 1, 2, 6, 207 - 213, 218
passive voice: 27, 31 - 34, 50, 57 - 59, 81, 82, 85, 90, 91
past continuous: 27 - 41, 81, 82, 90
past form: 27 - 42, 46, 64
past participle form: 27 - 42, 81, 82
past perfect: 27 - 41, 81, 82, 85, 90
past perfect continuous: 27-41, 81, 82, 90
past tense: 27 - 41, 90, 93
patterns for words: 218, 221
perception verb: 58, 59, 89, 194
perfect continuous tense: 27-41, 81, 82, 85
perfect tense: 27 - 41, 81, 82, 85
periodic sentence: 201
person: 22, 23, 26
person and number: 26
personal pronoun: 22, 23
personification: 247
phrasal verb: 14, 67 - 80
phrase: 10 - 13, 81 - 89, 91, 111, 112, 123, 126, 127, 138, 139, 147, 148, 158, 164 - 177, 191 - 195, 201
phrase preposition: 140
plural: 20, 26
position of adjective: 101, 102
position of adverb: 124 - 127
position of determiner: 117, 118
positive degree: 102 - 105, 108, 132 - 134
positive form: 92, 103, 133
positive sentence: 46 - 48
possessive adjective: 22, 23, 117
possessive adjective form: 22, 23
possessive case: 21 - 23, 199
possessive pronoun form: 22, 23
post-modifier: 13, 112, 138, 148, 156
predicate: 9
prefix: 17, 240, 241
pre-determiner: 112
pre-modifier: 13, 105, 106, 107, 110, 112, 134 - 136, 148
preposition: 7, 10, 11, 67, 68, 137 - 146
prepositional adjective phrase: 11, 112, 139, 194
prepositional adverb phrase: 11, 123, 126, 139, 195
prepositional noun phrase: 11, 139, 195
prepositional object: 10, 137, 147
prepositional phrase: 10, 11, 112, 123, 138, 139, 142, 147, 148, 164 - 177
present continuous: 27 - 41, 81, 82, 90
present form: 27 - 42, 46
present participle form: 27 - 42, 53, 54, 81, 82
present perfect: 27 - 41, 81, 82, 85, 90
present perfect continuous: 27 - 41, 81, 82, 90
present tense: 27 - 41, 81, 82, 92
pronoun: 2, 22 - 25, 92
proper noun: 19, 116, 200
proverb: 14, 234 - 239
punctuation: 16, 159, 161, 162, 184, 197 - 200

Q

quantifier: 117, 118
question: 47 - 52, 184 - 188, 194 - 196, 197

question-word question: 48 - 50, 194 - 196
question-words expressing surprise: 50
quotation: 14, 239
quotation mark: 184, 198

R

reciprocal pronoun: 24
reflexive pronoun: 23
regular comparison: 103, 133
regular verb: 27, 42
relative adverb: 150 - 154, 180
relative clause: 152 - 154
relative conjunction: 150 - 157, 180
reported clause: 184, 198
reporting clause: 184, 198
relative pronoun: 150 - 154, 180
reported speech: see indirect speech
reporting verb: 186 - 190, 193
run-on sentence: 161

S

same word - different parts of speech: 6, 207 - 212
second conditional sentence: 53, 64
second person: 22, 26, 37
second person plural: 26
second person singular: 26
semicolon: 198
sentence: 1, 8, 13, 15
sentence structure: 1, 6-8, 29, 31, 37, 46, 47, 48, 51, 53, 56, 58 - 60, 63, 64, 104 - 107, 110, 133 - 136, 159, 161,162, 184, 191 - 194
separable phrasal verb: 68
short simple sentence: 158, 163, 164 - 177
simile: 17, 246

simple future: 27 - 41, 85, 91
simple past: 27 - 41, 81, 82, 90
simple preposition: 5, 139, 140
simple present: 27 - 41, 81, 82, 90
simple sentence: 13, 158, 159, 163, 164 - 177, 187
simple tense: 27, 35, 38, 40, 65 - 67
singular: 20, 26
slash: 199
split infinitive: 88
stative verb: 56, 89
stop + present participle: 54
structural element: 8 - 14, 48 - 50, 164
structural sentence types: 13, 14, 158 - 162, 173
structural sentences: 13, 14, 158 - 177
subject: 6 - 8
subject complement: 7, 9, 49, 61 - 62, 193
subject form: 22, 23
subjective case: 21 - 23
subjunctive mood: 27, 63, 64, 189
subjunctive sentence: 15, 63, 64, 189
subordinate clause: see dependent clause
subordinating conjunction: 150, 151, 154 - 157, 178 - 180, 205
suffix: 17, 240, 241
superlative degree: 102, 103, 107, 110, 132, 136
syllable: 1
synecdoche: 248
synonym: 17, 243, 244
synthesis of sentences: 163
(see transformation of sentences also)

T

tag question: 51, 52, 97, 205
tense: 26 - 41, 81, 82, 85, 90 - 96
tense and aspect: 27, 28
thinking verb: 59, 194

Index

third conditional sentence: 53
third person: 23, 26, 29, 37, 63
third person plural: 26
third person singular: 26, 29, 63
transformation of sentences: 111, 136, 164 - 177
transitional expression: 122, 182
transitive verb: 54, 55, 58
types of adverbs: 119 - 124
types (method) of transformations: 164
types of words: 1, 240 - 245

U

uncountable noun: 20, 24, 117
uses of be-verbs: 38, 39
uses of tenses: 35, 36

V

verb: 3, 6, 9, 26 - 80, 81 - 91, 92 - 97, 191 - 193
verb complement: 7, 9, 49, 55, 61, 62
verb form: 11, 14, 26 - 45, 63, 64
verb phrase: 148
verb pattern: 61, 89, 218 - 221
verbal phrase: 11, 12, 81 - 89, 148, 164 - 177
verbs of knowledge: see thinking verb
verbs of opinion: see thinking verb
voice: 27 - 34, 50, 56, 57 - 59, 81, 82, 85, 90, 91
vowel: 1, 20, 115

W

word: 1, 2
word groups: 17, 240 - 245
word types: see word groups

Y

yes/no question: 47, 48

Z

zero conditional sentence: 53
zero infinitive: see bare infinitive

2. Abbreviations - alphabetical order

A	Auxiliary	ObjC	Object Complement
adj	adjective	OC	Other Complement
AdjCls	Adjective Clause	PAdjP	Prepositional Adjective Phrase
AdjP	Adjective Phrase	PAdvP	Prepositional Adverb Phrase
adv	adverb	PNP	Prepositional Noun Phrase
AdvCls	Adverb Clause	PO	Prepositional Object
AdvP	Adverb Phrase	POS	Parts Of Speech
AV	Action Verb	PP	Prepositional Phrase
BV	Be-Verb / Being Verb	prep	preposition
CCn	Coordinating Conjunction	pron	pronoun
ClxS	Complex Sentence	prt	Participle
CpdS	Compound Sentence	PrtP	Participle Phrase
conj	conjunction	PV	Perception Verb
CV	Causative Verb	QW	Question Word
d	determiner	RA	Relative Adverb
DO	Direct Object	RCn	Relative Conjunction
exp	expression	RP	Relative Pronoun
fp	first person	S	Subject
fpp	first person plural	SC	Subject Complement
fps	first person singular	SCn	Subordinating Conjunction
GP	Gerund Phrase	SmpS	Simple Sentence
IAdjP	Infinitive Adjective Phrase	sp	second person
IAdvP	Infinitive Adverb Phrase	spp	second person plural
inf	Infinitive	sps	second person singular
INP	Infinitive Noun Phrase	SS	Sentence Structure
interj	interjection	tp	third person
IO	Indirect Object	tpp	third person plural
IP	Infinitive Phrase	tps	third person singular
LV	Linking Verb	TV	Thinking Verb
n	noun	v	verb
NCls	Noun Clause	V	verb
NP	Noun Phrase	VC	Verb Complement
O	Object / Direct Object		

3. Abbreviations - topic-wise order

POS	Parts Of Speech		SmpS	Simple Sentence
SS	Sentence Structure		CpdS	Compound Sentence
n	noun		ClxS	Complex Sentence
pron	pronoun		GP	Gerund Phrase
adj	adjective		PrtP	Participle Phrase
d	determiner		IP	Infinitive Phrase
A	Auxiliary		prt	Participle
v	verb		inf	Infinitive
V	verb		INP	Infinitive Noun Phrase
adv	adverb		IAdjP	Infinitive Adjective Phrase
prep	preposition		IAdvP	Infinitive Adverb Phrase
conj	conjunction		fp	first person
interj	interjection		fps	first person singular
S	Subject		fpp	first person plural
O	Object / Direct Object		sp	second person
DO	Direct Object		sps	second person singular
IO	Indirect Object		spp	second person plural
OC	Other Complement		tp	third person
SC	Subject Complement		tps	third person singular
VC	Verb Complement		tpp	third person plural
ObjC	Object Complement		QW	Question Word
NP	Noun Phrase		AV	Action Verb
AdjP	Adjective Phrase		BV	Be-Verb / Being Verb
AdvP	Adverb Phrase		LV	Linking Verb
PO	Prepositional Object		CV	Causative Verb
PP	Prepositional Phrase		PV	Perception Verb
PNP	Prepositional Noun Phrase		TV	Thinking Verb
PAdjP	Prepositional Adjective Phrase		CCn	Coordinating Conjunction
PAdvP	Prepositional Adverb Phrase		SCn	Subordinating Conjunction
exp	expression		RCn	Relative Conjunction
NCls	Noun Clause		RP	Relative Pronoun
AdjCls	Adjective Clause		RA	Relative Adverb
AdvCls	Adverb Clause			

NOTES

The End

To follow us on facebook: **https://www.facebook.com/spcEnglishGrammar**

The End

To follow us on facebook: https://www.facebook.com/spgEnglishGrammar